THE NEW DEAL ART PROJECTS

AN ANTHOLOGY OF MEMOIRS

THE NEW DEAL ART PROJECTS

AN ANTHOLOGY OF MEMOIRS

Edited by FRANCIS V. O'CONNOR

Smithsonian Institution Press · Washington, D.C. 1972

Designed by Crimilda Pontes. Printed in the United States of America.

Library of Congress Cataloging in Publication Data
Main entry under title:
The New Deal art projects.
Bibliography: p.
1. Federal Art Project. I. O'Connor, Francis V., ed.
N8838.N4   709'.73   72–181525
ISBN 0–87474–113–0

"The New Deal's Treasury Art Program: A Memoir" by Olin Dows
previously published in Arts in Society, vol. 2, no. 4 (1963–1964).

The Authors and Editor join in dedicating this anthology
to their colleague
AUDREY McMAHON
in recognition of her contribution to American art

CONTENTS

LIST OF ABBREVIATIONS

AAA	American Abstract Artists
AFL	American Federation of Labor
CAA	College Art Association, New York City
CCC	Civilian Conservation Corps
CIO	Congress of Industrial Organizations
CWA	Civil Works Administration
ERA	Emergency Relief Administration
FERA	Federal Emergency Relief Administration
MOMA	Museum of Modern Art, New York City
NAACP	National Association for the Advancement of Colored People
NRA	National Recovery Administration
PWA	Public Works Administration
PWAP	Public Works of Art Project
Section	Treasury Section of Painting and Sculpture (Later Section of Fine Arts)
TERA	Temporary Emergency Relief Administration
TRAP	Treasury Relief Art Project
UAA	Unemployed Artists' Association
WPA	Works Progress Administration (After September 1939 Work Projects Administration of the Federal Works Agency)
WPA/FAP*	WPA Federal Art Project

* This is a modern composite abbreviation employed along with "Project" and "Art Project" throughout the text to refer to the WPA Federal Art Project (1935–1939) which became the Art Program of the Work Projects Administration of the Federal Works Agency (1939–1942) and ended as the Graphic Section of the War Services Division (1942–1943).

Introduction

FRANCIS V. O'CONNOR

Ten of the memoirs contained in this anthology were commissioned in 1968 as reports to a research project I was directing under a grant from the National Endowment for the Arts. This project, titled "Federal Support for the Visual Arts: The New Deal and Now," was designed to study the cultural and economic effectiveness of the New Deal art projects in New York City and State. All of these reports were used as background material, and excerpts from several were incorporated in the manuscript and published versions of my final report.[1] Subsequently these accounts were reshaped by the authors and myself into their present form. The first memoir, that by Olin Dows, is reprinted here, with slight revisions, from the 1963/64 issue of *Arts in Society*.[2] The anthology concludes with a dialogue between four of the authors and myself derived from about four hours of taped conversation which took place in July 1968.

In selecting the authors represented here, my first concern was to find persons intimately involved in the New Deal art programs who would be able to discipline their memories with research in the primary source documents I was uncovering and organizing in the course of my research project. I needed, and found, persons who could handle the difficult task of encountering in the sources the realities behind their recollections. Using this method, it has been possible to eliminate most of the inevitable telescoping of time and place and the distortions of relationship to which memory is prone, though not always contradictory versions of the same event. Only at the very end, when the authors had completed their research, was a tape recorder used to capture their free associations. Consequently, the general reader should find these memoirs both lively and informative and the scholar should find primary source documents capable of prompting and supporting further investigation.

There is a tendency among former employees of the Work Progress Administration's Federal Art Project (WPA/FAP, 1935–1943),[3] and to a lesser extent among those who worked on the Treasury programs, to disavow or obscure their relationship with them. As Audrey McMahon notes, for some of those who began now successful careers on these projects—especially the relief projects—to have created a mural for a prison or post office, or an easel work for allocation to a public hospital, is a source of embarassment today. There is also fear, the roots of which are discussed by Lincoln Rothschild, that association with the "WPA" will in some way insinuate their affiliation with "subversive" organizations. I hope the time will come when all those who worked on the projects will be proud—and feel safe—to admit having done so. I hope, further, that the example of this book will hasten that day.

The illustrations were chosen wherever possible to fill the visual needs of each memoir. Supplementary material has been included to provide a glimpse of the wide range of creative activity on the projects. The illustrations constitute in themselves the first extensive visual anthology of New Deal art to be published since the projects ended in 1943.[4]

Although the Treasury programs and the WPA/FAP were nationwide federal undertakings, this anthology is essentially about New York City and State. The New Deal art projects spent a large part of their annual budgets there and assisted a proportionate number of artists. New York thus constitutes, with its vast urban center appended to a basically rural state, an excellent microcosm of the entire nation. Also, New York City was then, as it is today, the "Paris" of our national culture. To understand what was happening there and on its projects, is to understand the most advanced artistic situation in the country during the 1930s. This does not mean that important and original enterprises were not undertaken by the New Deal projects in other parts of the nation or that this book does justice to all points of view concerning the New York projects. I hope that this anthology will serve as a stimulating model for similar collections of memoirs from the New York region and other key areas such as Massachusetts, Illinois, Michigan, the Pacific Northwest, New Mexico, and California.[5]

In themselves, however, these memoirs, and the concluding dialogue, constitute the first attempt to publish in depth the recollections of artists and administrators who worked on the New Deal art projects of the 1930s. Of the several anthologies about the period published in recent years, only Studs Terkel's moving *Hard Times* provides any testimony about the projects, and that is limited and without context. Indeed, even standard histories of American art barely mention the art projects and when they do it is usually to disparage their achievements and confuse their identities.

With this in mind, perhaps it would be useful to outline briefly the nature of these enterprises. They are often mistakenly recalled as the "WPA" projects, primarily because the WPA/FAP was the largest and most creative of those which existed between late 1933 and the spring of 1943.

There were three distinct government art projects set up under the Treasury Department. These are discussed in detail by Olin Dows, who also gives some basic facts about the WPA/FAP. For clarity's sake—and to introduce you early to the flavor of New Deal alphabet soup—these Treasury projects were: the Public Works of Art Project (PWAP, 1933–1934) which received its funds from the Civil Works Administration (CWA), the Treasury Relief Art Project (TRAP, 1935–1939) which was funded by the WPA, and the Treasury Section of Painting and Sculpture (Section, 1934–1943) which was funded essentially from appropriations for public buildings. There was also another government agency, the Federal Emergency Relief Administration (FERA) which helped artists indirectly between the end of the PWAP in June 1934 and the start of the WPA/FAP in the fall of 1935. This ran parallel with, and was partially funded by, New York State's Temporary Emergency Relief Administration (TERA), which in turn funded the pioneer work-relief program for artists which had been operated by the College Art Association (CAA) in New York City since about 1932.[6]

The WPA/FAP, however, was the most far reaching of the four art projects. It sponsored on a nationwide basis separate divisions dealing with all major visual art forms and activities. Audrey McMahon, the former director of its New York region, supplements the raw facts supplied by Olin Dows with an incisive description of how the WPA/FAP was organized and operated and gives her account of its basic problems and achievements. These two memoirs form Part 1.

Part 2 consists of memoirs of the creative divisions of the WPA/FAP. Edward Laning leads off with a broadly painted account of his experiences as a muralist on the Project—and also on the Section. Joseph Solman describes how the WPA/FAP easel division provided the impetus behind a small group of expressionist painters known as The Ten and gives, in the process, a good insight into the New York gallery world that the easel painters had to depend on at the time. Robert Cronbach recalls his experiences on the sculpture division and compares them with working for the Section. Jacob Kainen tells of the graphic division and what it was like to survive as a creative artist and a human being in the uncertain bureaucratic world of the Project during those difficult years. Finally, Lincoln Rothschild recounts the history and contribution of the WPA/FAP's Index of American Design, which not only helped to preserve in images our heritage of folk art and craft, but put to creative use the talents of unemployed commercial and academically trained artists.

Throughout these memoirs other important aspects of the WPA/FAP are also discussed, such as its extensive and highly effective art education program in public schools and settlement houses, the "loan artists" program which sent experienced New York artists to culturally underdeveloped regions, the flourishing program of traveling exhibitions circulated through the Project's network of Federal Art Galleries and, finally, the all-important Community Art Centers, which brought original art and art classes to isolated corners of the nation during a period of bleak distress.

Other ramifications of the WPA/FAP are discussed in Part 3. Here Lincoln Rothschild shows how the artists organized, along lines similar to the labor movement, to fight for their rights and adequate recognition. Rosalind Browne demonstrates how that most controversial of art styles—abstraction—was nurtured on the Project and how the country's first art organization devoted to abstraction, the American Abstract Artists (AAA), grew out of its membership. Olive Gavert reveals how the major American world fairs in this century can serve as a barometer of cultural development and how the WPA/FAP's World's Fair exhibitions revealed a new attitude toward the arts unique to the 1930s. Finally, Marchal Landgren's account of the Municipal Art Galleries' exhibition program provides an excellent example of the indirect influence of the Project on local cultural programs, as well as giving a description of the role of the exhibition in the life of the individual artist and his public.

The closing dialogue between Audrey McMahon, Marchal Landgren, Jacob Kainen, Olive Gavert, and myself, sums up many of the themes implicit and explicit in the various memoirs and provides, I think, an eloquent insight into the impact the projects made on American culture, and individuals concerned with that culture, during the 1930s.

Art in America did not always flourish as it appears to do today. Indigenous artistic expression was incredibly narrow and conservative at the time the market crashed in 1929. Whether one listens to Mrs. McMahon describe the purile contents of provincial museums, or Jacob Kainen the repressive hegemony of the etching societies, or Mrs. Gavert the essential irrelevance of art at early 20th Century Fairs, one cannot escape the reality that something very vital—indeed, something revolutionary—happened to American culture during the 1930s. Nor can one ignore the idea of essential democracy which permeates these memoirs: democracy in the employment and competition procedures of the various projects, democracy in the structures and policies of the artists' organizations and unions, democracy in the exhibition concepts employed at the World's Fair or the Municipal Art Galleries, democracy on the picket line itself! That all this should be parallel to the political, economic, and social revolution of Roosevelt's New Deal and the struggle between international communism and fascism, is not surprising. Yet it remains to historians of art and of ideas to delve more deeply than they have into the relationship between culture and politics over the last forty years.

Today is not an inauspicious time to begin. Certainly many aspects of our present period have eerie resemblances to the crises-wracked Depression decade—a fact not unnoticed in some of these memoirs. Our economy is unstable. The conflict in Indochina divides a new generation with passions similar to those engendered by the Spanish Civil War. The relatively localized problem of the "dust bowl" is replaced by almost universal erosion and pollution of natural resources. Dissent against big business and banking has grown to dissent against Big Brother with attendent "police riots" and sit-ins. Marcuse replaces Marx in the reading of young radicals.

If art prophecies the deepest tendencies of the period in which it is created, it might be useful if the art of the 1930s was seen, not in comparison with what it eclipsed or what transcended it, but in terms of its own cultural function. Art is too often discussed solely in terms of critics' theories of quality, fashion, and pedigree. Only history confirms prophecy. The present conventional wisdom, discounting the earlier achievements of Milton Avery, John Marin, Stuart Davis, Ben Shahn, Reginald Marsh, Marsden Hartley, John Sloan, Arthur Dove—to name but a few outstanding artists of the 1920s and 1930s—would have "great" American art begin in the mid-1940s. Abstract Expressionism, the child of European Surrealism, is seen as a pragmatic (or puritanical) American version of the "mainstream's" insight and sensuality. This put America "on the map" as an international art center and it has been there ever since. Yet how few really wonder how those presumably benighted young artists, isolated on the WPA during the 1930s, ever managed to do what they did during the 1940s and 1950s. Some sort of reaction against what is naively called "social realism" is presumed, yet surely such a reaction must have been of profound dimensions to produce an art of such human intensity.

This is not the place to explore the details of this problem and expound new theories. I want only to outline a new problem with questions.

If it is so simple to see the art of the 1960s—Pop Art, Op Art, "post-painterly" Color Field Art—as the reaction of the rationally pure against the emotional solipsism of Abstract Expressionism, if a new generation of artists can preen themselves on this oft-proclaimed difference, which they deem profound, then what depths of insight—and suffering—must have accompanied the Abstract Expressionist's reaction against the 1930s which nurtured their youth and art? It is easy—indeed, natural—for sons to reject their fathers; is it so easy for mature men to reject their past? Or did they? And if they did, was that rejection caused by refined esthetic discrimination or by the ramifications of political disillusion? The artist of the 1930s, whether his style was American scene or regionalism, social scene or expressionism, surrealism or abstraction, was constantly called upon to justify his social relevance. As Jacob Kainen says in the Dialogue, to be a good colorist would not have been sufficient—nor one surmises, would

5

exclusively personal expression have sufficed either. Could it be that the 1930s saw the end of a certain superficiality in America? Could it be that it saw our last look at the landscapes and cityscapes which so dominate our past art? Could it be that a unique conjunction of artistic permissions and political upheavals, in which the individual artist saw for the first time in America his essential irrelevance when it came to the social import of his creations, drove him deep into himself—into his unconscious—into the processes of his art? Could it be that the 1930s is the psychological watershed of American art? Could it be that the polar archetypes of this profound change are Thomas Hart Benton stating "I am an American" and his pupil Jackson Pollock saying "I am nature?" Could it be, finally, that the essential tension between social concern and self concern so palpable during the 1930s has been resolved on the side of the self—and that true art, from now on, can only serve society as a sacrament of integrity, as a celebration of the inner life, as a prophecy of where stability lies beneath shifting intensities of chaos?

Art during the 1930s, drab in style, grim in subject and constricted in scale though much of it was, expressed the conflict between the individual artistic personality and the mysterious inner forces of society. For the most part this was accomplished within the conventional vocabulary of pre-Surrealist art. The art of the 1930s must, therefore, be seen in terms of that function and that background. These memoirs provide a basis for such vision.

In conclusion, I would like to thank the authors for their unfailing enthusiasm and assistance, especially in helping to acquire photographs to illustrate their contributions. I am indebted to Dr. Joshua C. Taylor, Director, National Collection of Fine Arts, and the Smithsonian's Office of Academic Studies for a visiting postdoctoral research associateship at the National Collection, under which this anthology was completed. A special word of gratitude must be expressed to Dr. David W. Scott and Dr. Belisario R. Contreras for unstinting assistance and encouragement. I also want to acknowledge the help of Francis Bowie Duncan, Irving Marantz, Garnett McCoy of the Archives of American Art, and William B. Walker of the Library of the National Collection of Fine Arts. Finally, my thanks go to my former research assistants Eleanor Harris, Lucy Leitzell and Ellen Eisenberg, and to Joan Horn of the Smithsonian Institution Press, who have all seen the manuscript and its editor through various metamorphoses.

FRANCIS V. O'CONNOR
Research Program
National Collection of Fine Arts
Smithsonian Institution
December 1970

1. *Federal Support for the Visual Arts: The New Deal and Now* (Greenwich: New York Graphic Society, 1969), 226 pp.

2. Vol. 2, no. 4, pp. 2–40. Published by the University of Wisconsin, University Extension Division, Madison, Wisconsin. This memoir was written before the establishment of the National Foundation on the Arts and Humanities. Thus, some of its references to the present state of government support for the arts are dated.

3. The abbreviations in parentheses following the first full citation of the titles of government agencies and private organizations will be used consistently hereafter throughout this anthology in the interest of brevity. See also the table of abbreviations on page ix.

4. For other visual material concerning the projects, see my *Federal Art Patronage: 1933 to 1943* (College Park: University of Maryland Art Gallery, 1966) and "Memoirs of a WPA Painter" by Edward Laning and "A Sampler of New Deal Murals," selected by Francis V. O'Connor, *American Heritage* (October 1970), pp. 38–57.

5. I am presently editing for publication *Art for the Millions*, an anthology of essays written by WPA/FAP artists and administrators from all regions of the country between 1935 and 1940.

6. For a basic history of the New Deal art projects, see my report cited in note 1 as well as my "New Deal Murals in New York," *Artforum* (November 1968), vol. VII, no. 3, pp. 41–49. See also the bibliography on page 331.

PART 1

THE ADMINISTRATION OF
THE NEW DEAL ART PROJECTS

OLIN DOWS was born in Irvington-on-Hudson, New York, in 1904. As a boy he took painting lessons with C. K. Chatterton. He attended St. Marks School and Harvard College. For two years he studied painting with Eugene Savage and Edwin Cassius Taylor at the Yale Art School, and briefly gave a course on Art History at Wesleyan University. During the 1930s he worked closely with Edward Bruce on the Public Works of Art Project and the Treasury Section of Painting and Sculpture. He was one of the sponsors of the first survey of Section mural designs, *Art in Federal Buildings*, published in 1936. From 1935 to 1938 he was Chief of the Treasury Relief Art Project, which operated under the Section with WPA funds. After leaving this position, he won Section competitions to paint murals in the post offices of Rhinebeck (1940) and Hyde Park (1941), New York. During World War II, while a sergeant in the Army Engineers at Camp Meade, he was sent as one of three war artists to the European Theater of Operations. In 1949 he wrote and illustrated *Franklin Roosevelt at Hyde Park*. He continues to paint and has works in a number of public and private collections. His last New York agent was the Macbeth Gallery. In 1950 he married Carmen Vial de Señoret. He lives in Rhinebeck, New York, where he has always lived, and owns a house in Washington, D.C.

FIGURE 1. Jury judging the "48 States Competition," 1939. From left to right: the painters Maurice Sterne, Henry Varnum Poor and Edgar Miller; Olin Dows, Edward Bruce (seated), and Edward Rowan. They are looking at a mural study submitted by Ward Lockwood of Texas. Above it is the entry of James Baare Turnbull of Missouri. (Courtesy of Dr. Belisario R. Contreras)

The New Deal's Treasury Art Program: A Memoir

OLIN DOWS

The New Deal Art Projects

In discussing the Roosevelt administration's Treasury Art Program, I should like to characterize each of the New Deal's individual art projects.

What I have to say may not be very lively: during World War II, I gave a talk to an art school in London about these United States government programs when Sir Herbert Read was in the audience. I was told afterwards he complained that I did not talk like an artist at all. Indeed I did not. I talked like an administrator, a bureaucrat, and I shall be writing like one now. The pertinent points of this discussion are: How was the program handled? How was the work obtained? How much did it cost? What kind of work was done? Who did it? What were its fruits, human, artistic, and social?

Although this article is not an artistic appraisal, I shall incidentally and inevitably make judgments. I do want to get the facts down as I remember them, relieved by some of the imponderables that suggest the way those of us who ran the programs felt, the reasons we acted as we did, how we solved our problems. This kind of material can only be obtained now, and very incompletely at that, by reading the documents, voluminous correspondence, and releases on file in the National Archives in Washington. As our government may again undertake some kind of art program, and as we are in the middle of what is called a cultural boom—which the government programs of the thirties did much to stimulate—it seems timely for me to add what I can to the record.

Human economic relief was the motive behind all the New Deal's art programs. That is why they were so easily accepted both by the public and the

Reprinted with permission from *Arts in Society*, volume 2, number 4 (1963–1964).

politicians. If it had not been for the great Depression, it is unlikely that our government would have sponsored more art then than it had in the past.

There were four programs: 1. The first was called the Public Works of Art Project (PWAP), a crash relief program administered without a strict relief test in the Treasury Department. It lasted six months from December 1933 to June 1934, employed about 3700 artists, and cost about $1,312,000.

2. The Section of Painting and Sculpture, later called the Section of Fine Arts, was the second program, also administered by the Treasury Department. It obtained painting and sculpture to decorate new federal buildings, largely post offices and court houses, by anonymous competitions. Inaugurated in October 1934, it faded away in 1943. It awarded about 1400 contracts and cost about $2,571,000.

3. The Treasury Relief Art Project (TRAP) financed in July 1935 by an allocation of funds from the WPA to the Treasury for the decoration of federal buildings, was administered by the Section according to the same relief rules as was the WPA. It employed about 446 persons, 75 percent of whom were on relief. It cost $833,784 and was discontinued in 1939.

4. The Work Progress Administration's Federal Art Project (WPA/FAP), a large relief program devoted to the plastic arts (which concern us here) was part of a wider program called Federal Project No. 1, which included drama, music, and writing. It started in August 1935, was administered according to the relief rules of the WPA, lasted until June 1943, and cost about $35,000,000. Slightly over 5,000 persons were employed at its peak.

I shall be writing about the first three of these projects and will call them the Treasury programs. I make no distinction between relief and non-relief artists, as there should be none. Some of the best work was done on the relief program. What I have to say about the WPA Project is given from an outsider's point of view.

Many people believe that government should not get mixed up in art patronage. Although they may be right, I believe it should. In the past it has ordered works of art, built public buildings and monuments, and decorated them with painting and sculpture, all paid for with tax money. I think it is suitable and socially and artistically beneficial that this historic policy be continued and amplified. I am convinced it will become necessary to have a national policy about art and a program to implement it.

As I also believe that the effective way to stimulate a living art is by purchase, commission, awarding prizes, and scholarships, I want to see as much variety as possible in the sources of these stimuli. I believe that no matter how

12

stuffy, limited, "chi-chi," or pedestrian the administration of fine arts bureaus may be (and this goes for museums and foundations as well), it is better to have them than not to have them. The greater diversity there is in their points of view and administration, the better.

Museum, foundation, and official commissions, purchases and awards rarely go to the very great. For one reason, there are few men of genius at any given period of time; sometimes there are none. For another, those who decide, the other professionals, the hangers-on of art, museum directors, critics, collectors, and amateurs, do not always recognize genius. What we do recognize, is ability, competence, and sometimes superlative professional performance in recent fashions of visions. Admittedly, the distinction between superlative professional performance and genius gets blurred with time.

There must be a broad base for a national art. The world is richer both for the work and the social contribution of the competent professional artist. Fundamentally it is he, egged on by outside forces, who sets the artistic climate or fashion. I have lived long enough to have seen several such fashions greatly influence our profession. To mention only three, Eugene Savage, Josef Albers, and now Jack Tworkov have succeeded each other as head of the Yale School of Fine Arts; they are examples of the talented and able professionals who at a certain time are bought by the museums, win the prizes, head the important schools. There are other artists, often rather obscure ones, whose expression is difficult, limited, or does not appeal to the current fashion; whose personalities are retiring and little disposed to influencing others. They too are important to a national art. For example, I recently visited the Smithsonian to see the annual exhibition of the Washington Water Color Society. A small wash drawing called *The Married Couple* by Aaron Sopher of Baltimore was the picture I most enjoyed. I was glad to see that Sopher had grown, and continued to develop his own satiric, acid, yet compassionate vision. I had not seen his work since 1940, when Forbes Watson gave me his thin book on the artist, published by Theodore Taub of Baltimore. Sopher's work has great personal distinction, which, in my opinion, has still not had sufficient recognition, though he is represented in the Cone, Phillips, and Dumbarton Oaks collections and has been reproduced in the *New Yorker* and the *New Masses*.

The importance of the Treasury programs, as well as its salutary effect on our national art, is largely owing to the fact that it included such artists as Eugene Savage, Gifford Beale, and Sidney Waugh, and at the same time—in the nineteen thirties, remember—Aaron Sopher, Bradley Tomlin, and Saul Baizerman. Being something of an artistic "mugwump" I am skeptical of the final validity of all artistic fashions and believe in the widest representation possible of artists and styles.

The Public Works of Art Project

If the first crash art program had not been so carefully thought out and expertly organized, I doubt that other programs would have been undertaken. The man mainly responsible for this was Edward Bruce. He was absorbed by the idea, and in a certain sense killed himself making it materialize.

The idea itself was already being discussed. American artists traveling in Mexico had been impressed with that government's immensely successful mural program, employing its best artists in public buildings at workman's wages. George Biddle wrote his Groton schoolmate, President Roosevelt, proposing that he and a group of distinguished American painters, Thomas Benton, John Steuart Curry, Reginald Marsh, Henry Varnum Poor, Boardman Robinson, and Grant Wood decorate the new Department of Justice Building in Washington for plumber's wages. The building itself was designed by his friend and fellow Philadelphian, Charles Borie.

This letter was passed on to Edward Bruce, who in 1932 had come to Washington to represent former clients in the solution of the practical issue of Philippine independence. He was also an advisor to the Treasury and had been sent to the London Economic Conference as our delegation's silver expert.

Edward Bruce was uniquely equipped for implementing the idea of government participation in the arts. He was a former Columbia football star, an honor graduate from the University's Law School, and a successful lawyer practicing in New York and then in the Philippines (where he owned the Manila *Times*). As promoter and president of the Pacific Development Company, he had lived in China for several years. When this experiment in oriental trade failed, he decided to take up painting as a profession; he had painted with J. Francis Murphy and Arthur Parton while at college. Consequently at the age of 44, having turned down a number of tempting offers in banking and the law, he and Mrs. Bruce went to Italy where he worked seriously with his friend Maurice Sterne in Anticoli. He destroyed his first year's work; had an exhibition of his second year's output in New York, and sold every picture. From then on he painted successfully for almost ten years. It was at the end of this period, when he was 53, that he came to Washington and became practically involved in the idea of an art program.

I first met the Bruces when we found ourselves visiting former Secretary of the Treasury Andrew Mellon's apartment to see his collection. We became friends. They asked me often to their Nineteenth Street house, where a stimulating company of politicians, administrators, experts, journalists, and artists were invited. It was a wonderful house to go to. I remember with the greatest pleasure the good and informal talk and the really delicious food. They were a vital pair: Mrs. Bruce handsome, outspoken, strong, almost a pioneer type; Bruce heavy, humorous, loving to tease amiably, enjoying ideas, throwing them out by the dozens and drawing them from others; both of them warm, generous, and kind.

Bruce and his friends were deeply involved in politics and various projects of the New Deal. He was well informed about events and plans. In March 1933 President Roosevelt had asked the emergency session of the Seventy-third Congress to provide several essential relief measures: the Civilian Conservation Corps (CCC), to take the employable young men off the streets and into the national forests for needed reclamation and conservation work; the Federal Emergency Relief Administration (FERA), a straight relief program; and the PWA. The Public Works Administration, needing careful preparation and planning, inevitably got off to a slow start. In November, Roosevelt created the Civil Works Administration (CWA) with Harry Hopkins as administrator. It was a crash employment program intentionally temporary, to last during the winter months of 1933–1934, to create short-term employment on small public works projects, to take as many people off direct relief as possible, and to pay them a minimum wage so that this infusion of purchasing power would help prime the pump of our stagnant economy.

As Bruce knew that both white collar and manual workers were being included in this new CWA program, he believed it was also suitable to employ painters professionally. Knowing many artists well, he realized how hard a time even the most successful ones were having. So with a couple of young New Deal lawyers he outlined and set up, in the Treasury Department, the first government program for the arts, the Public Works of Art Project (PWAP). The funds for the program were allocated to the Treasury by the CWA. Being a lawyer, business man, and economist, and knowing most of the important politicians and administrators informally, Bruce would talk to them in their own language, and so inspired their confidence in what he was trying to do. This was undoubtedly one of the main factors in getting the first program off to a good start. We also tend to forget today how much political courage it took for President Roosevelt to authorize and Secretary Morgenthau to assume the administration of this first program. The sympathetic interest of Harry Hopkins and the Secretary of Labor, Miss Perkins, and other highly placed individuals in the administration also helped this and later programs.

Bruce called the first organizational meeting at his home in mid-December 1933. It consisted of museum directors and important people in the field of art from all over the United States, men and women whom he had chosen as being best fitted to direct this first experiment. It was an outstanding group, and I was much interested to meet Mrs. Juliana Force, Forbes Watson, and many others for the first time. Bruce outlined his plan and asked for suggestions. These men and women were all aware of their artist neighbors' difficult professional situations. They generally approved the plan and had constructive ideas about how to operate it. Mrs. Roosevelt sat at the table from which Bruce was directing the meeting, knitting steadily, and every once in a while interjecting a pertinent remark or a question.

I find it difficult here, as elsewhere in this article, to convey the sense of hope, excitement, and enthusiasm that the early New Deal days inspired. Edward Bruce personified it at its best. He was no starry eyed "do gooder," though he couldn't have been a finer man. He was practical, successful, able, with a first rate mind, a realistic man of affairs who threw himself into this project with his whole being. Some of his enthusiasm went with many members of the group when they left his house that afternoon to return to their various cities to get the project started. I still feel a kindling of the spirit when I think of this meeting, what it meant, and how it was instrumental in what followed.

To simplify its organization, the CWA had divided the country into 16 regions instead of the usual 48 states. The PWAP used the same divisions. It had a professional Treasury paymaster in each region; also a volunteer committee of museum curators, painters, and other persons interested in the arts who directed each regional program. Edward Bruce directed it from Washington, with Forbes Watson as advisor, and Edward Rowan as assistant. Bruce asked me to go on the local regional committee which included Washington, Maryland, and Virginia. As I was the youngest and the least important of its five members (Charles Bittinger, Powell Minnegrode, Duncan Phillips, and Law Watkins were the others) and as I owned a model T Ford, I did much of the leg work in the region, with the help of an intelligent, able, and charming Junior League girl, now Mrs. Alice Korff.

Most of the work produced in ours, as in the other regions, was placed in tax-supported buildings, schools, hospitals, public libraries, and museums. Some was sent to Washington headquarters where it was used for decorating Congressional and administrative offices. You still see pictures done under this first program in Washington and throughout the country. The PWAP employed about 3,750 artists at low daily wages. They produced over 15,600 works of art. There was no question of or test for relief in this employment, and I think there were a number of distinguished painters who, being enthusiastic about the idea, went on the project for a nominal period or who directly contributed one of their works to it. The total cost was approximately $1,312,000, which makes the cost per artist about $350.00. At the end of six months a large exhibition of painting and sculpture from all over the country was held at the Corcoran Gallery in Washington. It was a great success: even my Republican friends acknowledged the government had received its money's worth. Knowledgeable people were impressed both with the quality and its geographical spread. There were older painters living in distant communities whose work received national attention for the first time; and there were younger ones like Frank Mechau or Herman

FIGURE 2. Chaim Gross (b. 1904). *Poddlers.* Mahogany woodcarving
in Irving, Pennsylvania, Post Office. Section, 1942. (National Archives)

17

Maril who started their national reputations here. It was the broad base, the fact there was much good painting and sculpture being produced throughout the country, that marked this exhibition. It was only a token of what the PWAP had produced everywhere. By a magnificent and practical gesture the government had strengthened our art and culture. It was a healthy influence. Under the pressure of events local artists were encouraged to leave their ivory towers, and they responded enthusiastically by carrying American art to a practical degree of social consciousness never achieved before.

Edward Bruce and Forbes Watson made a dynamic team. They believed in the importance of American art and the essential social fairness of opening its benefits to as many artists as possible and of making their product available to as many communities as possible. They were both articulate, disinterested, and men of deep convictions. Bruce was an extraordinarily talented administrator, generous in his delegation of authority and confident in the abilities of those who were working with him. He was interested in results, not in a method. He often used the old cliche, "there are many ways to skin a cat." If he found one way ineffective, he would try another, but always thoughtfully, carefully, and with great attention to detail. He ran his office at PWAP, and later in the Section, with a jovial informality that instilled everyone working with him (from executive to file clerk) with real team spirit. He would often pack a critical wallop in a joke. He never spared himself, and he expected the best from everyone else. On the whole he got it, for our small staff accomplished much.

Forbes Watson had a critical yet enthusiastic mind. His lucidity in speech and writing, his intimate knowledge of the art situation throughout the country, the respect in which artists held him (even when they didn't like him or what he wrote), his rock bottom integrity, and his personal style added an essential strength and quality to this and subsequent programs.

The regional committees also had much to do with the PWAP's success. There were men like William Millikan, busy director of the large, rich, and growing Cleveland Museum, who really knew his local artists and had already initiated important programs for their benefit; women like Miss Charlotte Partridge, head of the then small Layton art center in Milwaukee, who was able to accomplish so much through her hard work, good eye, and enthusiasm.

On the whole, our advisors on the Eastern seaboard were less interested in our program than their colleagues in the Middle and Far West. I felt the political attitude of rich museum trustees in the East carried unnecessary weight with their professional staffs. Some of these professionals also found it difficult to detach themselves from what they felt were "standards." A project as inclusive as this one did not appeal to them.

In the last analysis, however, the success of this program was due to those painters and sculptors who contributed to its various social purposes and produced some of their best work for it. The PWAP ended in June 1934. Some of the strictly relief aspects of the program were, nevertheless, carried on by other relief organizations, which were finally merged and coordinated in August 1935, when the WPA Federal Art Project was organized by Holger Cahill.

The Section of Fine Arts

In the summer of 1934 I spent several months with the Bruces in Vermont. Besides an active day painting—in the studio in the morning, outdoors in the afternoon—Bruce would dictate a voluminous correspondence during his lunch hour; and in the evening we would discuss together or with visiting friends the possibilities of government patronage and what form it should take.

That autumn he set up the second program, the Section of Painting and Sculpture later called the Section of Fine Arts, again in the Treasury. Since the eighteenth century, the Secretary of the Treasury has been responsible for federal buildings, with the supervising architect as executive officer. Naturally then, the Section was placed under the architect's direct jurisdiction. In the thirties he was Louis Simon, an efficient and careful administrator. Under the Director of Procurement, Admiral Christian Joy Peoples, Simon was in charge of a huge emergency program for building post offices and court houses all over the United States. Secretary Morgenthau issued an administrative order authorizing the expenditure of one percent of the total cost of each building for embellishment, if on completion, funds were still available. In practice this money materialized for only about one third of the new buildings. On the larger post offices and court houses the amount actually spent for painting and sculpture was usually less than one percent of the building's cost. This nevertheless made a respectable sum. The work was obtained by anonymous competitions, usually open. The winning artists received contracts, as in any other government job. There was no question of relief. The government was simply doing what it had always done, up to a point: decorating some of its public buildings. Now, however, it was doing so in a different way and on a larger scale than ever before. Ironically enough, from 1934 to 1938 the Section of Fine Arts spent about $537,000 on 375 contracts for painting and sculpture, which was a smaller sum than a few sculptors had received for the architectural sculpture on the Triangle Buildings in Washington under the previous Republican administration.

In the past, what decoration was done in government buildings was awarded through architects of those buildings. The Section's policy was to acquire, on as broad a base and in as fair a manner as possible, the best available painting and sculpture for the new federal buildings. As we were part of the supervising architect's organization we were able to see the plans of new buildings in their early stages.

19

In addition to the regular force of civil servant architects and draughtsmen a group of twenty or more prominent architects from all over the United States had been engaged by the procurement division to help make plans for the new post offices. In many cases they brought their staffs with them, and were set up as small designing offices within the larger organization. We worked most of the time with these two groups in the necessary but sometimes reluctant collaboration that was the basis for our program. Some architects were new to governmental regulations, and often found red tape troublesome. Besides the routine of the procurement division, they had to consider the special demands of the Post Office Department, for whose essential service the buildings were to be erected. Moreover, since the overall building program was designed to increase employment generally, the architects also had to put up with the Section's importunate insistence on placing murals and sculpture in their buildings.

The Section, inaugurated in October 1934 trailed off during the war, curtailed by President Roosevelt's budget message of January 3, 1941, eliminating all non-defense projects. It ended in July 1943.

During those nine years of activity the Section awarded 1,124 mural contracts for which it had paid $1,472,199 and 289 contracts for sculpture costing $563,529. One hundred ninety-three competitions were held, and 1,205 individual artists placed their work in federal buildings. The average price for the mural commissions was $1,356, and for the sculpture $1,936. Administrative costs were $393,516.

Edward Bruce was named director of the Section, with Forbes Watson as advisor; Edward Rowan was in charge of the states west of the Mississippi, and I in charge of those to the east. Miss Maria Ealand and Inslee Hopper were the other members of our staff. Under Bruce's cohesive direction we worked as a group, discussed our mutual problems, and collaborated on important letters or decisions. Fundamentally we were agreed on what we were trying to do, and this unified our efforts. We had decided that competition was the fairest way to acquire work for the public. Although it is a wasteful method, and open competitions may not attract some successful artists, we believed it to be the best solution for our purposes. We kept our juries as varied as possible, and also awarded many contracts for recommended but non-winning designs. I still believe this is the fairest way to proceed in acquiring art with public funds.

Our first large and important competition was for the new Department of Justice and Post Office Department buildings in Washington, D.C. Both were finished, and funds remained available to the Section for their decoration. As mentioned above, most of the sculpture had already been completed under the previous administration. The architect of the Justice Department, Charles Borie, was enthusiastic. He had in fact designed some superb mural spaces. William Delano, the architect of the Post Office Department, though not too pleased, I suspect, with the way we were going to obtain the work, collaborated graciously with his usual understanding, charm, and courtesy. We appointed a committee of nineteen museum directors, art experts, and painters (who would be *hors concours*), and asked them for lists of the twenty-two painters and fourteen sculptors (the number of spaces available) who in their opinion could best decorate the two important buildings. When the confidential lists were sent in, we tabulated the results and found that eleven painters and two sculptors had received three more votes than the others. To this group we gave contracts. They were painters Thomas Hart Benton (who later withdrew), George Biddle, John Steuart Curry, Rockwell Kent, Leon Kroll, Reginald Marsh, Henry Varnum Poor, Boardman Robinson, Eugene Savage, Maurice Sterne, and Grant Wood (who resigned on account of previous commitments) and sculptors Paul Manship and William Zorach.

The remaining artists who had received votes were invited to a national competition for the remaining eleven mural and twelve sculpture commissions. The painters were divided into nearly equal groups, each group being assigned specific subject matter.

All of the 107 sculptors suggested by the advisory committee were asked for photographs of their work. This material was reviewed by a jury consisting of Paul Manship, Maurice Sterne, and William Zorach, who recommended forty-eight sculptors divided into groups of four, each group to make scale models of a mail carrier from a specified period in our history.

A jury of six painters, Leon Kroll, Bancel LaFarge, Jonas Lie, Ernest Peixotto, Henry Schnakenberg, and Eugene Speicher, and three sculptors, Alice Decker, Paul Manship, and William Zorach, as well as the architects of the buildings, William Delano and Charles Borie, spent three days examining 315 mural sketches and sixty-two sculpture models. The following artists were awarded contracts: painters Alfred Crimi, Karl Free, George Harding, Ward Lockwood, Frank Mechau, and William Palmer; two other artists were appointed, Doris Lee and Tom Lea, and both were asked to redesign their submissions. Sculptors chosen were Stirling Calder, Gaetano Cecere, Chaim Gross, Arthur Lee, Carl Schmitz, Louis Slobodkin, Heinz Warnecke, and Sidney Waugh. In addition to these winners, eighty-two painters and sixteen sculptors were invited to design and were awarded contracts for other post offices.

All the judging of sketches was by number. The artist's name was pasted on the back of each sketch in a sealed envelope, which was opened only at the end of the three-day session when the jury's decisions had been made. The fact that we awarded additional commissions as a result of sketches submitted in this competition made it clear to artists that they were not wasting their efforts in a one-shot raffle. These awards helped to mitigate one of the greatest drawbacks to the competitive system.

From our point of view there was one great advantage in this system. Artistic and political pressure could be courteously satisfied by inviting the recommended artist to the next competition. A young Texan artist had been strongly recommended to us by an important Congressman or Senator from his state. We invited him to the national competition described above. As it turned out, one sketch intrigued the jury increasingly over the three-day judging. It contained an unusual solution of the mural space and a certain nineteenth century *Harper's Magazine* look; it was beautifully executed. The jury gave it an award, but recommended redesigning. When the envelopes were opened, one of us thought the name was somehow familiar. We looked up the file and discovered that it was the young painter recommended by the Texas politician, his name Tom Lea!

I go into this competition in such detail because it set the pattern and established the Section as a responsible professional outfit. Architects like William Delano who, though they may not have approved of the method we were following, realized that what we were trying to do was neither superficial nor ill-advised, and that it did bring forward new and talented artists who had something personal to say in solving these problems. They discovered somewhat later that these painters and sculptors, though not specially trained for architectural work, could execute and install their jobs competently, professionally, and on time. The care and integrity of the jury also had an influence on the artistic community. These things get around.

We held a number of large national competitions like the ones described above. One such was for a new small post office in every state which we called the 48 State Competition. Others were held, open to artists living in the states west of the Mississippi, and again for those living to the east of that river.

The greatest number of our competitions, however, were what we called local, that is, for panels on which the appropriation would be from two to five thousand dollars. We would invite a museum director, head of an art association, or some technically equipped person who lived in the vicinity of the post office or court house we were to decorate. He acted as chairman and ran the competition, being paid a nominal fee for his expenses (between fifty and two hundred dollars). We asked him to appoint a jury, always including the architect of the building. We sent him a form announcement specifying the size and location of the panels to be decorated, the amount of money to be paid, the terms of the competition, the scale of the sketches, etc. He returned this form, filled out with the names of his jury and any suggestions he had to make on the competition and especially on local subject matter. This form was mimeographed in quantity and returned to the chairman with blue prints of the spaces in competition. He and his committee then notified the eligible artists (sometimes from one state, sometimes from several, depending on the artistic population). There would also be announcements in the local press.

FIGURE 3. Leon Kroll (b. 1884). *The Defeat of Justice.* Study for mural in a lunette of the Attorney General's Office, Justice Department Building, Washington, D.C. Section, c. 1936. National Gallery of Art. (National Gallery of Art)

FIGURE 4. Peter Blume (b. 1906). *Grape Vine.* Study for mural in the lobby of the Geneva, New York, Post Office. Section, 1941. Collection unknown. (National Archives)

The competitors submitted their sketches (anonymously, with names in sealed envelopes, as described above) usually after a designing period of three months. At the jury meeting the sketches were numbered and the local jury sent their recommendations and all the sketches to our office without opening the envelopes. If, after studying the designs, the Section staff had any doubts about the choice of the local committee, they were discussed by letter. In practice, however, we rarely questioned a local decision. If we disagreed, we awarded the next good job that came up in that region to the designer who had, in our opinion, been passed over. This was rare, too, for our jurors were knowledgeable. Moreover, these competitions often produced several good designs which the local jury would recommend. Only after the final decision was reached would the envelopes be opened and the name of the winning artist disclosed.

Technically we had few failures. Almost all commissioned artists on any of the programs gave competent professional performances. One fact materially helped the juries attain this record: it was that a three foot square full size detail was often asked for in addition to the two or three inch scale sketch. This decreased the possibility of a painter's winning a competition with a slicked up sketch he would afterwards be unable to execute adequately.

We urged the local committees to exhibit designs and models. This clarified the Section's activities, interested the communities in their artists, showed the latter how different designers had solved the same problem and, in so far as the jury's opinion was concerned, how the designs had been judged and the individual sketches had failed or succeeded. The price paid for murals was based on the rate of $20 a square foot. The time alloted for the completion of a contract was about two years, but in practice this was flexible.

A variety of activities were undertaken by the Section during its eight-year life. Besides the competitions just described, we held at least one, I remember, to which a limited number of artists were invited. There was a $6,000 appropriation available for decoration on a new building in the Carville, Louisiana, leper colony. Through his friend Frederick Keppel, Bruce obtained another $3,000 from the Carnegie Corporation and held a watercolor competition for the purchase of 300 watercolors at $30 each. The watercolors were to decorate rooms in the leper colony.

Other competitions were held by the Section for the interior decoration of the Maritime Commission's new ships. Among others, Bernard Perlin's winning design actually went to sea.

Edward Rowan had charge of a group of young painters who found themselves in ccc camps throughout the United States, and who were encouraged by their officers to paint a record of camp life. These pictures were sent to the Section. Some of these men later made national reputations.

24

The Section also published a mimeographed bulletin, edited by Forbes Watson, which was sent free to over 5,000 interested persons. It contained full information about the competitions, biographies of the winners, appointments, and articles of general interest. Its purpose being to report and inform, it was intentionally non-critical.

All contracts with artists contained a clause that a photograph and negative of the completed mural was to be supplied. These became the property of the Section. A practically complete pictorial record was made. It contained these photographs of completed murals, an incomplete photographic file of the PWAP, the pictures taken at the Section's own photographic shop of competition sketches sent to Washington, and those taken of the TRAP work (discussed below). All this material is now on file in the National Archives.

As the country prepared for World War II, the Section did some work for the Red Cross and also employed eight distinguished painters to make a record of war production. My attempt at this time to have the army take on a group of painters to make a record of the war is another story; I mention it only because here again the staff of the Section was involved in the proposed planning.[1]

Treasury Relief Art Project

Never a large program, the Section had started promptly and produced its first competitions and commissions in the autumn of 1934. It was not set up to engage in widespread relief. The following winter and spring, the Roosevelt administration studied various means of meeting the necessity for national relief. The WPA (created May 1935) was the outcome of these deliberations. The Treasury was asked to administer a large relief art project that was to be part of this national effort. Neither Secretary Morgenthau nor Edward Bruce wanted to undertake a program on the proposed scale, especially as it was to include not only the plastic arts, but music, drama, and writing as well. So the WPA went ahead with its own plans.

From one point of view the Section made a mistake in not directing this larger program. It would have given unity, which it never attained, to the government's effort. On the other hand, a healthy rivalry developed between the WPA and ourselves which stimulated each of us to outdo the other. This situation was like so many other administrative anomalies under the Roosevelt administration, possessing its good and its bad sides. It is also ironic to think that we described the Treasury program as "permanent." It turned out to be more so by only one month! We also suggested that the Treasury was after "quality," while the WPA offered "relief," but the public has never made any distinction whatsoever. You still hear remarks about those WPA murals in post offices; and as to quality, both programs produced fine jobs. In fact, the inclusive net of WPA employment quite often achieved first rate results. It cost more, but then that money would presumably have been spent on relief anyhow. Who remembers the ditch diggers and leaf rakers? But David Smith and Jackson Pollock are and will remain memorable talents of our cultural heritage whether you like them or not.

As the Section was ready to handle additional funds in July 1935, the WPA administration made a $530,784 grant to the Treasury for the decoration of federal buildings. TRAP was to operate under the same employment rules as the WPA, i.e., 90 percent of the personnel on relief, 10 percent non-relief (six months later changed to 75 percent relief, 25 percent non-relief), with a "going wage" which varied from $69 to $103 a month for 96 hours' work.

I was in charge, with Henry LaFarge as my assistant and Cecil Jones as business manager. We had three supervisors: Bernard Roufberg in California, Mrs. Elizabeth Lane in Boston, and Mrs. Alice Sharkey in New York. Like almost everyone who worked on any of the art projects, they did a devoted and enthusiastic job. Our New York program was numerically (as in the other plastic arts programs) about one-third of the whole country's. Mrs. Sharkey showed much tact and sympathy, and possessed a discerning and keen eye; she handled our New York office with great skill, produced distinguished work, and did so without perceptibly treading on toes. One artist told me that it was always a pleasure to go to Mrs. Sharkey's office, because she behaved as if she were about to hand you a cup of tea. New York City's situation was a difficult one to handle, both administratively and artistically: the Artists' Union was strong and vociferous and our project was partially dependent on the city relief administrators as well as on Mrs. Audrey McMahon, the dynamically able head of the WPA art project in New York.

The TRAP held a rather special position in the country owing to the skill of administrators like Mrs. Sharkey and to the relations the Section had in one year established for itself with professional artists. Outside the jurisdiction of our three supervisors, artists dealt either directly with our office or sometimes through a volunteer friend, such as a neighboring museum curator. Ours was considered a privileged program, and indeed it was. Being small, it could afford to be considerate and flexible. I do not know how many artists realized that much of our smooth operation was due to Cecil Jones, an enthusiastic Georgian, who knew many of Washington's administrators and, more important, their secretaries. It was rarely that even the most unusual or troublesome piece of procurement stumped him. He dashed around government's red tape with ease, and got things through channels in record time.

Most of our jobs in TRAP, like those of the Section, were for post offices. There were many buildings, old and new, without appropriations for decoration but possessing fine spaces for painting and sculpture. We chose those buildings which were situated in the vicinity of an available artist or group of artists. We allowed two trips to the building, if it were a question of transportaton. A master artist would be put in charge, sometimes as a result of winning a Section competition. After designing and having the sketch approved by the architect, local advisors, and our office, he organized one or more assistants to help him execute the mural. Materials were supplied; work space was rented, lent, or the work was done directly on the walls.

In this way eighty-nine murals and sixty-five sculpture projects were produced. A number of these appointments were made as a result of Section competitions. Although the pay was low, many painters preferred to do these overall mural schemes for a post office lobby rather than a single panel that was more highly paid. The problem involved is an almost irresistable temptation to a painter. I regret that the Treasury programs could so rarely award more than a one-or-two-panel commission. There were, however, a number of reception rooms in U.S. Marine hospitals and post office lobbies (especially entrance lobbies in the larger post offices), which allowed for fine overall schemes. If there had been more, it would have enriched the whole program. I remember original and personal overall murals created on both the TRAP and the Section by Ray Boynton, Kenneth Callahan, Howard Cook, Gerald Foster, Xavier Gonzales, David Granahan, Frank Long, Henrick Martin Mayer, George Picken, and Stephen Mopope. Mopope, with a group of Indian painters, decorated the Anadarko, Oklahoma, post office with murals which are in much the same style as he and William Crumbo used in the Interior Department, Washington, D.C.

There were also about 108 painters doing easel pictures and prints, and forty-nine receiving miscellaneous employment: some drafting, some working in the photography and framing shops attached to our Washington, D.C., office.

After TRAP had been running for about a year, the WPA decided it would no longer allocate funds to projects outside its jurisdiction and would withdraw such funds as had not been spent. We felt that our commitments were to individuals, and that it would be a mistake to change the work conditions in the midst of progress. So for the first and only time I asked to see President Roosevelt professionally. (I knew him as an old friend of my family.) I called Mrs. Roosevelt and explained to her what was disturbing me. She asked me to lunch the next day and said she would try and let me see the President for a minute afterwards. When I went into his oval office, I showed him a dozen photographs of work that was under way, explained what we considered the personal commitment and the relatively small sums involved. Marvin McIntyre, his secretary, hovered nervously in the background, fearing, I expect, that I would waste the President's time or needlessly disrupt his tight schedule. F.D.R. obviously had other things on his mind, but he looked through the photographs and listened to what I had to say. He asked a few questions, nodded his head and said, "I see." Scrawling an undecipherable hieroglyphic on a chit of paper about the size of a hat check, he told me to give it to the Director of the Budget. I departed, went straight to the Budget Director's office, was admitted and handed in my chit. The matter was settled, the jobs completed as planned; our program kept the unspent funds, and we even got supplementary appropriations later without much difficulty.

Although our original appropriation had allowed us 500 jobs, as the WPA art program had started its wholesale relief employment only a month after TRAP and had taken on many of the artists capable of doing murals, we considered our appropriation as essentially a sum with which to produce needed work of a certain kind. Hence we were selective. The New York City Artists' Union had heard, however, that the project had been allowed a total employment of 500; so Stuart Davis sent us a sizzling manifesto, attacking our handling of the funds and the employment quota. Mrs. Sharkey, Mrs. McMahon, and I had a stormy session with the union's committee in New York. It was grotesque and an anomaly to have artists unionized against a government which for the first time in its history was doing something about them professionally. However, as there was some justification in the Union's contention that the WPA had not been able to take on relief all competent artists, we did increase our personnel in New York. Among this group which we took on under pressure there was one young painter who had sent sketches to several Section competitions and had tried to join the New York TRAP, both unsuccessfully. I remember that his work when he joined TRAP did not add greatly to our program; yet he has since achieved, quite justifiably, a considerable reputation. Such an occurrence in the inevitable exercising of judgment makes one diffident. But like jury decisions, individual judgments do have to be made.

In addition to the work already mentioned, there was considerable variety in other aspects of the TRAP's program. A number of federal agencies needed different kinds of "art work" which we were in a position to supply. This was done on the workshop principle already discussed in relation to the post office murals, with a painter or sculptor in charge of a group. In this way TRAP produced important murals and sculpture for six of the PWA housing projects (Public Works Administration, Secretary of the Interior, Harold Ickes' outfit). The largest of these was designed by Archibald Manning Brown, in Harlem, New York. Like most of the architects in charge of such housing, he was pleased to have our collaboration. There were no funds under the PWA for extras, and these great congeries of low cost apartments urgently needed some kind of accent. Heinz Warnecke undertook this Harlem job for us and with Mrs. Sharkey discussed the work needed with the architect. Warnecke started his group working individually on sketches, so that each member should understand the problems involved. Handsome symbolic figures of a man and a woman were designed for the main gates; appropriately rounded animals, tumbling bears and penguins, which children could play on, were placed in the gardens. Richmond Barthe carved two sensitive low relief panels for an outside stairway. Inside Miss Elsie Driggs, Domenico Mortellito, and Algot Stenbury executed, respectively, murals of playful animals, low relief colored linoleum panels, and an abstracted city landscape in small play and reception rooms.

When this work was well under way, several members of the Harlem committee, representing the future tenants, voiced deep resentment that the symbolic male figure was naked to the waist and held a cog wheel. These individuals believed it was undignified and a slap at the colored race. They wanted a frock coat or business suit on their figure. We called a meeting in Warnecke's studio; present were Langdon Post, New York housing administrator; Walter White, the able and intelligent head of the NAACP; the architect; Mrs. Sharkey, of course; the Harlem committee; all the painters and sculptors working on this project, and an invited group of important negro artists. The meeting was bitter and unpleasant, because of the conduct of only two members of the Harlem committee. It did no good to point out that symbolic figures were usually partially or wholly nude; that Rockefeller Center was plastered with them; that no disrespect had been intended; that the sketches had been approved and were well under way. The two furious committee members were not convinced; but because they saw that the Negro artists backed up the suitability and quality of the figures so wholeheartedly, the matter was settled and work went ahead.

Work on the other housing units went smoothly enough. Only once did the Housing Administration actually question a completed design. But there were a number of administrators who were fearful of newspaper criticism and several times they expressed grave doubts about the advisability of our doing this kind of embellishment. I always felt this was our headache, not theirs. After all, we were spending the money. The particular decoration that was questioned was by Miss Edna Reindel for a small reception room in the Stamford, Connecticut, housing project. It was an attractive, elegant, rather surrealist domestic mural which would have looked well in any fashionable house. The suitability of the design was questioned just because of these very qualities. Fortunately it was installed, and we heard later that the tenants were proud and pleased with it. Henry Kreis carved a dignified group for the garden of this same project.

Edgar Miller was in charge of important sculpture for Holabird and Root's Chicago housing; William McVey carved Paul Bunyan reliefs for an auditorium wall in the Cleveland project, with independent murals for children's rooms by Charles Campbell and Earle Neff. George Aarons and Aaron Douglas in Boston, Daniel Olney in Washington, D.C., and the Misses Grace and Marion Greenwood and Ahron Ben-Shmuel in Camden, did personal and characteristic work.

The most difficult and complicated mural space undertaken by the TRAP was the dome of Cass Gilbert's old New York Custom House on the Battery. Reginald Marsh organized eight or ten artists to help him with this large job. According to one of his helpers, Marsh who set the example by working long hours himself kept everyone's nose to the grindstone. There were few artists who put in only the stipulated ninety-six hours a month, and many assistants sent us easel pictures because they also wanted to be represented individually. Marsh painted the dome, from a fifty-foot movable scaffold in fresco secco. The murals consist of large New York harbor scenes in color, separated by grisaille figures of explorers, whose names were already carved on the dome. It is lively and vital, and when in downtown New York I often go in to look at it.

Both the Department of Commerce and the Post Office Department use series of posters in their relations with the public. Edward Buk Ulrick, with the help of a large group, produced many dozens of smart posters by silk screen printing. For the State Department we copied historic portraits and painted screens; some easel pictures and prints were sent to our missions abroad; others

FIGURE 5. Reginald Marsh (1898–1954). Murals in dome of U.S. Custom House, New York City. View shows eleven of the sixteen alternating fresco secco panels depicting New York harbor scenes and grisaille portraits of great navigators. (National Archives)

to various federal institutions in this country like Howard University, Washington, D.C.; the leper colony in Carville, Louisiana; and the narcotic farm in Lexington, Kentucky. One of the most interesting and useful of all TRAP projects was in placing the young painter, Paul Wilhelm, in the industrial reformatory at Chillicothe, Ohio, where he taught some of the prisoners art and organized some inmates to decorate their mess hall. Wilhelm did an understanding and an immensely useful, if difficult and taxing, job; he likewise produced pleasant and appropriate decoration. The warden, Sanford Bates, showed me the prison during an inspection tour of our projects. I still remember that day as one of the most interesting and impressive I have ever spent.

The Imponderables

For several reasons the Section of Fine Arts was stronger than was warranted by its subordinate position in the Treasury Department's table of organization. Many officials knew that President and Mrs. Roosevelt and Secretary and Mrs. Morgenthau were interested. The latter especially kept in close touch with our activities. Her wise, sympathetic and intelligent advice was a great asset. Although she helped to solve a few difficult administrative matters, there was never any question of professional interference or pressure.

Edward Bruce carried weight with key members of both political parties and many administrators. He was greatly respected and liked both personally and professionally. Those who knew him were aware of how much he was sacrificing to do this job. His unique combination of qualities gave a stability to the Section which it is impossible to overestimate. With the exception of Forbes Watson, the rest of us were relatively obscure, but that too was an asset: there was no jockeying for position and none of us were prima donnas. Nor did we wish to see the Section become more important politically. We felt it was most effective where it was. Our preoccupation was to do the best job possible under the circumstances. We all believed in the importance of American art (most of us owned work by living American artists). Moreover, our personal tastes varied considerably, and this too helped diversify the Section's collective judgment. We presented no official esthetic dogma.

Edward Rowan joined the PWAP from the directorship of the Cedar Rapids, Iowa, museum, where he was engaged in a pilot project of the Carnegie Foundation. There he had done an outstanding job, promoting and interpreting American art and artists in a community that previously had had little contact with the subject. This experience, his knowledge, and his enthusiastic personality, were very valuable to the Section. Inslee Hopper had done some writing on art, had a variegated group of artist friends, and brought to the job a keen, critical point of view. Henry LaFarge was an old friend of mine, scholarly, quiet and

31

careful, with excellent judgment and a remarkable capacity for getting essentials done without fuss. Miss Maria Ealand, our office manager and Edward Bruce's niece, developed real understanding and sympathy for art and artists. She was a tower of strength and a magnificent catalyst in keeping the office moving and everyone in it in good spirits.

To say that the art critic of a New York newspaper and editor of what I still consider the liveliest and most satisfactory art magazine ever published in the United States, is uncommitted, may sound a bit far-fetched. Paradoxically, Forbes Watson was, I believe, committed to not being so. If I understood him correctly, he felt that the field of painting and sculpture was wide, that there was much talent, much good work produced all over the country, and that the finest artists were not always those most prominent at the moment. His campaign in *The Arts* against the National Academy was not directed at artists so much as against the academy's exaggerated power and vested interests in the American art world. He felt that power was out of proportion to its artistic achievements, just as John Canaday does today, I suspect, in his writing about the academy of the Abstract Expressionists. Watson's differences with the National Academy, though leaving behind a residue of permanent hurt feelings, was an old story by the thirties.

With the exception of Ned Bruce we were all inexperienced in government procedures, but we did our best to conform to them. Treasury officials seemed to respect our efforts and were amused by the Section, which struck a rather eccentric, casual, free and easy note in the administrative machinery of procurement. There was one occasion I remember with some embarrassment. The Secretary's office had telephoned to say that he was to see the President that afternoon, and would like an architect's name to fill a vacancy on the Commission of Fine Arts. We sent a note over immediately, suggesting whoever it was we considered the best person for the position. Next morning Admiral Peoples called me to his office. He told me gently but firmly how surprised he was to hear of the appointment to the commission, although he had sent no such recommendation. I felt thoroughly ashamed for my blunder; it was a stupid and unnecessary breach of procedure; worse, it was bad manners to an able and excellent chief. This was the worst break I remember making.

Matters of this sort, relations with Congressmen or top administrators, appropriations and budgets were handled by Bruce; it was he who would advise how they could best be handled. During the period of his serious illness, or if he was away, when I was in doubt as to a course of action, I would ask to see Leo Martin, executive officer of procurement, a gifted administrator who really understood the huge organization. He always found time to explain clearly and simply any administrative matter which I did not understand. If I followed his advice, the matter would go through smoothly and quickly. This first-hand ex-

FIGURE 6. George Biddle (b. 1885). *Tenement*. Study for fresco panel
in fifth-floor stairwell, Department of Justice Building, Washington, D.C.
Section, c. 1935. University of Maryland (University of Maryland)

perience as part of a great government department has given me lasting respect for administrators like Martin, who have the character, ability, and energy to go far in private business, yet prefer to work as civil servants.

The Section's work involved much paper: the drafting of proposals and reports, a large correspondence and many interviews (with those who wanted something from the Section, with those from whom we wanted something), and of course, endless business on the telephone. All this was but a means to an end. I found satisfaction in doing it adequately. What really made the job a pleasure was the relationship with the painters, sculptors, architects, and museum men, the give and take of the jury meetings, and the feeling that all this activity was actually producing results. Ideas, information, and programs from all over the country flowed into the Section, as they do to any agency which is placed in a strategic position in government. From that central position they were diffused and sent out again, a process that is stimulating, productive, and creative.

Three Controversies

I remember three major controversies during the time I worked on the Treasury programs. George Biddle's mural for one of the Justice Department staircases was the first sketch we sent to the Commission of Fine Arts for its approval. This commission, created by Theodore Roosevelt, passes on all schemes proposed for official Washington: buildings, monuments, painting, sculpture, and landscape gardening. It is the watchdog of L'Enfant's plan. Although it was set up to advise, in practice, its disapproval had always been accepted as a final veto, and it disapproved the Biddle sketch. The Section decided to buck the commission and to authorize George Biddle to proceed. We were not entirely happy about having this particular mural as the basis of our first fight with the commission and we were irked by an interview which the painter had just given to *The New Yorker* magazine about himself and about the controversy.

As it turned out, this was, I think, the first and only Section mural sketch categorically turned down by the Commission of Fine Arts. After revisiting the Washington murals this winter I feel that both our own and the Commission's lack of enthusiasm in Biddle's case has not been justified by time. His mural stands up very well, indeed; it is personal, has character in its color and design, and is interesting in its subjects. It looks better to me now than many jobs I preferred thirty years ago.

Our main objection to *The New Yorker* article was our belief that any controversy would hurt the Section. We did our best to keep out of the limelight and especially not to publicize an internal jurisdictional disagreement with another government agency. As you will see in the following case, we were quite wrong. It is better to be talked about, even unfavorably, than to be ignored.

Rockwell Kent was painting two panels for the Post Office Department; one showed the carrying of the mail in Puerto Rico, the other in Alaska. Directly in the center of the Puerto Rican mural, one person is giving another a small white piece of paper to read. When Kent installed the mural he tipped off a journalist friend that written on this letter was a message in Icelandic suggesting, I think, that the Puerto Ricans revolt or declare their independence, or some such sentiment. The story, published in a Washington newspaper, broke with enormous effect. Secretary Morgenthau's and Admiral Peoples' desks were deluged with letters in the many thousands. *The New York Times* ran the story on its front page for almost a week. We were angry and appalled, feeling the whole program and the work of other less publicity-minded artists was endangered. As no one could read the Icelandic message, Ned Bruce sent it, slow mail, to a great Icelandic scholar in Denmark, to be translated. In the meantime the publicity died down, and the story was forgotten, when, months later, the message was returned, officially translated. Eventually the words on the white piece of paper were painted out. On seeing this mural recently I found it hard to believe it could have raised such a rumpus.

The written message, of course, had nothing to do with the mood of the mural. It was applied, a stunt. The last thing in the world we expected was to have such publicity help our program. But it did. The powers that be were impressed that an unimportant Section's activity could hold *The New York Times'* front page for a week and cause such torrential correspondence. Our official status rose perceptively. This fear of having the program hurt by publicity was the reason we avoided it and asked artists not to give unauthorized interviews. Thomas Benton, in an otherwise excellent article in the Sunday *Times* (October 28, 1962), implied that we were "aesthetic egg heads," afraid of being disagreed with or even of having our judgment questioned, since we had worked so hard to achieve our opinions. Had this been the case I think we would not have urged the local committees to exhibit all the sketches in a competition, exhibited them ourselves whenever possible, distributed our Bulletin where all names and facts were published, or produced at our own expense *Art in Federal Buildings* (1936)—the latter financially ill-advised but well worth doing, as it contains the most complete outline of our procedure now available.

Time may prove us wrong for not valuing Benton's work as highly as he naturally does. If I remember correctly, Biddle and Borie's first plan for the decoration of the Justice Department proposed that Benton paint the ceremonial stairway, the finest mural space in the building. We asked Boardman Robinson to decorate it. Although it was late and Robinson was not at the height of his powers, I still believe it was the right decision. He painted a distinguished and intelligent mural. Benton painted expert and characteristic sketches for the two panels he was awarded in the Post Office Department, but he never executed

35

them. He obviously found the Section irritating to deal with, and he had a larger and more interesting commission in the Missouri State Capitol.

The third controversy concerns one panel of Maurice Sterne's series of twenty on "The Law" for the Department of Justice's library. The panel in question symbolized "cruelty" by a rather abstract treatment of trial by fire. It showed a man carrying two red hot irons, collapsing at the altar where he is supposed to place them after having walked three paces. A group of medieval churchmen look on. A Roman Catholic priest campaigned against this mural as being offensive and untrue. He did his best to keep it from being installed, and succeeded in doing so for a long time. This affair also was taken up with relish by the press. It dragged on and on.

At the time, I went to see a great churchman, scholar and art lover, and an old friend, Father John LaFarge about it. My impression was that the controversy subsided shortly afterwards, but from the account Francis Biddle gives of the incident in *In Brief Authority*, it continued and the murals were finally installed very much later. Superb and fascinating as are the drawings, design, and intellectual scheme of these panels on "The Law," in revisiting the library I found the murals themselves cold, and subdued. Again I marvel that they could have caused so much heat and feeling in the thirties.

Subject Matter and the Problems of the Mural Painter

For its local competitions the Section suggested subject matter dealing with local history, past and present, local industry, pursuits, or landscapes. We noted that the postal service was active communication and need not be symbolized by the obvious train, coach, or plane, but might take on considerable human and dramatic significance as a concrete link between every community of individuals and the federal government. This may not sound very inspiring, but it allows considerable latitude, and most painters were able to express themselves adequately, some very well indeed, within these limitations. Straight landscapes made fresh, original, and personal murals, like those of Aaron Bohrod for Vandalia, Illinois; Clarence Carter for Ravenna, Ohio; Mrs. Georgina Klitgaard and Charles Rosen for Poughkeepsie, New York, and Richard Zoellner for Portsmouth, Ohio. Informal arrangements of working or playing figures against landscape backgrounds were also effective, such as *de Toqueville's Visit* for Wappingers Falls, New York, and *Winter Sports* for Lake Placid, New York, both by Henry Billings; Louis Bouché's auditorium backdrop screen for the Interior Department, Washington, D.C.; Guy DuBois' *Racing Scenes* for Saratoga, New York; Wendel Jones' *Settlers Cutting Down Roof Tree* for Granville, Ohio; *Whaling Scenes* for New London, Connecticut, by Thomas LaFarge; and David Stone Martin's *Power Line* for Lenoir City, Indiana. Some of these subjects were worked out with the collaboration of interested local citizens. This did not make them effective murals, but it did give them a certain local status not to be sniffed at.

The problem of subject and its effect on a painter is well and clearly expressed in a letter to Edward Bruce by Henry Varnum Poor. With the latter's permission I quote:

I think that the basis of any great mural, as of all great painting, is a sense of the pictorial necessity, a visual freshness and reality, which speaks more clearly than any other thing. So a complicated or highly intellectual idea is a great drawback—something to surmount rather than a real help.

Examine the purely intellectual content of any great mural and you'll find it almost nil. Or a truer way to put it would be to say that what the artist contributes to the original story is something which could not, ahead of time, be expressed in words or conceived in words. When it is accomplished, it may be the result of the finest wisdom, so endless words and ideas can play over it, but they could not help in its creation.

In Masaccio's "The Tribute" you will find the simplest possible illustration of the subject. The painter's contribution is just in the air and light which bathes the figures, in their grouping, in their types and in their gestures. These things hold the finest wisdom, but it is created out of visual sensibility, not out of ideas.

Da Vinci's "Last Supper," from the most intellectual of painters, does not contribute one idea—it only clothes the story in the most profound human understanding, expressed through types and groups and gestures again. This would hold true for Giotto, Della Francesca —almost all the great mural painters.

There are a few painters who live with a great deal of pain, in the heroic mold, and who have given concrete form to involved or abstract concepts. But this heroic or Michelangelesque tradition has given us a long series of the world's worst murals, from the hands of painters not of this real heroic mold.

My suggestion, then, is that the wisest thing to do is to find, if possible, a connected or related series of simple incidents, or places, or people, or conditions of living which, in themselves, may not express the whole idea of social security, but might do so through the humanity and insight with which the artist shows them. This it seems to me is the most sound way of doing.

My conviction that this pictorial freshness is the first quality of a mural was formed while serving on the 48-States jury. That quality came through most directly. The problems of architectural and special composing are perhaps even more important and rarely understood, but they are not as basic and are of course nothing for laymen to become involved in.

The subject matter referred to by Poor was for the new Social Security Building in Washington, D.C. Philip Guston and Ben Shahn, among others, won contracts in the competitions for its decoration. The scheme proposed for its murals or any other suggested or defined subject has little to do with the quality of the painter's conception. It may stimulate his dramatic, decorative, or plastic imagination. It can do no more than that for him, although it makes the mural vastly more interesting to the general public. Here lies one of the mural painter's special problems,

FIGURE 7. William Gropper (b. 1897). *Construction of the Dam.* Mural in Department of Interior Building, Washington, D.C. Section, c. 1937. (National Archives)

this matter of subject, of communication. Although there have been misunderstandings in the past between mural painters and their public, the general acceptance by both of certain beliefs, with their attendant symbols, made communication easier. Today the painter creates the visual symbol as well as interpreting the ideas that form the framework of his mural. Because the period in which we live is so chaotic in its beliefs or lack of them, in its forms of expression or lack of form, the painter's problem is compounded. Traditional symbols like halos, scales of justice, or swords are weak not only because few significant painters have chosen, or been commissioned, to use them, but also because our understanding of their meaning has changed. They are stale. The newer experimental symbols such as monumental clasped hands, the cock streaming banners with quotations from revolutionary prophets and poets, though they often appear more lively, have not yet acquired the weight of general acceptance. They smack of the political cartoon. The social and spiritual beliefs of our democracy are hard enough to express in words. They are much harder to express in visual or plastic symbols. Perhaps that is why so many modern mural painters lean on explicit quotation. Personal freedom, justice, equality, good will, reason, decency, fair play, the desire to live and let live with its essential base in compromise, these classic and Christian ideals that give our society much of its spiritual strength are not often adequately expressed in painting. It is easier and more

38

effective to paint scenes where these fine ideals have failed. The truth of the matter is that the failures, serious and disgraceful as they may be, are less important than those social and political achievements which are immense and impressive, yet so hard to express.

The current demand for painting is big and active. But today, the buying of a picture because one likes it, or because it looks well on one's wall is too frequently of less importance to the buyer than the consideration of its possible increase in value. The ownership of old masters has always had this financial motive as well as its value as a symbol of social status. This point of view has increasingly invaded the purchasing of contemporary painting. Whether or not treating pictures as speculative stocks has pushed painters to their present extravagant pursuit of originality, esoteric expression, and experiment is hard to say. But there is no doubt that the current fashion in these characteristics is excessive; for example, the large sums paid for much of what is called "pop" art, or the enthusiasm for Ad Reinhardt's series of six black panels, now being exhibited in New York's Museum of Modern Art. When feeling cynical I wonder if the only bona fide demand for the painter's craft today is not for portraits (the club, posthumous, and board of directors variety) and commercial art. There is a certain malaise in the atmosphere that surrounds the profession today. We are selling too much snake medicine; we see too many suits on the Emperor.

Although the demand for murals is larger than it was in the nineteenth century, it is still special and sporadic, and is complicated by the unhealthy climate just suggested. The active demand for pictures during the last century helped support a successful group of professional painters of great quality and variety. During the same period there was only one painter of significance (and that a minor one), Puvis de Chavannes, who might conceivably be described as a professional mural painter in the same sense that Giotto's pupils, Ghirlandaio or Boucher, were. Professional decorators, these men produced superbly competent wall paintings. Similarly, in periods like the Byzantine or Romanesque, the work of great groups of decorators was in demand. I might add that in the long period from, say, the fourth or fifth century to the fourteenth there was a feeling for a wall which showed up even in small scale works of art. This is hard to define. I can only suggest it by noting that in the most "unmural" of countries, William Blake, who rarely did a picture larger than twelve square inches, has this mural quality. It is obvious if you throw a slide of one of his engravings for *The Book of Job* on a wall.

A traditionally wall-conscious society helps create a profession of mural painting and a sense of craft, which the somewhat artificial stimulus of the Mexican and of our own government programs or the uncertain modern commercial demand has failed to create. What will always exist are painters who, when commissioned to paint a wall, have a special talent or feeling for it, like Delacroix, Orozco, LaFarge, or under the Treasury Program, among others, Rico LeBrun, Henry Varnum Poor, and Anton Refregier. There are other painters of the greatest distinction (like Bonnard in his mural at Assi) whose way of painting and point of view does not seem to be at ease as an integral part of a wall. This discussion is so subjective that I can only suggest my point by these specific examples.

Another problem the mural painter must consider is that of working in a particular and relatively permanent space, often within an elaborate architectural setting which frames his work and which may create a mood and rhythm, friendly or inimical to it. The wall itself implies a certain craft in the handling of paint. Consequently, many painters feel an urge to use fresco or work directly on the dry plaster. As this is not the normal equipment of a painter's education today, even so interested and expert a technician as Reginald Marsh studied fresco with Olle Nordmark before undertaking his panels for the Post Office Department in Washington, D.C.

How much each individual working for the Treasury Program was restrained by his own inner sense of fitness or tact in painting on a public wall; how uncertain he may have been technically; how disturbed or stimulated he was by the architectural setting, by what he thought the public expected of him, or what a particular jury, in the case of a competition, would accept—all this is impossible to ascertain. It would be especially interesting to know how painters like James Brooks, Philip Guston, or Willem de Kooning, whose styles have changed so radically since the early thirties, felt then. I do remember that, during my three consecutive years' association with the Treasury, very few abstract sketches were submitted in competition.

On the whole, the mural program was successful. Many painters produced murals that were consistent in quality with their total output. Some for various reasons did not. No one produced an incompetent job. There were a number of painters whose murals will look well beside those painted in any country, at any period of history.

Juries

The whole program was based on the Section's jury system. Final decision on the smaller competitions depended not only on the local jury, but on the Section's staff as well. This had not been true of the first local competitions. With these the chairman had been asked to send only his jury's three or four first choices to Washington, with its recommendation for the winner. In one of these early competitions, immediately after the jury had held its meeting and before their choice of sketches had reached our office, we heard through the grapevine that a number of reputable painters in the region questioned the jury's recommendations. When the three or four placed sketches arrived the local jury's award seemed quite reasonable to us. Acting on what we had heard, however, we asked the chairmen to send all sketches to Washington. When they in turn arrived, we found that several, which had not been sent to us, were considerably more interesting than those the jury had at first recommended. In other words, we felt the critical artists had been quite right. The Section awarded the contract to the local jury's first choice, but it promptly gave contracts to several other painters whose solutions of the problem had been overlooked. From that time on, all competition sketches were sent to Washington. I don't think we ever reversed a local jury's recommendation; but we did award other contracts, as in the case cited, and sometimes these awards were for a more interesting mural space carrying a larger payment than the original commission.

I am not implying that some local juries behaved improperly; there are always honest differences in point of view. Nevertheless, the result of this experience was important to the Section, for from then on all sketches were reviewed twice by different and unconnected groups of professionals. This insured a fairly wide variety of opinion, and, in the case of the Section's, one that was completely detached from local considerations.

With national competitions like those for the Post Office and the Justice Department bulidings, the Section appointed juries with as much variety in point of view as possible. Although the architect of the building was always a member, the others were always professional painters or sculptors. This was not equally true of our local juries, for there each chairman appointed his own. Besides, local painters and sculptors who did not want to enter the competitions were not always easy to find. As the chairmen throughout the country had varying attitudes toward art, we were assured of considerable variety in the juries they appointed. As with the PWAP volunteer committees, those men and women who handled the local competitions for the Section did outstandingly objective jobs and contributed greatly to the success of the program.

From my experience on juries, which thirty years ago was considerable, I have found they do their utmost to make the fairest decisions possible from the work submitted to them. In most jury meetings, when there is a relatively high level of competence in work submitted, the half-dozen or more entries which remain for the final discussions really become a matter of personal taste with each juror. It is rare indeed that any juror's first choice is not kept for this final consideration. But at this point the joint decision on a winner may not be the first choice of any juror, or may be that of only two or more members of a five man jury.

In the case of the Section's anonymous mural sketches the situation was complicated by the fact that some juror might recognize a competitor's style and so be influenced by his estimate of that painter's other work or reputation. It was surprising, however, that although the authority of an accomplished painter usually carried over in a mural sketch, a strong personal style in other work often did not. A juror's first choice of a mural sketch can be influenced by what he understands by scale, or by what he considers suitable treatment for a wall. No two painters on a jury may think alike on these questions. Such very personal and subjective factors can be decisive. In spite of the eternal complaints about compromising juries, I wonder if, in the long run, better decisions can be reached through any other method. On the whole, the painters and sculptors believed in the Section's jury system. They had sufficient confidence in it to make it work well and produce results.

The WPA Federal Art Project

In the early summer of 1935, Mrs. Ruth Reeves brought a well thought out plan to the Section's office. Painters were to record our indigenous decorative arts by watercolors and drawings of certain limited sizes. The pictures were to be attractive likenesses of folk art objects from private and public sources. The program was to be nationwide. It was an excellent idea.

Being an aid to employment which would at the same time yield useful and enduring results, it was an invaluable idea. However, since we felt it was not properly within the administrative or financial scope of the Treasury's program, we referred Mrs. Reeves to Holger Cahill, who was just beginning to set up the WPA art project. He was personally sympathetic to Mrs. Reeves' scheme because he really knew and loved Americana, and pioneered in its appreciation. As an administrator he took brilliant advantage of this idea in employing artists, and implemented immediately what became known as The Index of American Design. It had centers in thirty-two states and employed about 500 painters, who produced over 23,000 watercolors and drawings. These are now in the National Gallery of Art in Washington, where you may usually find a few hanging in the corridor leading to the cafeteria. They make a unique and beautiful collection, and one which has made a permanent contribution to this country's cultural resources.

The figures on this one important item in the WPA's program clearly illustrate its extent, as do the following statistics from studies perpared for *Collier's Yearbook* by Miss Dorothy Miller: (1) Over 2250 murals, including frescos, mosaics, and photo murals, were prepared for tax-supported public buildings (for example, the four large panels in the main hall of the New York Public Library, painted by Edward Laning). (2) Over 13,000 pieces of sculpture were produced, ranging from small ceramic figures for public schools and libraries to monuments for parks, housing developments, and historic battlefields. Remember that the sponsoring agency, be it a village board, trustees of a public library, city council, or art society, paid a large part of the cost for materials on each project. (3) Over 85,000 paintings, out of the over 100,000 easel pictures produced, were allocated on permanent loan to public institutions. Many art teachers in distant rural districts had rarely seen an original painting. (4) A total of 239,727 prints from 12,581 original designs were completed. The New York project developed the silk screen process as a vital expressive medium for artists and in a mimeographed handbook on this subject made a pioneering effort of real importance. The carborundum print was likewise developed on the Philadelphia project. (5) About 500,000 photographs were produced as well as two educational films, one on the painting of a fresco, the other on making a mosaic. (6) One-hundred and three community art centers (mostly in the South and West) were organized. I visited a number of these centers when I inspected some of our Treasury projects, and was always much impressed by their vitality and the public's interest in them. They were usually run by a painter, who organized lectures, demonstrations, adult and children's classes, and exhibitions. The space—sometimes an unused store, an apartment, or even a whole house that was lent by the municipality or a private source—would be in the business section of town, where the public could conveniently drop in.

An excellent handbook on how to set up a small art center and a simple inexpensive exhibition gallery was mimeographed by the project. These centers have had an influence of lasting importance in this country's art appreciation and on our present "cultural boom."

The extent of local support from state and municipal governments, Chambers of Commerce, Rotary and women's clubs, art and educational societies, can be gauged by the fact that about one million dollars was contributed to these centers by the communities from 1935 to 1941. During these six years more than eight million individuals participated in the activities of community centers, and the WPA had an exhibition service which prepared 450 complete traveling exhibitions for them. A number of these centers were continued by their local communities after the WPA had folded, and many were also taken over as recreational centers for the armed services during the war.

In 1941 the WPA's activities were generally used to produce work for the armed services and the Office of Civilian Defense. These included all kinds of experiments in the making of visual training aids for the War Department and Air Force, as well as posters, arm bands, and portable altars. The project likewise supplied instructors for recreational art classes in the camps.

These notes give the merest hint of the project's scope. Our relations with the WPA were essentially cooperative on both sides, with a dose of sharp rivalry mitigated by respect and friendship for the administrators with whom we dealt personally or through correspondence.

It would be hard to overemphasize the importance of the art centers, the Index, or the print medium experiments. I viewed a certain number of excellent murals done in schools and other public buildings. The program produced easel paintings as good as any painted in the country during those years.

Holger Cahill was an outstanding administrator, warm, enthusiastic, careful, and understanding. He had a sensitive eye for quality and he fostered the best work possible under the circumstances. Much of it was very good indeed, and without doubt many painters felt happier and succeeded in expressing themselves more fully on the easel program of the WPA than in murals for post offices: there was more freedom to experiment and develop new techniques. Almost all of today's prominent painters and sculptors worked on the WPA program, and many of them worked on the Treasury programs as well.

Influence and Outlook

The great mass of painting and sculpture produced during the nine years of the government programs described above inevitably increased the general public's familiarity with the plastic arts. Since local artists often did this work and they, not administrators, ran the art centers of the WPA, community interest was often generated in art projects. This tended to weaken the overwhelming influence of the large metropolitan centers, especially New York City, which I suspect has

FIGURE 8. Kindred McLeary (1901–1949). *Wall Street.* One of eight mural panels depicting Manhattan street scenes in the Madison Square Post Office, New York City. Section, 1939. (National Archives)

by now profited indirectly from the increased audience in the provinces. At any rate, this work done for the public, combined with a considerable amount of administrative activity, influenced the profession as a whole and the point of view of many individual artists. I became aware of this difference during World War II in England, where, although the British government had instituted extensive programs, the attitude of the British painters and sculptors I met remained far less socially conscious, far more subjective, than that of American artists in general. Mural painting, for one thing, will never be the same in America as it was before the programs. The murals painted for public buildings on the WPA and those done through competitions of the Treasury Department's Section resulted in new attitudes, significant experiments, and some original talents, as well as far more commissions than ever before.

The relief aspect of the program is not likely to recur. When these programs were a necessity, they kept an important if small number of the country's unemployed professionally active in work which, to say the least, was socially beneficial. All political parties and our social system cannot afford, ever again, to have fifteen million unemployed. But since unemployment as a result of automation and other causes has neither been solved nor produced a joint policy between government and industry, it is not impossible that some large scale professional service employment program might be undertaken again. In such an event the art programs of the thirties will have value as precedent.

Except for a relatively few successful individuals, the artists' profession is marginal. Since the government art programs ended, there has been some political pressure for their revival; but in number of votes, this pressure has been ineffective. The most powerfully articulate and richest segment of the artistic community—the museums, foundations, and collectors—would, in my opinion, be opposed to any such general employment of artists. Yet the government has always had some need for the plastic arts in its public buildings. It has also become conscious of all the arts' importance in international public relations, as they give the world an image of our life, culture, and civilization. Our artists make significant personal contacts abroad. Too many of our neighbors, some with cultures older than ours, tend to look down their noses when talking about mass-produced art. Though they will probably continue to do so, it is useful to show this international public what we actually produce. Once shown, it can see and judge for itself. This use of a national art has become a not unimportant aspect of foreign relations.

In consequence, the government needs both a program and a policy in this matter. How much this should be used to stimulate a living national art, and, if so, in what proportions the government and private or semi-public associations should participate—or whether the government should participate at all—are questions that can be discussed endlessly. Both the Republican and Democratic administrations have willy-nilly taken certain actions that in themselves tentatively create a program. The government also has had to take a policy position about traveling exhibitions and artists, international scholarships, and performances of music, drama, and ballet. President and Mrs. Kennedy had personally made important gestures in general patronage, awarding ceremonial honors to art and artists. For Pablo Casals to play, and for Edward Hopper to be hung in the White House, was an honor to these distinguished artists as well as to their professions. They, and other artists like them, shed their own glamor. Since honor and prestige run on a two-way street, appreciation or ownership of a celebrated artist's work is likewise an honor—and a status symbol—for the individual and the country who honor them. I understand that an important advisory committee on the arts is to be appointed, probably by the time this paper reaches print. There was one also under the preceding Republican administration. These things are admirable gestures; but, unfortunately, at the present time they have rarely gone beyond using and discussing mostly accomplished facts and reputations already established. As such, they are well worth doing. It adds to our national prestige that they are being done with such style. It is, however, essential to do more: art is not all window dressing or public relations. To get at the root of the matter, to really affect or stimulate our national art, to be creative and productive, our government policy and program should be larger, more experimental and dynamic.

Sooner or later, under this or some succeeding administration, our government will be forced to formulate a policy and to organize a program for the arts. I would prefer to see each artistic activity that is used by the government managed in the department using it. This seems to have been the policy of the Kennedy and Eisenhower administrations in their token efforts, the State Department being involved with the exportation of exhibitions and of performing artists and their productions. Doing this and attempting to stimulate or subsidize the performing arts nationally is a problem so distant from, for example, the acquisition of painting and sculpture for public buildings, that there is no reason to have them managed in the same governmental department. Separation, like that between the Section and the WPA program, would give each activity a smoother base of operation: it would be quieter politically; and being better able to control publicity, administrators could get more done. Eventually, however, I expect the pressure to create an important directorship of fine arts, as well as an administrative tidiness in having all such activities included in one government agency, may prevail. If so, let us hope that it will be on the high professional and non-political level of the Bureau of Standards.

In the meantime, there is the precedent of the thirties. I submit that the Treasury's Section of Fine Arts was important, not as a palliative for social dislocation, but as a proved and effective method of acquiring painting and sculpture for public buildings. Its organization was sufficiently flexible to be contracted or expanded as needed to include any related activities. Its program was then, and would be now, a modest and reasonable one for a country of our wealth and power. Should such a program be undertaken, its policy should be catholic in taste, not overly committed to a particular esthetic aim, and large enough to make this broad base reasonably workable. The individual commissions should cost somewhat less than the equivalent private ones would. I believe that competition is still the fairest way of awarding such commissions, but I do not want to be dogmatic about it. No doubt, the success of the Section's competitions and the high quality of the participating artists' work was partly the result of the almost total lack of other jobs at that time. In any case, it is essential that competing artists respect and support the juries, and that a majority of each jury consist of working painters and sculptors. The mechanics of selection depend upon the situation. How many competitions should be held; how many jobs awarded as a result of each competition; the nature of the competition itself—whether open, geographically limited, or invited as the result of the review of an individual artist's work (as with the American Academy in Rome, the Tiffany and Guggenheim foundations); whether the artists should be selected from tabulated votes and lists, or from photographs of sculpture (as in the case of the Post Office Department already described)—all this may be decided pragmatically.

Today the rift in vision between abstract expressionists and relatively realistic painters makes it difficult for juries to equate and judge the works of both kinds of artists against each other. It might be possible, however, to try two different juries for making awards. I have already noted the advantages which the Section found in its competition system; there is little doubt that it gives a sense of participation throughout the national artistic community, and affords opportunities to the younger and the less well-known members of the profession.

In preparing this paper, I reread some of our enthusiastic and positive statements made about the programs in the thirties. With the skeptical mind and eye of the sixties focused on essential facts, I do not want to overstate the case now, though I thank God for that enthusiasm. Still, much of the discussion and writing on this subject, foot dragging and apologetic as it is, fails to suggest or even to understand the significance of the programs. If a carefully chosen collection, representative of either the Section's work or of all the programs of the thirties, were assembled, or if a generously illustrated book of the work done between 1934 and 1942 were published, it would stand up very well indeed beside a similarly selected collection of contemporary work taken from the nation's art galleries, the national exhibitions and museums, and the murals and sculpture commissioned during the last nine years.

Such an imaginery collection would constitute a visible report on the government programs. Some of the work done under their auspices will reflect the variety, vitality, and spiritual strength of our country's painters and sculptors. Their work *is* the program and its principal fruit. But the administrative enterprise I have described here also shows us one small but not unimportant solution to the great and urgent problem facing our own and succeeding generations; namely, how to consolidate and organize our fantastic knowledge and power over nature and to distribute its benefits more evenly throughout our nation and the world. It is the practical problem of government, ranging from the question of race relations to the distribution of wheat; the quality of its solution has been, is, and will continue to be an outward and visible sign of our own inward and spiritual grace.

1. To someone who knows his work, an artist's name conveys a certain image. The following very incomplete list of painters and sculptors not already mentioned or illustrated will help to emphasize the fact that the Treasury Programs included artists who were already prominent in the thirties as well as those to become so later, and that the esthetic and professional variety was reasonably inclusive, ranging from Phil Dike and Ogden Pleissner on one side to Victor Candell, and Willem de Kooning on the other. With over 1,400 contracts awarded, not to mention the work produced on the TRAP, one can see that this list with the names mentioned in the article itself and the illustrations only suggest the programs' scope and variety.

Victor Arnautoff	Nathaniel Dirk	John Heliker	Barse Miller
Bernard Arnest	Alexander Dobkin	Eugene Higgins	Bruce Mitchell
Milton Avery	Lamar Dodd	Stefan Hirsch	James Penney
Rainey Bennett	Stephen Etnier	Malvina Hoffman	Robert Philipp
Hyman Bloom	Philip Evergood	Peter Hurd	Hugo Robus
Oscar Blumenschein	Jerry Farnsworth	Mitchell Jamieson	Umberto Romano
Cameron Booth	Dean Fausett	Joe Jones	Theodore Roszak
Louis Bosa	Ernest Fiene	Ibram Lassaw	Lewis Rubenstein
Fiske Boyd	John Folinsbee	Sidney Laufman	Paul Sample
Robert Brackman	Karl Fortess	Ernest Lawson	Helene Sardeau
Manuel Bromberg	David Fredenthal	Pietro Lazzari	Zoltan Sepeshy
Byron Browne	Robert Gates	Julian Levi	Niles Spencer
William Calfee	Harry Gottlieb	Edmund Lewandowski	James Turnbull
Vincent Canade	Morris Graves	Jean Liberte	Polygnotos Vagis
Nicolai Cikovsky	William Gropper	Erle Loran	John Von Wicht
Howard Cook	Louis Guglielmi	Louis Lozowick	Franklin Watkins
Randall Davey	Walker Hancock	Peppino Mangravite	Max Weber
Adolf Dehn	Minna Harkavy	Fletcher Martin	Harold Weston
Edwin Dickinson	Lily Harmon	Henry Mattson	Milford Zornes
W. Hunt Diederich	Marsden Hartley		

AUDREY McMAHON was born in New York City. She received her early education in Paris, holds a degree from the Sorbonne, and has done graduate work in the fine arts and social work in the United States. During the years before her marriage to the art historian A. Philip McMahon she worked as a creative writer for a number of small publications. In the late 1920s she became director of the College Art Association and editor of *Parnassus*, as well as managing editor of the *Art Bulletin* and *Eastern Arts*. She also initiated a very large traveling exhibition program which gave many colleges and museums their first shows of original works of art. During the very early years of the Depression she got permission from John Shapley, President of the CAA, to set up a rental system and gallery for artists. Later she and Frances Pollak, who was associated with the CAA and later became editor of the Index of Twentieth Century Artists, sought and obtained municipal, state and ultimately federal emergency relief assistance to employ artists and models. Because of her unique experience with these first work-relief programs for visual artists, her advice was sought by Harry Hopkins in the early planning stages of the WPA Federal Art Project. Inevitably, she became its director for the New York region when it began in 1935, and she continued her supervisory role through to the liquidation in 1943. Since then she has worked actively in social service agencies.

FIGURE 9. Berenice Abbott (b. 1898). *Audrey McMahon*. Photograph made by Miss Abbott while she was on the New York City WPA/FAP. (Courtesy of Berenice Abbott)

A General View of the WPA
Federal Art Project in New York City and State

AUDREY McMAHON

The WPA/FAP in New York City

In the early days of the Depression the hopes and purposes of millions of people were frustrated. A job was clung to, tooth and nail; when it, too, dissolved, all was lost. New jobs were non-existent. But even the basic necessity to eat, the bread lines, the apple venders on street corners, the day-in-day-out hopeless searching for employment, the innumerable suicides, the cloture of long-established, well-known concerns and that of the neighborhood grocer or pharmacy, the pervading despair, did not make the "dole" acceptable to millions of people. Nevertheless, in the early days, it was the only form of "relief" and subsistence.

It did not help the situation that, in the beginning, the dole was distributed "in kind," food, clothing and household goods handed out in Lady Bountiful fashion. Rents and basic utilities (no telephone was permitted) were paid by a system of vouchers, also a denigrating action. To present a "relief voucher" in a shop was to advertise destitution, and many merchants took advantage of the desperation of the "voucher" client to shortchange or humiliate him. The "voucher" system presupposed the inability of the individual to handle his own funds, merely because he had none of his own to handle. This degrading situation was eventually modified and presently payment by "relief check" inaugurated.

In order to be eligible for "home relief" as it was called, a searching investigation had to be undergone, to make quite certain that the recipient had no property or means of support, and that neither he nor his family, including in-laws, had property, savings or insurance that could be "cashed in." After payment by check had been established, investigators still invaded homes for room-to-room check-ups of refrigerators (surplus food), closets, and general family status—a child might have secured a newspaper route or someone might be babysitting clandestinely.

Neighbors were queried about the relief client's comings and goings and conduct; even small savings accounts were still taboo. A brother-in-law who was working was still the occasion for being "dropped" from the relief rolls, and idleness, as a prerequisite for receiving help, was enforced as it was essential to be up and doing nothing when the investigator appeared.

Among the residents of New York, there was a corps of civic-minded wealthy people who held the view that many persons would rather work for a living than receive this sort of hand-out. These were the originators of the privately financed Gibson Committee, one of the earliest—if not the earliest—of the work-relief programs to function in this community.

At that time the College Art Association (CAA), of which John Shapley was president, was intimately aware of the plight of the artists, largely through its association with them in a broad program of traveling exhibitions. The CAA deplored the situation of the artists, which had always been precarious but was now acute, and cast about for ways to help.

Frances Pollak, an earnest CAA volunteer worker who became editor of the *Index of Twentieth Century Artists*, approached members of the Gibson Committee and enlisted their support. The CAA became the dispensing agency for Gibson Committee funds to artists. The stipend the artists received was meager and, if I remember correctly, funds were available for employment only on an alternate-week basis. Nonetheless this was a tangible step toward the alleviation of both dire need and enforced idleness.

It was at this time that a number of us came into contact with Harry Knight. He seemed, to all of us, to have the qualifications required to fill the position of technical supervisor of an art program, and he held this post first with our CAA project and, after the fall of 1935, with the WPA/FAP until 1939, weathering changes in program, administration, and sponsorship. He was kind, wise, forbearing, and discerning, and I cannot recall that any artist or supervisor ever took exception to him.

Mrs. Pollak assumed direction of the mushrooming teaching program, which, at that time, was set up primarily in settlement houses. Under the supervision of Harry Knight, creative artists in various media were employed, as were craftsmen and allied workers, and a framework was developed on which the WPA/FAP in New York was later patterned.[1]

As unemployment continued, the Gibson Committee found that the demands exceeded those which a private organization could hope to meet, and its activities were absorbed by the Emergency Relief Administration (ERA). This was a state-based organization, which later became the Temporary Emergency Relief Administration (TERA) and received participating funds from the federal government. Our art program was transferred to these agencies and the employment of artists increased as more funds became available. In New York City, Mayor LaGuardia was the official sponsor, and employment quotas for artists, models, and allied personnel were allocated by his office to the CAA. For the first time adequate provision was made for supervision. The ERA art unit included primarily easel and mural painters, sculptors, graphic artists, artisans, models, and teachers. Early supervisors were Harry Knight, on an over-all basis, Burgoyne Diller, for mural painting, and Frances Pollak, who was finally put on a payroll, and whose teaching program expanded rapidly when Alexander Stavenitz became her assistant. I was placed in general charge, without stipend, as my services were donated by the CAA until the inception of the WPA/FAP.

During this period the CAA continued and extended its own program of assistance to artists. The landlord of the building on East 57th Street, in which the CAA was located, donated a floor for artists' activities, and the October 1933 minutes of a board meeting of the association, contain a lengthy statement by President John Shapely, outlining the CAA's activities on behalf of needy artists. In this report, Mr. Shapely promised cooperation "until the necessity for it disappears." He says in part:

The formation of the College Art Artists' Cooperative is another new undertaking arising from the special need of the artists. . . . The nature of this enrollment may be of interest. The artists have become members of their own cooperative and are asked to indicate on which side of the fence they are—whether they need help or whether they wish to give it. As its initial step the Cooperative purchased seven paintings last season. The second step was taken on September 1st, when a series of one-man shows was, not borrowed, but rented for a nominal compensation to the artists. Although the amount is small, this is a step in the right direction. Developing this plan of rental of paintings from the artist, there is being inaugurated, on October 1st, the Rent-a-Painting plan, which is an attempt to alleviate the present condition of the artists, and to make it possible for people who are not ready to buy paintings to have them in their homes on a monthly rental basis. This plan will be under the management of John Davis Hatch, Jr., former director of the Seattle Art Institute, and while similar plans have been undertaken (for example at the Art Alliance in Philadelphia, and at the Dayton Art Institute), this is the first plan of which we are aware which intends to charge more than a nominal fee and to devote the entire proceeds to the artists. In this way we can take a small step toward discharging a debt of gratitude toward the artists who have helped us for years in lending paintings for our exhibitions, and we will have an opportunity of furthering art appreciation among the middle class population of New York City.[2]

In the ensuing years Katherine Schmidt, working with the Artists' Union, continued the effort to secure rentals or royalties for artists from the museums, for the "use" of their paintings. But the opposition she encountered appears to have been overwhelming and in the end this plan was defeated.

53

Although the Temporary Emergency Relief Administration's larger allocations for the employment of artists enabled the CAA to expand the program, it still failed to meet the need. In the January 1935 issue of *Parnassus*, which I had the joy of editing for the CAA, Forbes Watson, who had been administrator in Washington of Edward Bruce's PWAP, comments bitterly on the fact that although the CAA, "the closest student of the relief problems of the artists of New York, and the most active worker on behalf of relief," was employing 300 artists through the FERA, there were "over 1400 artists in New York City, carefully classified by the College Art Association, who were in need, and not on relief." Rather naively, I feel, Forbes Watson wonders how "a city, where hundreds of expensive bars flourish and which supports millions of automobiles" cannot keep its artists from "undignified distress."[3]

The awareness of the inadequacy of the existing relief programs to alleviate the need of an unemployed nation were apparent to others besides Forbes Watson, and early in 1935 the Works Progress Administration was inaugurated under Harry Hopkins. In July of that year, the WPA set up the division of professional and service projects, headed by Jacob Baker. The federal art, music, theater, and writers' projects were the original quartet included in WPA Federal Project No. 1. Somewhat later the Historical Records Survey was added, and in 1939 the Federal Theater Project was terminated.

At this time a national director was sought for the WPA/FAP, and I had the honor of being invited to this post. Unfortunately for me, I was obliged to decline for personal reasons. I suggested, and was requested to approach, my great friend Francis Henry Taylor, then director of the Worcester Museum, but Taylor declined. Holger Cahill, at that time at the Newark Museum, was recommended for the WPA/FAP directorship by Edith Halpert, Alfred Barr, and others. His intense interest in, and knowledge of the American art scene, together with his museum background, which included exhibition activities in the field of American art for the Museum of Modern Art, made him ideal for the job. He had many close friends among a wide range of artists, was greatly concerned with their plight, and all of us in the field were pleased that he accepted the position of director. I became one of five regional directors of the project, with responsibility for New York City (administered as a separate state by the WPA), New York State, New Jersey, and, for a brief time, Philadelphia. I resigned from the CAA directorship.

The briefings received in Washington and the collaborative sessions with Harry Hopkins, Holger Cahill, Jacob Baker, the regional directors, and many others, added to my previous experience in art relief, stood me in good stead in this large undertaking.

The WPA/FAP was originally Washington-based, and Holger Cahill's authority in professional and technical matters pertaining to the Project was absolute.

Probably due to the size of Federal Project No. 1 in New York City, however, a local administrative representative was appointed, and although he took direction from Washington, he also came under the authority of the city WPA administrator, Colonel Brehon Somervell. This was never a happy situation, either for the Washington representative or for us.

Looking back over our structure and procedures, I am increasingly convinced in my belief that our efforts through the fall of 1935 on the CAA unit, though puny, set the general tone. In New York, the existing CAA staff was retained, enlarged, and absorbed into the WPA/FAP structure. The guidelines as to who was employable as an artist and in what category were continued in substance and broadened to encompass new categories. Artists who wished to work in the "creative" bracket were asked to submit examples of their work, copies of clippings, evidence of one-man shows, or participation in group exhibitions. It was also helpful to belong to the stable of a known art dealer so that a broader view of the artist's work might be obtained.

As I recall, the committee which passed upon the qualifications of applicants when the WPA/FAP was firmly established was composed of the top division supervisors. This group included Burgoyne Diller for murals, Girolamo Piccoli for sculpture, Russell Limbach and later Gustave von Groschwitz in the graphic arts, and Alexander Stavenitz for teaching. They were supplemented by other supervisors and members of the CAA staff who had worked for a number of years on the selection of material for traveling exhibitions, as well as the pre-WPA/FAP relief programs and the Artists' Cooperative. We also employed a sizable staff for local administration. Teachers, for the vast and enormously effective teachers' program, which eventually reached hundreds of thousands of children and adults annually, and which proved to be one of the most effective arms of the program in its impact on the public, were recruited from artists who had experience, as well as those who could not "make" the creative artist bracket, or who were interested in the chance to teach and had appropriate personalities. Still others, who seemed to be natural teachers were persuaded to join those ranks. It was certainly less demanding to work in one's own studio; therefore it was not easy, in the early days, to secure enthusiastic cooperation from artists for these admittedly difficult teaching assignments. However, the eloquence of the indefatigable and dedicated Alexander Stavenitz, who was a very able, verbal persuader, and the exciting experiences of fellow artists in this remarkable program, helped the cause.

Assistant artists, who aided muralists or architectural sculptors and who fell into the "skilled" bracket, consisted primarily of young painters and sculptors with aspirations toward mural painting or large sculptural projects of their own. Other categories were similarly established, and the minimum of strife in this touchy area must, I feel, be credited to the almost superhuman tact and patience which Harry Knight always evinced, and the respect which the artists accorded our committees and my administration.

It is my belief that it was Holger Cahill's concept, as it was ours, not only to give basic employment to artists, according to the government mandate, but to furnish them with *lebensraum* for artistic expression and development, and it is my after-the-fact conviction that this was accomplished. That this had come about within inhibiting and arbitrary boundaries did not alter our effort to provide the artist with artistic freedom. It is gratifying to note, these many years later, that almost all of the painters, sculptors, graphic artists, and muralists who recall those days remember little or no artistic stricture. There are, to be sure, many artists whom I remember well as members of our group, who have become so successful and well known that they admit no recollection at all of their affiliation with the WPA/FAP. It is safe to say that their development also was not inhibited.

The fact that, at its peak in New York City, almost three thousand artists worked in comparative freedom, must not be taken to imply that our own administration was similarly fortunate, except for two halcyon years during 1937 and 1938, when we succeeded in being taken over completely by Washington. Prior to this time we functioned under the thumb of the local WPA administrator, Colonel Brehon Somervell. To say that Colonel Somervell did not like and did not understand the Project or the artists is a vast understatement, and to indicate that this distrust was mutual is not more than the fact. He was not only of the school of critics who felt that "his little Mary could do as well" as, shall we say, a distinguished painter like Ben Shahn or Stuart Davis, but, in addition, he had a profound conviction that to create "pictures" was not "work."

Added to this was the Colonel's equally deep-seated belief that the projects were a hotbed of communism and that he had been appointed not only to administer them (his cross) but to "clean them up." Of course he and I were diametrically opposed and, looking backward, I realize with a certain amount of joy that I must have been as great a burden to him as he was to me.

Although the artists were fully aware of this situation, and helped immeasurably to bring about the change to direct Washington administration, they were not, at that time, burdened with many of the Somervell strictures, which were siphoned through and watered down by our own New York set-up. In the early years, the Colonel's antagonism took the form of obstruction; after 1939, he went happily to work on his mission of breaking us down.

The two major units of creative and non-creative work into which the program was broadly divided, were supplemented by many adjunctive services. Easel painters, sculptors, both architectural and those who made free standing works, graphic artists, silk-screen poster and other designers, "master" muralists and certain mavericks like George Pearse Ennis, who headed a stained glass studio, comprised the creative group. Copyists for the wonderful Index of American Design (originated by Ruth Reeves), mural assistants, teachers, and a host of other aides, fell into the second category. Artists could be, and often were, transferred for a period, or "permanently," from one of these categories to the other. There were additional brackets and rates of pay governing the employment of models, frame makers, "service" workers who assisted in the more manual phases of silk screen printing, such as pushing a squeegee, and poster and lithograph printing. Then, of course, there were the categories of administration, supervision, and assisting technical personnel.

The standards and procedures used for employment in the rest of New York State were not substantially different from those used in the city program, and were in the hands of Geoffrey Norman, with whom I covered hundreds of miles by car and had many interesting experiences. In the early and formative days of the WPA/FAP, we were permitted a 25 percent non-relief quota in New York City, for the dual purposes of establishing appropriate supervision for large mural, sculpture, and other important projects, as well as to enable us to employ needy artists of known caliber to give leadership and to provide goals for others. In New York State, the non-relief quota was 10 percent, and it was not long before the New York City non-relief quota was reduced to this figure. This barely allowed for administrative and professional supervision and the employment of "master" muralists or sculptors who headed large projects. It also caused real deprivation among many artists who could not quite meet the "needs" test, which was even more stringent in the rest of the state than in the city. (I will discuss the New York State project in greater detail below.) In addition, a horrifying uncertainty as to the duration of Project employment, which, hard as we tried to act as buffers, still seeped down to the artists, was vastly detrimental to their efforts and morale. As bad as this uncertainty, or even worse, was the foreknowledge of being laid off after eighteen months' employment, which became a regulation in 1939 and subjected the artist to all of the difficulties and trauma of requalifying for home relief, and reapplying for work on a project which, by the time he was eligible, might well have a decreased quota. Hard as we fought each step of the way, all of us knew that we were doomed.

For reasons not clear to me then and obscure now, we were continually moving our headquarters. We were, very likely, undesirable tenants, even in those days of tenant shortages, because of our vast number of comings and goings, and the turbulent manifestations to which we were prone. At one time we were on East 39th Street, where we had many difficult, and even disastrous, mass gatherings; we were on 42nd Street, unwelcome neighbors of a number of reactionary tenants, including the *Daily News* which, of course, despised us and vilified us whenever possible, and where our problems were complicated by a contiguous restaurant which would give no service to Negroes. We had a couple of well-arranged, large lofts and enjoyed anonymity on King Street; we had vast space in the Port Authority Building—one of our happier homes—and lastly, and disastrously, we were housed in Colonel Somervell's headquarters on Columbus Avenue.

By some miracle of youth, solidarity, and determination, we took these changes in stride, but in considering them objectively after thirty years, I cannot believe that they were helpful to artists whose tenuous tenure in their own homes, in those black days, must have mirrored our own gypsy pattern.

Through all of this a straight line of standards for employment and assignments was, rather miraculously, maintained. Production regulations varied, according to the category of work. Easel painters, for example, were accorded four to six weeks' time, at the end of which a painting of a given size was due. An honest effort was almost never rejected, and any assumption that this work had to be "allocable," that is to say acceptable to a public sponsor, would be incorrect.

Graphic artists were a little more tightly held, as they were obliged to submit a sketch of their planned work before obtaining a go-ahead signal. Whether this arose from the fact that the medium made it possible, or whether it was motivated by the greater propensity of the graphic artist to be a commentator, and that this was feared, I do not recall. There is little evidence that the latter was the case; indeed the consensus indicates quite strongly that easel painters, graphic artists, and sculptors of free standing figures experienced a remarkable degree of freedom in their work. Supplementing the graphic art was a printing unit which, as its name implies, printed the editions of works that were to be circulated or allocated. Each edition numbered about twenty-five, in addition to trial proofs and three "good" prints, which were given to the artist.

The sculptor discussed the subject of his project before beginning it—largely because of the time and cost of materials involved. While it is true that the supervisors and I conferred often with creative artists whose work might have been in demand for public allocation, had it not been considered by the sponsor's representative to be overly controversial, or grim—such as a depiction of a bread line—there was no imposition of ideas on this group. If they could not or did not care to modify their approach to the daily scene, they were left free to work in their own way and another artist's work was submitted to the putative sponsor.

Allocations to tax-exempt institutions were, of course, of great importance, since artists' materials, even when "home-made" in our own excellent laboratory, were expensive. As the recipient of any work of Project art reimbursed the Project for all materials involved, expenditure for non-reimbursed materials was subject to both Washington and New York City or state administrative survey, and was certain to draw censure. The files are filled with such reprimands, of which I was the recipient. We did not permit this criticism to limit our activities, but were always happy when it could be avoided. The Washington administration, which sponsored national traveling exhibitions, siphoned off our best small creative works and was continuously and very tryingly critical, seeking "excellence," originality without controversy, and quantity. They showered us with a hail of censure in this area. It seems to one now, as it did then, that even Washington, which was by far the most liberal of our "bosses," sometimes lost sight of the basic purposes of the program and problems inherent in it. I refer to voluminous files, now in the National Archives in Washington, which are filled with plaintive demands from Holger Cahill for "more and better work," and I think back to those problem-filled days and marvel that we did so much and that it was so good. Credit is due the artists who made the most of their opportunity, and to the supervisors who held the line.

Muralists and architectural sculptors did not enjoy the freedom of the creators of small works insofar as subject matter and mode of execution were concerned, since their output had to be acceptable to a sponsor and to the Municipal Art Commission in order to take final form. These projects were usually the subject of lengthy conferences, as in the case of the wonderful mural by Arshile Gorky for the Newark airport, now unhappily destroyed.

Fortunately, thanks to careful planning and the flexibility of the artists, rejections of large works were few, although modifications, irritating and incomprehensible to all of us in some cases, were frequently requested by the sponsors, who might have pet phobias or special, undisclosed longings which had not been divined. Diplomacy and firmness in the supervisor, and the support of the Municipal Art Commission won the day in the majority of instances. Adverse action by the art commission was happily rare, even in the days of the ultraconservative and somewhat didactic Jonas Lie; when his successor, dear Ernest Peixotto, took over, peace and encouragement of young talent reigned.

It may be of interest to examine, in some detail, the manner in which a large mural for a public building was undertaken and executed in those free-wheeling days. Let us begin with Burgoyne Diller, the talented and indefatigable top supervisor. Diller, as he was known to all of us throughout his lifetime, and his scouts, had the job of finding the space, the building, and the sponsor. They were constantly on the prowl for good tax-supported locations and receptive sponsors. This was no mean problem; the idea of wall decoration and reimbursement for materials, scaffolding, and other incidental costs had to be sold to the sponsor; a plan suitable for the space developed; an artist who painted in the genre which the purpose of the building demanded enlisted; a subject suitable to all involved determined, research into the subject to be depicted undertaken; and preliminary sketches prepared and approved by our own committee, the sponsor and his group, and the Municipal Art Commission, if a city

FIGURE 10. Arshile Gorky (1905–1948) painting one of ten mural panels for Newark Airport. WPA/FAP, c. 1935–37. (Courtesy of Museum of Modern Art)

building was involved. A homogeneous group of assistant artists was then assembled, and on-the-spot working facilities arranged, if the work was being done on location. If the mural planned was to be a large one, such as that of Edward Laning in the 42nd Street public library, with cumbersome scaffolding, this often became a public nuisance, and the cooperation and interest of the sponsor was essential. Happily, it was usually available. Finding space for large murals on canvas, or other major works which required studio facilities, was a frequent part of the supervisorial chore, as the artists' studios, if any, were rarely large enough to accommodate a series of large canvases and a group of workers.

The presentation of work for the preliminary approval of the Municipal Art Commission was but the first of many submissions. From its beginning each major project was followed assiduously by Mr. Peixotto who counseled and commended or objected, but never won anything but respect and affection from artists and supervisors alike. I still see this man in his seventies ploughing up long flights of stairs to visit an artist who was working in a studio. There he and the rest of us spent an hour or so in intimate discussion with the artist (often crowding a smallish studio to the bursting point). At the close of the conference, Peixotto would turn to me, saying, "Whom do we see now?" He was unassuming and indefatigable, and enormously interested in youth, its efforts and tribulations. I am certain that he waged battle with other less-yielding members of the art commission on our behalf, since the murals had to be accorded final acceptance by this body as a whole, but we were never inhibited by the knowledge of these problems. After he had given preliminary approval of subject and style, he espoused our cause, often congratulating a recalcitrant sponsor on the wisdom of his choice.

The process followed by the architectural sculptor was, in great measure, similar to that of the muralist, allowing for the differences in media. We did not have as valiant a champion in Paul Manship as we had had in Ernest Peixotto, but Manship, too, was sympathetic. The battles to be waged on behalf of sculptors were less strenuous because the character of the work to be undertaken was governed by the character of the building, and caused less controversy. In this area competence was all-important, and the larger works produced were sound and solid, if not inspired. Some of the smaller pedestal sculptures were magnificent, such as those by David Smith, José de Rivera, Eugenie Gershoy, and an occasional superb Nakian.

It is incorrect to think of the WPA/FAP in New York City as dedicated primarily to the execution of creative works, even though these aroused the most comment. The program was highly diversified, and included a variety of "service" projects. Of these, the teaching program, headed by Alexander Stavenitz, was the largest and one of the most effective. The records from January to June 1937 for instance show approximately 800 teachers having held 3,295 classes, whose average attendance was 30 students each. These figures are indicative of classroom activities until the project was cut back.

This significant program was the heir apparent of the early days of the CAA endeavors, and many original locations and basic procedures remained unchanged. It had been the wise policy, even then, not to try to make artists of the students, but rather to encourage free expression and foster appreciation and understanding of art through exposure. Mrs. Pollak was no longer with us, but the cooperation of the settlement houses and similar agencies in which young people gathered for classes was maintained. In addition, entrance into the school system's continuation and adult education classes was achieved. The direct effects of this were profound and far-reaching.

Before the New Deal art projects began late in 1933, when one of the aims of the CAA was to reach a broad public, traveling exhibitions, sponsored by the Association, had been sent to museums, colleges, libraries, schools, and many other public and semi-public places. The distribution of these exhibitions brought us into contact with many curators and art teachers, and was extremely revealing. The teaching of drawing and painting, outside of the urban area (and sometimes within it) was primarily in the hands of genteel, highly uninformed ladies, who had demonstrated "talent" but many of whom had never seen an original work of art! Museum collections, in smaller centers, were apt to be of very low caliber, if they existed at all. It is understandable that the purchasing budgets of these institutions, when there were any, did not make provision for the acquisition of contemporary American art. Indeed even the modest fee for rentals was hard to come by if the work was "modern," and almost unattainable if, in addition, the artist was American. An exhibition of Maurer's painting, beautifully assembled and lovingly prepared, was returned to us unshown by one of our great eastern universities, because Maurer's figures were considered overly "distorted."

Snobbery, born of ignorance, is hard to overcome, and in the area of teaching the lack of a college degree and the presence of a middle-European accent would have disqualified even the most excellent practitioner. The traveling shows of the CAA, the American Federation of Arts, and other art organizations, were entering wedges; the broader program of the WPA/FAP, which sponsored community art centers and traveling shows, hastened the learning process. When the Project closed, and for many years thereafter, former Project artists could be found in almost every museum, college, and university. The artist as a teacher of his own craft and the museum worker who is also a practising artist have come into their own, to the vast advantage of those who seek to see, to enjoy, and to learn. A by-product of this progressive step is that artists who wish to teach seem to have accepted a new way of life in which formal education also plays a role. A two-way street which still functions has been opened.

In addition to the more usual form of art instruction for children and adults, the New York City art teaching program undertook many experiments. Classes were held among prisoners in the house of detention for women and on Rikers Island, among convalescents in many hospitals and in a variety of settlement houses, homes, and other institutions.

The cover of a leaflet published by Bellevue Hospital in February 1939 reads: "ART AND PSYCHOTHERAPY: An Exhibition Jointly Sponsored by Bellevue Hospital and the WPA." This exhibition was held at the Commodore Hotel on the occasion of the annual meeting of the American Orthopsychiatric Association, and consisted of "work done by the Art Teaching Division of the Federal Art Project, under the supervision of the psychiatrists of the hospital staff." Dr. Loretta Bender, senior psychiatrist of the hospital, said: "Graphic art is a means of establishing rapport with children who are not spontaneously expressive (some of these boys and girls had not spoken for long periods of time) . . . who are reluctant to discuss their intimate problems, or who are taciturn or withdrawn." She continued: "It is a means of obtaining an insight into the child's unconscious life . . . he may unwittingly reveal his fantasies or emotional drives of which he, himself, is unaware . . . . This knowledge may be used in our plans for psychotherapy for the child's social adjustment . . . often, however, it seems that the mere expression of unconscious fantasies is of psychotherapeutic value" although she admitted, in this same foreword, that there were practitioners who did not consider this non-verbal form of expression therapeutically valid. The little catalogue gives an extraordinary listing of the twenty-three categories into which the paintings on view were divided, including such headings as "Sexual problems in adolescent girls," "Hypochondriacal adolescent boys," "Use of primitive form principles with mentally defective children," and the simple heading "Schizophrenia." There were well over twenty-three classifications and one hundred carefully annotated entries, primarily by children. There were also some adult inclusions.

Let me stop the more or less chronological order of this report to state here how the Bellevue teaching project was terminated.

Late in 1939, when the program had again been placed under the administration of Colonel Somervell, and my title changed from that of "Regional Director" to "Assistant to the National Director," Colonel Somervell decided to include a survey of some of our activities in his weekly inspection. Bellevue was selected as an example of the teaching service (one of the few forms of our work in which he professed to believe) and although we were filled with misgivings, Harry Knight and I had no choice but to accede to the colonel's wishes. We were driven in pomp to the hospital, where the colonel viewed with marked disdain some teaching classes which were in process. A member of the hospital staff, who, of course, accompanied us, locking us in and out (the only part of the excursion which appeared to intrigue the colonel) then decided to take us into some of the wards of adult patients who formed part of our student body but whose classes were not scheduled at that particular hour. What his purpose was, I do not know, nor did I foresee that this would spell doom.

We were ushered into a small male ward, containing four or five patients. Our group was introduced, and then our guide chanted impressively enough to reach even those clouded minds, "and the administrator, Colonel Somervell." A patient, who had been slouching in a corner and was hitherto unnoticed, arose, stood at attention and saluted. The trouble was that he was minus the trousers of his hospital pajamas, and that his jacket was flapping wide.

The colonel turned on his heel and strode out without a word, while we straggled behind, attempting to make a decent exit and suppressing wild mirth. This was ill-placed, for as we reached the official car, the colonel turned to me with "Mrs. McMahon, that project is closed." Closed it was and closed it remained. Our explanations and supplications and the eloquence of hospital authorities were unavailing. The Army had spoken.

This is but one example of the petty authority with which the colonel enjoyed plaguing us. He was constantly on the alert for opportunities "to put those so-called artists [and Reds] in their place," which he would have preferred to have been the guard-house.

Ralph Guttieri was supervisor of the Project's photographic unit. The creative aspect of this part of the program was of major significance, producing photo-murals, and independent photographs of which the Berenice Abbott prints are the outstanding examples. A selection of these photographs by this master craftsman was published by E. P. Dutton in a book entitled *Changing New York* (1939) with text by Elizabeth McCausland, and I am proud indeed to have written its preface.

This project had enlisted the interest of I. N. Phelps Stokes and Harding Scholle, then Director of the Museum of the City of New York, who aided it throughout. It portrayed "the contrast of old and new, of beauty and decay. . . . Scenes which were here two years ago and are gone today, and changes which are taking place are recorded in their relationship to the environment which remains. A truthful, sometimes humorous and often bitter commentary ensues."[4] What I did not say in this preface, and might have added, was that this superb photography will stand up through the years.

The photographic division also made "record" photographs of all major and many of the minor works produced on the Project and a large number of these are happily extant today in the Archives of American Art even though the paintings and murals themselves may have disappeared in the final holocaust.

Each aspect of this highly diversified program had its own internal and inherent objectives, and even the smaller units had practitioners who numbered in the hundreds. Some of the lesser known subdivisions of the Project were formed primarily on a service basis, and were enormously important to the prosecution of our work. One of the most significant of these was the group concerned with techniques and materials. Headed by Raphael Doktor, this unit not only made the great quantity of artists' supplies which the Project employed at a cost considerably below commercially available materials, but so improved the standards that better and more lasting results were achieved.

The design laboratory, headed by Josiah Marvel, later director of the Springfield Museum, was established with the assistance of the eminent Gilbert Rohde and Ruth Reeves, whose textile expertise was an important factor. This was a contemporary Americanized form of Bauhaus undertaking. It flourished for four years and sponsored some extremely interesting and original efforts, but was one of the first programs to succumb in 1939.

Another important activity was the vigorous exhibition program whose purpose was to have a showcase for presenting the work to the public. Our Federal Art Gallery functioned for most of the duration of the Project, and its work was seen by thousands of residents and visitors. It was not always liked.

There is the memorable occasion when doughty Mayor LaGuardia of New York, who made no secret of his dislike for modern art, said, of a mural sketch by Arshile Gorky, that if that was art he "was a Tammany politician," a statement which was gleefully noted by a reporter from the *Daily News*, who did not fail to do it justice in the pages of his paper the next morning.

The exhibitions in New York City afforded dealers and the public an opportunity to see works by hitherto unknown or little known artists, with constructive results, which carried far beyond the life of the program. Washington emissaries, too, always seeking the "best work" for their traveling shows, found these displays helpful.

An important adjunctive service unit was, of course, the professional models group. On one never-to-be-forgotten evening, Colonel Somervell visited his wrath on it in a particularly harsh manner.

The occasion was a lie-down strike in the early days of the program when its headquarters were on 39th Street. I cannot recall the reason for this particular protest, but I do remember that one evening, after hours, when the colonel had commanded my presence elsewhere, he ordered that the premises in which the models were staging the strike be vacated by the police. This was done by means of dragging them out feet first. To evict them in this way, it was necessary to pull them the length of a long, narrow corridor, and several of these young people were hurt, and one seriously injured, by gratuitous banging of heads against the walls. The tactics of the police today and those of thirty years ago are grimly similar, and if the artists and the public have progressed in understanding and respect for their fellow man, the police surely have not.

It is difficult to convey the flavor of those days. An eighteen-hour day was the rule rather than the exception. I believe that it was excitement, as much as anything, that sustained us. Each morning, in fear and trembling, I approached a mountain of mail, divided into categories by painstaking secretaries. Each morning my terror was justified, and what kept me—and I think all of us—going was the basic conviction that what we were doing was both right and well done, and the belief that, except for the dreaded lay-offs, every obstacle was surmountable.

In a recent brief visit to the National Archives I was appalled to come upon files of my correspondence with the powers-that-were. I realized with a resurge of the panic that so often beset me during the 1930s, how much we had been at the mercy of the written word—there were unending directives from a variety of sources, complaints from all and sundry, new procedures which were often replaced by others before we could put them into effect, requests from artists, sponsors, families of artists, the press, the public—indeed every conceivable source. I haven't the faintest idea of how we managed all of this; it appears, however, that we did.

It has been felt by many of those who have commented on the WPA/FAP, that the administration was hampered in the execution of its program by the Artists' Union and the Artists' Congress. Our work days were complicated by these groups, it is true; but I always felt that their basic purpose was similar to, if not identical with mine, and I stood in neither fear nor awe of them. Nevertheless, the fact that we were more often than not on the same side of the issue under discussion did not serve to soften many bitter encounters.

I believe that it is safe to say that in the early days, the presentation of grievances was as new an experience for the artists as hearing them was for me. At the start, all artists who objected to anything sought to present their case en masse, and I well remember several hundred men and women pushing into a rather small office, in which two or three of us, who were trying to adjust a complaint, were backed up against a wall! All were talking at once, trying to make or refute an unintelligible point.

With the growth of the program, and under the tutelage of adept leaders in their own ranks, such as Hugo Gellert and Stuart Davis, aided by personnel practices which were worked out jointly, these grievance committees gradually became modified, and we were able to establish a procedure in which five artists, plus the complainant (if there was one), and five representatives from the administration met at a stipulated time. This procedure invariably broke down whenever there was a quota cut or any other emergency.

Despite the procedures, a number of sit-in and lie-down strikes similar to the one on East 39th Street took place. The most publicized was that held on the premises at 42nd Street, in which the artists and models took over the building one day during office hours when all of us, including Harold Stein, Washington's representative for Federal Project No. 1, were present. We were treated somewhat as prisoners, accompanied to mens' and ladies' rooms, and slept on desks and files. I do not recall how long a time we were there, probably not as long as it seemed. I remember that I didn't really mind any of this, but Mr. Stein was horrified and against my wishes had us bailed out by the fire department. I do recall vividly the constant demand that he and I call Washington to tell the national administration that we were imprisoned and to demand that the quota curtailment be rescinded. If we complied we must have realized that this was an empty gesture.

Picket lines were, in actuality, almost as trying as strikes. Many an office session had to be adjourned to a public place to avoid crossing picket lines, and with the increase of the distribution of "pink slips," harbingers of dismissals, both picket lines and mass protest manifestations increased. For weeks on end I was even picketed at home, and forced to use a back entrance, if I was not to cross the line.

If the activities of the Artists' Union and the Artists' Congress were beneficial to the artists and to the projects in many ways, they did not help the image of the Project in the public eye. Some picket lines had their amusing sides. One of these took place in front of the colonel's office at Columbus Avenue, while I was there in conference with him. The colonel was furious, denouncing "those Reds" and boiled down to the street with me, to give them a piece of his mind. There we encountered not one, but two picket lines, and they were not at all in harmony with one another. Each line started its march from an opposite corner of the street and converged in front of the door of the building, at which point they glared at each other and returned to their respective starting points. The Artists' Union pickets (the colonel's "Reds") carried signs reading "McMahon employs armed guards" which I was dismissing with a laugh, when the colonel assured me it was true. He had placed a guard complete with revolver outside of my office, and I had known nothing about it! Signs carried by the other picketers said "Send McMahon back to Moscow—McMahon is a 'Red'." The colonel was delighted.

The WPA/FAP in New York State

As I stated previously, the New York State WPA/FAP functioned as a separate state program, apart from New York City, but both were under my jurisdiction, as was New Jersey. Since there had been various relief programs in New York City which antedated the WPA/FAP by three or four years, there was not the same basic difficulty in gaining comprehension of artists as paid workers that there was in New York State. As the general WPA program upstate was being operated on less than marginal wages, however, there was little concept of the economic needs of the professional worker and little patience with any demands—theirs or ours—for increases. Whatever Washington and the New York State WPA administration established as the correct rate for any professional worker was applied to the artist. I believe that the figure was approximately $76.00 a month in comparison to New York City's $95.00, with, of course, an increase in rate for the non-relief supervisors, of which there were only a few.

In New York State we were held rigidly to the 10 percent non-relief quota, which was used exclusively for supervisors. To tell the truth, this posed less of a problem than did 25 percent in New York City. There were two reasons for this: in the first place although all the artists outside the city were poor, most of them owned their own homes and could "manage" as far as food was concerned through barter. Clothing also was far less important in the country than in the city, and schooling involved less expense. Only Buffalo and Albany were exceptions to this. In the second place, we could not have employed more than 10 percent of the artists as supervisors, because there was not a sufficient concentration of personnel outside the two aforementioned cities, Dutchess County, Westchester, Long Island, Woodstock, and Syracuse. Individual artists, employed on a non-relief basis to guide and supervise others, as they were in New York City, were not prepared for such positions in a state where each man had been his own boss all his life and knew no other way of working.

To get onto the relief rolls, however, was ever so much more arduous in the state than in the city where poverty was both visible and accepted. In the first place the requirements were very rigid and the rules petty. Then too, there was a reactionary and backwoods attitude toward need throughout the state so that the dole truly carried a stigma, and many artists who were in dire want never "made" the relief rolls or the WPA/FAP because they could not bring themselves to apply. Of course, some of these were absorbed by the PWAP and later TRAP, but there were still a great number who preferred genteel starvation. These, added to the reactionary citizenry of a small community, were basically inimical to the program and became the kind of thorn in the flesh that we later encountered in Woodstock.

Although relief checks emanated from Albany, they were distributed through WPA sub-headquarters in such places as Kingston and Poughkeepsie. There were of course, sub-offices maintained by the WPA for their program as a whole and these took care of the isolated Project member.

With the exception of the ownership of a home, relief requirements were far more stringent in the rest of the state than they were in New York City, and the rumor department was at its most active and vicious in reporting people who were allegedly "chiseling." Many a private grudge was settled in this horribly unfair fashion. Relief investigators descended on homes unheralded and their prohibitions started where their written instructions ended. They functioned much like a secret police and might lead someone on by accepting a drink and then criticizing them to their superiors for indulging in luxuries. This autocratic attitude varied with the individual conditions which were better in some places than in others, but the general attitude of the relief supervisor was to treat his client as an offender and to try to catch him malingering or cheating.

The artists as a whole were submissive, with the exception of those in Buffalo, who were politically alert; Woodstock, which was socially aware; and the metropolitan area, which was kept informed by New York City. If the picture seems uneven, so were the circumstances.

This was not, however, the intent of the administration, which had unification and "leveling" as its goal. In Albany, we had a number of administrative people, of whom I remember Eric Branham best. He became my fast friend and ally, and with his advent the entire situation became more reasonable, though he could not liberalize it. When things got too bad, as they often did, Governor Lehman was invariably available, so that small reforms, brought about in a most unorthodox way, must have been most trying to local WPA administrators.

Because of the Woodstock program, which was composed of some of the most distinguished modern artists in the East, Holger Cahill had a soft spot for the New York State undertaking. This was heightened by the fact that his beloved Index of American Design flourished throughout the state due to the quantity and quality of source material available, the excellence of many upstate artists as draftsmen and their incapacity for work in the creative area.

Mr. Cahill encouraged me to appoint a state supervisor and was delighted with the choice of Geoffrey Norman, a wonderful person, but mediocre as a muralist. He was ideal for the job as his painting was academic (he later became the President of the National Society of Mural Painters, a truly conservative organization).

Although the state directors of the WPA/FAP had, in theory, responsibility only for the technical aspects of the program and enjoyed technical authority, this was never true in New York City where we were snowed under with a vast administrative avalanche. This is not officially recognized now and was never truly recognized by Holger Cahill, though the fact itself is not surprising when one considers that at the peak over 2,000 people were on the New York City payroll. In the rest of New York State, however, we had neither administrative responsibility nor authority, and the lack of any authority in this area was often extremely trying. For example, even a paint brush had to be requisitioned "through channels."

The burden of these duties devolved entirely on Norman who was probably one of the most tactful people I have ever met, and whose legitimate English accent was an asset. He made periodic trips to Albany and was a wonderful go-between. It was not long before I abandoned administrative visits almost entirely and, with Norman's assistance, confined my traveling through the state to technical supervision.

One of the areas in which Norman waged continuous battle was the impositions of the timekeepers on the artists, a scourge added to that of the itinerant relief investigator. The time-keeper was a petty official who would descend upon the artist without any advance notice, of course, and be horrified that the artist wasn't "creating." The fact that a painter might get involved in his project and work for twenty-four or thirty-six hours without a stop was totally unacceptable; it had to be a nine-to-five day. A project which called for night execution, such as a night scene, "should be done in the daytime from a photograph." Norman used his tact to show the small political hacks and wardheelers who had these time-keeping jobs that too much fuss might render them jobless, since we had Washington's ear, so that we operated under some sort of a truce in which they saw and didn't see unless suddenly offended by something particularly "Bohemian."

Hiring followed procedures similar to those in use in New York City with requirements basically the same, but modified to adapt to community potential and needs. There were some teaching programs in centers like Poughkeepsie and Buffalo, a few mural and sculpture projects and some arts and crafts, but by and large the program was limited to creative painters, portraitists, graphic artists, and the Index of American Design.

On the whole the quality of the work was excellent; far higher than the average turned out by New York City, although it never reached the peak of the best work that the city artists produced. After all, the city had Ben Shahn, Arshile Gorky, James Brooks, Byron Browne, Benjamin Kopman, Jackson Pollock, Stuart Davis, the Soyers, George Constant, José de Rivera, Eugenie Gershoy, Elie Nadelman, Reuben Nakian, and a host of others, and while Woodstock boasted big names also, it produced few luminaries such as these. Local prejudice was one of the most difficult obstacles to overcome, and in this too, the state project differed widely from New York City, where local prejudice if any, was not vocal. In a small community what one person thought of another was extremely important and when this grew to what one faction thought of another the situation was really hazardous.

There was a striking example of this concerning the investiture of Eugene Ludins as supervisor in Woodstock. Like most of upper New York State, the citizens of Woodstock were reactionary and opposed to both the state and national administration politically. Ideologically also, the people with vested interests down to small shop-keepers felt that art was neither really work nor respectable. There were many areas where a model could not pose and a model in the nude would have been taboo on the Project even in "advanced" Woodstock. Woodstock was more accepting of the artists than most other communities, in part because of its history, and in part because the presence of the artists was of year-round benefit to the shop-keeper. Then too, artists were property owners of a sort, and, most important, were a catalyst for a growing summer tourist trade. This did not prevent their being a sore spot to the general population, however, because with all their "qualities" the artists were still "advanced and different." In addition, and of major importance, there was a group of "conforming" artists who painted in the academic manner and the fact that they were really mediocre, even compared to New York City academicians, only increased their spleen. Actually they were the Project's most vicious critics.

There was a small gallery in Woodstock used as an art center by the Washington office. This was being lent to us to show some Woodstock Project art and also to celebrate Ludins' becoming the local project supervisor. Rumors reached New York that there was going to be trouble and perhaps a public demonstration to try to prevent us from putting Ludins in. It was also said that the show would not be allowed to open. Harry Knight, my assistant in New York City (whose brother was a Woodstock painter), Norman, and I conferred with Ludins to see whether he wanted to run this gauntlet—after all, he had a home and a family and didn't really need the work desperately as he was not, of course, on relief. But Ludins decided that he would not only take the job, but come what may he would hold it for at least a year, and we respected this decision. So we hied ourselves to Woodstock the night before the big day.

By some strange coincidence, Juliana Force, director of the Whitney Museum of American Art, was also in town. Norman was Ludins' guest; I stayed elsewhere. That evening, before the gallery opening, and Norman's official taking over, there were fiery crosses on the surrounding hillside. I received a number of threats and the local police, who were friendly to us, advised that we should accept their protection. To prevent a fracas we did so and walked into the doors of the gallery with a police guard. In the gallery, the project's artists and the police were a friendly, homogeneous and sympathetic audience throughout the speeches. Outside, the townspeople and the opposing artists' faction hooted and booed.

The troubles of those days differed from those of today, in that nothing but words were thrown at us, and there wasn't any physical violence. However, the intent was similar. That evening, Knight, Norman, and I had the unprecedented experience of not being served any dinner in a public restaurant in which Mrs. Force was entertaining friends. We decided that we were doing Ludins no favor by staying any longer and left for the city. I am of the opinion that the fact that "foreigners" from New York City came up to "take over" the official job of bringing him in caused part of the resentment against him and if I had it to do again I would see that my opposite number from Poughkeepsie or Kingston were present. A state of warfare continued throughout the year Ludins was there, although it became a set of known tactics with which we learned to cope. It must have been a very trying time for Eugene Ludins and his family, but he was always an excellent supervisor and a gracious host.

In Buffalo, Albany, and the outlying districts, as in Woodstock, technical supervision was conducted by periodic visits by Norman and myself as a team and we covered hundreds of miles and saw hundreds of canvases and discussed problems with a great number of artists. Norman traveled most of the time between upper New York State and New Jersey, of which he was also assistant regional director, and I traveled about a week each month, although I was never absent from New York City seven consecutive days, but rather, took flying trips. We traveled by car to save money, since two of us could go on the 5 cents per mile allocated to us, and also brought back canvases for Washington or other allocation. We took supplies with us when they were not locally available. Our overnight expenses were strictly governed by Albany regulations and I, at least, was never able to take a trip without incurring a financial loss. We used our cars alternatively and later on Josiah Marvel and I followed the same pattern. Marvel assumed the New York State position when Norman joined Cahill's staff in Washington.

Artists who had to be visited individually were seen routinely by Norman and occasionally alone by me if it was not felt worthwhile to take the time of both of us. The only occasions when we did visit them as a team was when there was trouble. When we traveled together, Norman might see the local administrators and be busy ironing out some problem, while I would perhaps be looking at the work produced and discussing it with the artists. This procedure was reversed as we thought it advisable. In Albany, it was almost always I who attended to the administration because I had long-term associations of a friendly nature and greater authority which could be exercised in moments of stress.

In 1939, when the Congress became openly unhappy about the WPA in general, and the Project in particular, we began the systematic and unhappy lay-offs.

Woodstock reacted as did New York City with protests and strikes. Elsewhere, in the state, there was only minor protest; where there was no concentration of artists, there was none. As almost all of the work not wanted by Washington was allocated locally in each community, we were spared the debacle which took place in New York City. The Project died relatively quietly—many of the artists went on to glory, others continued to work as they always had.

Liquidation

In 1939 Colonel Somervell's objective was, at least, out in the open. He had been instructed to liquidate us and was planning to do so. The orders from

FIGURE 11. Officials gathered at dedication of James Michael Newell's mural *The Evolution of Western Civilization* in the library of the Evander Childs High School in New York City, November 1938. From left to right: Mrs. Ellen S. Woodward (?), Assistant Administrator, WPA Federal Project No. 1; High School principal (?); Holger Cahill, WPA/FAP National Director; Audrey McMahon, New York City WPA/FAP Director; James Michael Newell; Mrs. Burgoyne Diller; Dorothy C. Miller; Mrs. Newell; and Burgoyne Diller, Supervisor of the New York City WPA/FAP mural division. (Holger Cahill Papers, files of Federal Support for the Visual Arts: The New Deal and Now, Library, National Collection of Fine Arts)

Washington were, to be sure, that this be done on the basis of a gradual decrease in quotas for which he could disclaim responsibility, since the directives came from on high. As a matter of fact, the Project continued for four years on a steadily diminishing basis, and was not liquidated until 1943. But the growing unease in the Congress concerning the size of relief appropriations and the prevalent conviction that the WPA in general, and Federal Project No. 1, in particular, were Communist dominated, presaged our demise. The fact that some of our artists liked and emulated revolutionary Mexican painters including Diego Rivera, Orozco, and Siqueiros, lent fuel to the flame.

This was the period during which "Investigating Committees" and "Witch Hunts" flourished and the colonel had me on the carpet repeatedly, demanding to know names of Communists on the Project, and requiring their summary dismissal. My naive, but truthful assertion that I was not overly politically minded, and had no idea of the political tenets of our project members, was written off by him with angry belief as being the idiotic methods to be expected from a woman. As it happens, it was the truth and, what is more important, it worked a great part of the time.

The time that it did not, which caused all of us anguish, concerned our head supervisor, Harry Knight, who had signed some harmless petition (for a playground in a housing development, I think) but which also was backed by a Communist front organization. There was no redress to be had. Knight's defection was grist to the mill of Art Project Enemy No. 1 and Knight was summarily dismissed.

The fact that my husband was a rather conservative person, and a college professor to boot (a circumstance which would not have today the connotation it did then) "saved" me from many an investigating committee. The conservatives were certain I was a "Red"; the liberals thought I was conservative. Both were wrong. Emotionally and practically I was dedicated to helping artists in distress and to furthering the WPA/FAP. Politically I was totally committed to the Roosevelt doctrine.

After 1939, although we were doomed, all of us put out a great deal of resistance against dying. The constant arrivals of directives to cut back the Project were met by the artists with heightened defiance, and I feel sure that the delaying tactics which were used slowed down the liquidating process appreciably. During these difficult and heartbreaking years, when destruction loomed, many of the artists became my friends, conscious as they were of the fact that we shared similar hopes and goals, suffered from similar antagonisms, and experienced the same despair. In 1942 our program became the Graphic Section of the War Services Division; mural painters designed and executed camouflage patterns for tanks, ships, and many military objects, and graphic and poster artists were of great help with propaganda. For the most part the artists lent themselves to this undertaking with conscientious ingenuity. By the end of January 1943 our program was liquidated and I resigned.

The final disposal of Project works was not known to me when it occurred. I had ordered the unallocated works placed in storage, and had been assured that there would be no destruction but that they would remain there pending ultimate distribution. What did happen is shameful history. I have long experienced a measure of guilt in that I failed to remain on the scene. Where Holger Cahill was at the time, I do not know, but I am certain that he also was unaware of what was taking place. Had we known, I feel certain that we would have been united in the end, as we were in the beginning, in the defense of American art and the rights of the American artists.

It is not possible for me to provide figures on allocation, as these records are unhappily missing, but thousands of works found their way into public buildings, and a great many of these are still to be seen on location today. With sufficient time at one's command, this information could be compiled from the day to day records available in the National Archives. Some student, who really cares more about where there are examples of contemporary art exercising an influence on the public than he does about the halo of an eleventh-century Madonna, might find research in this area productive—historically this data would be invaluable. The work produced should be located, recorded, and cared for. If the work is in use today, it should remain where it is: if it is not, it should be placed where it can be seen by posterity, in a building dedicated to this form of American culture. To place a representative collection of the work of the WPA/FAP in the National Collection of Fine Arts in Washington, D.C., would be to give it a fitting home where it could serve as a reminder of the past and an inspiration for the future.

In the 1930s each one of us in the vast middle class of a nation in which the middle class dominated had been hit in the solar plexus by the worst phenomenon of a great financial depression—the inability to secure employment. All of us had been educated to feel that work, in addition to being a necessity, was the good way of life. (With me this "took" and thirty years later I am working still.) To be robbed of this opportunity was to be robbed of our rightful heritage.

That we had a political administration which subscribed to this, and would not humiliate us by a dole, but offered us a chance to ply our crafts, was the most wonderful possible circumstance, and that there were public places where the fruits of our labors were wanted and, indeed, needed, was balm to our souls. So, naturally, we did the best we could, and that best was very good.

Indeed, I believe that the WPA Federal Art Project should serve as a model for the years ahead, for the artists and the public of tomorrow. I hope broad public patronage of the arts may, some day, be repeated, for never in the history of any land has so much cultural progress been achieved in so brief a time as in the New Deal years. People without hope, at the end of their resources, were given freedom to work by a great man who believed in freedom, and in America freedom pays off.

1. For further details see Audrey McMahon, "May the Artist Live," *Parnassus* (October 1933), pp. 1–4.
2. Archives of the College Art Association.
3. "Art and Government in 1934," pp. 15–16.
4. Elizabeth McCausland, *Changing New York* (New York: E. P. Dutton, 1939), pp. vi–vii.

PART 2

THE CREATIVE DIVISIONS OF
THE NEW DEAL ART PROJECTS

EDWARD LANING was born in Petersburg, Illinois, in 1906. He studied at the University of Chicago, the Art Institute of Chicago and the Art Students League of New York, where he was the pupil of Max Weber, Boardman Robinson, John Sloan, and Kenneth Hayes Miller. During the 1930s he was employed on the early College Art Association relief project and later, from 1935 to 1939, on the WPA/FAP painting murals on Ellis Island and in the New York Public Library. He also won Section competitions for murals in Rockingham, North Carolina, and Bowling Green, Kentucky. During 1943 to 1944 he was an artist correspondent for *Life* magazine in the Aleutian Islands and in Italy. He has taught at the Art Students League of New York from 1931 to 1932 and from 1952 to the present. From 1945 to 1950 he was head of the Department of Painting and Drawing of the Kansas City Art Institute. He has also taught at Cooper Union Art School, Pratt Institute, and the National Academy Art School. He has held Guggenheim and Fulbright Fellowships, has work in leading public and private collections including the Metropolitan Museum of Art and the Whitney Museum of American Art, and is currently represented by the Bernard Danenberg Galleries in New York. He is now (1970) the president of the National Society of Mural Painters. Excerpts from Mr. Laning's memoir appeared in the October 1970 issue of *American Heritage*.

FIGURE 12. Edward Laning painting a section of his Ellis Island mural. (Holger Cahill Papers, files of Federal Support for the Visual Arts: The New Deal and Now, Library, National Collection of Fine Arts)

The New Deal Mural Projects

EDWARD LANING

It was in 1926, during the "era of wonderful nonsense," that I came to New York, a drop-out from Amherst College, and enrolled at the Art Students League (where else?). I was twenty years old and an intellectual snob, and I chose to study with Max Weber (who else?). At the end of the year I went out to Taos, New Mexico, to paint on my own, and I discovered that away from Weber's spellbinding presence I had nothing to go on. When Weber did not return to the League the following year, I tried to study with Walt Kuhn, the League's next most *avant garde* teacher, but Kuhn, too, failed to show up and I was offered the monitorship of John Sloan's class. I considered Sloan old hat and was condescending in my attitude toward him. For want of anything more stylish, however, I remained with him for two years. He was, of course, a great artist and a great teacher, and in my second year with him I came to recognize this. Afterward for many years, whenever I reached an impasse in my work, something Sloan had said would come back to me as the answer to my problem.

In the summer of 1929 I went to Europe. I went looking for Cézanne and Renoir and discovered that all the Cézannes and Renoirs were in America. But I learned that if I loved Renoir I loved Rubens more. I stood before the *Descent from the Cross* and determined I would be a mural painter. There was an influence from Thomas Hart Benton in this (I had not studied with Benton, but I had read his remarkable essays in *The Arts*, "The Mechanics of Form Organization in Painting"[1]). But above all it was to Kenneth Hayes Miller that I turned with a sort of conversion. I had resisted Miller's influence for three years and had been outspokenly hostile to him at the League. When I went back to New York in the fall, Miller's students howled in derision when I entered his classroom.

I really went to work then. I knew that if I was to form any comprehension of Renaissance and Baroque art, I must work with Miller and work hard. He had a way of talking over one's head that was bewildering but somehow momentous. It was like following a voice in the dark. I didn't catch up, but I knew I was on the track. It was my good fortune that Isabel Bishop was still in Miller's class at this time, and when I was thoroughly mystified, I would turn to Isabel for an interpretation. It was around this time that Miller brought Reginald Marsh and me together in his studio (Marsh had been his student until the year before I enrolled in the class) and said to us, "I want you to know each other. Each of you has something the other lacks." (Years later Marsh told me he had never been so jealous in his life!) I took a studio in 14th Street near Miller's and Bishop's studios. Marsh was in 12th Street. We visited each other and criticized each other's work. My education continued. After two years in Miller's class, I had the invaluable experience of accompanying Miller and Bishop on a tour of the galleries of London, Paris, and Madrid. When we came back to New York, Miller took a year's leave of absence from the League and turned his class over to me.

I was invited to join the Dudensing Gallery, and my work was exhibited in their splendid new quarters in 57th Street. The newly formed Whitney Museum of American Art invited me to exhibit in the first Whitney Annual, and my painting was purchased for the Whitney's permanent collection. *Creative Art* (March 1933) made me the subject of a laudatory article, with reproductions of my work in color. I was invited to join the prestigious Society of Painters, Sculptors, and Gravers. I had arrived! I was part of the Art World! I got married. I moved into a big skylight studio in Greenwich Village. My only unrealized ambition was to be a mural painter, and, lacking a wall to paint, I embarked on a series of big panels—scenes of New York life.

There was no money problem. My sister and I owned a couple of Oklahoma oil wells. I recall sitting in the lobby of a hotel in Genoa in the summer of 1929, reading in the Paris *Herald* about the economic depression in Europe and thinking how lucky it was to be American and assured of eternal prosperity. But even then I was aware of trouble. When I would return to Illinois to visit my beloved grandfather, I found him saddened and perplexed. As we drove through the rich Illinois farm land, past fields which were unplanted and unplowed because farmers could not sell their produce except at ruinous prices, my grandfather said to me, "All our troubles come from back there where you are," meaning New York and Wall Street. And back there my own friends were unsure where their next meal was coming from. (John Sloan used to describe for us a terrible holocaust in no-man's-land. It was a black night, and the blasted landscape was lighted only by shellbursts and flares. Over the side of a shell crater scrambled a millionaire, seeking refuge from the bombardment. When, at the bottom of the hole, his eyes grew accustomed to the darkness, he saw that he was not alone. Another figure was lurking there. "Who are you and what are you doing here?" demanded the millionaire. His companion replied, "I'm an artist. I *live* here.")

There was a spirit of rebelliousness in the air which quickly swept up most of the intellectuals of the time. (This was the early thirties, and now, in the sixties, I have lived to see history repeat itself.) As the bread-lines formed and the "Hoovervilles" sprang up, writers and artists turned passionately (if vaguely) "socialist." Because I had taught for a year at the Art Students League, the John Reed Club asked me to serve on the board of their newly formed art school. The club occupied two floors of a loft building on 6th Avenue in the Village, with the school on the upper floor. The lower floor served as meeting room and gallery and was dominated by a big table at which the officers sat. It was at this table that John Reed had written *Ten Days That Shook The World*. On the walls, in changing exhibitions, I showed there, along with William Gropper, Raphael Soyer, Walter Quirt, George Biddle, Jacob Burck, and many others. The *Yale Record* printed a cartoon showing big red roses springing up in the garden of art—and the red roses were labeled Laning and Burck.

I attended meetings of the club for a while in the hope that my work would gain a deeper social content, but I never heard a relevant word. Bill Gropper would drop in, gentle and smiling and radiating good will toward all mankind, and Raphael Soyer would sit there dutifully night after night, silent and expressionless, while up at the table the officers (honest-to-Godless Reds, I presumed) harangued the meeting in an effort to persuade someone to go out to a plumber's union meeting in Canarsie to give a chalk talk. I decided that John Reed's table was all the John Reed Club possessed, and I departed in boredom and frustration.

My own notions of form and content in painting owed nothing to these "left-wing" associations, nor even to Marx and Lenin, though I tried unsuccessfully to read *Das Kapital*. (That, I suppose, was just more intellectual snobbery.) But one day in the New York Public Library I got the word. I found Bukharin's *Dialectical Materialism* and read it from beginning to end with mounting excitement. I learned that nothing in the universe is static but all is change, and this change is no mere flux but is ordered and predictable. I learned that Marx had adopted Hegel's "dialectics," his doctrine of change through a process of "thesis-antithesis-synthesis," but had "stood Hegel on his head" and put materialism in the place of Hegel's idealism. (I remembered saying to Miller once as we walked along the Prado in Madrid, "In the beginning was the Word," and Miller snorted, "Nonsense. In the beginning was the *Thing*.") I went on reading in Bukharin that everything is what it *is* because it *was* something else, and that it is in the process of becoming something else again. As I read Bukharin, I was back there in Antwerp standing before the *Descent from the Cross*. This was the greatest exposition of Baroque esthetics I could imagine. I already *had* the word—and had had it all the time. The word was *Rubens!*

Undoubtedly I was a very callow youth. Perhaps I hadn't suffered enough (there were those oil wells). About this time I met Ernestine Evans, who was the first person in the United States to write about the Mexican mural painters, Rivera, Orozco, and Siqueiros. Ernestine was a revolutionary, too—a *Mexican* revolutionary! She introduced me to Diego Rivera when he came to New York in 1933 to paint the big fresco at the entrance to the RCA Building in the new Rockefeller Center. Nearly every afternoon Ernestine and I would join Rivera's wife Frieda Kahlo and the gang of friends and hangers-on in the living room of his suite at the Barbizon Plaza. Around four o'clock Diego would amble in from the next room, vast and sleepy-eyed, looking like a great unmade bed. Ernestine and I would bundle him into a taxi and take off for the RCA Building. He blinked, wordlessly, as we drove through the New York streets. One day we took him to see my show. On the way Ernestine asked him what he thought of New York. "A great commercial city," he mumbled. He looked at my paintings and muttered, "Very good." Then night after night I stood below his scaffold watching him paint. I wanted to learn about fresco painting from someone who knew. I watched and I talked to his assistants and plasterers, principally a young Japanese, Hideo Noda.

Rivera began his day's work around four or five in the afternoon and painted steadily until one or two in the morning. Night after night as I watched from below Nelson Rockefeller sat beside him on the scaffold. After Diego climbed down to the floor, the faithful would escort him to some Village restaurant, where he would eat his one Gargantuan meal of the day. We would nibble and chatter while he silently stowed away vast quantities of food. One night someone said to him, "Nelson Rockefeller sits up there beside you night after night while you paint. What does he talk about?" Rivera munched silently for a while and then answered, "Tonight he said, 'I'm of the last generation in which a great fortune will be in the hands of a single family.'"

When he was barred from the Rockefeller Center scaffold because he insisted on painting Lenin's head into the fresco, Rivera went down to Fourteenth Street and proceeded to paint a series of smaller fresco panels on the walls of a Trotskyite school—the "New Workers' School"—in a dingy loft building. I followed him there and learned a lot more about fresco at close quarters than I had been able to gather in the vast spaces of the RCA Building.

In protest against the banning of the Rockefeller Center fresco, a rally was held in the auditorium of the New School for Social Research in West 12th Street. Rivera addressed the assembly in Spanish. George Biddle interpreted. Rivera would say a few words; then Biddle would put these words into English for us. After one passage Rivera looked toward Biddle and said, "I didn't say that," and proceeded to tell us in perfect English exactly what he meant—something quite ungenteel and un-Biddleish.

Later, when the Rockefellers broke up the fresco, Ernestine and I, together with Suzanne LaFollette, shot down a big American exhibition which Holger Cahill was arranging for the grand opening of Rockefeller Center. We spent several nights on the telephone calling all the artists who were invited to participate and urging them to boycott the show in protest against the destruction of Rivera's fresco. Most of them went along with us, and when the show finally opened it was a poor thing indeed, with nobody much in it. "All the talent is on our side!" exclaimed Ernestine. Then she came to my studio to see my own work and she was shocked. "Knowing you," she said, "one expects your work to be bitter, but it's cheerful and optimistic!" I told this to Charles Locke, the great painter and graphic artist, and I said to him I didn't understand it myself. "I *feel* bitter!" I said. Charlie said, "You mean you blow it in sour and it comes out sweet!"

This early optimism is today much impaired, but I came by it naturally. I was born and raised a Jeffersonian Democrat in a rich agricultural community in the Middle West where it was easy to feel, with Hamlin Garland, that "the more smiling aspects of life are the more American." I moved to the city when I was young, and while it's true that you can't go home again, it's also true that you never leave home. During New Deal days I used to visit old Edgar Lee Masters at the Chelsea Hotel, where he spent his last years. (The author of *Spoon River Anthology* came from my own home town.) One day Masters said to me, "The America of Jefferson is dead. The old Court House America is dead. And the beginning of the end was the rise of the Republican Party after the Civil War." I rejected this pessimism. I preferred to believe in Progress. Progress wore a smile.

By the time Franklin Roosevelt was inaugurated in March 1933, the economic depression had become more severe, and month by month the desperate situation grew worse. The catastrophe for artists took the form of a dearth of sales and commissions which, by 1933, had created a desperate situation. At first only private funds were available to help unemployed artists. Sometime during the summer of 1933 Harry Knight came to my studio and asked me if I would like to paint a mural. Harry was supervisor of a work-relief program started in December 1932 and administered from the offices of the College Art Association on 57th Street. Mrs. Audrey McMahon, the Director of the CAA, was running this with the assistance of Mrs. Frances Pollak. It was Mrs. Pollak who gave me the first assignment which I can recall. She had approached the directors of the Bowery Savings Bank and gained their willingness to consider sketches for murals in the bank's Romanesque building on 42nd Street. I believe several artists were asked to make sketches for the Bowery bank. My own never pro-

ceeded beyond a couple of elaborate pencil drawings, and I don't recall that anything was ever submitted to the Bank's officers by anyone.

The next assignment I was given was the lowliest task I was asked to perform, one which was in some ways the turning point from aimless doodling in the dark to something like purposeful mural decoration. The CAA agreed to undertake the renovation of a shabby church in East 27th Street, a church with the improbable name of St. Illuminator's Armenian Cathedral. My part of the work began with the cleaning and restoring of some big religious paintings of very indifferent quality but of superstitious value to the congregation. My friend Ralph Mayer advised me how to proceed in this. When the silly paintings were finally clean and bright and uglier than ever, I proceeded to clean and restore the polychromed altar. Finally the fat Armenian priest, who didn't speak a word of English, indicated the space over the baptismal font, handed me a little chromo card representing the Baptism of Christ (the sort of cheap little card given to children in Sunday School) and by sign language showed me that he wanted this picture painted life-size for the font's embellishment. I painted this foolish thing in my own studio, improvising where the priest's little card was too vague or discolored to follow. I put gold-leaf halos over the heads of Christ and St. John and took the painting to the priest, who beamed with approval at everything but the halos. These, it seemed, were no part of Armenian iconography. I painted them out and my first mural painting was installed. Soon after, I discovered that my little card was a wretched reproduction of Guido Reni's

FIGURE 13. Edward Laning. *Building of the Union Pacific Railroad.* (Above) One of eight mural episodes whose overall theme was the "Role of the Immigrant in the Industrial Development of America." Painted in the Alien's Dining Room, Ellis Island, New York, WPA/FAP, 1937. (Courtesy of the artist) (Below) Overview of the Aliens' Dining Room. (Archives of American Art)

Baptism. If I had known this earlier, I could have made a straightforward copy, which would have been much less fun.

Next, Mrs. Pollak introduced me to Dr. John Lovejoy Eliot, the venerable founder and director of the Hudson Guild, a settlement house in West 27th Street. Dr. Eliot wanted a painting representing the work of the settlement house in the Hell's Kitchen neighborhood where he had labored for the welfare of the poor for many years. He told me that any mural painting in the Hudson Guild would have to be sturdy. He showed me wallboard partitions in the corridors through which the neighborhood boys, to demonstrate their strength, had poked holes with their fists. I told him the answer to that was fresco, and he told me to go ahead. Hideo Noda, who had plastered for Rivera, was assigned to me as a plasterer, and together Hideo and I, assisted by Joseph Pandolfini, proceeded to paint a nine by fifteen foot wall. I made a sketch which Dr. Eliot approved, representing the guild's playground and the supervised play and recreation that went on there.[2] Hideo would come in early every morning for a couple of hours and plaster as much of the wall as I could paint in a day; then he would go on to a project of his own (he was making designs for a mural at Ellis Island) while I painted through the afternoon. I recall that George Biddle visited me there one day while I was working and asked me to tell him how to paint in tempera. I described the technique while George took notes. Then he departed.

As I recall it, the New Deal art projects originated with George Biddle (and they may be said to have ended with him, too). Soon after Roosevelt's election in 1932 I went with Reginald Marsh to Biddle's house in Croton, New York, where we were joined by several other artists whom Biddle had invited to discuss his plan for organizing a group of artists along the lines of the Mexican "syndicate"—Rivera, Orozco, Siqueiros, Charlot, *et al.*—to paint murals in the Justice Department and Post Office buildings in Washington, D.C. I remember that Maurice Sterne, Henry Varnum Poor, Boardman Robinson, and Thomas Hart Benton were involved in the scheme (though Benton later withdrew). Biddle told us during these meetings that he had discussed his plan with the President, who was favorable to it. He explained that the money to pay for such decoration was already available without any appropriation because under the terms of an act of Congress passed during the presidency of Theodore Roosevelt one percent of the cost of all government buildings was set aside for embellishment with painting and sculpture, and in the case of most federal buildings this fund had never been drawn upon. He showed us blueprints of the halls and corridors of the Justice and Post Office buildings, and we discussed the allocation of wall spaces and the appropriate subject matter. I was the youngest artist involved in this project (I'm sure it was Marsh who persuaded Biddle to include me). I believe that to Biddle's mind it may have seemed politic in a public project of this kind to include a young man. In these early days Biddle frequently called me from Croton and asked me to run errands in the city related to the details of launching the enterprise. Eventually the plans were drawn up and Biddle submitted a detailed proposal to the President. Then one day he asked the artists involved to meet him again in Croton. He showed us the report which the Washington Fine Arts Commission had made to the President regarding his proposal. It was written, we guessed, by Eugene Savage, the painter-member of the commission, and it was harshly and contemptuously negative. It dismissed the artists whom Biddle had named as "easel painters of incidental merit" and added, darkly, that some of them had involved their patrons and sponsors in embarrassing situations. (This last, we decided, was a scare tactic designed to raise the specter of Rivera and the Rockefeller Center debacle.) Scrawled across the last page of the commission's report were the words, "This looks bad for Modern Art!—F.D.R." We were cheered.

It was to be expected that the Old Guard would resist the invasion of the Biddle Boys. Dating back to the neo-classicism of the Chicago World's Fair and centered in organizations like the National Academy, the Architectural League, the Beaux Arts Institute of Design, and the National Society of Mural Painters, these artists had long monopolized official art. They had eminently respectable antecedents deriving from artists like John La Farge. Their dean in the early thirties was the academic allegorist, Edwin Blashfield. They conducted the Yale School of Fine Arts in their own image. They controlled the American Academy in Rome. Artists like Barry Faulkner, Ezra Winter, Hildredth Meière, J. Scott Williams, *et al.*, decorated America's state capitols and battle monuments. The sculptors among them—Manship, Jennewein, Wheeler Williams, and others—carved those huge Victories, and Columbias, and Giants of Labor and Industry, which abound in Washington, those enormous muscle-bound horses with Babylonian manes and tails at the approaches to bridges, all that genteel and tiresome stuff for which nowadays only Henry Hope Reed, Jr., can find an excuse (though considering what passes for a public building and its decoration now that the Museum of Modern Art has succeeded to the tyrany, it is sometimes difficult not to wish that Henry could revive the Bozart!).

Not all the Old Guard were bigoted and reactionary. With the development of the various government art projects, the National Society of Mural Painters saw the handwriting on the wall, as it were, and decided that if it couldn't lick 'em, it would join 'em. Its members, led by Ernest Peixotto, realized that if they were to retain any leverage with the New Deal they must bring new blood into the organization. A number of Young Turks, myself included, were invited to join. Hildredth Meière organized a mural class at the Beaux Arts Institute with a unique and intelligent program. Architects came to the class and presented problems, usually projects which they actually wished could be carried out in some building they had designed. A professional mural painter discussed various possible approaches to this problem. The class executed sketches or *projets*. Finally architect and mural painter returned and criticized the designs of the students. It was an academic routine based on the practice of the École des Beaux Arts in Paris. I attended this class and gained valuable technical knowledge from it. But by and large the effort came to nothing, as much through the government's failure to cooperate in any way as through any fault in the methods of the course. As the New Deal art projects were developed, other members of the Old Guard made substantial, if often thankless, contributions. Men like Ernest Peixotto and Dean Cornwell, as members of the Fine Arts Commission of the City of New York, were genuinely helpful to young and "unknown" painters. And of course Leon Kroll, urbane and ageless and above clique and faction, was consistently helpful to everyone concerned. Old timers like Peixotto, Meière, and Kroll sometimes seemed almost to be "traitors to their class"!

The meetings of the Mural Painters Society at this period always sent me home with a headache, though in retrospect they seem hilarious. Open warfare was the rule, but even while opposing him I was lost in admiration for Ernest Peixotto's dexterity. He wore a monocle, the only monocle I ever saw outside the movies. At the height of the din, Mr. Peixotto, the president of the society, would rise smiling, his glass flashing. He would wait a moment until he had the attention of the meeting, when suddenly his monocle would fall. Had it fallen to the floor and broken to pieces? Was he blind without it? And what was it just now I was so concerned about? After exactly the right pause, Peixotto would reach for the monocle at the end of its black cord and replace it in his eye. He had restored order—his order. He was a superb actor, and the artists in his audience recognized a master. You might suppose you hated him, but you had to respect him, and this respect was very close to love.

George Biddle's ambition was not immediately to be realized. For political reasons his plan for a small group of selected artists moving into preferred positions was abandoned, or, rather, postponed, while something more politically viable was worked out. A bureaucratic structure was set up within the Treasury Department (originally the Public Works of Art Project, later the Section of Fine Arts), headed by Edward Bruce, a wealthy Washington lawyer who worked for the sugar interests, and an amateur painter (as a pupil of Maurice Sterne he had painted a picture of a cherry tree). In New York the Public Works of Art Project was headed by Mrs. Juliana Force, director of the Whitney Museum of American Art, assisted by Lloyd Goodrich. I have remembered for many years a design I made showing a group of matrons scratching and clawing over a bargain table with the figure of Walter Winchell flying above them, microphone in hand, and the legend, "Wake Up America" on a banner over all—and I've wondered why I did it. Now I discover from a report I wrote to Mrs. Force on January 7, 1934, that I had been asked to make designs for the four large wall spaces on the third floor of the New York Public Library. In this report I outlined my ideas of subject matter and treatment. The project had been initiated only a month before I wrote this report, and I believe I was connected with it from its inception. My report ends, "P.S. I was informed by Mr. Goodrich, on Thursday, that it is unlikely that any project for the Public Library can be carried out. He told me that he would assign me, early this week, to another project but that I should continue with the present project in the meantime." This letter from the past reassures me that my "Wake Up America" was a joke, a harmless exercise in the void, and that I had had no serious intention of trying to set up John Reed's table at the center of the Great Hall of the library!

After the collapse of the Dudensing Gallery I was approached by a couple of bright young men just out of Harvard, Alan Gruskin and Francis Healy, who told me they were organizing a "cooperative" gallery, to be called the Midtown Gallery, in the quarters of another defunct establishment on Fifth Avenue. "Cooperative" meant that the artists would pay ten dollars a month for the privilege of exhibiting there. Isabel Bishop was invited to join them at the same time. Gruskin and Healy asked me to recommend other artists and I advised them to approach Paul Cadmus and William Palmer. At the new "cooperative" Midtown Gallery I exhibited my five panels of New York scenes.

My recollections of the next year, 1934–35, are very hazy. I know that sometime in 1934 I went broke like nearly everybody else. The oil wells went dry and word came from Illinois, "That's all there is; there isn't any more." I borrowed money from friends who still had some (and repaid them, for the most part, with paintings). My landlord, Eugene Schoen, kindly waived my rent for a number of months. In the meantime the plight of all artists was growing desperate. The John Reed Club folded and was replaced by The Artists' Union. (I had no part in the organization of the union and never attended one of its meetings.) A demonstration was held in front of the Whitney Museum in 8th Street, complete with placards and chants and shouted imprecations, and was dispersed by the police. My friend Karl Free, a curator of the Whitney Museum and one of the most brilliant artists of the time, leaned out of an upper window of the beleaguered Museum and called to many of the demonstrators below, "I know *you*, So-and-So, and *you*, Such-and-Such," implying that he meant to blacklist them forever. Mrs. Force was tough as long as she could play the great lady, but this was no time for ladies. I visited her one day in her fabulous apartment above the Museum and she told me of the outrages she was experiencing. As I bade her goodbye in the entrance room of the apartment (a room with walls of purple metal foil and a floor of lacquered chintz), she told me of a delegation of destitute artists she had recently received. "They stood on this very spot," she said, "and howled insults at me. And as they turned to go, one of them *spat* here, right at my feet!" Mrs. Force threw in the sponge and the Public Works of Art Project came to an end.

In October 1934, the Section of Painting and Sculpture was established under the Treasury Department, and when the commissions to decorate the Justice Department and Post Office buildings were awarded, most of the original Biddle gang were assigned their allotted spaces—except me. George called me to say that it was felt that I was too young. But he went on to assure me that other spaces in the Post Office Building were to be allocated on the basis of a competition and that it was his understanding that if I would take part in this competition, I could be sure of an award. I was crushed at first, but I allowed myself to trust him. I confess that my conscience was untroubled by his suggestion that the competition would be rigged in my favor. Perhaps my baroque esthetic made these tergiversations seem comprehensible.

I made a great effort with these sketches for the Post Office (my preliminary drawings for two spaces in the Post Office rotunda are in the permanent collection of the Whitney Museum), but when the judgment was announced I received no award. George called again to explain that one of the judges, Eugene Speicher, had felt that my color sketches lacked "surface quality." (This meant simply that I did not display the old Woodstock fuzz, that blur as of carpet sweepings which was the hallmark of Speicher and McFee, the leaders of the provincial Woodstock school.)

A member of the National Council on the Arts and Government said to me in the summer of 1968 that the prospects for public support of art seem brighter today than in the thirties because there is now a more widespread public interest and appetite, whereas the government sponsorship of the thirties rested solely on Franklin and Eleanor Roosevelt's love of Art. I doubt the validity of either term of this proposition. I don't believe either of the Roosevelts cared about art at all. What is true is, first, that they were great humanitarians and, second, that they were loyal to their friends. George Biddle was an "aristocrat" who had gone to school with Roosevelt. He could walk into the White House and be sure of a gracious personal reception. When his ambition to paint a mural was satisfied, he exerted little further influence, but he did establish a precedent and a principle. The Section of Fine Arts persisted until 1943, when it was swallowed up in the Second World War. The principle upon which the Section was based was one of selectivity. Its establishment was merely another changing of the guard; the Beaux Arts-Yale School axis was supplanted by the Whitney Museum-Woodstock axis. (If Nelson Rockefeller's presidential aspirations had succeeded, we would see the Modern Museum-*Art News* axis in official control.) It was the same thing when Charles Le Brun ran the show during the reign of Louis XIV—*Plus ça change, plus c'est la même chose*. I remember visiting Washington in the early days of the Section and being invited to a tea party in the studio of Ed

Rowan, Ned Bruce's assistant. I took a New York friend with me, and we found ourselves in the midst of a lot of old Washington biddies. Ed Rowan was a man of ageless boyish charm and a fast man with a teacup. The old girls were exclaiming to each other, "Isn't he utterly delightful?" (which he was), and when we left, my friend said to me, "I feel as if I had been in a well of treacle!" So much for Franklin's and Eleanor's friends (and friends of their friends).

The Roosevelt's humanitarianism was a more serious matter. Their loyalty to friends made them permissive; their humanitarianism made them passionate. Their true concern was with social welfare. Another man who could call at the White House at will was Harry Hopkins, with whom Mrs. Roosevelt had been associated in welfare work in New York City. I believe it was on Hopkins' advice that the other art project of the New Deal, the Federal Art Project, was organized under the Works Progress Administration. The national emergency was critical; it was urgently necessary to put unemployed Americans to work for wages; a pump-priming operation was required. But highways and dams and bridges, schools and hospitals, require long and careful planning before men can be employed to build them. Hopkins knew that there was one segment of the population that could go to work tomorrow—the artists. They didn't require a capital outlay. They already had paints and brushes of a sort, and they carried the plans for their next painting in their heads. I've known only three art institutions in my life that I've had any respect for: the old Society of Independent Artists, the Art Students League of New York, and the Federal Art Project of the WPA. All the rest have been establishments within the Establishment. These three alone have been disestablishmentarian. The secret principle of each was that it had no principles. I've always considered this principle ineffable, something which can be maintained only if the Establishment is looking the other way or is temporarily paralyzed. Today, thirty years after the end of the WPA, I am awe-inspired by the dissident students at Columbia and Berkeley, who seem to have grasped this elusive principle—when the Establishment says to them, "But what is your program? What are your principles? What do you propose to establish in the place of the institutions you oppose?" they answer, "You can't put us in *that* bag. We don't have a *program; we have demands!"*

Speaking of demands, one day I received a call saying that Mrs. McMahon, who by this time—the fall of 1935—had graduated from the old CAA project to the directorship of the New York WPA Federal Art Project, wanted to see me. Mrs. McMahon was a formidable person (as indeed she had to be to ride the whirlwind of these projects), and it was no joke for an artist to be called to her office. I was scared. The Federal Art Project was now my sole means of livelihood. It was more. It was my life as artist and mural painter.

Mrs. McMahon told me that Hideo Noda, who had been assigned to make sketches for a long wall in the administration building at Ellis Island, had disappeared without leaving any word. Hideo, a gentle boy of poetic temperament, had found the resident Commissioner of Immigration impossible to cope with and in despair had run away. "The commissioner *is* difficult," Mrs. McMahon added (and I thought to myself that if *she* thought so, he must be a dragon). She went on to tell me that Ellis Island was important to the whole Project. She had secured the commissioner's consent to look at sketches, on approval. The administration building at Ellis Island was federal property, and it offered possibilities of more than one mural series. A number of artists had already been assigned to Noda as assistants, and *their* jobs were in jeopardy. Would I take on this assignment?

It wasn't, of course, a request, it was a command, but I accepted with alacrity. Why did I? Looking back on what I involved myself in, I know that any sensible person would have avoided this whole business like the plague. Who was it, then, who said yes and undertook this ghastly ordeal? At the age of 62 I have concluded that an artist doesn't speak for himself. An artist is a carrier (a carrier of his talent), a sort of Typhoid Mary. Audrey McMahon, whom her assistants in the Art Project office called "Arsenic and Old Face," may have been an unlikely Muse (but that's only because we have been taught to think of the Muse in terms of ancient Greek idealism). I don't think either Audrey McMahon or I knew what we were doing; I don't think either of us *counted*. We were, quite simply, doing the Will of God.

I was asked to meet with the artists who had been assigned to Noda's project as assistants. It was an awkward moment. The Federal Art Project was a *relief* project. The regulations required that three-fourths of the artists employed by it be drawn from the relief rolls. For an indigent artist not to be accepted for employment by the Art Project meant work as a ditch digger or leaf raker, and Mrs. McMahon's office made every possible effort to give employment to every qualified artist. In practice this presented administrative problems. The whole New Deal had a bad press, and no part of it was subjected to such constant abuse as the Art Project. Most of the newspapers and magazines in America were Republican and anti-Roosevelt, and they made what capital they could out of traditional American Philistinism. The Art Projects were scorned as "boondoggling." Under this constant and relentless attack it was necessary to develop work projects that could be defended as "worthwhile." For the Project to have sent every artist home to paint his own pictures in his own way without supervision or accountability would have invited disaster. Mural projects were a little less liable to charges of boondoggling than easel painting. They were relatively public and subject to scrutiny and criticism. In the early days of the Art Project this led to a certain amount of padding where the personnel of mural projects was concerned. When I met with the artists who had been assigned to Noda as Ellis Island assistants, they were wary of me at first. Their looks told me that they wondered if I would be such a damned fool as to ask them to work for *me* (even this one ritualistic meeting was a tribulation for them—it required them to leave their easels and waste an afternoon uptown), but we all played it straight. I told them I looked forward to a pleasant and productive association and we went our various ways. I believe it's a fair measure of the situation I am describing to recall that two of these "assistants" were the distinguished painters Joseph Solman and Herman Rose.

I went out to Ellis Island to look at the walls in the aliens' dining room, avoiding any contact with the commissioner, and began to make sketches. The Project let me pick a couple of assistants of my own, James Rutledge and Etta Fick, and they sent me a model, Albert Soroka. In the beginning Jimmy and Etta busied themselves in the research I had to do. The Ellis Island dining room was a hundred feet long, and I undertook to depict along one of the long walls the role of the immigrant in the development of America. It meant learning how railroads were built and sawmills were operated and coal was mined and steel was manufactured.

While I was working on my sketches, another assistant was assigned to my project, a charming girl I'll call Helen. I wasn't aware that I needed her—but that's how much I knew. She had no artistic talents or pretensions, but she was the wife of a struggling commercial artist and she was a vigorous organizer for the Artists' Union. She was very bright, and when she wasn't out on Union business she made herself useful to my work. While Jimmy and Etta tracked down pictorial material I needed, Helen would check historical references at the library.

When I had completed designs for half the episodes I hoped to represent, I rolled them up and headed for the Commissioner's office on the island. Helen went along for the ride. It was a delightful trip across the harbor and Helen's interest and curiosity helped to calm my jitters, but the venture nearly ended in disaster. The commissioner was a big gruff man with a red face and white hair. He scowled at me when I approached his desk. It was bad enough that I was a boondoggling artist, but I took what comfort I could in the fact that at least I wasn't Japanese. The commissioner allowed me to unroll my sketches. He looked at them and growled, "You don't know much about railroading, and you don't know a damned thing about coal mining!" He began to shout. He turned purple. I muttered, "Yes, Mr. Commissioner, yes," and was prepared to be thrown bodily out of his office, when Helen maneuvered around the side of his desk, caught his eye, and said with a sweet smile and fluttering lashes, "But we're only trying to please *you*, Mr. Commissioner." To my amazement, he went to pieces completely. All his bluster vanished. He turned to me and said, "They didn't use clean-cut railroad ties in 1869. They left the bark on them. And go home and study up on coal mining." I said I would do that and be back soon.

Helen smiled at him and we departed. After that, I never went back to the island without her.

I completed my series of designs, a sequence of areas between and above the windows of the dining room, and went back to Ellis Island. I wanted the commissioner's approval of the general plan. I meant to tell him at once that I hadn't yet had time to make the revisions he had demanded, but he didn't wait for explanations. "Now that's more like it!" he roared. "Now you've got it!"

I painted the Ellis Island murals on canvas in my own quarters in East 17th Street. My wife and I occupied a top floor loft for which we paid forty dollars a month. The place had two skylights in the roof and banks of iron pipes which kept us snugly warm from Monday morning through Friday afternoon. For winter week-ends there was a pot-bellied stove and a big coal bin for which I carried coal up four flights of stairs. A young cabinet maker, Giorgio Cavallon, who was employed by the Project as a carpenter, built me a sturdy movable partition on which I stretched my canvas. (I think this name alone is sufficient refutation of the charge that the wpa Federal Art Project coddled incompetents.) This marvelous contraption took up most of our living quarters. I could have done the work directly on the wall at Ellis Island, of course (and there was a second Ellis Island group, developing another mural, which did attempt to work out there), but the inconvenience of eating and sleeping with my mural seemed better than being under the surveillance of the terrible-tempered commissioner.

I was pretty well along with this work when friends began to call me to express their concern for the disaster which had befallen me. "It must have been humiliating," they said. "What an outrage!" "What in the world are you talking about?" I asked them. "I read about it in this morning's *Tribune*," they said, "and want you to know I'm sorry." I rushed out to buy the paper. It was the leading article on the front page: "Commissioner throws artists off Ellis Island. Charges waste, incompetence and indolence. Says that yesterday he walked in to inspect the progress of a 'mural project' which the wpa/fap had set up in the administration building there and found that no work had been done, the artists were sitting around doing nothing, one man was fast asleep. He says this sort of thing cannot go on under his administration. He ordered the "artists" to get off the island, told them if they didn't clear out at once he'd have them thrown out," etc., etc. Then the newspaper went on to tell its readers that the Ellis Island mural project was inaugurated several months ago, it was being painted by Edward Laning and a group of assistants, the theme was announced to be "The Role of the Immigrant in the Development of America," and the Tribune recapitulated much of what they had printed when my project was started.

I rushed down to the new headquarters of the Art Project on King Street and demanded to see Mrs. McMahon. "This is an outrage," I said. "Why didn't the

Tribune consult us? You know that I have never worked at Ellis Island for a single moment and this business, whatever it was, had nothing whatever to do with me." Mrs. McMahon said, "They did call me and I told them I had nothing to say." I couldn't believe my ears. "But Whitelaw Reid is our friend," I said. "I'm going to call him. I'm going to protest this and demand that the *Tribune* retract it. This is libelous." Mrs. McMahon fixed me with her baleful glare and said, "You aren't going to call anybody. You aren't going to say a word. You aren't going to open your mouth."

My first reaction, of course, was to hate Mrs. McMahon as I had never hated anyone in my life. I could only think of myself as the victim of a wholly gratuitous sadism. But I was helpless. And I began to realize that Mrs. McMahon knew why I was helpless. She hadn't canceled my mural project. All she had done was to tell me to go home and paint—and shut up.

In 17th Street we went on with our work. Etta and Jimmy ground pigments with a muller on the top of a big marble-slabbed butcher's table we'd picked up at a Village auction and laid ground colors on the canvas. At noon we'd stop for an hour for lunch at a table near the window. We would discuss the mural which crowded over us while we ate. Albert, my model, would ask us to criticize the painting which he had made at home and brought in for our consideration. One day Albert said to me, "If you would recommend me to the office as an artist, and ask for me as an *assistant,* I would be glad to go on posing for you until the mural is finished and you wouldn't have these interruptions when they make me go pose for someone else." I took his paintings to the Project office and said that here was someone who should be granted an artist's status. This was agreed to, and I had a first-rate model—and student—until the Ellis Island mural was finished. A few years ago I ran into Albert on 42nd Street. He told me he now has his own advertising agency and has more work than he can keep up with—and if I ever need a job I must come and see him.

We finished the painting and asked the commissioner to come in to inspect the work—as much of it as we could stretch out for his inspection in the limited space on 17th Street. He brought his daughter with him. Away from *his* territory and as a visitor to *mine,* he was graciousness itself. He might have been Charles V in Titian's studio. Arrangements were made for the installation of the canvases at Ellis Island.

Raphael Doktor, the Project's technical director, and his crew met me in the Ellis Island dining room on a Thursday morning. I had asked him to use white lead as the adhesive for mounting the canvas on the plaster walls, but Doktor dismissed this as old fashioned. He assured me that he had a new plastic adhesive of superior quality. His men prepared the walls and proceeded to apply the miracle glue. By the end of the day's work about a fourth of the mural had

FIGURE 14. A section of Laning's Ellis Island mural. (Courtesy of the artist)

been fixed to the wall and trimmed in the corners and around doors and windows. All looked well and I went home in high spirits.

The technical crew only worked from Monday through Thursday, and I didn't return to the island until the next Monday morning. I saw immediately that the marvelous adhesive was a serious failure. It had dried as hard as stone, but in the process it had swelled and blistered in places and had created ugly bumps and hollows in the canvas surface. We found that no rolling or pressure would smooth out these unsightly swellings. There was no cure but to cut through the painting at many points, dig out the blistered lumps of hardened glue and patch the injured painting as best we could. That night I went home in despair. Next morning on my way back to Ellis Island I picked up the *Tribune*. There I was again: "That big mural at Ellis Island won't stay put," wrote the *Tribune*, and went on to present a slapstick account of our troubles. On the Ellis Island ferry that morning I leaned over the rail looking at the waters of New York Harbor gliding past and thought it might be better to slip over the side and have the agony over with. Something in the water caught my eye—a condom. Suddenly I was aware that the harbor was a mass of floating condoms—thousands, millions of them. I decided to wait and die some other way.

We repaired the damage after many days of hard work, and the remainder of my canvas sections were mounted successfully with white lead. I believe it was in the spring of 1937 that the completed mural was finally unveiled. The Project invited a small group of interested people to attend. Ernest Peixotto was there representing the Mural Painters Society. Mrs. McMahon and the Com-

missioner greeted each other cordially. Holger Cahill, the national director of the Project, said to me, "Well, this puts you among the big contenders—though I'm not sure who they are!" I don't recall that anybody was there from the *Tribune*.

In December 1935, following the judgment of the competition for the Washington Post Office Department murals, Ed Rowan, of the Section of Painting and Sculpture, wrote to me that the advisory committee which had awarded the post office commissions had recommended me for an appointment under the Section's program and that the Section wished to offer me the commission for the Rockingham, North Carolina, Post Office.

The records show that the original plan for the post office and court house in Rockingham called for three panels, one panel ten feet high by ten feet wide directly behind the judge's seat in the court room and two over the doors on either side. This was later reduced to a single ten by ten panel. Finally the mural space which was offered to me consisted of an area eight by twelve feet at one end of the post office lobby. I was given a year and a half in which to do the work.

I accepted the appointment and explained that because I was already working very hard on a rather ambitious project I would ask for the full year and a half and be finished in June 1937. I added that Rockingham, North Carolina, was in the one section of the United States I knew nothing about but that it *was* in the United States and nothing human, I hoped, was alien to me.

The Congressman from the Rockingham, North Carolina, district expressed an interest in the project and appointed a local committee to work with me on

97

the question of subject matter. For a long time I could get no word from the committee. When at last they responded, it was to tell me that Rockingham was a mill town—the one fact I had been able to unearth at the public library. The committee advised me to write the county historian, and his reply was that nothing much had ever happened there!

I wrote to the Section suggesting a general post office theme, Good and Bad News, or one dealing with the manufacture of cotton textiles. The Section favored the first idea. I recall that I was preoccupied with Ellis Island at this time and the little southern post office didn't fire my imagination. I made a hurried sketch which didn't excite the Section, either! I reworked it and they called it handsome in color and admirably suited for the lobby of the building in question.

This was in mid-February 1937. I was nearly finished with the Ellis Island work and I started in on Rockingham and painted it in three months. In June I set out from New York in a new Chevrolet, bought on the installment plan. In the car with me were my wife, our friend Dorothy Allen, and Mr. Fred Crittenden, an expert paper hanger. Lashed to the top of the car was the roll of canvases (the mural was in three parts) and a lot of molding.

We drove down through New Jersey, across Maryland and Virginia, and into the pine barrens of North Carolina to Rockingham. Mr. Crittenden and I met the Postmaster; we prepared a wall and pasted up the mural, trimmed the edges of the canvas and framed the three sections with a molding. I had very little retouching to do, and while Crittenden worked on the scaffold, I stood on the lobby floor with the Postmaster. As the mural unrolled, the local citizens wandered in and out, buying stamps and mailing letters. Everybody greeted the Postmaster by name, then looked up at the mural. "What's that?" they asked. The Postmaster said, "It's a mural painting," nudged the vistor and nodded in my direction and whispered, "This is the artist." To a man—and woman—the response was a loud and polite exclamation, "Well, it sho' is mahty purty!"

With Rockingham and Ellis Island behind me, I drove west and spent the summer traveling over the country, as far as California. When I returned to New York, I began preparing sketches for a Section competition. This was a big project for the decoration of the new San Antonio, Texas, Post Office—a series of lunettes running around the four sides of the post office lobby. It was the sort of mural project I enjoyed most, the story of the Pioneer West, and I studied Texas history assiduously. When the competition was judged I did not win the award, but Reginald Marsh, who was on the jury, reported to me that I was among the last three in the running when the decision was made. He also told me that Maury Maverick, the colorful Congressman from the San Antonio district, had attended the meeings of the jury of selection and had expressed a decided preference for my sketches. The Section then invited me to paint a

FIGURE 15. Edward Laning. *The Post as a Connecting Thread in Human Life.* Mural in Rockingham, North Carolina, Post Office. Section, 1937. (National Archives)

mural for the Springfield, New York, Post Office, a space about seven by ten feet in area, and I declined. I wrote to Ed Rowan that it was heartbreakingly difficult to say no to them about anything but that I had taken part in six of their competitions (I've now forgotten what the others were), that I had come close to winning at least two of the most important ones and that the Springville offer seemed to me an inadequate reward. I heard nothing more from the Section of Painting and Sculpture until 1941, when they invited me to paint a mural for the Bowling Green, Kentucky, Post Office.

In the meantime the WPA office called me in to discuss an important project. I believe this was soon after my return from California, in the autumn of 1937. Mrs. McMahon, Harry Knight, and Burgoyne Diller told me that they had for a long time tried unsuccessfully to secure the walls of New York's public libraries as locations for mural decoration, but the library board had steadfastly declined to cooperate. They had decided on a frontal assault. If they could succeed in securing the main building on 5th Avenue and 42nd Street, the branches should fall into their hands without trouble. With this aim, Diller had approached Mr. Isaac Newton Phelps Stokes, a member of the Board of Trustees of the Library and Chairman of the Art Commission of the City of New York, and had told him bluntly that it appeared that Mr. Stokes was hostile to young artists and indifferent to their fate. Mr. Stokes had been shocked by the charge and had denied it. Diller said that Mr. Stokes should prove his good faith by agreeing at least to look at sketches for those big empty spaces in the library's third-floor hall, spaces designed by the architects Carrere and Hastings to contain mural paintings but left empty through the years. Stokes agreed.

It must have been an interesting confrontation. Burgoyne Diller was an abstract artist's abstract artist. He was a dark, intense young man, utterly serious and dedicated. (Ten years later when I visited Philip Guston in St. Louis, Guston and I were recalling the days of the Project and we mentioned Diller, who was a close friend of Guston's. Guston told me, "Max Beckmann says, 'Some painters paint to make the visible visible. *I* paint to make the *invisible* visible.'" And Guston went on, "Burgoyne Diller paints to make the invisible invisible!") Perhaps Stokes saw something of himself in Diller. As an old man, Stokes resembled (as *Time* magazine put it) an El Greco cardinal. In the background of Sargent's portrait of Mrs. Stokes, in the Metropolitan Museum, the young I. N. Phelps Stokes is a lot like Diller—dark, intense, and humorless.

This was the formidable task Mrs. McMahon and her Project supervisors charged me with. I believe they selected me to spearhead their scheme because I had demonstrated at Ellis Island a capacity for endurance. Even Ned Bruce, who never liked my work because I was not of the Eugene Speicher-Maurice Sterne school, had once written to me, "I can say this for you, that what you start you finish." When I met Mr. Stokes, I knew at once what I was in for. He was the greatest stickler for detail I ever knew. This extended to every aspect of the library project from beginning to end, from the punctuation of the contract between the Art Project and the library to the last detail of my paintings. I hung on by my teeth.

Stokes was one of the most remarkable men I've ever known, and my association with him was one of the most difficult but also one of the most rewarding of my life. He had been an architect in his younger days—the Brummer Gallery on 57th Street, one of the loveliest small buildings in New York, was his work. (It still stands, and since the closing of the Brummer Gallery it has housed a number of other businesses, including that of Mr. John, the milliner.) His life work was an incredible series of volumes, *The Iconography of Manhattan Island*, in which he literally catalogued the physical history of New York City, building by building and block by block, from the Battery to the Bronx. When I knew him, he was a solitary old man living out his days in an apartment in the East Sixties to which he had moved from Greenwich, Connecticut, after the death of a wife whom he adored. From the beginning he made the library murals his own project, and I believe that while the work went on, it was almost as much his concern as it was mine.

I went to him with two suggestions for subject matter or theme: first, a series of four American literary masterpieces—perhaps *The Scarlet Letter, Moby Dick, Huckleberry Finn,* and *An American Tragedy;* second, the story of the Recorded Word—Moses and the graven tablets of the Law, the Medieval Scribe and his manuscript, Gutenberg and the Printing Press, and Mergenthaler and the Linotype. Stokes immediately rejected the first as lacking in dignity and enthusiastically approved the second. I proceeded to make sketches in crayon and wash, and he approved these without change. What he haggled over was the terms of agreement between the library and the Art Project. I carried these papers back and forth time after time. The Project supervisors were worn out before Stokes finally decided the details of this agreement were ready for submission to the Board of Trustees. He told me to put my sketches under my arm and meet him in Wall Street on a certain day in front of the Bank of New York. "I want you to be there on the sidewalk at the curb in front of the bank's entrance, facing east. Be there at exactly 2:45. At 2:50 I'll approach from the east and will turn into the bank. When you see me go in, I want you to follow me. I'll go directly through the bank and open the door to the directors' room. Follow immediately behind me into that room."

All went according to plan. Mr. Stokes appeared—tall, gaunt, and elegant in a gray suit and gray coat. Without glancing at me, he turned into the bank and I followed. He closed the door to the directors' room. This was where the Executive Committee of the Library Board met once a month. It was a big room, paneled in dark wood from floor to ceiling. Stokes pointed to an enormous

Renaissance table at the end of the room and said, under his breath, "Put the sketches there." I lined them up; he nodded, and murmured, "Go along now and call me at home precisely at five o'clock." He wanted me well out of the way before Mr. Morgan, Mr. Root, Mr. Polk, and the other members of the committee arrived. I wandered about the financial district until five o'clock, unable to concentrate on anything but the meeting in Wall Street. At five I called Mr. Stokes from a public phone and was told that the committee had approved and would submit the project to the Library Board at its next meeting. He told me to call at the Bank of New York the next morning to pick up my sketches and to take them to the office of Dr. Lydenberg, the director of the library, at a certain hour on a certain day.

Dr. Lydenberg was a little dry old man who had been helpful to me in my research. When I reached his office, he proceeded toward a big door, which he unlocked. He led the way into what must be one of the most splendid rooms in America, richly paneled walls, a great carved marble fireplace, and paintings by Stuart and others, including Du Plessis' portrait of Benjamin Franklin and Rembrandt Peale's "Porthole" portrait of Washington. Again I was directed to set up my sketches and to disappear. As I turned to go, Dr. Lydenberg whispered, "I hope you get what you want!"

Under Mr. Stokes' sponsorship the sketches were approved by the full Board and the project was launched. A few days later, the Project office called me in and explained that in drawing up the agreement—that agreement over which Stokes had pored with such concentration on detail—a slight clerical error had been made. According to the usual procedure, the institution receiving a mural painting was to pay the cost of materials; the artists were paid a weekly wage by the Project. In the case of the library, the cost of materials was estimated at four hundred dollars, two hundred for canvas and two hundred for paints, brushes, etc. Through some oversight only two hundred dollars had been indicated—enough for canvas or for paints and brushes, but not for both. I was told to return to Mr. Stokes and ask him to increase the allotment by two hundred dollars.

I called at his apartment and explained the difficulty. He looked more solemn and grave than I'd ever seen him. He sat in silence for a long time and then said quietly, "If I had the two hundred dollars I would put it up myself. But I don't have it. I would go to Mr. Baker for it, but unfortunately Mr. Baker is dead. I would ask Mr. Harkness, but Mr. Harkness is dead. I would ask Mr. Morgan, but Mr. Morgan was one of a minority on the Board who weren't very favorable. Mr. Morgan said, 'Those wall spaces have been vacant all these years. What's the hurry? If we wait, maybe someone will *give* us some murals.' I don't want to go back to the Board about this. We have their approval now, and if we reopen the question there's always the possibility they may reverse themselves. No, I don't think there's anything that can be done about it." I took this word back to King Street and the Art Project found the two hundred dollars and we went ahead.

My first work location was in an abandoned church on 10th Avenue where the Federal Theatre Project had built a paint-frame for the use of scene painters. This was a platform about twelve feet above the floor which ran across the width of the church. There was a protective railing at the front of the platform, and behind it four great wooden frames suspended on pulleys from the ceiling and balanced with counterweights. We stretched our four canvases, each about nine by eighteen feet in area, on these frames. I borrowed Reginald Marsh's projector and enlarged my designs to the full scale from lantern slides made from my drawings. To paint the top of the picture, I had only to lower the entire canvas toward the floor. To paint the lower part, I raised the picture toward the ceiling. While we worked on our platform, the Theatre Project's actors, dancers, and musicians rehearsed on the floor below us. It was an ideal situation, and the work went rapidly forward. Lloyd Goff joined me as assistant, and together with James Rutledge and Etta Fick we ground our own colors (with invaluable technical advice from Ralph Mayer) and proceeded with the underpainting of all four panels simultaneously. Dr. Lydenberg came in from time to time to watch our progress. (Romona Javitz, director of the picture collection, laughed when I told her this. "You know something?" she asked. "Dr. Lydenberg is color-blind!" I told her that didn't matter because the work was in a monochrome so far.)

Mr. Stokes visited us frequently and took particular interest in the Mergen-thaler panel. It pleased him that I pictured the Brooklyn Bridge out the windows of the New York Tribune Building where Mergenthaler first installed his lino-type machine. "I was the first person to walk across the Brooklyn Bridge," he told me. "I was about fifteen years old, and I stood all night at the Manhattan approach to the bridge. A great crowd gathered, but I was in the forefront, and when the ribbon was cut, I made a dash for it and reached Brooklyn ahead of anyone else!" One day he came in to tell me that he had been thinking about the kerosene lamp I showed hanging over Mergenthaler's machine. "I remember," he said, "that in 1880 I went with my father to New Jersey to visit Mr. Edison, who was in my father's employ. He had made a clock for my father which, in-stead of striking the hour, said, 'Twelve o'clock and all's well.' He had incorpo-rated his newly invented phonograph in the clock. I know that by this time he had already invented the incandescent electric lamp. A year later, in 1881, elec-tric light was installed in Mr. Morgan's house next door to us, and in 1882 our house was wired for electricity. I'm sure that by 1883, the date of your picture, there would have been electric light in the Tribune Building." I painted out the kerosene lamp and painted in an electric bulb. Then he decided he might have been premature and sent me back to kerosene. This was his only active intervention in the painting itself, and I didn't mind the trouble it gave me because his reminiscences were fascinating. One day he talked about Sargent's portrait of his wife which was then on loan to the Brooklyn Museum. "I commissioned Sargent to paint it as my wedding present to her," he said. "To look at it you would think Sargent had dashed it off in a few days of brilliant brush work. Actually, we posed for it thirty-six times! At first Sargent had her right hand resting on the head of a greyhound dog, but he didn't like that, so he painted the dog out and painted me in instead. When he was finally satisfied, he touched his brush to his palette, backed away from the easel all the way across the studio, poised the brush like a lance and charged, shouting, 'Pis-tache, pistache, pistache!' and touched the painting. And do you know, the highlight on the engagement ring stood out a quarter of an inch! Many years later the Metropolitan Museum wanted the painting for a big retrospective exhibition of Sargent's work. Sargent had insisted on having the final word on what was to be shown, and I wired to him in Boston, where he was painting the murals in the Boston Public Library, asking his permission. He wired back, 'Certainly, but under no circumstances allow anything to happen to the highlight on the engagement ring!'"

Our work was interrupted when the Project lost its lease on the Church building. We rolled up the canvases and moved to an abandoned warehouse in West 49th Street, where we stretched the canvases on the wall and worked on a scaffold. Before we were quite finished, the warehouse was lost to us and the murals were rolled up and stored at King Street while a new work location was sought.

In the meantime, Harry Knight had said to me one day, "Are you eligible for relief?" I told him I certainly was, that I had no source of income except my weekly pay check from the Project. Up to that time I had been employed by the Project on a "non-relief" basis, which meant that I was not subject to investigation of my financial need. Harry explained to me that if I were "certified" as being in need, my job would be more secure; the "non-relief" category was subject to dismissal before relief workers were presented with the dreaded "pink slip," which was the official notification of being fired. I applied for relief status, was investigated and certified. I told the investigator the truth except for one small fact which I concealed, that my wife had a small part-time job as night supervisor at the Cooper Union Museum. She had had this position since the days when she was a student in the Cooper Union Art School, long before our marriage; she loved the museum; the job didn't pay enough, remotely, to support her. I saw no point in mentioning it. But it wasn't long until the relief investigator called and, after a few polite routine questions, said to me, "This morning on my way down here I passed a Woolworth's on Lexington Avenue where I

FIGURE 16. Edward Laning, *Mergenthaler and the Linotype.* Mural panel in lobby of Main Reading Room, New York Public Library. WPA/FAP, 1940. (Courtesy of the artist)

saw an artist painting in the window as part of some sales promotion. Couldn't you do something like that?" I told her I might be able to. I admitted I had never tried. I attempted to say something about the importance of the work I was engaged in. Then she calmly asked, "And what about your wife's job at Cooper Union? You said that neither of you had any source of income other than the WPA." I had no answer to this, and a few days later I received a pink slip.

I went down to King Street to try to reclaim my non-relief status, but I knew this would take time. The whole Project had been under fire recently. There had been a reduction in its funds, and many artists had been laid off. The response had been demonstrations culminating in a sit-in at the King Street office (a premonition of the sixties!), and the police had staged an attack, dragging the protesters from the building just as they do today in our universities. The Washington office of the WPA had appointed an army officer, Colonel Somervell, to direct the New York WPA, and the office in King Street feared the worst. My own situation seemed desperate. My murals had been rolled up and put on the shelf for weeks. I had no place to work; I had no job.

I went into the big factory-like room where dozens of Project clerical workers had their desks and saw Mrs. McMahon there. This was unusual; she rarely emerged from her private lair. I discovered that she was interviewing the non-relief contingent of the Project. I saw them called to her desk and heard her ask each in turn (Anton Refregier, *et al.*) how their projects were developing and how much time they estimated they would need to complete their work. Suddenly I lost my head and charged up to her desk, pushing the others aside. I began to shout and curse. I don't remember exactly what I said, but I know I yelled that it was a God-damned outrage that my project should be stalled like this while these others who were doing far less important work were coddled in this obscene manner—or words to that effect. The office force froze. Secretaries stood up and craned their necks. I raved on. "Arsenic and Old Face" stared at me for a moment in silence, then gave me her famous double-whammey. Her left eyelid came unhinged and began to flutter spasmodically. This device had unseated stronger men than I—it was calculated to freeze thy young blood, make thy two eyes like stars start from their spheres, etc.—but I was carried along on a wave of madness. I continued to curse loudly, and Mrs. McMahon retired to her inner sanctum. The crowd looked at me in silence. I turned to Refregier and the other non-reliefers and said, "Well, I guess I've played the fool." Refregier smiled and said, "That may very well be."

I was about to turn and go, resigned to my fate, when someone came to me and said, "Mrs. McMahon wants to see you in her office immediately." I thought I might as well get it over with then and there, and I followed to the inner sanctum. I hardly noticed the little man in the dark suit, seated in the corner. She sat at her big desk and let me stand. "Mr. Laning," she said, "what was it you were saying to me just now in the outer office?" Suddenly the whole wave swept over me again and I became vituperative. "You let me wait outside," I said, "begging to be allowed to continue my work, while you interview these others. I'm only interested in one thing in this world and that's to be allowed to get back to my job and carry it through"; and then I began to rant and rave again. She interrupted me, saying, "Mr. Laning, this language in my office would warrant my severing your connection with this project!" I answered that if I couldn't do my job, I wouldn't give a damn. "You may *go* now," she said, and I left the office.

Walking home, feeling defeated but purged, I reached Bleecker Street when I suddenly wondered, "But who was that little man who sat so quietly in the corner of her office while I blew my top?" And then I remembered—this was Colonel Somervell's representative in the Project office, Colonel Somervell's *Spy*. I had been *had*. Mrs. McMahon had *used* me. The charge the Establishment had been making against the whole Project was that the artists were lazy "boon-dogglers." My rebellion had offended her, but she had quickly risen above personal affront and had made me grist to her mill. Colonel Somervell's man would report to his superior that a WPA artist had dared all to be allowed to get on with his job. Mrs. McMahon had turned my attack against her into an advantage for the Project as a whole. Once again my personal hatred for her turned into awe for her selflessness.

Suddenly I was offered a new work location, an abandoned pier on the Hudson River. I was only one of many projects working in this vast space, and I finished my library panels quickly. One day we were visited by the redoubtable Colonel Somervell, who had Mrs. Roosevelt in tow. When he came to me and had introduced me to Mrs. Roosevelt, Colonel Somervell stepped out of the line of march to speak to me. "How is your project going?" he asked. I told him it was proceeding very well. "Do you need anything you aren't provided with?" he asked. I said I had everything I could require. He fell in with Mrs. F.D.R. and proceeded on his inspection of other work projects on the pier.

It was early in 1940 when my four mural panels and two lunettes were finished and we took them to the library. This time I had my way and the installation was made with white lead as an adhesive. The technicians would meet with me and my assistants about six in the evening, after the library was closed to the public, and we would work into the early hours of the morning.

When the lower walls of the library's Great Hall were finished, the Project staged an unveiling. Photos of the murals were released to the press. Emily Genauer of the *Tribune* pronounced them "sound as a nut," and Edward Alden Jewell, after quibbling about the library's neo-classical architecture, announced, "The Mausoleum is complete." The official unveiling was scheduled to be a ceremony in the auditorium, adjoining the Great Hall to the east. Mayor La-

Guardia promised to be there. Two or three hundred people gathered and waited. It was at least an hour beyond the announced time before the mayor appeared, but the crowd, though restive, kept to their seats. People who remember Fiorello LaGuardia will recall that he went everywhere, and was always late. He came in escorted by Colonel Somervell.

Holger Cahill opened the ceremonies. Then I was called on to say something. I told the audience this was not the first time I had seen Mayor LaGuardia confronted by a work of art—or, I added, a work of art confronted by Mayor La-Guardia. At this point the Mayor looked up at me quizzically, as if to say, "What the hell are you up to?" I went on to recall a recent opening of an Art Project easel painting show, when Burgoyne Diller had brought the mayor and Arshile Gorky face to face before a Gorky painting and had asked Gorky to elucidate his Kandinsky-ish painting to the mayor—and LaGuardia had turned on his heel and walked away, saying, "I'm as conservative in my art as I am progressive in my politics!" I hesitated a moment while the audience laughed. I looked at LaGuardia, who seemed relieved. I added, "I thought it was good at the time, but now I'm not so sure!" I sat down and the Mayor came to the rostrum. He looked down at me with a fierce scowl. Then he beamed. He said, "If politicians could paint as well as Mr. Laning can talk, it would be a better world!" He went on to apologize for being late; he explained that he was a very busy man but that this was a more important occasion than he had realized. He led us into the hall and witnessed the unveiling of the murals, and he congratulated me.

Shortly before the murals were installed, Mr. Stokes said to me, "If we could get you up there, could you touch up the ceiling?" The ceiling in this monumental hall on the third floor of the library is a vault. It consists of elaborately carved moldings framing open spaces. At the center is a space about fifteen feet wide and forty feet long which had been painted to represent an open sky—pink clouds against a blue ground. In 1940 this ceiling painting was flaking badly and looked very unsightly. Mr. Stokes explained to me that the library's roof had become leaky but that this problem had finally been solved. "We succeeded in raising a million dollars for a new monel metal roof over the entire building," he said, "and there will be no further damage." I said to him, "If you can get me up there at all, why don't we paint something more interesting than pretty pink clouds in a blue sky? Why don't we do something more in keeping with the mural paintings we are installing below?" He told me to design something, and I made a sketch of Prometheus descending from Heaven carrying the stolen fire of learning and culture to Mankind below. At either end of the space I designed figures representing Man's reactions to Prometheus' offering: some aspiring toward the light, others putting down those who aspired, some lost in indifferent sleep.

FIGURE 17.   Edward Laning. *Prometheus*. Ceiling panel in lobby of Main Reading Room, New York Public Library. WPA/FAP, 1942. (Archives of American Art)

My sketch was approved by the Library Board, and on our abandoned Hudson River pier I prepared a full sized cartoon. The Project's carpenters made me a huge frame which we laced with crosswires. I placed my cartoon (which I had drawn on paper tacked to a side wall of the pier) on this frame, face down, and with ropes and pulleys we raised the cartoon overhead to a height comparable to the height of the library ceiling, about fifty feet from the floor. I studied my figures in this overhead situation and worked with them until I thought their foreshortening was convincing. I knew that when I painted the canvas against a vertical wall, this sense of overhead foreshortening would be very difficult to achieve, and once I had my cartoon right I held to it strictly. This necessity applied to the figures at the ends of the painting, figures which were represented as standing or sitting on rocky peaks seen from below. The figure of Prometheus at the center was another matter. Since he was suspended in air, I knew I could give him any attitude I chose. I decided that the figure in my cartoon was stiff, and I decided to improvise.

I had an excellent model working for me, a young man with a splendid physique and a somewhat less admirable character. I made a rough sketch of the figure I had in mind; the model looked at it and said, "Let's see what we can do!" He found a couple of pieces of stout rope, climbed to the top of our scaffold, fifteen feet above, and lashed himself by his wrists to the top beams. The strain was terrific, but for a short time I could see exactly the dynamic posture I needed. I painted furiously as long as he could hold out. The sweat poured from us both. He would collapse and rest at intervals, then return to his crucifixion. After a couple of days of this agony he would disappear, sometimes for a week. The Project's time-keepers would come to check on us, and I would tell them I had sent him off on an errand for me. After several days' absence he would come back rather sheepishly and tell me he had been on a binge and had run into a pretty girl. According to his accounts, his extra-mural activities were as athletic as any work he did for me. But he made up for these prolonged absences by brilliant performances on the scaffold, and Prometheus got painted.

In the meantime the library prepared to erect a scaffolding in the Great Hall. One day the custodian of the building, Mr. Fedeler, took me to the attic, a vast area of beams and cat-walks, above the entire building, two blocks long. One of the cat-walks passed alongside the top of my vault. We stood looking down on its curving sides, and I mentioned the expensive new roof and said I was glad there'd be no more leaks to contend with. "There was nothing wrong with the old roof," he said. "The new roof was an unnecessary expense. My maintenance men, going about their work up here, stop off at this spot, and urinate on this vault. I've tried, but there's nothing I can do about it."

Finally the scaffold was in place and we ascended to a giddy height and walked over loosely laid boards fifty feet above the marble floor. We cleaned the ceiling area and mounted our mural with white lead. It had been impossible to obtain a single piece of canvas large enough for this space, and my mural was painted in three overlapping strips. This had made its execution difficult, since these overlaps had to be painted out beyond each other four times, but it facilitated installation. It was only necessary to roll out each strip with a white lead paste and then cut through these overlaps and clean up the smears of white lead and retouch these seams. It wasn't a heroic task like the Sistine ceiling, but it was difficult enough.

By this time the Japanese had attacked Pearl Harbor, the country was at war, and the library began to worry about the scaffolding. The Great Hall was the entrance to the card catalogue room and the enormous main reading room, and it might have been difficult to evacuate hundreds of people through our forest of iron pipes. We were urged to hurry, and we ran a race with time. From my point of view it was essential to get it right once and for all, because I knew it would be a long time before I would ever get up there again.

In 1941 the Section of Painting and Sculpture, "on the basis of competent sketches submitted in the San Antonio, Texas, Post Office and Court House mural competition," invited me to paint a mural in the Bowling Green, Kentucky, Post Office. I corresponded with several people in Bowling Green, and the local newspaper had asked its readers for ideas about subject matter. The president of the Bowling Green Business University wrote, "Why not pictures portraying the 'Long Hunters' who camped near the country club on what is now the Warrener farm?" I prepared a design based on a story about Daniel Boone and the "Long Hunters": Boone, who enjoyed solitude, had wandered off alone and was absent for a long time. One day the Hunters heard a strange sound in the woods and followed it. They discovered Daniel sprawled out on the top of a hill, singing a duet with a Kentucky cardinal perched on a nearby limb.

This design was approved, and when the work was finished I sent Ed Rowan a photograph of it. He wrote, "I personally like it the best of any of your work that I have seen. I am confident that the lyric quality and competence will not be lost on the people of Bowling Green."

Mr. Crittenden and I installed the mural. I recently learned from a citizen of Bowling Green that when a new post office was built, my mural was a principal factor in the decision to save the old building and convert it to other civic uses.

With the war, the Art Projects quickly came to an end. The administrative agencies continued to operate for a short time, but it was their task now to "liquidate" the Projects. Federal support of the Arts ended with the emergency that had brought it into being.

About 1952 I ran into Joe Pandolfini, who had worked with me on my Hudson Guild fresco, and Joe asked me to come with him to the club. I knew what he meant—the 8th Street Club, the headquarters of the *avant garde*, the Abstract Expressionists, the favorites of the Museum of Modern Art and *Art News*. "Oh, come on," Joe said, "they're all your old friends!" It was a big meeting in a dreary loft on East 8th Street. There were about two hundred people present, and the occasion was a panel discussion, with Clement Greenberg and Alfred Frankfurter at the speakers' table. (It was a lot like the John Reed Club.) I looked around at the crowd. Joe was right. They were all my old WPA colleagues, and nothing, essentially, had changed. Ad Reinhardt got up during the discussion period at the end of the speeches from the table and directed himself to Greenberg. The burden of Reinhardt's harangue was that the current Whitney Museum show, a block to the west, had a few "objective" or "representational" paintings in it. (Before the war the abstract painters had had one or two galleries of the museum to themselves. By 1952 the "representational" painters were crowded into a dark corner and the "abstract" artists dominated the place.) Reinhardt challenged Greenberg about this monstrous fact that there should be *any* representational painters in a Whitney Annual. Greenberg looked at him scornfully (there was some personal feud involved) and said, "I'm not an artist; I'm only a writer. If you and your friends object, why don't you march down the street and tear up the joint?"

Then I knew I was back in the John Reed Club. But with a difference. The steam had gone out of the revolutionaries. What had made the change? It was the Stalin-Hitler pact of 1939. My old "revolutionary" friends had been left with nothing to paint. Stalin had pulled the rug from under their feet. With nothing left to say, they had decided to paint for painting's sake, merely to push and pull the paint on the picture surface. But their *Marxism* didn't die so easily; they remained revolutionaries, *avant gardistes*, rebels without a cause. And Nelson Rockefeller's Museum of Modern Art took up where the John Reed Club left off. "Historical determinism" is the common faith of the Chase National Bank and the Kremlin. Manifest destiny and historical necessity are one and the same thing. As a hand-lettered sign, carried before the Soviet Embassy after the Czechoslovak invasion read, just the other day, "The Pig is the Same All Over!"

Looking back, it all seems to me to have come 'round again, full circle. Have I learned anything? Not much. Let's see. It was 1932. . . .

It was the worst of times; it was the best of times. It was the best because it was the worst. Business came to a standstill, the banks closed, people everywhere were thrown out of work—and almost over night New York became the Great Good Place and America the Land of Promise. Until then, every man's hand had been against every man. Now, suddenly, all were kindly and helpful and filled with compassionate purpose.

I know now that it was our Golden Age, the only humane era in our history, the one brief period when we permitted ourselves to be good. Before that time, all was Business, and after it all has been War. But this Golden Age was an accident; it was nothing of our choosing. Business is the license to steal; War is the license to kill; and America is the Land of License. Two years of killing, during the First World War, were followed by ten years of riotous stealing. After World War I (we hadn't yet learned that war need never stop at all), Warren Gamaliel Harding cried, "Back to Normalcy!" and Calvin Coolidge said, "The business of America is business."

Then suddenly the country went broke. But the ensuing Golden Age was a fool's paradise. The stealing stopped, but only because there was nothing left to steal. Within ten years Business had discovered War, with a rapaciousness that led even a triumphant general to cower before the monster of our "military-industrial complex." Again as in 1929 we are assured that nothing can now stop the progress of this boom. But what we really know is that this time the bust will be complete and final. And there will be no hideaway for the artist—or the millionaire—at the bottom of the shell hole. There isn't going to be any refuge.

1. November and December 1926 and January to March 1927.
2. This mural, now destroyed, is reproduced in Audrey McMahon, "May the Artist Live," *Parnassus* (October 1933), pp. 1–4.

JOSEPH SOLMAN was born in Vitebsk, Russia, in 1909 and came to the United States with his family in 1912. He studied art at the National Academy of Design beginning in 1926. His first one-man show was held at the Contemporary Arts Gallery in 1934. During the same year he was employed on the PWAP and the CAA's art project. From 1935 to 1941 he worked on the easel division of the WPA Federal Art Project in New York City and for a short period at the Spokane, Oregon, WPA Community Art Center. He was also active on the editorial board of the New York Artists' Union publication *Art Front* and served as its editor-in-chief in 1936. Since the Project days he has lived in New York City and has devoted himself to painting interiors and portraits. From 1965 to 1967 he was president of the Federation of Modern Painters and Sculptors. At present he teaches painting at the City College of New York. A pictorial survey of his work, with an introduction by A. L. Chanin, was published by Crown in 1966.

FIGURE 18. Joseph Solman. *Self-Portrait.* 1941. Collection of the artist. (Photograph by Walter Rosenblum)

The Easel Division of the WPA Federal Art Project

JOSEPH SOLMAN

During the Depression years a series of attempts to alleviate the lot of the artist began in New York City as far back as 1931 with the Gibson Committee for the Unemployed. As one instance, I was sent along with six jobless architects to the Hudson Guild Farm in Netcong, New Jersey, to perform regulation farm duties in the morning. From noon on we were free the rest of the day to draw up plans, sketch, or paint. I believe it was a six-month make-shift program.

Later the Gibson Committee funded a project supervised by the CAA to help hungry artists. Harry Knight was liaison. From allocated funds one hundred artists were chosen for various teaching and decorating or mural projects. Joseph Pandolfini, later to become an easel painter on the WPA/FAP, told me of re-decorating a church on West 53rd Street along with artists Michael Loew, Boris Gorelick, and James Lechay. Since it was an integrated church the artists decided on the bold scheme of painting both black and white angels alongside each other. Thus the seeds of social struggle and enlightenment were even then being scattered by a naively courageous group of artists on the walls of a humble church.

From December 1933 to June 1934 the PWAP ran its uneven course. Early in 1933 George Biddle, a well-known painter and personal friend of President Roosevelt, had written him about the immense achievements of the Mexican muralists under government patronage and how such support could assist in this country to initiate a native mural tradition. With the proselytizing and advise of Biddle, the sympathies of Harry Hopkins, administrator of the Civil Works Administration and, later, the WPA, and Mrs. Roosevelt, the irons were in the fire and Edward Bruce was chosen as the national director of PWAP.

In order to be hired for PWAP in New York, the artists had to submit work to

Lloyd Goodrich and Juliana Force, both of the Whitney Museum. The artists who were chosen taught art in settlement houses and decorated everything from hospital walls to panels on the inside of a ferry boat that went back and forth to Ellis Island. Their weekly paycheck coming from Washington was $38.25. Reginald Marsh was in charge of the mural projects and their allocation.

When the PWAP was officially disbanded in June 1934, many artists had already been fired and once again joined the vast army of the unemployed. A group of artists, some of them members of the John Reed Club, and others, fresh out of work, decided to hold a meeting to discuss their problems. Joseph Pandolfini headed an ad hoc committee including people like Max Spivak, Boris Gorelick, and Phil Bard. With such committees, aided by other sympathetic artists, the first Artists' Union was born. About two hundred artists participated in the baptism of this fledgling organization.

The outcry of many artists in the land against the grim conditions of the Depression and the desire to participate as dignified citizens with their own creative skills which they wished to bring to the community at large, were factors that cannot be underestimated as an incentive to broadening the scope of the art program that finally, in 1935, became the WPA/FAP.

The PWAP and the Section of Painting and Sculpture emphasized mural decoration to dramatize the social uses of art for public buildings as had been the case during the Renaissance in Italy and in the recent efflorescence of the Mexican mural. Post offices and court houses as well as other public buildings were fortunate recipients of some fine murals. Thus, when the WPA was formed, the greatest emphasis was placed on mural work and art teaching, with easel painting regarded as a precious field for the rare few. Many painters like myself, whose obvious gift was for easel painting, spent months assisting highly skilled muralists in their designs for schools and libraries. Some of us were not in sympathy with their traditionalism or old master cast. It is true that some superb modernists were given an opportunity to try their wings on walls. Stuart Davis, Karl Knaths, Arshile Gorky, Byron Browne, Louis Schanker, and Willem de Kooning made history by being the first exponents of the modern or abstract style in American mural painting. It would be truer to say they initiated abstract mural painting in this country. It must also be noted that Ben Shahn's murals for the prison on Rikers Island, New York, created a storm of controversy because of their social sympathies. Shahn's natural monumental style had an effect on his own easel work as well as on the easel work of many younger contemporaries.

The easel project was at first very small. The Artists' Union, in a series of grievance committee meetings with Audrey McMahon and Harry Knight, both representing the WPA/FAP, successfully persuaded them to convince Washington that the easel division needed expanding. Among those easel painters representative of the Woodstock school of painting as typified by Alexander Brook and Kuniyoshi were Stuart Edie, Elizabeth Terrell, and Bruce Mitchell. They were primarily landscape painters of the American scene. Of the more romantic sea-scape and landscape painters were Joseph de Martini, Jean Liberte, John Loner-gan, Don Forbes, and the early Jackson Pollock. The social scene painters were legion due to the mighty economic upheaval of the period and the precedent of the Mexican mural movement. There were Philip Evergood, Gregorio Prestopino, Joe Vogel, Walter Quirt, Jack Levine, Joseph Hirsch, Robert Gwathmey, Boris Margo, Philip Reisman, and others too numerous to mention. The urban scene broadly delineated in expressionist terms was represented by Herman Rose, Jules Halfant, Jack Tworkov, Louis Nisonoff, Alice Neel, Louis Harris, Mark Rothko, myself, and others. Some of the abstract painters I mentioned previously in relation to mural making; however, many were represented in the easel divi-sion including Ad Reinhardt, William Baziotes, Irene Rice Pereira, Giorgio Cavallon, John Opper, Ralph Rosenborg, Jan Matulka, Joseph Stella, and the later work of Jackson Pollock. Rufino Tamayo, Marsden Hartley, and Milton Avery were connected with the Project for a comparatively short period, I be-lieve in the 10 percent non-relief quota. I recall seeing them in line of a Friday morning to sign in for their week's activity and payroll listing downtown at 110 King Street, New York City.

A pet device of museum directors and critics is to pigeon-hole or tabulate artists according to a school or movement. Artists as a whole despise it. When-ever I come together with them justifiable scorn is heaped on this IBM technique. I have just done something of the same in the above paragraphs, but I hasten to qualify. What I have cited are broad groupings primarily to show some of the diversity of the Art Project. Don Forbes, for instance, bedecked his storm-tossed scenes in rich jewels while Joseph de Martini used a spare palette to depict the loneliness of abandoned quarries. Other artists are even more difficult to pigeon-hole. Byron Browne was a highly baroque modernist while Balcomb Greene's work was more severe than De Stijl or Constructivism. (Both these men turned to highly original figurative painting at a later date; Browne with volatile, broadly-brushed portraits before his untimely death, Greene to large figures splintered by a sort of cinematic light.) Ben-Zion with his apocalyptic studies of prophets and Bible stories is a lone Blake-like figure on the American scene, and to mention an influence of Max Beckmann would be as pointless as to compare Stuart Davis to Léger. Douglas Brown, now deceased, created amazing water-colors on the Project of strange Louisiana, Mexican, and New Orleans scenes that someday may be rediscovered as being equal to those of Burchfield. They can no more be classified than the curiously original work of Loren MacIver and Alice Neel. Earl Kerkam painted exquisite still lifes and strangely defiant self portraits, combining elements of Abbott Thayer and Soutine in his own highly personal way. A painter's painter, admired by many colleagues, his work is not easily classifiable. But this memoir cannot take up the individual qualities of the work of many artists I have known, so I will return to the administrative procedures.

With an enlarged easel division, incorporating so great a diversity of styles, several WPA Federal Art Galleries were opened to show some of the outstanding work of these painters. One such gallery was located on 57th Street near 7th Avenue in New York City. New exhibits were installed monthly with an opening and invited guests. I cannot help recalling one exhibit where Rothko and I were invited as two of the participating artists. Max Weber, once Rothko's teacher, was one of the distinguished guests. So he called his former teacher over to show him his painting of a ghostly quartet engaged in playing chamber music. Weber eyed it indulgently and yet a mite critically; then, flicking some ashes from his lit cigarette into the palm of his hand, went over and rubbed them over the face of one of the players, saying "This spot should be toned down a little." For the moment Weber was back in the classroom. Rothko and I chuckled long after the master left. At many of these exhibitions work which was not too popular or allocable but contained originality and some creative spark, according to the administrative jury, was shown.

From many painters I have spoken to, the time allotted the easel painter for his painting went according to size; four weeks for a 16 by 20 inch or 20 by 24 inch canvas, five weeks for a 24 by 30 inch canvas, six weeks for a 24 by 36 inch size. Ben-Zion, who was one of the earliest to paint on a large scale, told me he received up to three months for a canvas five feet high. The general allotment for watercolors or gouaches was two per month.

The painter brought his finished work to the supervisor of his division at 110 King Street in Manhattan. A Mr. Lloyd Rollins, one of our earliest supervisors, was a stickler for conservative craftsmanship, so that the expressionist camp chafed considerably under his cold reception. Fortunately he was later replaced by Benjamin Knotts who took a kindlier view of the variety of styles projected by the artists. Knotts later on became an important figure in the educational department of the Metropolitan Museum in New York.

John Lonergan and Burgoyne Diller, two fine artists, also were supervisors and were highly encouraging to original talent. I recall Lonergan going out of his way to show me an early emotional abstraction, an oil on paper, of Jackson Pollock. He was truly excited by it. Diller had much to do with helping some of the abstract painters get interesting mural assignments. Four panels were done for station WNYC in New York by Byron Browne, Louis Schanker, John von Wicht, and Stuart Davis. The brilliant panel by the latter is now on permanent loan to the Metropolitan Museum.

Landscapes, street scenes, and still lifes done in the Woodstock tradition or the skillful academic manner were naturally allocated most quickly to those institutions eligible for them: schools, hospitals, libraries, and other tax-supported buildings. Only the modest price of stretcher and canvas was charged to them.

Some of the members of the administration were afraid that if an artist piled up a number of unused and unallocated canvases in the stockroom his position was shaky as an efficient project worker and it was then deemed advisable to switch him over to the teaching division. I recall one such instance when Audrey McMahon placed Sascha Moldovan, Alice Neel, and Max Schnitzler in just such a position. As head of the grievance committee of the Artists' Union at that time I came down to King Street with several other members of my committee to argue the cases. Fortunately I was very well acquainted with the work of all three artists, their long background, the unyielding individuality of their work, and the painterly merits that could not always be discerned by the well-meaning administration. After pointing all these qualities out the administration wisely gave in and the three artists remained on the easel division. They are all highly respected painters today. Alice Neel, in her 1968 show of scalpel-sharp portraits at the Graham Gallery, was acclaimed for her "unforgettable" images. Like many I have mentioned in this brief, she is a loner, unclassifiable and therefore receives no popular publicity such as some fourth-rate followers of the hard-edge school obtain.

There is scarcely any question of the profound effect the WPA/FAP had on the artist in America; and, in turn, the vast influence the artist had on the country at large; for instance, over 100 WPA community art centers were established between 1935 and 1943.

In 1938 I was sent for six months, along with two other colleagues from New York, to help develop a program for the Spokane art center in the state of Washington. I was designated as exhibition designer but I also taught art to adults one evening a week, conducted a Saturday morning children's class, and held a course of lectures on both art and music. The response was heartwarming, Hilda Deutsch, the sculptress from New York, remained on as teacher, eventually marrying the local director of the center, Carl Morris, a well-known abstract painter today—an example of American East-West cultural integration.

The WPA artist quickly became aware of his social environment; first, because he had to go through the gauntlet of home relief before he was eligible to be employed by the Project; second, he felt an inevitable alliance with the new surge of trade unionism for unskilled workers (CIO) sweeping the country; third, the heated discussions taking place everywhere concerning the New Deal, the welfare state, socialism and communism in the U.S.S.R., particularly as depicted by the heroic films of Pudovkin and Eisenstein. The artist became a self-esteemed citizen of his country feeling his product was a viable commodity and beneficial to it.

At this time the Artists' Union and the National Maritime Union (NMU) were two of the most active participants in aiding striking picket lines anywhere in New York City. If the salesgirls went out on strike at May's department store in Brooklyn a grouping from the above-mentioned unions was bound to swell the picket line. I recall some of our own demonstrations to get artists back on the job after a number of pink dismissal slips had been given out. At such times everyone was in jeopardy. Suddenly from nowhere a truckload of NMU workers would appear and jump out onto the sidewalk to join our procession. Cheers welled up from all sides. Those were spirited times indeed.

One time our identity with art and tradition was humorously pointed up. Late in 1935 about two hundred or more artists were picketing the offices used by the Project administration on the corner of 57th Street and Lexington Avenue. The occasion was a new round of firings. The police wagons appeared and this time they decided on a wholesale arrest, no one excluded. When we arrived at the 17th precinct, James Lechay led the long line of prisoners. "Your name!" bellowed an officer, pad and pencil in hand. "Jim Picasso" came the firm response. That was a sufficient cue. Cézanne, Da Vinci, and Peter Breughel followed. What an ego-satisfying game it was and with what relish everyone participated. When my companion Martin Craig gave the name of his idol James Joyce the policeman muttered, "How did an Irishman like you get mixed up with this mob?" Pandolfini was reincarnated as Bellini and Rosalind Bengelsdorf (Browne) as Rosa Bonheur! Even the names of Michelangelo and Van Gogh did not bring a spark of recognition to the eyes of our patrolmen. We could not call home but the police were willing to phone messages for us. Thus, when my wife, who with Craig's wife was expecting both of us home for dinner, answered the phone she heard this pronouncement: "James Joyce and Georges Seurat have been arrested and are at the 17th precinct." Our wives knew at once who had chosen each name and rushed over with the Union lawyer Martin Popper.

We were locked in cells in groups singing folk songs all the time. As the hours passed they released a small group of about four or five at a time just to drag the action out and teach us a lesson. The judge summarily dismissed the cases as they came up. One fellow in the cell with me had bolted our profession and given himself out as John Milton. As the officers came, now about three A.M., to release a few more prisoners to the judge and he called the names of Al Soutine, John Vermeer, and Eddie Degas, our fellow tugged at the bars madly and yelled "When are the poets coming!"

Besides the economic activities of the Artists' Union members (and there were now artists' unions all over the land), they arranged forums concerning the various art movements: surrealism, social art, expressionism, and abstract art. I recall one highly original slide lecture by Joseph Konzal (currently a teacher of sculpture at the Brooklyn Museum), entitled "Three great sculptors." Konzal proceeded to show examples of the painters, Ingres, Cézanne, and Picasso and explained sculptural form through these men. I hosted one called "Old and New" comparing Mirò with cave painting, Piero with Seurat, etc. Rosalind Browne presided over a slide lecture on cubism.

The gallery situation was vastly different than it is today. There were little over two dozen galleries in town compared to something like 350 today. Wildenstein, Demotte, and John Levy showed old masters; Durand-Ruel, the Impressionists, Valentine and Balzac housed established French moderns, while Frank Rehn, Ferargil, Stieglitz, the Downtown Gallery and the A.C.A. Gallery had their small stables of American art. The New Art Circle under the knowing care of J. B. Neumann exhibited Rouault, Klee, Chagall, Beckmann, Orozco, Max Weber, and even a few select old masters. Soon Pierre Matisse and Curt Valentin came along to feature international French and German moderns. With very few exceptions the galleries were located on 57th Street. The A.C.A. Gallery concentrated on the new young social painters and the Contemporary Arts Gallery and the Artists Gallery also concentrated on new talents. These were about the only places to which an artist seeking a gallery could go.

Pat Codyre, who originally worked behind the reception desk at the Museum of Modern Art, inevitably came in contact with many young and old artists who were anxious to have their work seen, particularly by a fresh modern institution. An enthusiast of native talent (he had been one of the first to purchase works by John Kane and Eilshemius), Codyre became friendly with a number of young Americans and showed examples of their work at the Hotel Marguery. His extracurricular activity finally got him ushered out of the Museum of Modern Art but he continued, along with Marchal E. Landgren, to help promote the varied romantic and expressionist painters whose gifts he felt to be outstanding.

The Contemporary Arts Gallery, managed by the selfless and devoted Miss Emily Frances, was the initial camping ground for Codyre. There he helped to introduce Mark Tobey, John Kane, Milton Avery, Mark Rothko, Earl Kerkam, Donald Forbes, and myself. Louis Harris and Louis Schanker also had their first one-man shows there as did Charles Logasa, who died in 1936. He was another favorite advisor to Miss Frances and a romantic painter who worked in the sombre hues—sort of an Albert Ryder syndrome—which afflicted many painters in our group. Roughly the years 1931 to 1934 covered the pioneer period just prior to the development of the art projects. Since none of the above-mentioned artists sold any pictures at that time, one may get a small idea of the remarkable boon afforded to painters by the PWAP and most of all, by the WPA/FAP.

When the WPA/FAP became an active institution, a number of talents who might otherwise have been "born to blush unseen" attracted the attention of

121

some gallery dealers, who, up to that time, harbored a carefully limited stable of artists. Edith Halpert, director of the Downtown Gallery, selected Jack Levine of Boston, Mitchell Siporin from Chicago and from New York, Louis Guglielmi, Gregorio Prestopino, Joseph Pandolfini, and Jacob Lawrence.

The A.C.A. Gallery promoted Philip Evergood, Aaron Goodelman, Philip Reisman, Elizabeth Olds, and William Gropper. Later they discovered Joe Jones, who had been painting in the Midwest and Robert Gwathmey, who had come up to Philadelphia from the deep South and was painting sharp social studies of sharecroppers and cotton pickers. The Artists Gallery, supported by Hugh Stix, gave its first showing of an American artist to Ben-Zion and soon after followed with shows of Adolph Gottlieb and myself. The Midtown Gallery under Mr. Gruskin's guidance, housed Paul Cadmus, Edward Laning, and William Palmer. As can readily be seen the WPA/FAP artist in many instances was entering the professional art arena and revitalizing it.

This gallery background is essential for the understanding of how the group of painters called The Ten came to be formed. Louis Harris and Mark Rothko (then Marcus Rothkowitz) became friends as classmates under Max Weber at the Art Students League. Since the Contemporary Arts Gallery followed a policy of introducing the very first one-man show of an artist, he must needs look for other, perhaps more reputable, galleries after his debut. This was not an easy matter, since any galleries that had handled American art for any length of time had enough to do to maintain their own stable. Moreover, since Codyre, Logasa, and Landgren, advisors to Miss Emily Frances, favored romantics and expressionist painting with free or dramatic brushwork, the chosen painters had in a way the mark of the damned on them and were homeless in the art arena. This was because the term expressionist was esthetically subversive at the time. The art climate was predominantly Woodstock (Alexander Brook), social protest (Shahn and the Mexican influence), and American Westerns (Benton, Curry, and Wood). We were outcasts on the scene; only John Marin and Max Weber, and to a smaller extent Stuart Davis, Hartley, Knaths, and Avery were tolerated as representative of the growing modern tradition. Pollock and de Kooning did not come on the scene till the mid-forties. Robert Godsoe, who for a time ran the Uptown Gallery, housing now and again some wandering waifs from these small galleries, set up his bastion on 49 West 12th Street sometime in early 1935 and dubbed it Gallery Secession. This name had been used by the rebel painters connected with Art Nouveau in Austria before and during World War I.

I recommended Ben-Zion for the gallery and Godsoe came over and accepted him on the basis of a powerful picture called *The Iron Bird*. I believe Louis Harris and Rothko brought Adolph Gottlieb in to Secession. Schanker, Tschacbasov, Byron Browne, Helen West Heller, and Balcomb Greene were other exhibitors. Godsoe was at that time given the estate of Alfred Maurer to handle.

FIGURE 19.
Mark Rothko (1903–1970)
Subway c. 1936
Collection unknown.
(Photograph by C. B. Ross,
Courtesy of Joseph Solman)

Maurer had been one of the lonely pioneers of modern art in this country, supported in part by the Weyhe Gallery and Bookshop before his suicide.

The WPA art project was in its initial ferment and the town was agog with new exhibitions analogous to the springing up of off-Broadway shows a few years ago in the theatre. A.C.A. was situated on 8th Street, Downtown and Artists Galleries on West 13th Street, Contemporary Arts on West 51st Street, and Gallery Secession on West 12th Street. Most of the new painters were on the Project and active to some degree or another in the Artists Union, the American Artists Congress or both.

Godsoe welcomed many an exciting new painter and was full of encouragement for his entourage. The front room was reserved for the one-man shows of the members and the large backroom held individual examples of everyone. For a time the gallery acted as an informal and amiable cooperative. Artists who had not known each other before then met, exchanged ideas, and became acquainted with each other's work. But after a while Godsoe began to overrun the gallery with too many painters, some of whom we considered too slight or specious for the character of the place. When Godsoe did nothing in response to our quiet pleas and protests a group of us seceded from Secession.

We discussed all our problems in my studio at 15th Street and Second Avenue and decided to form an independent group with the title The Ten. The original group consisted of Ben-Zion, Ilya Bolotowsky, Adolph Gottlieb, Louis Harris, Yankel Kufeld, Mark Rothko, Louis Schanker, Nahum Tschacbasov, and myself. That made only nine but we felt an open space was convenient and we could always invite a "tenth man" once we obtained a place in which to exhibit.

After knocking at many doors with dark photographs of dark paintings we received unexpected hospitality at a rather conservative gallery, the Montross at 785 Fifth Avenue. The exhibition, our first as a new group, took place from December 16, 1935 through January 4, 1936. Each artist showed four works.

Immediately following this first show, our new group exhibited from January 7 to 18 in the opening show of the Municipal Art Galleries, which were directed by Marchal E. Landgren. Edgar Levy, a good friend of Adolph Gottlieb, was included in this show as our "tenth man."

Some of our titles provided an interesting commentary. Ben-Zion, for instance, listed *Lynching* and *Abstract Landscape* though he was never a social protest artist in the sense of a Shahn or an Evergood and never an abstract painter at all. Bolotowsky's listing included *Sweatshop* and *Sewing Machine* though at that time he was more a precursor of abstract expressionism over a thin skein of subject matter. Later he was to develop his own brand of hard-edge color planes, a variant of the Mondrian and Glarner geometrics. Rothko exhibited *Subway* and *Seated Nude*, dark, mysterious pictures that hardly prefigured the lovely blurred rectangles for which he is known. Gottlieb's *Conference* and *Musician* evinced a quiet, tasteful palette and gentle deformations. He might at that time have been called the Otto Mueller of the group. Both Rothko and Gottlieb, close friends of Milton Avery, paid homage to his work. Schanker in *Three Clowns* and *Leap Frog* used a light playful form of cubism and I, in *El* and *World Series Scoreboard* was already immersed in my expressionist scenes of New York. Henry McBride commented on all this in the *Sun:*

Admittedly they have put a lot of raw meat on the table, but the flavor, decidedly gamy, leaves no doubt that it is meat. . . . These young artists are completely uninhibited and paint anything. They attack a canvas with as much fury and excitement as they spend in attacking a government. Some of them already said, 'Down with subject matter' and have become cubists. Some of them go into trances and paint dreams. Some of them mock politicians. One of them even goes deeply into social etiquette and discusses lynching. They dare any theme, and in a splashing, dashing youthful fashion get away with it.

A dark palette pervaded the pictures of the group interspersed with some bright firebursts in the canvases of Bolotowsky and Schanker. Ben-Zion carved out some lumbering black and white shapes as though the letters of the Hebrew alphabet had returned to imagery. There was an overdose perhaps of emotionalism, drama, expressionism, and what have you, but I think the present-day critic, showered with the hectic melodrama of Hans Hofmann and Appel, would smile indulgently at our excesses.

At this time we had ample opportunity to experiment and proliferate in our work through the remarkable opportunity afforded us by the WPA/FAP. How many of us and the other artists of the period might have been discouraged or derailed in their creative calling if the Project did not exist is speculative indeed. Yet I know through mutual discussions and activities that Bolotowsky, Rothko, Ben-Zion, Harris, Schanker and I found the WPA indispensable for our development as artists. Earl Kerkam and Ralph Rosenborg, who became members of our group when Kufeld and Tschacbasov dropped out, were completely dependent on the Project for a number of years and have expressed to me its importance in their lives. A five to eight year span, which was the period most of us worked in, cannot be underestimated in the development of artists fresh from their initial encounters with galleries. Louis Harris was only employed for three and one-half years. Adolph Gottlieb was employed for a shorter period of time under the 10 percent non-relief quota, his wife holding down a teaching job, so that he was able to remain casual if not indifferent to the benefits of the WPA/FAP. Kufeld turned from painter to paint chemist and dropped from our group though he continued to work for the Project in his new field. The brashness and opportunism of Tschacbasov alienated the rest of The Ten and we froze him out of the group after two exhibitions.

Shortly after our first exhibition we invited Joseph Brummer to one of our studios where we had gathered together representative examples of our work. Brummer had sat for Henri Rousseau, was now a successful dealer in ancient Greek art, and, once each season, held a large solo exhibition of a leading European sculptor like Brancusi, Despiau, or Lipschitz. We admired his great taste and knowledge. He looked our work over, was very encouraging but stated that in the general atmosphere of American regional art we might do well to get an exhibit in Paris and then come home, so to speak, as conquering heroes. He was willing to defray the shipping and rental costs of such a show and in November of 1936 we launched our second group exhibition at Galerie Bonaparte in Paris.

Waldemar-George, the eminent French critic and scholar, wrote the preface for our catalogue, starting his various comments with the refrain, "America, where are you headed?" He spoke of the clear influence of cubism on the work of Schanker and Solman, the geometry of Bolotowsky, Rothko's nostalgia for the Italian Trecento and the work of Tschacbasov, Kufeld, and Ben-Zion as oscillating between drama and caricature. The only note of joy he was able to find was in a canvas of Gottlieb's entitled *Man with Pigeons*. Chil Aronson wrote a lengthy review in *Les Arts* speaking of our tortured souls and our courage in pursuing our own visions as opposed to either brutal realism or an encroaching decorativeness in abstract art. An interesting comment from a French critic on the "scene" in the art world of the time.

We returned to the American scene again at the Montross Gallery precisely one year after our inaugural showing. This meant December of 1936 through January of 1937. Emily Genauer in the *World-Telegram* was kind to the group stating that "Their strong inward preoccupation with the quality of painting, on which they deserve a good rating, has been carried forward." Edward Alden Jewell's comments in *The New York Times*, December 20, 1936, gives a clearer picture of the critical atmosphere of the time. He wrote: "I do not believe I understand the American 'expressionists' so very well. Many of these paintings at the Montross I feel I do not understand at all. Often they look to me like silly smudges. And if a painting looks like a silly smudge, it is safe to conclude that you do not understand it."

In May 1937 we enlisted the sympathy of Georgette Passedoit, a gallery dealer who though handling French art thought it was time to handle some native talent. It is of some significance to note that our little band was helping some galleries in town to pay more attention to new Americans and along with other galleries like the A.C.A. and the Downtown Gallery who were selecting gifted Project artists, the WPA/FAP was a distinct force in broadening the American art scene. The French parade was dominant but we were getting into the march. It may also be mentioned that since sales for our group were as scarce as "hen's teeth" the Project was our lone lifeboat.

At the time of our Passedoit show Jacob Kainen, a fine WPA artist wrote occasional reviews. As a professional painter and printmaker he had a keener understanding of our aims. "Probably the most active painters in the city" he wrote, "from the standpoint of exhibiting work, are those who comprise the group of Expressionists known as The Ten. Expressionism in this case merely denotes a generally untrammeled attitude towards painting, with little respect shown for dreary repetition of outworn molds and plenty of respect for the really enduring qualities of design and provocative pictorial ensembles. In this sense The Ten is a really progressive group, sloughing off the superficial elements of

FIGURE 20. Joseph Solman. *Venus of 23rd Street.* 1937. Collection of the artist. (Photograph by Bernard Cole)

a literal realism and getting down to the heart of the creative problem." We showed at the Passedoit again exactly a year later in May 1938.

In November of 1938 our group decided cockily to challenge the hegemony of the Whitney Museum. Enlisting the sympathetic aid of Bernard Braddon who had opened up his Mercury Galleries at 4 East 8th Street we titled our show: "The Ten: Whitney Dissenters." In our catalogue of the same title we decried "the reputed equivalence of American painting and literal painting" and declared that "the symbol of the silo is in the ascendant at our Whitney Museum of modern American art." Most critics labeled us inchoate expressionists.

By this time we had added John Graham, Earl Kerkam, and Ralph Rosenborg to our group. Lee Gatch showed with us for a short time and Karl Knaths was a guest artist twice. Each of us was beginning to attach himself as a distinct member to a particular gallery. In 1938 the New Art Circle added Solman to its roster that already included among its Americans Gatch, Knaths, and de Martini. Along with Kerkam we were billed as "Five New American Painters" in May of 1938. The Artists Gallery favored Ben-Zion and Adolph Gottlieb with large shows. Each artist was graduating into his fixed gallery.

Our first tentative appearances in group shows, baptism under fire at Contemporary Arts and Secession, the foothold of independence that the WPA/FAP gave us and the formation of The Ten had matured each of us in only several years. Our last exhibition took place at the Bonestell gallery late in 1939. This catalogue notes David Burliuk as a fellow exhibitor. I have no recollection of his attending any of our meetings which took place about once a month, usually at a new studio each time so that we could see the latest work of our members. Though the pressures of individuality finally broke up our group sometime in 1940, we had given each other heart for a valuable period of time. We had been toughened and scarred in the art arena and remained undaunted thereafter.

Before I make a final summary of the importance of the WPA/FAP to the artists working at that period I recall a story that I believe illustrates in a strange way the curious relationships between movements and influences that would at first glance seem incompatible. An artist by the name of Axel Horn, who was a member of the mural division of the WPA/FAP and an early friend of Jackson Pollock told me this story. During the WPA days an experimental Mexican workshop was operated by Siqueiros on West 14th Street. The social trend of Mexican art was encouraged in New York by the beautiful Alma Reed, directress of the Delphic Studios. The murals of Orozco on the walls of the New School for Social Research and Rivera's frescos for The New Workers League on 14th Street had already created some commotion among the artists and citizenry of New York and elsewhere. Axel brought Pollock up to the Mexican Workshop to view work in progress. Pollock was witness to one of the experimental techniques Siqueiros was using, namely, a spraygun full of multiple colors being siphoned onto a canvas panel quite larger in size. When the first layers of accidental tones and colors appeared the artist would then reshape the colors while still in flux into the revolutionary subjects he already had in mind. Axel says that Pollock was so excited about this initial procedure that he begged his friend to take him back for another visit. Axel claims this was a determining factor in the development of the famous drip style. Since Pollock's expression and esthetic were in reverse to the Mexicans it is completely credible without taking one whit of originality away from Pollock. I relate the story in order to show how many influences were at work at the time to shape the course of art.

Another artist, Abraham Tobias, was on the mural division of the Project and was deeply involved in social painting. He developed at the time shaped canvases and panels perhaps in deference to particular wall space problems. He even exhibited several of these in Artists' Union exhibitions of the period. Out of necessity the shaped canvas was born thirty years ahead of its time.

J. B. Neumann had the courage to put on a three man show of Gromaire, Rothko, and myself at his New Art Circle in 1938 in order to show that American artists could stand alongside of well-known French painters, as Julian Levi was

FIGURE 21. Adolph Gottlieb (b. 1903). *Seated Nude.* In an exhibition of The Ten at the Municipal Art Galleries, January 1936. Collection unknown. (Courtesy of Marchal E. Landgren)

soon to do with the work of Arshile Gorky in relation to the surrealists his gallery was handling. And Pierre Matisse had already included on his roster the work of the poetic Loren MacIver, another Project artist.

In asking a number of my old colleagues about the old WPA days many were nostalgic, a few complained about spot-checking methods by roving supervisors, but there was practically a unanimous verdict on the important opportunity the job gave to them. Ben-Zion's comment was "Look what an artist could accomplish on $23.86!" Herman Rose, whose work is represented in many museums and had a full-page rave review in *The New York Times* of his last show at Zabriskie Gallery stated flatly: "I do not know if I could have even continued to be an artist if not for the WPA."

Many artists unfortunately fell away after the Project ended because of the tough and unrewarding factors of the profession. Some of them found it necessary to go into commercial art like the gifted Jules Halfant, who is at present the art director for Vanguard Recordings.

Despite the great publicity art receives today, the larger availability of teaching jobs, and the momentous prices paid to a dozen or so stars like Warhol, de Kooning, Rauschenberg, Johns, etc., an economic survey taken at this very moment of the annual income of the practicing artist in America today would probably average out to a surprisingly low total. It is manifestly untrue to say that the weakest are weeded out. Examples like that of Modigliani abound; and the hardships and hack magazine work that many of The Eight in America had to go through is well chronicled. I have given an account of one small segment of the artists that worked for the WPA and it will be readily recognized that most of these are today of museum stature as well as leaders of contemporary art movements. My case rests.

Ads from 1936 issues of *Art Front*

ROBERT CRONBACH was born in St. Louis, Missouri, in 1908. He studied at the St. Louis School of Fine Arts and the Pennsylvania Academy of Fine Arts during the late 1920s. In 1930 he worked as an assistant in the Paris and New York studios of Paul Manship. From 1935 to 1939 he was employed on the sculpture division of the WPA/FAP in New York. He also won a Section competition in 1940 for two heroic bronze sculptures for the Social Security Building in Washington, D.C. Except for the war years, he has worked continuously as a sculptor and maintains a studio in Westbury, Long Island. From 1947 to 1961 he was on the art faculty of Adelphi College. He has exhibited widely, has works in a number of distinguished public and private collections and has received many important commissions, including one in 1960 for the wall sculpture outside the Meditation Room in the United Nations General Assembly Building.

FIGURE 22. Robert Cronbach working on sculpture for Willert Park Housing Project, Buffalo, New York. WPA/FPA, 1939. (Courtesy of the artist)

The New Deal Sculpture Projects

ROBERT CRONBACH

I was first employed on the WPA/FAP in January 1936, about six months after the Project began, and left it in August 1939, just before the time of the drastic curtailment of WPA employment. I believe that my stay covered the most active, creative, and interesting period of the Project.

At its peak time there were about 175 to 200 sculptors on the New York City project. To be so employed, most of them had to qualify for relief, as well as to show that they were "professional" sculptors. I was one of a minority, however, who had no relief status. The rationale for the employment of this non-relief minority was that their technical skill and experience was necessary for the successful development of the Project and for the efficient employment of all the sculptors. The non-relief sculptors were paid the same wage as the other artists.

In the beginning I worked in my own studio on a number of sculptures. Several of these were studies or *maquettes* for large architectural sculpture; the rest for free-standing pieces.

I particularly remember two works. One, *Industry,* was carved directly from a block of plaster about 18 inches high. Along with a companion piece by Milton Hebald, it was designed to be carved in rough limestone or cast in concrete on a large scale for the New York State Building at the 1939 World's Fair. This scheme never came through, but the *maquette* made a quite successful small sculpture. It was widely exhibited, and when Harry Hopkins left his post with the WPA, the New York project presented him with a bronze version along with some other works.

The second work was a high relief (really engaged full round) sculpture of basketball players, designed for the pediment of a rather neo-Georgian gymnasium building at Brooklyn College. I made both a small study and an eight-foot version in plaster. Both were exhibited and the large one was eventually used in a public school building. The final version to be executed in glazed ceramic as originally conceived, would have been gigantic and could only have been carried out if the WPA/FAP had lasted.

One must remember that the WPA/FAP was subjected to continual violent political attack. This was one of the major factors in the whole scene. As a result of these attacks, the minority of non-relief artists in all media was constantly whittled down. By the end of 1938 very few non-relief artists remained on the Project. Some qualified for relief—this was still the Depression. I was kept on because of a special situation. The Project had an opportunity to make some sculpture for the Willert Park housing project, which was a United States Housing Authority-assisted program in Buffalo. The sculptor would have to be self-supervised as the Buffalo WPA/FAP was not staffed or equipped to handle this work. I was offered the job and accepted. For this reason I was kept on the sculpture division until the job was finished. I returned to New York during the summer of 1939.

In the Willert Park situation the phrase "self-supervised" was no empty label. I planned the sculpture with an architect, found a suitable vacant city-owned building and arranged for its use as a studio, worked out the casting and installation procedures for the tamped concrete sculpture with the concrete contractors who were working on the housing project, and brought a fellow Project sculptor, Harold Ambellan, from New York to join me in carrying out the work. Naturally, the New York City project had to approve all the important esthetic or procedural decisions, but except for the initial sketches this was done at a distance and rather infrequently.

The important qualification, "a professional sculptor," needs some discussion. As soon as one thinks about it seriously, it is an almost impossible definition, in sculpture as in all the arts. Various elements—professional training, professional experience, ability to earn one's living in this profession, public or professional recognition—all these enter in. But almost immediately one can think of many great artists who would lack one or more, sometimes all, of these qualifications. And conversely, one can call to mind many thoroughly qualified mediocrities. Nevertheless, the weakness of this key definition did not prove a major obstacle to setting up an art project.

The whole concept of these WPA art projects in the thirties, during the Depression and during the enthusiasm of the New Deal, was to employ artists in the mass, not just the "good" artists, but all serious working artists. On this basis a whole field of related art activities was set up and artists were used in many ways. Some made "architectural" or socially planned art, some made individual "easel" or "pedestal" art. Some were technicians, some were assistants, some taught, some helped run the various Project exhibits, etc. The pay was approxi-

FIGURE 23. Robert Cronbach. Seven-foot high tamped concrete wall relief at Willert Park Housing Project, Buffalo, New York. WPA/FAP, 1939. (Courtesy of the artist)

mately the same in all categories—$23.50 per week—and it was not much different from the pay for non-art projects of the WPA. For this reason there was no great pressure on even the most sympathetic supervisor or from the most zealous Artists' Union Committee (more about this later) to employ obvious artistic incompetents, and to a great extent common sense could prevail. This probably sounds too good to be convincing. Upon thinking about it carefully, however, I cannot remember any serious artists who could qualify for relief status and was then unable to get on the New York City WPA/FAP nor, on the other hand, that there was any more "dead wood" than one encounters in any large organization, private or public.

Unlike the painters, who could work in the easel division creating individual studio pieces or in the mural division designing wall paintings in various media for public buildings, the sculptors were all in one division. There were several reasons for this. Relatively few sculptors—one to two hundred—were on the Project, compared to over a thousand painters at peak employment. Sculpture by the 1930s had still not developed a clearcut separation between individual, gallery sculpture made to be exhibited independent of environment, which I shall call "pedestal" sculpture, (the equivalent of "easel" painting) and "monumental" or "architectural" sculpture designed for a particular fixed environment.

At the start Julian Bowes was head of the sculpture division, but during most of its life Girolamo Piccoli was head and George Thorpe, his very able assistant. Together they made a very good team, with Piccoli as administrator and general planner and Thorpe in charge of most technical phases. The only other assistant I remember was Mitchell Fields. In addition, William Zorach acted as an unofficial adviser in the stone-carving section of the central workshop. Louis Slobodkin became head of the division, some time after my separation from the Project. All these men were sculptors themselves. George Thorpe had been employed first as a sculptor; later he became head of the WPA/FAP in Chicago.

There were central workshops and storage space at the main office, but all the sculptors, whether engaged on pedestal or architectural work, maintained and paid for their own studios. Their working materials were supplied by the Project. They were required to work fifteen hours a week on sculpture which was to be turned over to the Project. The sculpture supervisors visited the individual studios to check on the progress of the work. Obviously the whole matter of checking and evaluating art, either from the point of view of quantity or of quality, is most difficult. As this matter is directly related to the success or failure of the whole Project I shall discuss it at length later on.

The techniques employed and the facilities available were consistent with the working procedures current in the 1930s. These had changed very little in the previous seventy-five years. The sculptors worked in their own studios, generally in clay to make plasters for casting in bronze, cast stone, or terra-cotta. Following the Paris trend of 1910 to 1925 toward direct materials (exemplified in this country by Flannagan, Zorach, and Chaim Gross), some carved directly in stone or wood and, as something of an innovation, worked in direct plaster. David Smith and José de Rivera were almost alone in developing Gonzalez' (Paris 1935) pioneering efforts in the direct working of steel using welding torches and industrial tools.

The central workshop had facilities for casting in plaster, concrete (cast stone), and enlarging scale models in clay, plaster, and stone. It also offered some space for sculptors executing large architectural sculpture. It had no foundry or large ceramic kilns, but on occasion could arrange to have bronze castings or terra-cotta architectural sculpture fired. Some technical innovations were worked out in the shop, principally in the development or redevelopment of materials for casting, such as magnesite (an improved cast stone), the use of all the superhard plasters, some plastics and papier-maché. The real technical as well as esthetic growth, however, came out of constant interchange of ideas and practices among the project sculptors. In this respect one cannot ignore the presence and constant activities of the Artists' Union. For example, David Smith gave a welding demonstration at one of the many Union forums. A great deal of imagination and energy went into the construction of floats, effigies, and banners, etc.—generally made in frantic, continuous working sessions of twelve, thirty-six, forty-eight hours—for the innumerable parades and demonstrations of the period. I remember particularly an excellent float made for a parade by de Kooning and Martin Craig. All this activity gave many Project artists considerable familiarity with many new techniques, as well as a bold approach to possible combinations of materials, and was, I believe, one of the underlying factors in the burst of new American sculpture in the forties and fifties.

The sculptor working in his own studio on "pedestal" sculpture simply carried out his normal creative work, and there were no directives from the Project as to the nature of this work. If the finished work—or fifteen hours' worth of it— had been simply dropped in the Project warehouse, this would indeed have been a frustrating activity, a kind of high-level boondoggling. There was, however, a very energetic exhibition program, once more the product of collaboration between the Artists' Union and the Project administration, which gave a basic validity to the "pedestal" sculpture program.

I believe a few examples will make this clear. The New York City WPA Federal Art Gallery held forty exhibits between December 1935 and June 1939 and many more thereafter. In the period cited three were all sculpture; many others included sculpture. "New Horizons in American Art," an exhibit at the Museum of Modern Art during the fall of 1936 included eight sculptors, five from New York City. The American Museum of Natural History held an exhibit of work by artists of the New York City WPA/FAP which included twelve sculptors. In 1938 the Public Use of Art Committee of the Artists' Union gave a show, "Subway Art," to demonstrate the possible use of Project art to decorate subways. "Frontiers of American Art" at the de Young Memorial Museum in San Francisco included ten New York City sculptors. *The New York Times* reported on May 24, 1939 that "Eighteen exhibits of work of the WPA Federal Art Project are scheduled for workers' organizations and will be held in the summer and fall." The Metropolitan Museum of Art's "Work in Use" exhibit in July 1941 showed about sixteen project sculptors. And finally, it should not be forgotten that many individual works—paintings as well as sculpture—were loaned to municipal, state, and federal organizations to decorate schools, offices, courthouses, and hospitals.

I have given this list in some detail to show that there was a broad and vigorous exhibition program. The artists represented were chosen sometimes by the Project, sometimes by the client, sometimes by a joint committee of the Project administration and the Artists' Union. This exhibition program did not always work out fairly—some artists were shown little or not at all—but it was active and large enough to give life and validity to the "easel" and "pedestal" art program, both from the point of view of the Project and of the artist.

As noted above, permanent allocations were also made of individual works from the pedestal sculpture project to schools and other public institutions. This policy might be considered an extension of the exhibition program, since it involved sculpture which was executed in the individual's studio, and which was not planned for any particular purpose. On the other hand, the pieces were given permanently to the various institutions and the suitability of the sculpture for its setting—both physical and social—was taken into account.

The program for "architectural" sculpture destined for a particular site was somewhat different. When a possible sculpture project came up, the supervisor called in one or more sculptors to discuss the problem and its possibilities. If they were interested, they would take the assignment and begin by working out a study and scale model. Sometimes there would be a small, interproject competition and several models would be presented. The supervisors saw but did not have to approve the model before it was presented to the client, who was sometimes the architect, sometimes the director of the tax-supported building for which the sculpture was intended. Once the model was approved, the sculptor went ahead with the sculpture. If it was a particularly large piece, he made an intermediate model which was likewise subject to approval. If the sculpture was to be in or on a city-owned building or on a city-owned outdoor site, such as a park or bridge, it was also necessary to have it approved by the New York City Art Commission.

This was a considerable gauntlet for the work to run, and consequently work done as pedestal sculpture was of a much broader range than work done on the architectural projects. There were, however, a number of alleviating circumstances. If the sculptor did not like the particular program, he need not take part in it, or if he entered a model which was not accepted, he could return to pedestal sculpture, in each case with no loss in pay. So the sculptor could afford to be casual, daring, experimental, or enthusiastic, without being exposed to any economic threat. The only reward for winning, or penalty for losing, a commission was esthetic and, to a lesser degree, one of status among one's fellow sculptors. There was not much point in entering a dull, pot-boiling model. At the same time, neither the architect's building budget nor the client's funds were drawn on to pay the artist or his shop costs (although sometimes they bore the charge for a minimal amount of materials). So both could afford to be more tolerant and open to new ideas.

I have already mentioned the fact that the sculptors owed fifteen hours of work each week to the Project, and that the supervisors came around to the artists' studios to check on their work. Obviously such a system is very open to abuse. For example, a sculptor could turn in a fragmentary sketch and claim it took 60 hours, or the administration could refuse to accept a painter's Marin-like water color—the fruit of two weeks' work—claiming that it took much less than a day to paint. The striking thing about the whole WPA/FAP in New York City is not that such abuses did not occur—of course they did—but that they occurred so seldom. To explain this one must describe the whole art and social world of the time, the whole ambiance in which this Project existed.

In 1936, in the middle of the Depression, the private market for contemporary art—painting or sculpture—was almost nonexistent. Private galleries, individual collectors, museums, all were practically frozen as far as sales were concerned. Architectural sculpture—sculpture designed to embellish a building or complement a particular site—was in the same situation.

Suddenly, as a result of the general agitation for measures to relieve unemployment, agitation in which the artists' organizations had been deeply involved, the artist on the Project found himself in an unusual position. He was being paid a regular weekly wage to work in his studio as a freely creative artist. Often his immediate reaction was that this was a lucky break, a sinecure which did not require him to put forth much effort. Gradually, however, it became apparent that he was in a unique position. Whereas for the unemployed artisan or professional in other fields, the WPA projects were a poor substitute for their normal employment, for the creative artist the WPA/FAP marked perhaps the first time in American history when a great number of artists was employed continuously to produce art. It was an unequaled opportunity for a serious artist to work as steadily and intensely as possible to advance the quality of his art.

The physical fact of the Project brought the artists together a great deal. In fact, between the Project, the Artists' Union, and other societies, most artists who were in New York City during the late 1930s feel today like alumni of a common university.

At the same time the art journals and the general intellectual world were busily debating such questions as art as a collective activity, art as a social force, the limits of 19th-century art, should the artist remain in his ivory tower. The Mexican muralists Rivera, Orozco, and Siqueiros made a great impression, Siqueiros having a collective "experimental" workshop on 14th Street and the other two having painted murals in the city.

I may appear to have wandered far afield in trying to explain how a supervisor could evaluate fifteen hours of art work. These remarks, however, are pertinent, because as a result of all these factors the Project sculptor felt that he was part of an important art movement; that his Project work would be seen by, first, his peers, and also by a fair section of the public and the art world; that there were no other equally valid outlets or markets for his work at this time; that both for selfish and social reasons his Project sculpture should at this time be his major sculpture.

Against this background it is easier to understand how the attitudes of the artist and the supervisor (often also an artist) were easily reconciled. In fact, when the artist—sculptor or painter—became deeply involved in a major project, he frequently completely disregarded the fifteen-hour rule and worked forty to sixty hours a week. I know that I, and many others, did. When I talked recently to James Brooks, who was one of the most effective mural painters on the Project, he confirmed these impressions.

Any intelligent review or description of the sculpture made on the Project must take into account the trends and influences which prevailed in American sculpture during the 1930s. There were the contemporary "modern" figurative sculptors—Maillol, Despiau, Epstein, Lehmbruck, Barlach, and Kolbe in Europe; Lachaise and Zorach in the United States. They had in common their rejection of Rodin (although they had grown out of him), and of the pictorial or "painterly" in sculpture; a rediscovery of primitive archaic art; an emphasis on "sculptural," architectonic qualities. Nevertheless, they were all still within the 19th-century French tradition. Then there were Lipchitz, Zadkine, Archipenko, Moore, abstractionists influenced by cubism, but who still based their work on the human image. There were also the purer abstractionists, ranging from Brancusi to the constructivist Pevsner. Finally there were the American academic sculptors, sometimes unashamedly literal and pictorial, at other times archaistic and mannered. Of this school Milles (whom I am considering as an American), Manship, and MacMonnies mark the high points.

Cutting across all these styles, challenging them and sometimes making use of them, was the general discussion and ferment—political, social, and esthetic—which I have tried to describe before. What is the role of the artist? Should art frankly "tell a story"? Should there be an emphasis on idea, representative content, as opposed to the formal, plastic values stressed by the school of Paris? Should there be an art of protest? Should art be immediate and social in its effect? Should the artist be a part of a collective group, as opposed to his role as an individual? The effect of these ideas on artists of all schools and on the art they produced was very strong, especially when the artists were employed on a collective basis, when the continuance of the project on which they worked was in jeopardy every few months, with every change of policy in the administering of the relief programs. It would be absolutely incorrect to imply that there was any sort of directive or pressure from the Project—or even from the Artists' Union—to make any particular sort of art. But to say that artists were not influenced by the climate of the times during a period in which the Rockefellers commissioned Diego Rivera to execute a mural (later destroyed) for Radio City, when as cool and self-possessed a sculptor as Noguchi went to Mexico to make concrete reliefs as part of a Mexican collective program, when Picasso painted the *Guernica* mural for the Spanish Republican Pavilion at the Paris Fair—to say that the artists were not affected by this atmosphere would be absurd.

Probably the figurative sculptors represented the largest group on the Project. The effect of the socially conscious trend I have described was an emphasis on expressionism. Minna Harkavy's sculpture is a good example. The work of Lipchitz and Zadkine had a great influence, sparked particularly by several good exhibits between 1937 and 1938. A number of sculptors fascinated by cubism and abstract sculptural qualities and at the same time wishing to project a clear, obvious, dramatic image, tried to evolve a synthesis based on Lipchitz's work of the 1930s. Much of this work was hopelessly pedestrian, but at its best it was probably the nearest thing to a genuine Project style. The work of Harold Ambellan, Milton Hebald, Herzl Emanuel, and my own work might be considered in this category.

Meanwhile a group of artists, who although few in number were highly respected by all the other artists, continued to work on pure abstractions, constructions, and surreal objects. Two examples are Ernest Guteman, who made very precise geometric metal constructions, and David Smith.

The sculpture project did not use any pressure or give any directives to the individual sculptor, who had complete freedom to work in his own studio on pedestal sculpture in whatever style he wished to and on whatever subject he chose. Sculpture of every style was executed, was cast in the Project shops if necessary, and was shown in the many exhibitions I have mentioned.

These prevailing attitudes and ideas had both more and less effect on the architectural sculptural projects as compared with pedestal sculpture. The more violent and immediate "protest" art was unlikely to get even the preliminary approval of the various administrative bodies involved. On the other hand, most of the sculptors carrying out large projects, the administration, and the client all agreed that the work should have some social content, or clear, direct image. When carried through literally and on a pedestrian level, this produced much of the typical "WPA mural art" in sculpture and in painting. Better artists, however, almost immediately began to develop the plastic and emotional aspects of the ideas involved. Sometimes this work was quite readily accepted (particularly when there were not too many boards involved). At other times there were quite fierce conflicts, during the course of which the sculptor and the project supervisor tried to educate the client. A number of good architectural sculpture projects were actually executed. A few notable examples are José de Rivera's highly abstract stainless steel *Bird* for the Newark airport (now in the Newark Museum), a series of cast stone play animals, the work of several sculptors, for the play court of the Harlem housing project, the sculpture for the Willert Park housing project in Buffalo, already mentioned, Cesare Stea's large frieze for the exterior wall of a community center in the Queensboro housing project, a statue of Columbus for Columbus Square in Queens, and a series of small sculptures for Bellevue Hospital.

However good the immediate results—and they were good—the long-range effects were even more significant. This was a period in flux. The focus of the Western World was moving from Europe to America, quite literally in the case of many outstanding artist-refugees or exiles (e.g., Lipchitz, Zadkine, Hans Hofmann, Georg Grosz). In this situation several thousand artists, including several hundred sculptors, were being paid to work continuously at their own profession, working in their own studios. This was a stimulating environment of excitement and challenge, and of comradeship.

I believe the outstanding result of the New York City WPA/FAP was the burst of art activity and discussion which it stimulated and supported. I believe too that this marked the beginning of American (New York) leadership in the world of art. From being a basically provincial center, a "following" place, New York became the actual center of the art world, the source of energy, ideas, and art production, and it has maintained this leadership for the past thirty years. From

FIGURE 24. Sculpture exhibition at the WPA Federal Art Gallery, New York City, March 1938. Dominating the gallery is José de Rivera's stainless steel *Bird*, created for Newark Airport and now in the collection of the Newark Museum. (Archives of American Art)

an even purely economic point of view, this result has justified the existence of the Project many times over.

Two examples of this leadership which come to mind are the makers of direct metal, welded sculpture, and the abstract expressionist painters. Direct metal sculpture was initiated in Europe by Gonzalez and Gargallo. It was developed in this country by David Smith, and has since grown in many directions; but the principal exponents are the sculptors of the New York school—David Smith, José de Rivera, Seymour Lipton, Herbert Ferber, David Hare, Theodore Roszak.

Abstract expressionism, which has been called the first international style initiated in America, was the work of New York artists associated with "Tenth Street" and the Artists' Club. The fact that these artists, their club, and their whole style were in violent opposition to the characteristic Project art, the art of the 1930s, and the sociopolitical position of the old Artists' Union in no way nullifies my thesis of origins. A true art center is, by definition, a center of thought and energy, broad enough in scope and strong enough in vital energy to have room for growth, revolt, contradiction, and synthesis within itself. Actually a great many of the painters and sculptors participating in these two activities—the Tenth Street group and the Artists' Club—were on the Federal Art Project and had been members of the Artists' Union. Among these were William Baziotes, James Brooks, Giorgio Cavallon, Martin Craig, de Kooning, Tworkov, Reinhardt, and Rothko.

There were other, less dramatic outgrowths. The Sculptors' Guild, the American Abstract Artists, the Federation of Modern Painters and Sculptors are specifically exhibiting groups, all of which started at about this time, and all of which are still active. I do not want this to become a directory of artists' organizations so I will say further only that most of the features of the present art world can be traced to this period.

The most immediate reasons for the end of the sculpture division, as well as all the other WPA cultural projects, were the end of the Depression, the rise of defense industries, and World War II itself. While unemployment still persisted, it was no longer the major problem. There was a general trend away from the New Deal, and the continuous attacks on all the Projects as being radical, socialistic, and boondoggling, naturally became more effective.

The war itself brought many important, if intangible, changes. Except among pure pacifists and members of the extreme right, this anti-Hitler war was probably the most popular and widely supported war in American history. The artists were as much involved as the rest of the nation. As a result, most of the emotion and drive which had really created the whole WPA program—including of course the sculpture division—and which would have been necessary to maintain the program in the face of attacks from its critics, were engulfed and dissolved in the general activities of the war. Many sculptors worked in war plants, for which their technical aptitudes particularly fitted them. Others served in the Armed Forces and in the Merchant Marine.

Through a series of curtailments and administrative changes, which I shall not describe, the whole WPA/FAP was reduced by the end of 1941 to one central shop. A few hundred artists worked there—not in their own studios—principally making posters and other accessories helpful to the war effort. On this basis the Project provided a livelihood, although a bare one, for the artists employed, but it was neither better nor worse than many expedients artists have used to keep going during modern times. The Project was no longer, as it had been earlier, an exciting and possible vehicle for an artist's major work.

In describing the sculpture program I have, quite naturally, tried to bring out its most positive qualities. It had also a number of weaknesses. The major defect was also a major element in the creation of the Works Progress Administration. This was the tie-in with relief projects, the requirement that almost all the artists, with very few exceptions, qualify for relief before their qualifications as artists, even as unemployed artists, could be considered. This meant that the whole life of the Project was tied to the ups and downs of the relief and welfare situation—the total number of artists employed; whether there should be a non-relief minority; whether or not two members of one household could be employed by the Project at the same time (which led to some rather involved matrimonial arrangements, particularly since the regulation was changed several times). Rulings on these matters changed almost from month to month and caused many of the artists to spend a tremendous amount of time and energy fighting them or their interpretation. This constant struggle was undoubtedly one of the causes of the great feeling of solidarity and comradeship, which was good, but it finally became a source of strain and uncertainty and, in addition, diverted a great deal of energy from more constructive work.

The relief basis on which the Project operated also accounted for its very low wage scale. The New York City rate, $23.50 per week, was the highest for the country. Even in the 1930s this was not quite an adequate wage. It is true that the whole concept of the Project as a mass employer of artists precluded a very high salary for the individual artist (as I shall bring out later in a comparison of the Treasury Section with the WPA/FAP), but even so the wage scale was really too low. That the Project worked as well as it did in spite of these handicaps is further evidence of the basic soundness and real appeal to artists of the original idea.

The final disposition of the pedestal sculpture as well as of easel paintings which has been executed on the Project was also discouraging to Project artists.

In this situation, however, considerable credit must be given to the Project administration. As soon as it was clear that the WPA/FAP was going to be terminated, the administration started, about nine months in advance, an energetic program of permanent allocation of all the stored paintings and pedestal sculpture to all schools, public buildings (including a few museums), and other tax-supported institutions in the New York City area which would accept them.

The permanent allocations I described earlier were a very positive and satisfying final use of Project art. There has been considerable careful planning, and each piece had gone to a place where there was assurance of responsibility for its maintenance and care. In this emergency of the Project's termination, however, the administration, correctly foreseeing that all work not already disposed of would be sent to the limbo of a government warehouse, allocated the art work as freely as possible. Sometimes this worked out happily, sometimes not. Undoubtedly a record of these allocations exists somewhere, but it would be very difficult to trace what finally became of all of the work. That this fear of indefinite government storage had a sound basis was confirmed a year or so later when a considerable number of Project paintings which had been stored in government warehouses was auctioned off as "used canvas." Many of these paintings were picked up by second-hand art dealers who were able to sell for a good profit work they acquired for pennies.

The general effect of this arbitrary dissolving of the Project was that for many artists several years of their serious professional work had simply evaporated. This was a terrible blow. Any further program should incorporate, at the very beginning, a built-in plan for final disposition of the work produced. Perhaps the artist should be allowed the option of re-purchase, which is his professional prerogative, as an alternative to destruction of the work.

The underlying concept of the Project, the mass employment of artists, with complete tolerance of and almost disinterest in any esthetic position, was always sound, and I believe would be important for future projects. Even here, however, were attendant weaknesses.

In face of the total social situation between 1936 and 1939 the Project was an exciting concept capable of engaging the best efforts and imagination of the artists and of the Project administrators. Once the situation was stabilized and artists were working, the real need was to move on, to expand and enlarge the whole idea. The tie-in with relief, which I have mentioned before, and the continuing political attacks made on the Project, necessitated a continuous battle to justify the existence of the Project on its original basis. The Project administration, as well as "project-minded" artists and the Artists' Union, became imprisoned in their original attitudes. The most sensitive and original artists, who had always been interested in the social and political aspects of the Project as a means to greater esthetic activity, rather than as ends in themselves, became disinterested. The real artistic action moved away from the Project and from government-sponsored art in general.

The Treasury Section of Painting and Sculpture sponsored a program for commissioning architectural sculpture and murals for federal buildings, principally through open competitions. Since I worked both on the New York City WPA/FAP and on the Section, and I was fortunate enough to win one of those awards in a national competition, I feel that I am in a good position to compare the two projects as public support programs for artists and as stimulants for a broad and lively growth of art. I have thought about it most carefully, and have in addition talked to many former project artists. The balance of opinion seems definitely in favor of the WPA/FAP.

The Section can be credited with some very specific achievements. It made it possible for the government to use the work of some outstanding contemporary "modern" artists on and in public buildings to a greater degree than had ever been done in the past and, to some extent, than has been done since. The government's awarding of commissions to this new group of artists broke a long-standing pattern. Until this time a closed circle of academic and conventional sculptors, mural painters, and architects had exercised complete control of all "official" art, so that the work executed for public buildings had become completely isolated from the whole stream of contemporary art. Actually the Section's awards were limited to commissions for federal buildings, and did not include work for state or municipal buildings. Nevertheless, the results were infectious.

The WPA/FAP, on the other hand, had a number of strengths which I think are more fundamental. Its program enabled a great number of artists to work continuously in their own field. Many of these artists had no interest in or flair for architectural murals or sculpture as such. Other artists might eventually have developed this interest, but needed time and opportunity to work and grow. And if one realizes that the most vital and important art of the last 150 years has been work that was non-official and non-commissioned, one must admit that to give a large number of artists of many different persuasions an opportunity to work steadily is a most important achievement.

The practice of having even an excellent jury choose the "best" work (which is the origin of most of the academies as far back as Louis XIV) has some inherent limits. Although it does make possible the use of some artists already known as "good"—even those recognized previously only by a professional minority—even under ideal conditions, this system can only recognize and employ already developed artists. It cannot enable new art to develop, or a wide range of art and artists to flourish.

Indeed, I believe that much of the best work accomplished for the Section was made possible because so many of the artists involved had had an opportunity, through the WPA/FAP, to work continuously and to grow and develop as artists. There is a psychological factor involved in the last point. There is something inherently sound and stimulating about the fact of a large number of artists working steadily at a flat wage which is neither disastrously low nor high enough to be of great importance. This puts the emphasis where it should be, on esthetic questions, esthetic competition, one's relationship to and status among one's peers, not on winning a money prize or a popularity contest.

After saying all this I must still admit that for the individual WPA artist, the winning of one of these Section awards was a great plum. The amounts paid to the artist, although quite reasonable according to the professional and commercial standards then prevailing, were princely compared to the $23.50 per week he had earned on the WPA/FAP. The publicity resulting from the award, and the knowledge that one had been chosen from a large field of contestants was very pleasant indeed.

This very triumph, however, had a built-in weakness. The fact that the original small-scale model, *maquette*, was the key to everything put entirely too much pressure on this stage of the design. One had to make the small model too well. The artist's highest point of esthetic tension and energy was reached with this *maquette*. Everything afterwards was a slight let-down. If one studies any example of large-scale monumental plastic art, from Michelangelo to Picasso's *Guernica*, one generally finds that many excellent rough sketches and studies were made for the work, but that no one has been followed exactly. It was difficult to use the maquette only as a springboard, as one must do if the large work is not to be a mere blow-up. In the case of architecture and of some present-day constructed "minimal" art, however, the blow-up works. The completed work is—or should be—mechanically executed.

It was easier to maintain a more flexible attitude toward large sculptural projects within the framework of the WPA/FAP than in the Section. It is true that a model in the WPA/FAP had to be approved, but it did not carry such an emotional and esthetic load. One could make a second sketch if the first one was not approved, or give up that particular project and go back to pedestal sculpture. In any event, the approval of the sketch had no financial or status significance, and was not of too much esthetic importance. It was merely a go-ahead signal. The real excitement came as the large work developed. Then the tension built up and a fresh and spontaneous development of the sketch became possible.

My particular Section commission was awarded to me after I was no longer

FIGURE 25. Robert Cronbach. *Independence*. Eight foot high plaster model of sculpture for the auditorium of the Social Security Building, Washington, D.C. Section, c. 1940 (Courtesy of the artist)

connected with the wpa/fap and, I believe, illustrates very well the joys and sorrows of the various New Deal art projects.

In the summer of 1940 the Section held a national competition for two eight-foot free-standing sculptures for the auditorium of the newly finished Social Security Building in Washington, D.C. (now the Department of Health, Education, and Welfare). Chaim Gross, Ralph Stackpole, and William McVey made up the jury.

I worked about a month on sketches and studies, then made the two required twelve-inch models in a four to five day stretch ending at about 5 A.M. on the day they were due. There was no time for shipping, so I took a train to Washington and delivered them in person about an hour before the noon deadline.

After the announcement of the award I had a conference with Edward Bruce and Edward Rowan of the Section in which the details of the contract were worked out. Sixteen thousand dollars was allowed for the whole commission. This was to include the cost of bronze casting, walnut pedestals, and delivery to the site. There were five payments in all, beginning with the agreement on the contract and ending with the acceptance and delivery of the sculptures.

The contract program included the making of intermediate 32-inch studies. I think this was a mistake. It was and is standard academic procedure. To state once more what I have said earlier, however, I believe that any dilution of the energy and spontaneity with which the sculptor attacks his actual final piece is bad. If the original has been carefully studied it is more than enough to work from.

The project took about 18 months and I worked principally with Edward Rowan and Forbes Watson. During the entire time everyone I dealt with in the Section was extremely understanding, cooperative, and efficient—that is, until the very end when the situation passed beyond their control.

The same cannot be said of the Washington, D.C., Fine Arts Commission. Because the sculpture was indoors the commission did not have full authority over it, but did have the right to "review and recommend." There were difficulties with the commission at each stage of the work—the original model, the intermediate, and full-size sculptures.

I am happy to say that the Section gave me complete support. The question was referred to the original jury (Gross, Stackpole, McVey), who endorsed the work saying that the larger stages were a just and satisfactory development of the original study. So I continued to work until one figure was cast in bronze ready for erection, the other finished in plaster, ready for the foundry.

By this time (January 1942), the war was in full swing, the Social Security Building was occupied by the War Production Board, and my two new shining bronze figures—if erected—would tower over desks where manufacturers would be fighting for allotments of copper, a critical material. The amount of metal involved was minuscule in a serious sense. (Later I worked in a war plant where more copper was wasted every week than would have been used for my two sculptures.) I realized that the gesture of placing the new statues in this place at this time would not have been a happy one.

In addition, although I was not then aware of it, the Section was in eclipse and would disappear within the year. I can only guess at the pressures involved. I know only that I was finally informed that the government did not see fit to erect the sculptures at that time. I was paid in full for my work except for the foundry costs for casting the second figure. The sculptures were delivered to a government warehouse.

After the war, when I returned from service in the Merchant Marine, I tried to revive the project. The Section was non-existent; Bruce and Rowan were dead. I had great difficulty finding anyone with any knowledge of the matter, let alone anyone with authority to initiate any action. For a year or more I tried to break through this Kafka-like impasse. Then I put the whole exasperating matter aside. Recently, I have learned that my two statues, the plaster one painted to resemble the one cast in bronze, somehow were allocated to an agency in Colorado! There is now talk of casting the plaster and installing both works in the auditorium for which they were originally designed. After thirty years, I will believe that when it happens!

To give a fair record of my experience with government-supported art, I should add that much later, in 1963, I was commissioned to make a large sculptured fountain for a Federal Office Building in St. Louis. This worked out very well and the water in the fountain is still flowing. Commissions of this nature awarded by the Public Buildings Service of the General Services Administration were a direct outgrowth of the Section's activity and continued until they were "temporarily" canceled by the Vietnam war.

This account of the New Deal sculpture projects is based almost entirely upon my own experience while working on them. I was never part of the administration and, although I had a good general knowledge of the major policy changes within the Project, I have made no particular effort to give an exact or complete calendar of them. My memories and impressions of this period were strengthened by conversations I have had recently with Audrey McMahon, James Brooks, Martin Craig, Joseph Konzal, Thomas Lo Medico, and Max Spivak.

It is hard to draw specific conclusions from my work on the New Deal projects. It was a rich and exciting experience, both esthetically and socially, and one I should have hated to miss. My work has grown and developed a great deal since then—it would be rather dismal if it had not. I think the WPA experience had an important effect on this development.

Federal support of the arts is possible and can be beneficial. It is most important that the nature of the support be flexible, imaginative, and adapted to the specific circumstances. It cannot follow any past pattern, but must be aimed at the present and developing situation both of the artist and the public.

Ads from January 1936 *Art Front*

JACOB KAINEN was born in Waterbury, Connecticut, in 1909. He received his education in the 1930s at Pratt Institute, New York University, and as a printmaker on the graphic division of the WPA/FAP in New York from 1935 to 1942. As a painter and printmaker, he has had twenty-two one-man shows, has exhibited in innumerable group shows here and abroad, has won a number of important prizes, and is represented in such distinguished collections as those of the Metropolitan Museum of Art, the Brooklyn Museum, the Library of Congress, the Phillips Collection, and the Corcoran Gallery of Art. In the early 1940s he joined the staff of the division of graphic art of the Smithsonian's United States National Museum and for twenty years, from 1946 to 1966, held the rank of curator. From 1966 to 1969 he was curator of the Department of Prints and Drawings at the Smithsonian's National Collection of Fine Arts where he is at present a consultant. He has published innumerable books, articles, exhibition catalogues, and book forewords. Two recent books are *John Baptist Jackson: 18th Century Master of the Color Woodcut* (1962) and *The Etchings of Canaletto* (1967), both published by the Smithsonian Institution Press.

FIGURE 26. Jacob Kainen. *Self-Portrait*. Drypoint, c. 1940. Collection of the artist. (Courtesy of the artist)

The Graphic Arts Division of the WPA Federal Art Project

JACOB KAINEN

When the WPA/FAP was established in 1935, printmaking in this country was just beginning to break loose from the deadening traditions that had kept it a timid, ineffectual echo of the past. The field was dominated by conservative artists who were concerned mainly with conspicuous technical competence, in the illustrative sense, at the expense of more expressive values. But for the first time, although haltingly and somewhat cautiously, a growing number of artists were beginning to make prints that showed a more independent outlook. It was on the clearly perceptible wave of this new desire for change that the WPA/FAP graphic arts division was launched.

In 1935 etching was still the major print medium. All the prominent print societies were made up of artists who worked in the copper plate media alone (etchings, engravings, drypoints, aquatints, and mezzotints). Only prints from metal plates were shown in their annual exhibitions, which were often open to outsiders who could pass their juries.

The most influential serial publication for printmakers was *Fine Prints of the Year*, which was subtitled *An Annual Review of Contemporary Etching and Engraving* (1923–1938). It reproduced and discussed British and American prints, and a few Continental ones, which had been selected for this honor. Only work in the metal plate media was considered. It was not until 1936 that *Fine Prints of the Year* began to include lithographs and wood engravings, although color prints and woodcuts were still excluded. The Society of American Etchers was even more reluctant to change. It waited until 1947 to broaden its policy. Then it took on the unwieldy name of The Society of American Etchers, Gravers, Lithographers, and Woodcutters, which it finally changed a few years later to The Society of American Graphic Artists.

Quite a number of printmakers were making lithographs and block prints although they were in the minority and were finding it difficult to win recognition. Art dealers were generally less hidebound than the print societies and made some effort to promote work in a variety of media. After its first issue in 1930, which showed only copper plate work, the publication of the Art Dealers Association, *Contemporary American Prints*, began to include some lithographs and block prints among its selections. *Prints*, a bi-monthly magazine that ran from 1930 to 1938, also had a liberal policy. This periodical carried brief articles on prints and printmakers, reproduced current graphic work in all media, ran advertisements, and was a clearing house in general for the print field. But little radical work was shown. Probably the most adventurous organization was the American Institute of Graphic Arts (AIGA). From 1925 until the 1950s it sponsored *Fifty Prints of the Year*, which it selected and circulated as a traveling exhibition. Work in all media was shown and every effort was made to run the gamut of esthetic approaches. Even in the 1920s the AIGA included prints by John Marin and the cubist-inspired Jan Matulka and Jolan Gross Bettelheim. In the 1930s this organization was probably the main agency for the exhibition of advanced tendencies in printmaking, although few examples were shown each year. Moreover, since dealers handled few radical prints, not many were available for selection.

In the early 1930s the United States was not so different from other countries in its largely conservative attitude toward prints. The greatest modern masters from Delacroix to Picasso, although acclaimed as painters, did not fit the standard backward-looking style of the print societies and therefore were not highly regarded as printmakers. Their work was considered too rough and offhand to a generation of print connoisseurs that relished conspicuous technical competence, which it equated with nerveless polish or the echo of an earlier master. J. H. Slater's *Engravings and Their Value* (1929 edition), which listed British and American auction prices, omitted such great printmakers as Degas, Manet, Gauguin, Munch, Bonnard, Vuillard, Redon, Picasso, and Matisse, among others. Obviously their work was not popular with print collectors.

Clearly, in 1935 printmaking was an unrewarding field for nonconformist artists. The growing body of American lithographers and woodcutters were fighting an uphill battle to win recognition from collectors and the professional print societies. Moreover, this group of artists, with few exceptions, worked in a fairly conservative manner. The major exceptions among the more prolific workers in lithography were Adolf Dehn, who employed a variety of fresh and novel textures in his landscapes and social genre; Louis Lozowick and Niles Spencer, who simplified their forms in the "immaculate" American manner; and Stuart Davis, whose independent cubist approach verged on abstraction. At the Art Students League, Kenneth Hayes Miller and his pupils took subjects from everyday life but arranged them in somewhat posturing Renaissance compositions. Will Barnet was added to the staff in 1934 and his classes in printmaking were encouraged to work in a freer manner than heretofore. There was also the earlier work of such personal artists as George Bellows and Childe Hassam.

In etching John Marin was so lightly regarded that he rarely printed more than a few impressions from each plate, and even such well-known printmakers as Hassam, Arthur B. Davies (who had died in 1928), and John Sloan were rarely patronized by museums or private collectors. When Hassam died in 1935 his widow found it necessary to distribute his unsold editions, which existed in bulk, to museums and libraries throughout the country. The prints of these artists could be seen only in the galleries of a few daring dealers such as E. Weyhe, J. B. Neumann, and Edith Halpert's Downtown Gallery.

When the WPA/FAP was established in New York City, Mrs. Audrey McMahon and her staff recognized the potential of printmaking as a popular medium for the public. Prints constituted the most portable and least expensive art form and it was clear that a graphic arts division, properly organized, could yield the bulk of allocations. One of the great achievements of this division was that it fostered the growth of lithography, the woodcut, and color printing on a large scale, expanded technical possibilities in these media and others, and broadened the concept of printmaking in general.

But before the printing of editions could be carried out on a scale that would keep scores of artists busy, a central workshop had to be set up. Here the problems were formidable. Mrs. McMahon enlisted the aid of Russell T. Limbach, an artist and printer experienced in all forms of the graphic arts. His job was to plan the shop for maximum working efficiency, to procure the equipment and supplies, and to find skilled printers. Equipment included different kinds of presses for printing in etching, lithography, and the woodblock media, a special tank and wooden grill for graining lithograph stones, and various kinds of tables for workshop operations. Supplies included lithograph stones of various grades and sizes, paper suitable for the different processes, plank and end-grain wood for the woodcut and wood-engraving media, copper plates for the intaglio processes, and tools and materials needed in all the techniques of printmaking. In addition storage racks had to be designed for storing stones, plates, and woodblocks.

It was not easy to obtain the equipment. Although money had been allocated for paying artists and obtaining supplies, there were no funds for presses. Fortunately, the technical apparatus was donated by sympathetic individuals. Thus, on February 6, 1936, the graphic division's studio workshop, the first sponsored by the government, was officially opened on the twelfth floor of the building housing the WPA/FAP headquarters at 6 East 39th Street. Demonstrations of the processes of etching, lithography, and block printing were carried out and a special lithograph, *City Hall*, by Harry Taskey, was printed and presented to Mrs. Henry Breckenridge, chairman of the Municipal Art Commission, acting for Mayor Fiorello LaGuardia.

Between August 1935, when work relief for artists was established, and February 1936, when the workshop was ready, the lithographs were printed mainly by Theodore Wahl. Together with Russell Limbach, he had been appointed by Mrs. McMahon at the suggestion of Bernarda Bryson (Mrs. Ben Shahn), whose counsel in the early stages of the Project was invaluable. But commissioned printers also produced editions, as well as artists who had access to outside presses. Among those involved were Will Barnet, Jacob Friedland, and George C. Miller. But until the workshop was in full swing, problems of logistics kept the printing output limited. About half of the artists, unable to get editions printed, were restricted to making drawings.

At that time Gustave von Groschwitz was supervisor of the graphic arts division, Russell Limbach was technical adviser, and Theodore Wahl was shop chairman. He did most of the lithographic printing, including his own designs. Albert Heckman, another experienced artist, supervised etching and block printing, with Arthur P. Snyder printing the etchings.

With the opening of the workshop, production began on an expanded scale. Several months later—April 30 through May 13, 1936—the first exhibition of prints was held at the newly opened WPA Federal Art Project Gallery, 225 West 57th Street.

Von Groschwitz described the early months of work:

A workshop, equipped with work-tables, and the presses necessary for printing, has been established at 6 East 39th Street in New York. To date, sixty-one men and women have been assigned to work here, with materials provided by the Federal Government, to make lithographs, etchings, wood engravings, linoleum cuts, and drawings. Their work, when finished, will be allocated to museums, schools, hospitals, and other tax-supported institutions at a nominal price. This price covers only the cost of the materials used. Thus the project will be in part self-liquidating.

Before executing a print, each artist makes a drawing which must be approved by the supervising artist and by the project supervisor to make certain that the subject is acceptable and that the finished print will have artistic value. The finished plate, block, or stone is printed in an edition limited to from 25 to 75 impressions.[1]

Along with the rest of the projects, the graphic arts workshop moved to 235 East 42nd Street in February 1937, and in September 1938 to its final quarters at 110 King Street. An administrative report dated September 29, 1938, lists Augustus Peck as shop chairman of the etching department and Theodore Wahl as assistant supervisor in charge of lithography. Both did creative work as well. Frank Nankivell, an older artist who had printed plates for Arthur B. Davies,

FIGURE 27. Jacob Kainen. *Drought*. Lithograph, WPA/FAP, c. 1935.
Collection unknown. (Archives of American Art)

now printed the etchings, and Isaac "Dick" Sanger printed woodblocks on a Hoe hand press and also produced his own prints. Two older craftsmen, Joseph Peroutka and Nathaniel Spreckley, worked full-time printing editions in lithography. I remember that Jacob Friedland made and printed his own lithographs and that Charles Hanke also printed lithographs. At that time, or shortly afterwards, Louis Schanker acted as a supervisor in color block printing, a field he had explored with distinction since the early 1930s.

The office force consisted of Anna T. Foley, assistant managing clerk, and Alexander Breckenridge, assistant to the supervisor. His main tasks were to file and record all the prints produced, fill allocation orders, and to assemble and catalogue prints for exhibitions. He also arranged for the periodic shipments of prints to Washington for national allocation. Lloyd Rollins also served in an administrative capacity. Before the artist could work on a plate, stone, or block, as Von Groschwitz stated, he had to submit several sketches, one of which had to be approved. He then received his block or plate and took it to his home. He also had the option of executing a lithograph or woodblock in the shop. If he worked in lithography he was notified when the stone would be delivered to his home by truck. After completing the work he notified the administration, which arranged for picking up the stone. When the schedule was set for proofing his block, plate, or stone, the artist would come at the appointed time to collaborate with the printer or supervisor on the printing. If changes had to be made the artist could do them on the spot except in the case of etching, which required extensive technical manipulation.

Usually six proofs were made and submitted to a committee of project supervisors. At times a representative of the Project artists sat in, particularly after the first year, and sometimes an outside expert (Carl Zigrosser was one) also attended. In the vast majority of instances the proofs would be accepted and a date would be set for printing the entire edition. As von Groschwitz stated, this ran from 25 to 75 prints, depending upon its artistic value or expected popularity. Most often the edition did not exceed 25. The artist, if he made the request, could obtain three proofs for himself with the stipulation that he could not sell them while on the Project. In general, the artist was required to produce one work a month, but proofing and printing the edition often took additional time. In lithography we could select our own stone, once the sketches were accepted. This liberty was important because certain kinds of stones were best for fine or broad treatment. We then ground off the design left from the previous printing and grained the stone to our liking. Since we watched and took part in all the print processes, we became familiar with the operation of a print workshop. This experience proved to be valuable later on when we had to qualify for jobs in the print field.

FIGURE 28. Stuart Davis (1894–1964). *Funnel and Smoke*. Lithograph, WPA/FAP, 1939. National Collection of Fine Arts, Smithsonian Institution. (Courtesy of Jacob Kainen)

Not many artists worked on blocks or stones at the workshop, for obvious reasons. It usually took several days, at the least, to finish the master image. At the shop the artist was without the comforts of home and moreover he had to work in a public situation, with people watching while he mulled over his compositions. He had the additional expense of going out to eat, to say nothing of the extra carfare. Also he had to work at stated hours, while at home he could work evenings if he wished. At both places the necessary materials were provided for the lithographer—crayons and heavy lithographic ink (tusche) and a barrel stave or another form of wooden bridge set over the stone to permit him to draw without the danger of getting his greasy fingers on the surface. Any trace of grease would attract ink in printing.

Doing woodcuts was more convenient at the shop because of the special tables available. These were set at an angle of about thirty degrees, with wooden cleats on the bottom and the left side to contain the blocks while cutting down with the knife or moving the gouge from right to left. The blocks were slightly higher than the cleats to permit the strokes to carry past the edges of the blocks. Etching was rarely done in the shop because of the acid fumes which would create an unpleasant and even toxic atmosphere for some workers. At home the etcher could bite his plate near an open window.

There were times when working at the shop was particularly rewarding. On one occasion I was drawing on a stone when Stuart Davis came by. I was twenty-six at the time. Inspired by his presence I made some bold decisions, almost reckless ones, that gave some verve and sparkle to the composition. It was probably the best print I made on the Project. I still remember with pleasure his kind words: "That's damn good." If more artists of Davis' caliber could have given us some personal attention, even if only to watch us work, I am sure we would have taken some unaccustomed chances and moved ahead in our art.

While work on the Project was exciting and stimulating, the hard facts of day-to-day relationships with the administration were generally unhappy. We realized that the Project administration was under pressure from its own administrative superiors, but that didn't alter the fact that we had to fight not only for reasonable working conditions but also for our economic existence. Political enemies and hostile critics, suspicious of cultural projects, made accusations of "boondoggling." In their zeal to obtain what they thought was full value for money received, they brought about regulations that were eminently in opposition to creative work. Most important among these were unrealistic supervisory methods, periodic firing of artists, and uncomprehending attitudes towards artistic creation.

In New York City, in the first years of the Project, an artist was required to go from his home each day to a central location and sign in by 9 A.M. He then returned home to work. This rule was not only wasteful of his time, it completely overlooked the fact that artists do not necessarily operate on a 9 to 5 schedule. One useful by-product of the signing-in practice was that it brought the artists together for a time to exchange pleasantries. I have a vivid memory of Stuart Davis standing in line behind me, around 1937. Pointing to the stout, gray, balding man behind him he said: "This is Joseph Stella. We both showed here in 1913." I then realized that the 69th Regiment Armory, where we were signing in, was the scene of the famous Armory show of 1913 that introduced modern art to America.

Artists were required to remain home at all times after registering in the morning. Periodically, timekeepers checked on them at unspecified hours. If the artist did not answer the door he was recorded as absent without leave. Consequently an artist hesitated to go out to get materials he needed, no matter how necessary, and even to visit the bathroom for fear the timekeeper might come during his absence.

If an artist wanted to go outside to sketch and gather subject material he had to notify the administration, giving the precise time when he could be found at a specified place. Often, a timekeeper was sent to make sure that the artist was on the spot. Naturally, this procedure wasted the artist's time and kept him from wandering about—the only way he could find unexpected subject matter. These timekeeping abuses, characteristic of the first few years, were later relaxed when it became evident to government officials, who dictated to the Project administration, that treating artists like factory hands was an unrealistic way to sponsor the production of works of art. If the administration bore the brunt of the artists' resentment it was because the artists had no way of knowing where the regulations came from and how and to what degree the administration resisted unreasonable orders from above.

Timekeeping methods were a nuisance and a bore but they were not the worst abuse the artist had to bear. Moreover they were eventually straightened out. The worst problem the artist had to face was the policy, begun in 1939, of firing Project members every eighteen months, ostensibly to allow them to look for private work. The policy was transparently fraudulent, since private jobs, especially for artists, did not exist. Actually the mass firings began as early as the fall of 1936. In July 1937 over seventy artists were dismissed with no advance notice. No apparent standards were followed in selecting artists for dismissal since those discharged included such prominent names as Joseph Stella, Julian Levi, Fritz Eichenberg, and Ben-Zion. Many in the group were non-citizens living in this country, including Chinese and Japanese who were specifically excluded from American citizenship by law at that time. Among those discharged was a large number of printmakers.

The arbitrary character of the firing aroused the indignation of many persons prominent in politics, religion, and the arts, and a Citizens' Committee for Support of WPA was founded. Among the members were Senator Gerald P. Nye, Edna St. Vincent Millay, Genevieve Taggart, Upton Sinclair, Van Wyck Brooks, Lillian Hellman, and Lewis Mumford. An exhibition titled "Pink Slips Over Culture" was held in the A.C.A. Gallery from July 19–31, 1937, and other exhibitions were held later. From that time on, artists awaited their paychecks with the disheartening expectation that a pink dismissal slip might be included. Morale began to deteriorate from that point, and became worse after the 18-months firing policy was instituted in 1939.

An artist could return to the Project, but the procedures for doing so were strenuous and demeaning. He had to declare himself a pauper and qualify for home relief. Then he had to wait in a home relief center every day of every week, sitting on a hard bench in a dreary waiting room together with other unemployed persons and homeless derelicts. He kept his eye on a blackboard, on which a clerk would occasionally list a job opening in white chalk. The artist remained there, if he was determined to get back on the Project, while such jobs as "dishwasher," "laborer," "porter," and the like were inscribed. When, finally, there appeared the words "graphic artist, WPA, 110 King Street," he made a mad dash for the exit and took the first street-car for his destination. It never occurred to us to take taxis; they were alien to our world and in any case we didn't have the money. The artist who got there first got the job.

To indicate the typical vicissitudes of firing and re-hiring I list my own record below:

Assignment 8-26-35	$103.40 per month	Termination 7-15-37
Assignment 9-2-37	$ 95.44 per month	Termination 8-31-39
Assignment 12-13-39	$ 87.60 per month	Termination 4-23-41
Assignment 5-22-41	$ 87.60 per month	Termination 5-6-42
		(Left to take job in the graphic arts field.)

I can state that the only reason for my being re-hired so regularly was my persistence in waiting in home relief offices. But it should be obvious to anyone that this sort of firing and hiring, in an economic depression, was frightening. It infected our thinking, consciously and unconsciously, and gave us the feeling of leading a transient existence. Certainly it created an uncertain and tentative atmosphere, one that was hardly conducive to the formation of a strong personal outlook, which must be built up in a careful and consecutive manner. This situation, in large measure, kept us from fully concentrating on our art and prevented us from expanding our possibilities naturally.

As one who joined the graphic arts division in its first month, I can testify to the enthusiasm and good will felt by participating artists. Aside from the relief at being able to survive economically, we were grateful to the government

FIGURE 29.   George Constant (b. 1892). *Triboro Bridge*. Drypoint, WPA/FAP, 1938.
National Collection of Fine Arts, Smithsonian Institution. (Courtesy of Jacob Kainen)

for recognizing that art was a public concern. It was good to know that we could function full-time as artists and work in a spirit of camaraderie with other artists and with master craftsmen. We had been given a strong professional motivation at a crucial time, and we appreciated it. One of the tragedies of the wpa/fap was that the artists were treated as beggars by the relief-orientated policies of the wpa (not by Mrs. McMahon and her staff), their creative problems were not understood, and their work was grossly undervalued.

But the experience of producing prints and having them professionally printed was a constant pleasure and made up for the numerous indignities. It was in the shop that the printmakers felt most truly at home. There they could proof their blocks, plates, and stones in company with outstanding professionals such as Stuart Davis, Raphael Soyer, Yasuo Kuniyoshi, Adolf Dehn, Louis Lozowick, George Constant, and others. There was no "star" system—we were all in the same boat. We were stimulated by each other's presence and by the fact that productivity was a common requirement.

No pressures were placed upon the artist to work in any specific direction. He was free to select his own subjects and to treat them in any manner he chose. Thus a wide variety of approaches lay open to him although the prevailing mood was one of concern with his immediate milieu. While much of the work was labored and illustrative the strongest examples reflected some of the major stylistic developments of the period. The first wave of modernism in America had subsided and cubist and post-Cézanne composition had been replaced by overtones of surrealism, Mexican proletarian art, and European expressionism, particularly Rouault. The graphic artists were naturally less *avant garde* as a whole than the easel painters since printmaking had a more conservative tradition. Most of the printmakers had little knowledge of the vital work done by Paul Gauguin, Edward Munch, and the German expressionists. In fact, most of them knew little about art history, past or present, and this group formed the hard core of the uninformed, unadventurous, routine practitioners. But even those who had some degree of sophistication could not resist the prevailing concern with the American scene even though they had no sympathy with the outstanding members of this art movement: Thomas Hart Benton, John Steuart Curry, and Grant Wood. The movement symbolized an effort to break with traditional European sources and find inspiration in American life and culture. In a way, it asserted that an honest and informed naiveté constituted a fresher approach for American artists than a transplanted Europeanism. The economic crisis, which the artists shared with the American people, gave point to this outlook. Thus many, without meaning to do so, became American scene artists or social commentators simply by reacting to their environment.

But the strongest printmakers, even when they produced work that reflected the Depression, showed an awareness of modern tendencies. Joseph Vogel and

Boris Gorelick incorporated elements of surrealism in their social indictments, with the former using strong abstract forms allied to Picasso. Older artists (anyone thirty-five or over was considered an older artist then) such as Stuart Davis and Louis Lozowick continued in a modified cubist vein, while a host of others, including Chet LaMore, Harry Gottlieb, Blanches Grambs, and Elizabeth Olds, showed a kinship with Orozco. The most pronounced expressionists were Adolf Dehn, Hubert Davis, Bernard Schardt, Will Barnet, Hugh Miller, Nan Lurie, Joseph Leboit, and particularly Louis Schanker and Benjamin Kopman. Independent artists included Ida Abelman, whose fragmented memories of childhood had an irrational, dreamlike quality, George Constant, whose poetical, beautifully nuanced drypoint vignettes represented a fresh approach to the medium, Yasuo Kuniyoshi and Chuzo Tamotzu, with their feathery Japanese touch, Anthony Velonis, an elegant semi-abstractionist, Eugene Morley, who employed vigorously abstracted elements in his compositions on social themes, and Albert Webb, a rollicking drypoint artist in the vein of "Pop" Hart. All the artists mentioned, and many more, were individualists and not camp followers of any current style. If they had been granted a little more time than five chopped-up, harried years, they might well have produced an even weightier contribution to American printmaking. If the full production of some of the stronger artists could be assembled (and much of their work has been lost), a new chapter in American printmaking could be written.

The graphic arts division probably reached its peak in 1937 and 1938, when an expansion of technical possibilities took place. Early in 1937 it had been announced that artists could work in color lithography, with Russell Limbach as technical adviser. Limbach had worked in the medium since 1930, and had made and printed the first color lithograph on the Project, *Trapeze Girl,* in 1935. It must be remembered that original printmaking in color was not common in America, particularly in the complex technique of color lithography. The 19th-century process of chromolithography had been strictly a craft method of reproducing paintings and had not been adapted to the fine arts, as in Europe. About the middle of 1938 (the catalogue is undated) an exhibition took place which included twenty-three color lithographs by sixteen artists. Held at the Federal Art Gallery, 225 West 57th Street in New York, the exhibition was titled "Printmaking: A New Tradition," and showed 143 prints in all media. The catalogue included a foreword by Carl Zigrosser, an "Explanation" by Gustave von Groschwitz, and a description of color lithography by Russell Limbach. To indicate the high quality of the prints, all made after April 1937, it was emphasized that ten had been selected for *Fine Prints of the Year.* But while only four of the 120 prints in black and white were marked "Edition exhausted," five of the editions of twenty-three color lithographs were so marked. Von Groschwitz therefore felt justified in stating:

The reaction of artists and other visitors to the Graphic Arts Workshop who have seen the color lithographs being made there indicates that this heretofore neglected medium may eventually achieve a mass popularity such as it has never had even in Europe, where it has been used by some of the best known artists.

In September 1938 a silk screen unit was set up in New York as a branch of the graphic arts division. It was headed by Anthony Velonis, who had produced silk screen posters for the poster division, had worked in commercial shops, and was thoroughly familiar with the medium. As Carl Zigrosser points out:

He became more and more struck with its possibilities as a color print medium for artists. He was aware of the growing popularity of color woodcuts and color lithographs produced on the Project by means of expensive technical equipment beyond the means of the average artist, and he set out to perfect a more fluent and less expensive color printing process. Encouraged by the Project, he and other artists experimented with the new technique and adapted it to the artists' needs.[2]

He adds: "There Velonis taught and gave technical advice to many artists. The first six artists, besides Velonis himself, were Elizabeth Olds, Harry Gottlieb, Ruth Chaney, Louis Lozowick, Eugene Morley, and Hyman Warsager." Velonis wrote two handbooks, the first in 1939, which were mimeographed by the WPA/FAP and were widely sought by interested artists. As the idea spread, artists outside the project took up the medium and in May 1940 established the Silk Screen Group in conjunction with Project artists. Printmakers throughout the country began working in silk screen (named *serigraphy* by Carl Zigrosser to distinguish it from the commercial method), and a new artists' color process was launched.

Exploration of the color woodcut was also carried out in 1938 under the leadership of Louis Schanker. Some excellent work was done by such artists as Hyman Warsager, Joseph Leboit, Ruth Chaney, Bernard Schardt, and Schanker himself. Hyman Warsager describes this undertaking in his unpublished essay for *Art for the Millions:*

Few color woodcuts had been attempted in this country, and in general they were marked by a banal imitation of early Japanese prints. The Art Program [WPA/FAP] artists took to this medium with rare enthusiasm. Large blocks from plank wood were introduced, usually whitewood, poplar, gumwood, cherry, and in some instances redwood for it presented a very sympathetic and useful grain. The large blocks permitted bold work, color was used in large simple areas but subtle uses of overprinting colors were employed. The quality of the grain of the wood itself gave the print a unique character. Raising the printing surface of the wood with cement and lowering it slightly with sandpaper varied the color intensity adding desired textures. A very rich print often resulted by engraving one block on end grain and adding color from plank wood cuts.

FIGURE 30. Louis Schanker (b. 1903). *Circus Scene*. Color Woodcut, WPA/FAP, c. 1936. National Collection of Fine Arts, Smithsonian Institution. (Courtesy of Jacob Kainen)

The administration was not only open to suggestions for technical exploration in color but it obviously took pride in this aspect of project work. It encouraged the production of color prints and publicized this advance in American print-making. In a WPA/FAP press release dated January 1, 1939, which contained a report to Holger Cahill summarizing three years of activity up to November 30, 1938, Mrs. McMahon stated:

Work in color lithography has passed the first tentative stages of its development by Project graphic artists. Four and five-color lithographs have been printed with signal success. But what is even more important, this impetus given to the revival of color lithography is evident in the renewed interest on the part of the public and artists all over the country. Recent experimentation in color-woodblock printing has revealed possibilities of technical and esthetic achievements. At the present time printmakers in the Graphic Arts Division are opening new avenues of approach to graphic media and are also reestablishing the values of techniques that have been neglected.

In the same report, Mrs. McMahon gave statistics of production for the three years up to November 30, 1938. Graphic artists in New York were reported to have completed 1,840 original works from which 36,571 prints were made. Allocations to public institutions numbered 9,282, in contrast to 3,925 allocations from the easel division. In summarizing Mrs. McMahon noted:

The works produced by the Graphic Arts Division have been exhibited in all the major print exhibitions and have consistently received prizes in these shows. . . . The largest number of the 9,282 prints allocated have gone to the following institutions: Brooklyn Public Library, Queensborough Public Library, Evander Childs, De Witt Clinton, and Brooklyn Technical High Schools, New York Post Graduate Medical School and Hospital, the United States Naval Hospital and the Fourth Battalion of the United States Naval Hospital.

Von Groschwitz the first supervisor, left the Project late in 1938, to be followed by Lynd Ward, Werner Drewes, and Oscar Weissbuch. I can say that all the graphic art supervisors were liked and respected by the artists. They showed sympathy and understanding and stood up for the artists under the pressures of the Project administration, which in turn was under political pressure. I remember an afternoon late in 1940, I believe, when a committee of supervisors was holding a session in an adjoining room. Artists in the workshop could hear the voice of Werner Drewes raised in vehement protest. When the meeting ended Drewes emerged, his face red with fury. When we asked what had happened, he said: "You now have another stupid regulation. You have to make finished drawings before making your prints. And by finished I mean that you must anticipate exactly what tones, lines, and textures you will use in your final print. In other words, you must copy your preliminary drawing exactly." Drewes went to a table where a stack of prints rested, then lifted them and threw them high into the air. They floated all over the workshop. Then contritely he began to pick up the prints.

Around the end of 1940 the Project began to disintegrate. The war in Europe and Asia, and the obvious determination of the government to discourage artists from continuing on the Project, were reflected in a growing demoralization and loss of focus. No more editions were printed. Artists were encouraged to make posters supporting the Allies, and were asked to print their posters in both silk screen and color lithography. The lithographic printers, Peroutka and Spreckley, were asked to train a number of artists to print. As elderly craftsmen with jobs to lose, they were understandably reluctant and deliberately gave the wrong information. Thus fledgling printers found their lithographic images disappearing, or turning solid black. There was much recrimination and the supervisor was constantly asked to make the printers see reason. The printers stoutly asserted that their instructions were absolutely correct, but that the students were slow and not too sensitive to the subtle techniques required to bring the stones to life. It was a mystery why the administration chose inexperienced artists instead of those who already knew how to print, the only explanation being that the seasoned lithographers showed understandable reluctance at the thought of becoming printers. So the administration picked younger artists avid to learn how to print lithographs, particularly in color.

After war was declared in December 1941, a greater emphasis was placed on the "war effort." More artists produced silk screens (additional screens and tables were made) and a smaller number made posters in color lithography. Artists now generally reported to King Street and wandered around the premises watching others work and helping where they could. Occasionally they made small paintings in poster colors (I and some others did them) as private works just to keep busy. Sometime in December 1941, a sign shop was set up to satisfy the need for proclamations and simple instructions relating to the war. But little was done in this area and the sign shop was discontinued after a few months. Then in March 1942, the whole WPA/FAP was re-named the Graphic Section of the War Services Division. By May 1942, when I left to become a museum aide in the division of graphic arts of the United States National Museum in Washington, D.C., it was obvious that the project was in its last stages.

The catalogue of the M. H. de Young Museum's exhibition *Frontiers of American Art* held in San Francisco in 1939, states "Although only 250 artists are employed in the Graphic Arts Section of the Project [nationally], production in this field totals 84,350 prints of 4,000 original examples in lithography, etching, wood engraving, color prints, and other media." Recalling Mrs. McMahon's report that by November 30, 1938, in New York City alone, 36,571 prints had been made from 1,840 master designs, we can see that almost half the total production in the country came from New York. The progress report of the Federal

FIGURE 31. Aline Fruhauf (b. 1907). *Martha Graham's Dancing Class.*
Lithograph, WPA/FAP, c. 1936. Collection of the artist.

172

Art Project in that city, dated February 15, 1936, listed seventy-seven print-makers and, in ensuing years, probably not over eighty-five were at work at any one time.

While the level of the better artists was high, and while their work was a marked advance in American printmaking, the potential existed for a still more exciting advance. The artists were ready and the time was ripe. Here the Project had a major weakness, one that could be attributed to the administration's interpretation of its mission. This mission was "art for the people," based upon the assumption that the people were not ready for unfamiliar expressions. The administration did not discourage adventurous work but neither did it encourage it. Perhaps the supervisors felt it was not their province to take sides on esthetic matters, or perhaps they feared political repercussions. Of course the WPA/FAP was under attack mainly by conservatives. But I am sure that if the administration had indicated that it welcomed esthetic as well as technical exploration a great step forward could have been taken sooner in American art.

By 1940 quite a number of artists were ready to cut loose. Special meetings and seminars to discuss the esthetic quality of our work could have been arranged. Ideas could have been exchanged and we would all have profited by coming to grips with basic problems. As it was, we had an uncomfortable sense of working in isolation, despite our occasional meetings at the shop, and the feeling that the administration had an aloof attitude toward our production. In a real sense, we found ourselves working in a vacuum. We created our prints, and that was the end of it. We never received information about the allocation of our work, and to this day most artists don't know where their prints can be found. The artists needed encouragement, a little nudge now and then to stimulate them to bolder efforts, but the administration gave no sign.

Certainly the artists were waiting to be informed that they had *carte blanche*. But if the administration did not take the initiative, and it was perhaps too much to have expected it to do so, neither did the artists. Probably they would have done so with another year of work. They were thoroughly familiar with their media and in fact had begun to take greater liberties by 1940. But just when the propitious time arrived for exploring new paths, the Project began to disintegrate. For more than two years the artists were economic prisoners receiving salaries, but kept from fruitful production. It is surely no accident that the big change in American art came shortly after the collapse of the Project, when former Project artists once again could work consistently. But without their years of work on the Project it is doubtful that the change would have been so rapid and so far-reaching.

Today, when printmaking is so widely carried out in the United States, we should not overlook the importance of the WPA graphic arts division in providing the initial impetus. The project artists bridged the gap between the old mori-

FIGURE 32. Joseph Vogel (b. 1911?). *Vision*. Lithograph, WPA/FAP, 1939.
National Collection of Fine Arts, Smithsonian Institution. (Courtesy of Jacob Kainen)

174

bund etching societies and the unprecedented flowering of the graphic arts that has taken place during the past two decades. The printmaking workshops that were set up in the 1930s were pioneer centers for technical and artistic growth, and the artists who worked there formed a solid basis for further development. They popularized lithography, the woodcut, serigraphy, and most of all color printing. When the projects ended they joined the staffs of schools and universities which increasingly added printmaking departments. These artists knew how to set up workshops and they knew all the media. And so, for the first time in the history of American graphic arts, students found a large number of instructors who practiced and welcomed fresh approaches. When Stanley William Hayter came to this country in 1940 to open his experimental graphic arts studio, Atelier 17, he found the artists ready.

The Projects created a new audience, also. The public, on a national scale, had been educated to accept and collect prints, which they had become familiar with through the WPA collections in schools, libraries, hospitals, military bases, government offices and through exhibitions in WPA/FAP community art centers. Prints to them were no longer the rare and inaccessible etchings, created in a mysterious fashion, that could be seen only in museums and a few art galleries. Nor were they the stuffy and tiresome depictions of game birds in flight or polo encounters that could be seen in the offices of doctors and lawyers. The public had learned that prints could be as imaginative and original as paintings, and much less expensive.

Most artists remember their Project days with mixed feelings. It was good to be able to work every day and to participate in the printing procedures. There was a warm feeling of boon companionship in a common enterprise, even though we didn't recognize that it was for high stakes. Even the constant threat of dismissal, while damaging to our art, was bearable so long as we could return to the Project and thus continue as artists. But the social, political, and artistic climate was not inviting. It was, in fact, restrictive, as we came to realize many years later. We were young and had a great opportunity, but circumstances prevented us from taking the steps we might have taken. We were too ignorant and too concerned with economic survival to take full advantage of our opportunity. I am sure that the feeling of lost possibilities, of youth spent without cultivating our deepest talents, lies at the heart of the bitterness we all feel, despite the fond memories. "In art," Henry James said, "there is no second chance."

1. "Making Prints for the U. S. Government," *Prints*, vol. 6 (February 1936), pp. 135–142.
2. "The Serigraph, a New Medium," *Print Collector's Quarterly*, vol. 28 (December 1941), pp. 447–448.

LINCOLN ROTHSCHILD was born in New York City in 1902 and was educated at Columbia University, the Institute of Fine Arts of New York University, and the Art Students League where he studied painting under Kenneth Hayes Miller. He started to work on the WPA/FAP in New York in 1935 and from 1937 to 1941 was director of its Index of American Design. He was also very active in the Artists' Congress. He has taught at Columbia University and City College and was chairman of the Art Department at Adelphi College from 1946 to 1950. From 1951 to 1957 he was national executive director of the Artists Equity Association. He is the author of four books among which are *Sculpture Through the Ages* (1942) and *Style in Art* (1960), and innumerable articles. He also edits his own private newsletter, *The Pragmatist in Art*. Currently, he is writing a study of his former teacher, Kenneth Hayes Miller.

FIGURE 33. Lincoln Rothschild (seated third from right facing audience) at the opening of an exhibition of Index of American Design plates, Federal Art Gallery, New York City, May 1939. (Archives of American Art)

The Index of American Design of the WPA Federal Art Project

LINCOLN ROTHSCHILD

The concept of an "Index of American Design," adopted as part of the national activity of the WPA/FAP late in 1935, shortly after its inauguration, arose from a new interest in American cultural antecedents that grew apace with new concerns for the arts generally. Stimulated by intensified contacts with the more art-conscious European scene following World War I, some Americans were content to ape the sophistication that centered in Paris, while others looked for inspiration closer to home. Holger Cahill mentions three people in his richly detailed introduction to Erwin O. Christensen's *The Index of American Design* (1950) whose various backgrounds and personalities contributed to a crystallization of this new concern for the arts in America.

Romona Javitz was director of the circulating Picture Collection of the main branch of the New York Public Library. This is a vast number of reproductions of illustrations and photographs, mostly clipped from periodicals and filed according to the subjects represented. Artists in need of information about the appearance of an object to be depicted in a creative assignment are permitted to borrow this material for use in their own studios. In discussing their special needs it became evident to Miss Javitz that a collection illustrating the tradition of American crafts, the particular appearance of objects used in the formative period of the nation, would similarly serve the artists' new search for knowledge about America's past.

Ruth Reeves was a textile designer noted for her ingenuity in developing new motifs. She might be thought of as one of these artists. Under a Guggenheim fellowship she had searched among primitive sources in Guatemala. A series of designs she created for a commercial manufacturer, based on scenes of the Hudson River valley, received considerable attention and demonstrated her concern for indigenous cultural reference. Miss Reeves saw that a program to employ artists with federal support and nationwide scope, could compile images of native American ingenuity in the crafts as inspiration for present and future designers, and her enthusiastic drive was instrumental in bringing the idea to the attention of those who could approve its inauguration.

Because of his own special concern with Americana, on which he had worked on several projects with John Cotton Dana, noted director of the Newark Museum, Mr. Cahill immediately recognized the possibilities of pictorial research in this area, and appointed Constance Rourke as national editor of the Index of American Design. Miss Rourke had written several books of American biography (from Horace Greeley to Charles Sheeler) and had prepared the material for a detailed study of American craftsmanship and culture from which Van Wyck Brooks compiled a volume titled *The Roots of American Culture* after her death in 1941. It was to her knowledge of the field and her organizing skill that the initial plans of operation were largely due. She was especially concerned with the vast opportunity for cultural and educational advantage that would accrue to the student, the artist, the collector, and the general public from a coordinated collection of accurate illustrations.

Quite independently, Peter Larsen, a craftsman-designer in metals, had proposed to Mayor LaGuardia the employment of artists to record designs of architectural decoration in iron and bronze that were being lost in the constant rebuilding of New York City. Mr. Larsen became one of the special supervisors on the staff of the Index in charge of recording metalwork.

As the program grew, a broad spectrum of various aims was conceived and promoted by different individuals involved in planning the Index. The competition of ideas enriched its program, and the momentum of participation in a larger operation carried it through the trials of early experimentation.

Some of the local administrators regarded the Index, to a degree, as a convenience in providing assignments for artists who were not accustomed to following their own inspiration. The employment program of the WPA included a mandate to give people on the relief rolls work in which they had training and experience, in order to conserve skills that might otherwise deteriorate from disuse during the period of economic emergency.

Among the most highly skilled artists, from the viewpoint of the Index, were those whose training had consisted in the development of a coordination between eye and hand capable of producing visual reproductions, such as architectural renderings or illustrations for catalogues. Such orientation toward the object, and experience in producing an accurate image, were exactly the requirements of the Index program. This special need fitted in with the problem of assigning personnel on the WPA/FAP in a manner that is clearly, if somewhat bluntly, indicated in a letter from Mrs. Frances Pollak, assistant director of the

Project for the New York region in charge of educational and service programs. On September 24, 1935 she wrote Cahill "I am so eager to have the Index approved since it offers a catch-all for a large number of artists not suitable and usable for any other purpose."

More idealistic, less immediate aims were conceived by the staff of the Index itself in terms of the potential interests of three separate types of clientele. A corpus of information such as the Index would attempt to compile could not help being of paramount importance in the parochial, but quite extensive and growing activity of collecting American antiques. Solving problems of authentication and classification could be vastly facilitated by a handy coordination of authoritative reference material, while the gradual accretion and circulation of information dug from recondite sources could help the connoisseur and intrigue the neophyte. This would also insure against accidental loss and destruction of the original material.

It was further hoped that as the program progressed and became generally recognized, the Index plates would afford artists and scholars a growing contact with works in private collections. Scholarship would also be advanced by making possible side-by-side comparison of a number of widely distributed objects.

A broader and more practical value would accrue to artist-designers and the commercial producers by whom they were employed. The need for new designs in some areas, such as printed textiles, is incessant and manufacturers who attempt to promote their products as superior from an esthetic point of view are always alert for new approaches that go beyond meaningless and superficial modification of age-old motifs. The Index would supply them not only with material having a distinct element of novelty but also some pertinence to whatever might be special about American, or pioneer, or democratic culture. It was hoped also that the designs of early hand-craftsmen, who worked directly with material and sculptural problems, might in some way help to restore a sense of authenticity in the work of industrial artists, who design more abstractly for machine production.

Potentially the greatest intangible value of this program lay in the possibility of enriching American culture by illuminating its past. The program of the Index would clearly reveal the existence of an ingenious and highly respectable tradition of genuine, spontaneous creativity early in our history. Its prompt success was hailed in *Fortune Magazine* for June 1937. Such recognition of the worth of the Index program was especially significant in view of the generally antagonistic or disdainful attitude toward the WPA/FAP taken by most of the "conservative" section of the populace reached by this publication. The article began:

One thing every sophomore knows about the tradition of American art is that there isn't any. American art is an importation. It has no roots in the depths of the American soil. It has no relation to the lives of the American people. It rests on no peasant handicrafts, no popular taste, no anonymous workmanship. It arrived ready-made from Europe. And the best of it arrived on the Ile de France within the last decade in a case marked "Picasso: use no hooks." To the sophomore, therefore, the illustrations on this and the following pages will come as something of a shock. For on this and the following seven pages are presented a few of the 7,000 renderings of early American decorative arts made by WPA's Federal Art Project and entitled The Index of American Design. They cover a period from the settlement of the country to the end of the nineteenth century. And they indicate that if the American sophomore and those who teach him both by books and by lectures have failed to find a tradition of popular art in America, the fault is not in America but in themselves.

Regarding the decay of taste in patronage of the fine arts that took place with the rise of the industrial tycoon toward the end of the 19th century, the article continues:

The popular arts, the practical arts, the arts which always must exist in a living society, whether the critics find them or not, survived and were vigorous. . . . What the Federal Art Project has done in its exploratory and memorial work is to present to the American people a few reminders of their true artistic past. . . . If the publication of the plates does not profoundly influence the work of modern American designers of articles of use, the loss will be ours, and the designers'.

A footnote explained that "WPA has not yet arranged for the publication of the plates. They will be available in museum exhibitions."

The imposing scope of these objectives inspired a vast array of skilled and informed ingenuity in bringing about the eventual program of the Index. Not all of the ideas and impulses were completely compatible, but the experience of dedicated professionals, working unhurried in pursuit of deeply felt social benefit without thought of immediate personal gain, succeeded in evolving a program that earned general respect.

Availability of artists and material suitable for the program made New York City and Boston by far the largest and most important centers of production. Since the main objective of the WPA/FAP was to get operations and employment under way as promptly as possible, work was started according to various interpretations of the few general directives that could be circulated immediately, with a minimum of "clearance" between the various regional units.

The New York unit was started under the directorship of Charles O. Cornelius, previously of the Metropolitan Museum of Art's American Wing. Conscious of the need for information to explain the images made by the artists, he set up a staff of well-informed experts to supervise selection and documentation of material in their respective categories, as well as a research section to help in collecting pertinent technical and historical information.

Early plans had envisaged the Index as a cooperative endeavor of the Federal Art Project and the Writers' Project. This did not prove feasible. At the outset, however, a group of people familiar with libraries and research was assigned from the rolls of the Writers' Project and placed under the direction of Mrs. Phyllis Crawford Scott, who had a graduate degree in librarianship from the University of Illinois and had been an editor for the H. W. Wilson Co., publishers of indexing services.

A factor, which reinforced the emphasis on research of the Index program in New York, was the limited ability of many of the artists supplied to the Index in the early days of intensive recruitment for the WPA/FAP. Interest centered in the easel and mural divisions, which drew most of the more skillful artists. Pressure from organized recipients of "home relief," as locally appropriated funds for the unemployed were called, resulted in some cases of employing underqualified personnel, who were generally assigned to the Index—Mrs. Pollak's "catch-all."

At the same time, it was possible in New York to fill the non-relief quota of supervisors with a group of specialists highly qualified in various fields of Americana, such as Helen McKearin, who with her father, George Skinner McKearin wrote several authoritative works, including *American Glass* (1941).

A natural consequence of these circumstances was the emphasis given by the New York unit to collecting significant information rather than to creating striking images. This included conscientiously digging out information for the "data sheet," which was a mimeographed form included in the original WPA/FAP manual of instructions for setting up Index units, on which was recorded pertinent factual details such as a precise description, period or date, style, original owner, where and by whom designed or made, sources of all information, and present ownership and location.

Besides filling out individual data sheets, interesting studies were made of the careers of noted craftsmen, methods of manufacture, and histories of the growth of particular industries. Some of the research workers simply went through early newspapers, copying out fashion notes and other references to the arts and crafts from the news columns and advertisements for whatever value they might eventually prove to have. In the very early days even more ambitious independent projects were undertaken by the research staff, such as a glossary of furniture terms, to be illustrated by outline drawings traced from the plates. Pictorial charts of the evolution of style in the various categories were also given considerable attention, but these efforts apparently had to be terminated before fruition.

Occasionally heads of other divisions would ask me to have my research staff "look up" something for them. Girolamo Piccoli, head of the sculpture division, indicated he often received requests for portrait busts to be allocated for use in schools, libraries, and hospitals—usually of individuals the institutions were named after. When they just wanted to fill a niche, he hated to be forced to pick out just another general or politician. I talked it over with Scott Williamson, then in charge of the research group, and within a few weeks we had a list of one hundred historically significant individuals and a reference to some sort of pictorial image for each. A little pamphlet was mimeographed and stapled inside a tasteful cover that the poster division had printed in color by the silk-screen process. It was used in promoting the allocation of sculpture.

Partly because of the uneven level of ability among the artists, it was felt advisable to attempt only simple, flat, almost diagrammatic drawings, which actually were deemed preferable by those dealers and collectors who felt more complete representation might serve for the manufacture of fake antiques.

Another consideration that tended to keep the plates of the New York unit as simple as possible was the greater facility of reproducing such designs by some sort of *pochoir* or stencil process that would be less costly than the highly efficient modern methods of photomechanical reproduction. Whereas no funds were available for such expenditures, the New York Project did have the poster division's silk-screen set-up. This process, requiring relatively simple equipment and depending mostly on labor, could have been enlarged to reproduce some of the Index material.

In her original proposals for the Index, Miss Reeves, who served for a time in supervisory and consultant capacities both in Washington and New York, frequently referred to the noted French publication, Racinet's *L'Ornement polychrome*, published in Paris between 1869 and 1873, in which a vast number of motifs from designs of the past are reproduced as flat patterns with little or no reference to the nature or modeling of the articles on which they originally appeared. The silk-screen medium was used later to produce a portfolio of such designs from plates illustrating the "Pennsylvania Dutch" style. In general, however, the process was inadequate for the higher quality eventually achieved in Index plates.

Superior interest and ability were found in the representational quality of the plates in Boston, which was the other large center of production in the nationwide program of the Index. Suzanne Chapman, a staff member of the Boston Museum, was loaned to the Index to develop a uniform, accurate and, at the same time, attractive style of rendering. According to Mr. Cahill's introduction cited previously, she had learned the methods of accurate representation that had been taught for many years at the Boston Museum School by Demman Ross. Joseph Lindon Smith had used these methods for making records of archeological finds on the Museum's Egyptian expeditions, where photographic equipment was unavailable or inefficient.

Miss Chapman wrote the first technical manual for the Index, issued several months after the program had got under way. Artists in New England were trained from the beginning to create accurate, handsome representations, which were larger than those first made in New York.

A procedure was developed, for example, of laying a lightly dampened sheet of blotting paper under a water color drawing so that washes would not dry too quickly. This resulted in softening the edges and giving a truly textural feeling to pictures of woven and embroidered materials. Early development of the textile industry in New England, as well as the widespread practice of domestic manufacture of hooked rugs, crewel embroidery, patchwork quilts and other needlework, made these categories an important resource of the Boston unit.

After the Project had been under way for about a year or so, Holger Cahill made a nation-wide tour to inspect the progress of operations. Among the things he noticed was the contrast in emphasis between the two major units of the Index, and he decided that the program might be enhanced by recognition of both of their divergent emphases. Consequently, he stimulated more serious use of the "data sheet" in Massachusetts, affirming the importance of fully establishing the historical and technical background of each object. An exhibition of plates from New England was sent to New York to promote development of a more handsome and completely accurate style of rendering, and Miss Ingrid Selma-Larsen of the Boston staff spent several weeks in New York to offer what suggestions she could. Some of the New York people became disaffected in the fear that this meant a desertion of their carefully built standards of scholarship, but this did not ensue.

An attempt was made to find a supervisor in New York capable of instructing artists in the methods of superior representation and coaching them throughout the process. James McCreery was selected to serve as "technical supervisor" with this responsibility. He had earned an architectural degree from the University of California at a time when such training heavily emphasized draftsmanship and techniques for attractively "rendering" the designs, as well as exhaustive copying of noted models from the past. Arriving in New York at the outset of the Depression, Mr. McCreery had found employment in an architectural office unobtainable, but he was able to expand his technical skills to create some opportunity in book illustration. With the establishment of the WPA/FAP he was on the relief rolls and wound up as an Index artist. When the push came for improvement of "style" in the New York unit, his skill as well as his ability to help other artists was recognized. He was later assisted by Ernest Busenbark, one of the authors of a book on silk screen printing, and Peter Larsen, the technical supervisor for metalwork.

The New York unit finally achieved a high standard in all phases of presentation. Although nothing was sacrificed in the way of accuracy in order to enhance the picturesque quality of the objects represented or the attractiveness of the plates, the unstinted pressure for solidity and texture as well as correctness of structure and detail achieved a high esthetic quality. The following is a description of the various steps:

Material was picked in accordance with an editorial program based in part on practical considerations of concentrating available personnel to develop a few areas in depth. Expert supervision was needed for the fields covered, and special effort was made locally to present the most typical objects or designs of the region. In New York, however, the wealth of material in the museums and other collections expanded the coverage beyond these limitations.

The chief editorial prescription was to select handwork made before 1870 that was not predominantly imitative of European sources. An exception to this date was a special survey of Victoriana, which was also the only area in which assemblies of objects were shown. Perkins Harnley, a specially gifted artist, did amusing views of a Pullman diner and an ornate stable as well as more ordinary interiors.

Objects were assigned insofar as possible according to the skill or special aptitudes of particular artists, each of whom was visited by his supervisor several times in the course of the plate's development to insure adequate representation of the most significant points. Meanwhile a data sheet to be attached to the finished plate was worked up. Eventually the roster of artists stabilized at about 150 but this was gradually decreased in succeeding quota cuts.

Artists were generally assigned where facilities for work were available, such as the Brooklyn Museum, the Metropolitan's American Wing, the Museum of the City of New York, and the New-York Historical Society. Studio equipment was set up at Project headquarters for about two dozen artists, who worked from small objects that could be borrowed from private collectors, or from the few types that could be done from photographs, such as ironwork. A few artists worked in their own studios.

All artists had to be available at definitely scheduled hours in the proper location, both for visits from the supervisors and for random "spot checks" by the Project timekeepers. At the beginning of each week, all of the artists were required to report to headquarters with their work for a group criticism by the technical supervisor. He also visited as many artists as possible each week at their "field" locations for coaching on their particular problems.

Each plate was given a completion period according to the estimated difficulty of execution. The range was from two to six weeks; but brief extensions, usually of a week or less, were allowed, and some very difficult pieces required eight to ten weeks. The artists in New York were paid the top WPA "professional" rate of $23.50 per week. Negotiations with the Artists' Union arrived at fifteen hours as reasonable performance for this amount.

An artist worked consistently on objects in the same category. Consequently each supervisor became familiar with the skills of his staff and their most effective application, while the artists' abilities grew with repeated handling of the same material.

Although early prospectuses for setting up local Index units repeatedly prescribed use of photography to record objects for which it might be considered "most suitable," this practice was never developed to any great extent. Color was considered a problem in photography, especially since the Index was designed as a permanent reference. For a time silverware was rendered photographically in New York, but even this was discontinued as the skills of the staff developed.

Photographs were occasionally made as a guide for artists where it was not possible for them to spend full time with the object or where special technical problems were involved as in the area of architectural interiors. This work was discontinued in the early days of the program when it was judged on a higher administrative level to duplicate the efforts of the Historic American Buildings Survey which used unemployed architects to make measured drawings of structures in this category.

Those who are not familiar with creative practice often inquire wonderingly, "How did an artist make an Index plate?" as though it were simply a matter of mastering some quasimagical formula. Of course, there was no such procedure. A successful Index artist had to be familiar with a range of methods and materials generated by the tradition of factual rendering. Transparent watercolor was most generally used, but opaque or "gouache" proved superior for certain materials, and pencil was sometimes used where color was not involved, especially in castiron objects like trivets and some lighting devices.

Careful manual application by brush was the standard, but highly effective textural effects could be produced, for example, in the case of the rougher ceramics, like stoneware, by judicious application of "spatter." The "wet blotter" technique described previously, was sometimes used to achieve a softness of outline appropriate for textiles and embroidery. Many artists used devices they had picked up or developed as the result of their own particular training or experience. The only touchstone was persistent application under knowing and sympathetic supervision, until the desired result was attained.

One unusual method mentioned in the manual but little used, was developed by Mr. McCreery, who demonstrated its special value in rendering several types of objects. Chinese ink is made in small tablets, the surface of which must be ground with water to produce a highly transparent, somewhat warm black. It was found to be subject to precise control for rendering smooth objects with delicately modulated surface tonalities, like glassware and silver. It also possesses the valuable property of drying harder than gum water colors, hence the need for grinding. For complex objects like costumes, it could therefore be

FIGURE 34. An Index plate of a combination crimping and flatiron is begun with a pencil drawing.

FIGURE 35. An Index artist makes color notes to be used in creating a plate of this antique.

FIGURE 36. Artists in Project studio complete Index plates from drawings and color notes or from the original object—here antique toys and wallpaper—loaned by private owners, dealers or museums.

FIGURE 37. An early American stoneware jug poses for its portrait.

FIGURE 38. An Index artist making a careful watercolor rendering of a spirited 19th-century weathervane.

FIGURE 39. Finished plates are inspected by a committee of Index supervisors before being catalogued. (Figures 34–39 in Holger Cahill Papers, files of Federal Support for the Visual Arts: The New Deal and Now, Library, National Collection of Fine Arts)

used to develop the drawing and modeling of an object in a careful "under-painting" before getting involved with color.

No face masks or long white garments appeared in my "office" after lunch on Thursdays, no scalpels or forceps, but in essence it was similar to the obstetrical room of a hospital. For the delivery of an Index plate after a period of gestation lasting from two to six weeks was no simple matter.

There were few private offices at Federal Art Project headquarters, but the "dog leg" space assigned to the Index at 110 King Street was divided into sections, my desk and those of the field supervisors being in the narrow, windowless part. In the wide section, two or three dozen studio taborets and stools were lined up in several ranks in front of the continuous high windows facing north, for artists who worked on the premises. Between these two areas, getting some outdoor light but farther from the windows, was the clerical and storage section, where Tillie Shahn (who had been married to the noted artist Ben Shahn) presided over a group of girls typing data sheets and otherwise grooming the not inconsiderable quantity of records characteristic of government operations, that had to be kept and transmitted.

One after another the supervisors entered, solicitously depositing small stacks of drawings on their desks, and when the whole group was present someone would begin. "This came up last week and James [McCreery, in charge of technical supervision] thought the folds of the skirt could be made to look more substantial." "How about it, James?" "It's fine now. She is one of our best costume people and I think that was just an oversight." "Everybody agree?" Murmurs of approval and nodding of heads. "O.K. Tillie, it's all yours." "Where's the data sheet?" "Oh, yes. Here it is in my briefcase."

Another plate goes up on the easel for all to see. "Now this one has had its full six weeks, but I'm not too sure about it. Everything is perfectly correct, and yet it doesn't really look like an 'Index plate.' Could he do any better with an extension, James?" "Definitely. Those ruffled collars take a lot of time, and there is that detailed textile pattern to fuss with, too. I'd give him two weeks more." Two other costume plates were admiringly accepted and Dotty Mazo said "That's all I have this week."

"I get all the lemons," complained peppery Peter Larsen. "I can't do anything with this new guy at all. Look at that!" He thrust forward a drawing of a simple cast iron trivet along with the photograph from which it had been made. Not only was adequate accuracy wanting, but the margins were smeared with graphite from the pencils used for rendering this type of object. "I could clean it up, but it still wouldn't be right." "I don't think we should waste too much time on this man," Mrs. Shahn broke in. "He wants to get in the mural division, and they have accepted him, but their quota is full for the time being. Personnel doesn't realize how much our standards have changed from the early days. I'll check with them and see if he can't be placed elsewhere until the spot opens up on the mural division."

Peter next showed an early rushlight holder, and Helen McKearin, who also did lighting devices in her glassware section, said "It's beautifully drawn, Peter, but how about the metal quality? It's hard to tell just what material it is." Larsen, the metalwork expert, said "I can touch up those highlights with an eraser —that's all it needs." "We let the artists sign their own plates for a reason," Tillie objected, "and I don't think we should work on them at all"; but Peter had a way of insisting. "I never do much. Anyway, he's already started on another plate and I wouldn't want to break his stride for a little thing like that." "Well, bring it in again next week, and if it needs more than you think, you'd better give it back to the artist, anyway."

Tillie turned over a plate of a handsome stoneware jug that was enthusiastically accepted, and again demanded the missing data sheet. "I just want to check that date, but I was too rushed when I was at the New-York Historical Society yesterday." Carolyn Scoon apologized. "I'll have it for you before you get the plate photographed and cellophaned." And so it went, for an hour or two, until the current production had been reviewed. "Before we break," I said after the last assignment had been discussed, "a few administrative matters should be brought to your attention. You might like to know that a group of Index plates representing cast iron banks will be shown along with a few actual pieces Peter was able to borrow, starting Monday for three weeks at a Fifth Avenue bank, and Tillie is busy getting labels typed for the large Index show that will be hung at the New York World's Fair. Now—the personnel division has finally worked out the new quotas that have been assigned to New York, following reduction of the appropriation passed by Congress last month, and the Index will lose six artists, two clerical workers or research people, and one from our non-relief quota. During the past month two artists have left for jobs in private industry, a secretary is getting married next week, and you can inquire around to see if any others are leaving soon so we can avoid giving out any more pink slips than we need to. I'm afraid Dottie is the only non-relief person we still have except me, so I don't see how we can save her. We'll just have to phase out the Costume unit, and Esther Lewittes will take over what has to be done in the area, along with her work on textiles. Sorry we have to end on this sour note. Is there anything else? See you all next week."

Mrs. Shahn carried the stack of accepted plates back to her recording and storage center, added a serial accessions number to each data sheet and handed the various items around to those of her staff who would be working on them for the next week.

Accepted plates were matted, covered with a protective sheet of acetate, and filed with a data sheet attached to the back. A master file of data sheets was compiled separately, and a copy sent to the national office in Washington. Photographs of each plate were made for purposes of record.

As they carefully wrapped up those plates that were to be referred back to their artists, the supervisors hob-nobbed for a bit, as it was likely to be the only time during the week when they would see one another. Shifts in artists' locations were reported to Mrs. Shahn so that no errors would occur in the spot checks made by the timekeepers of the personnel division. Supervisors with the most far-flung groups checked with Joe Cleary, who drove a Project car assigned to the Index, so they could be sure of their transportation schedules. And so another infant batch of Index plates was born.

Two interrelated questions were frequently asked about plates produced for the Index. Can they be thought of in any way as "works of art" and "is anything gained by the lengthy individual effort applied to each plate beyond what photography might produce in a fraction of the time?"

It is notorious that the highest levels of technical facility do not always produce the greatest artistic satisfaction. An obvious example is the relative esthetic value of a still-life by Chardin as compared with a slick, highly detailed job by a 17th- or 18th-century Dutch still-life specialist, or the simple strength of a Breughel compared with the exhaustive fussiness of a 19th-century romanticist.

Therefore, there is obviously a *degree* of cultural advancement or sophistication in the enjoyment of recognition in art, and there is an *element* of art in a recognizable image that goes beyond mere technical accomplishment. No attempt will be made here to evaluate these two factors in relation to what may be presented in more consciously "creative" works of art. After all, the precise purpose of an Index plate eliminates some of the usual elements of a major creation. No representation of space is involved, except what is implied by the always well established solidity of the object. There is no "composition" or spatial relation of objects to one another since each plate concentrates on a single object. The classification of "art," however, is accorded many kinds of work with intentionally limited scope, like a line drawing or a black and white print; in literature, a sonnet, a couplet, or a *haiku* are considered "poetry"; in music, a sonata or an étude may appear on a concert program. All of these are certainly reduced in scope from an oil painting or a mural, a novel, a play or an epic poem, an opera or a symphony. Yet they are classified as "works of art."

The great oversight in discounting the exciting sense of actuality that may be found in a precise image, even as simply composed as an Index plate, is due to the fallacy that a work of art appeals only to the sense by which it enters consciousness. It would be ridiculous to eliminate rhythm from the analysis or evaluation of a musical composition; yet it has nothing to do with the ear, but appeals to the muscular or "kinesthetic" sense of motion.

Likewise the sense of mass that may be conveyed by a plastic image has nothing to do with values appealing to the retina, which are only light and color. It is the subtle and satisfying contribution of the artist that *brings out* the muscular intuitions of shape and weight in an object by subtle modifications of the purely visual image. Cézanne stated that this was his major objective. Even sculptors must make a special effort to achieve it, and the esthetic inferiority of much academic sculpture from the 19th century is due to dependence on structural formulae that failed to take into account the special attention needed to achieve a true sense of bulk, or to the opposite concern with surface considerations of interesting "play" of light and shade, somewhat as in impressionist painting.

The divergence of "tactile" and "optic" reality—recognizability to the hand or to the eye—becomes most obvious in the attempt to make an accurate, convincing representation of a *shiny* object. A glossy or highly polished metal surface reflects highlights of such a degree of complexity, especially in a well-lighted room, that virtually all sense of form is lost in a visually accurate image, even or especially in a photograph. Use of photography for accurate, commercial illustration of products as in a catalogue, involves a considerable amount of retouching, mainly to eliminate or simplify the highlights.

There are also other less obvious modifications, however, that an artist can make in the drawing of an object to bring out its shape. They cannot be formulated, and depend entirely on working toward a "sense" of the desired suggestion of plastic and structural reality. This is true also in respect to the textural quality. Index artists became so skilled in representation of textiles and embroidery that people seeing plates of such material in exhibitions frequently asked, "Is that a piece of cloth or a painting?", even expressing tentative indignation "if a beautiful antique was cut up like that!"

Although artists in other divisions had a condescending attitude toward Index work, and an occasional newcomer considered it a sort of "holding pattern" until an opening occurred for his transfer to the easel or mural division, the main body of Index artists unquestionably felt they were doing a creative job. This may be accounted for in two ways. Many of the artists assigned to this work were older people trained according to earlier standards, often under arduous discipline required abroad as the basis for all artistic crafts. These artists actually felt the finish and achievement of clear, objective standards of which they were capable was *superior* to the appearance of arbitrary, subjective, hit-or-miss character of work that is apt arbitrarily to be called "more creative."

The younger artists, without this sort of indoctrination, who stuck with the Index, were doubtless inspired by excellent morale within the division resulting from deep conviction among the supervisory staff that an important job was being done. Good work was desired, demanded, and recognized; adequate help was given, and these artists appreciated the value of such experience, both emotional and technical.

No precise plan for publishing the Index was enunciated at the outset. Various people had their own private views, and it became increasingly obvious that some form of multiple issue would be needed. Modern photochemical reproduction in color was the ideal, but other means were considered since no funds were available for the amount of initial investment this would have required.

In a letter of April 13, 1936 Mr. Cahill anticipated plans of publishing the Index in a series of lithographs by artists of the graphic division and printed on the hand-operated equipment which they regularly used! Jacob Baker who was then Harry Hopkins' deputy in Washington, asked Cahill in a letter dated March 24, 1936, about publication of the Index folio on Shaker products, the imminence of which he seems to have already announced, raising questions of editorial pattern that also had to be ironed out.

Because of the quantity of material available, and the desirability of presenting it in as great detail as possible both for the antiquarian and the designer, an encyclopedic series of volumes was felt necessary. It was generally thought that each of these would present a complete historical survey of a given category, such as Costume, Furniture, or Glassware. Although hopeful enthusiasm convinced the staff that one category or another was "nearly ready" for publication in the early days of the program, the problems of financing and editorial policy managed to defer actual production. Nothing had been published by the New York unit when the WPA program was suspended in the "Arsenal of Democracy" period just prior to the United States' entry into World War II.

The WPA was inaugurated primarily to solve the unemployment problem by putting people to work. Hence strict limitations on the amount of money that could be spent for materials or labor that was not actually on the relief rolls were written into the basic legislation. The staff of the Index thought at one point of getting some kind of subvention from private philanthropy, but the large foundations were hesitant, partly because the WPA/FAP was regarded generally as an emergency, hence temporary, measure. Questions of the authoritative character of the work would have to be satisfied with a time-consuming investigation; and there was definite resistance among the wealthy toward dispensing their largesse in areas presumably being "taken care of" by the government.

Widespread approval of the Index encouraged belief that publication could be made self-supporting "eventually," at least in respect to costs of reproduction.

It was obvious, however, that the initial investment needed for an encyclopedic series of bound volumes consisting largely of full-page, four-color plates, would be astronomical, even if the volumes were published singly at fairly long intervals. The price would have to have been fixed at a point which would have distorted the ideal pattern of distribution by precluding ownership of the volumes where most needed. The prospect was so discouraging that no actual calculation was ever made.

Problems of editorial plan and authenticity were equally inhibiting. The question of finality was one of the most serious. A monumental production would have to be authoritatively complete, to a degree substantially surpassing good handbooks available in many of the categories. Since every last object could not be included, perhaps not even known to exist at any given point, what would be "enough" and who would decide?

When the supervisors of the New York unit began to think a given category was "almost ready" for publication, work in that area would be favored. In fact, one of the earliest directories set up an editorial pattern under which "starting with Costume, the earliest century will be completely recorded!" Completion seemed to offer no problem, but it soon became evident that practical conditions such as availability and location of the material required other priorities.

The question of possible criticism from outside authorities on the editorial selection loomed on the distant horizon. Would the judgment of the staff be acceptable? Could it withstand criticism that might be inspired by the self-interest or emotional attachments of dealers and collectors? Might it not be advisable to secure in advance the approval of some sort of editorial council or advisory board from the official world of museums, publications, and other pertinent institutions? Might practical limitations engender rivalry among regions and categories within the Project for priorities in the schedule of publication?

Reference to an encyclopedic series of volumes on separate categories might be the most efficient procedure for factual research and comparison by experts. It might, however, prove inflexible and less handy for the designer or for the research worker interested in cross-reference to set up a view of a given period or locality, for example, and the size of illustrations would have to be reduced.

Even moderate public use over a period of time involves gradual or accidental deterioration. Repair or replacement of a complete volume in the event of serious damage would be difficult or excessively costly for small institutions.

Following my appointment as director, the New York unit began to work on plans for a more flexible manner of publication, which I conceived, in order to avoid the problems attached to producing an encyclopedic series of comprehensive volumes. In brief, I envisaged gradual release of reproductions of the plates in loose leaf folios averaging about twenty items at quarterly or more frequent intervals, which would be distributed by annual subscription.

Besides the standard Index "data sheet," printed on the back of each reproduction, each folio would present a narrative introductory text giving important
and interesting information on the particular area, period, and group of objects
reflected in the subjects selected. Considerable progress was made in developing
a cataloguing system whereby an ordinal letter-digit-decimal combination would
produce a number classifying each plate according to period, category, and type
of object, so that a cumulative reference file could be built up in which any
cross-section would be readily available. The file numbers assigned when Index
plates were sent to Washington was more like an accession number, giving the
region and category, but beyond that simply the order in which it had been
received. The categories established were Carving (CA), Ceramics (CER), Costume (CO), Furniture (FU), Glassware (GL), Metalwork (ME), Textiles (TE) including floor coverings, and Miscellaneous (MSCL). Provision was made for
breaking these categories down a bit further as for example Iron (ME-I), Brass
(ME-BR), Toys (MSCL-T), Dolls (MSCL-D).

The editorial problem of selection is immeasurably simplified by gradual
release of the material according to this plan. From the impossible challenge
of complete coverage, even of the outstanding monuments in any given field,
and of determining which they are, the requirement shifts simply to selection of
an interesting group of good plates. Yet the ideal of an exhaustive corpus is never
relinquished.

The financial problem likewise is virtually eliminated, because low unit cost
and increased serviceability could probably make the operation self-supporting
in this form.

An encyclopedic form of publication, besides reducing the number of agencies that could afford it, would undoubtedly limit the value of the Index to use
as a static source of reference for those experts familiar with its existence and
availability at some large, nearby institution. The dynamics of its appearance at
periodic intervals, on the other hand, would facilitate more intimate contacts,
even with a wide, previously uninformed public. Each folio received by a sub-
scribing agency then becomes material for a small, easily mounted exhibition,
before being filed permanently for reference, where the plates would still be
available for later exhibitions. Collectors, writers, artists, designers, and re-
searchers would find the feasibility of spreading out a particular selection of
individual plates for side-by-side observation a convenience immeasurably superior to a heavy, bound format. New editions of any given folio might be made
available for replacement in the event of physical deterioration as well as for
unit sales of especially popular subjects, and upon exhaustion could be reprinted
without incurring the great cost of an entire volume. Unfortunately, it was never
possible to realize this plan.

There are approximately 23,000 Index plates. The entire collection cost the WPA/FAP approximately $2,000,000 or an average of $88 per plate. Widespread enthusiasm for the Index program throughout the country during the 1930s made the preservation and continued accessibility of the plates mandatory when the program ended.

After liquidation of the WPA/FAP the Index eventually found its way to the National Gallery of Art, where it was set up as a separate department under Erwin O. Christensen. During the thirteen years of his curatorship, from 1945 to 1958, 3,800 people or an average of 300 a year used Index material at the gallery.

The present curator, Grose Evans, has an assistant and a secretary. Some help in handling the material is rendered by the extension service of the National Gallery. Under the circumstances, the use that can be made of Index material is far less than might occur if more extensive facilities were available. The record, however, of public response to the opportunities offered gives a clear indication of wide general interest.

The greatest amount of contact with the material has been afforded by means of circulating exhibitions and slide lectures. A small catalogue lists thirty selections of from twenty to seventy-five plates on various subjects, such as Shaker craftsmanship, the art of the Spanish Southwest, Ironwork, and Costume. They are assembled in specially prepared cases for shipment on loan to institutions. The extension service of the gallery offers sets of slides complete with notes on fields covered by the Index. Besides these slide lectures, 37,000 slides were made at the outset of the program at the gallery for permanent allocation in 684 sets to seventy-five institutions such as museums, colleges, and libraries; 375 sets were sent to U.S. Information Agency offices abroad.

Widespread interest in the fields covered by the Index is indicated by the increasing volume in all types of use since it began to function as a department at the gallery. The report for 1968 fiscal year gives the figures of 74 exhibitions and 154 sets of slides loaned and 371 individuals who personally consulted the collection. This record is achieved with a minimum of publicity.

An attempt to complete the Index should be made. In sixteen states no artists at all were employed to work on the Index program. In a recent memorandum, the figure cited by Dr. Evans is nineteen, probably because of the negligible quantity and quality of work done in three of the states represented. Even in those states in which acceptable work was produced, the available staff was not always sufficient for adequate coverage, and quality varies. Termination of the program blocked plans for proper coverage of various fields even in areas where the quality of work and supervision was adequate.

Two approaches have been suggested for "completion" of the Index. Mr. Christensen projected virtually full revival of the program based on employment of 200 artists in various centers, with an annual budget running well over a million dollars. He also suggested a more modest plan which was revised by Dr. Evans in a memorandum dated December 1964. It provides for a sort of "flying squandron" of three artists, each producing approximately ten plates per year, to be sent into regions or assigned to those subjects deemed most deficient in presentation of crucial material.

While this is a quite necessary stage for publication in the form of comprehensive bound volumes, the idea of completion could reasonably be deferred under the serial of publication developed in the New York unit as described above. A series of small, cohesive subjects would suffice until nearly all the plates of publishable quality are used. After a period of not less than five, and possibly ten years, the subscription list might develop to the point where funds to employ a minimum staff of artists might become available.

The widespread acceptance of the Index in educational and professional fields, as well as by the general public, emphasizes the necessity for finding some effective means to publish, and eventually to complete, this unique pictorial survey of American design.[1]

---

1. Since this memoir was written in 1968 it has been learned that Harry N. Abrams, Inc. will publish in the fall of 1972 a selection of about 900 Index plates in a book by Clarence P. Hornung titled *Treasury of American Design.*

PART 3

THE NEW DEAL ART PROJECTS
AND RELATED EVENTS

Artists' Organizations of the Depression Decade

LINCOLN ROTHSCHILD

Historical Background

The Depression represented a temporary setback in the rapid expansion of American industry, which greatly altered economic and social orientations in all walks of life. For the artist, paradoxically, new vistas were opened with indigence. In fact, a completely new concept of his professional role burst upon his horizon.

All artists, to be sure, were not affected in the same degree, but for a time so many were forced by circumstances into a pattern of mutual interest and dependence on the general resources of the community, that a new dimension was added to the function of creating paintings and sculpture. In a sense, its ancient dignity was restored.

The problem of personal welfare in the Depression so far exceeded the capacity of standard charitable organizations of a laissez-faire society, that a new concept of community responsibility arose. The degradation of the charity "hand-out," which had seemed to provide adequate social hygiene in the past, could not be inflicted on skilled craftsmen and experienced executives who were unemployed through no fault of their own.

Local governments and finally the national administration, felt the responsibility of providing gainful occupation for the unfortunate, as that term lost its derogatory connotation. Various operations were undertaken to employ them at jobs conceived to approximate as closely as possible the type of work for which they had been trained. For many artists, such integration with systematic patterns of production and remuneration represented a new way of life, or revived a long-forgotten function of contributing to the community in a substantial and responsible capacity.

198

In the earlier decades of the century, American artists had more inbred and parochial concerns. Opportunities to exhibit and to be free from the prejudices of the Academy and big museums, led to such organizations as the Society of Independent Artists (established 1917). Artists also banded together in the American Society of Painters, Sculptors, and Gravers, better known as the "Painter-Gravers" (established 1919), the Whitney Studio Club (whose origins go back to 1908 and which later became the Whitney Museum of American Art) and An American Group (established 1931). Typical of the artists' concerns was the "rental issue" which demanded that museums and major exhibitions pay fees to the artists showing in them. Muralists, sculptors, and printmakers also organized to promote their specific professional interests. With the onset of the Depression, however, other concerns began to dominate artists and new groups were founded.

Symptomatic of the crisis, perhaps, was the establishment of John Reed clubs throughout the country in 1930. Named after the author of *Ten Days That Shook the World*—an eloquent, eyewitness account of the Russian Revolution written in 1919—they were radical in outlook and composed mostly of Marxist orientated writers, though they had visual artists among their members and ran an art school in New York City for a time. Their cultural interests were generally focused on the "viewpoint of the new working class."

The two largest of the new organizations founded by the visual artists were primarily concerned with working out their newly felt relationship with the community in general and dealing with a single, powerful government employer in particular. To oversimplify the picture somewhat, the Artists' Union (later called the United American Artists) was primarily concerned with the second objective, negotiating with the federal administration on conditions of work, remuneration, schedule, and other such day-to-day problems; the American Artists' Congress applied itself to a somewhat broader and less specific program of cultural and professional growth.

The Artists' Union

Hampered by inexperience and inadequate resources, the various public agencies that attempted to fill the gap in employment were bound to make repeated mistakes of omission and commission, even when their intentions were of the best, which was not always the case. In New York City, Mayor Fiorello H. LaGuardia was highly sympathetic, but could not always get necessary funds from his city council. Son of a U.S. Army band leader, he was interested in cultural activity, and responsive to the plea of artists that they be included in his work relief programs.

The inevitable sense of being inconsiderately whip-sawed from hope to disappointment in a series of inadequate, experimental, impermanent and sometimes callously handled operations, gradually forced artists to join with one another to procure and protect some means of livelihood, and so fundamental a concern aroused great emotional force. The magazine *Art Front*, which was published by the Artists' Union and the Artists Committee for Action, reports, for example, that on September 24, 1933, twenty-five artists "threatened by discontinuance of the first white collar and professional Emergency Work Bureau . . . organized the E.W.B. Artists Group." This unwieldy name was changed to "Unemployed Artists Group" as their horizons broadened beyond the municipal scene.

They petitioned Harry Hopkins, who was President Roosevelt's close adviser in charge of the nation's welfare activities, and he set up the Public Works of Art Project (PWAP) to employ artists on creative assignments. The PWAP varied considerably from one area to another. Artists were employed at tasks calculated to last from one to six months at salaries ranging from $27.00 to $38.25 for a 30-hour week. As the agency closest to the living American artist, the Whitney Museum of which Mrs. Juliana Force was then director, was entrusted with local administration of this program in New York City. The Project lapsed after about six months.

Encouraged by recognition of their joint pressure, the artists' groups joined together in the Artists' Committee of Action, which spawned and then faded into the Artists' Union. Several demonstrations were held at the Whitney Museum to emphasize the limited scope of the PWAP and gain recognition of the vastly greater need. The Project was caught in an uncomfortable cross-fire from right and left when it was discovered that jobs were given to several well-known artists. The Union said, "They cannot need jobs as much as our members," while opponents of public expenditures for welfare and anti-administration politicians said, "These people do not need relief. It's just plunder of public funds!"

Lloyd Goodrich, later director of the Whitney Museum, who had been working there under a research grant, was placed in charge of operating the PWAP program as Mrs. Force's representative. He tells a very illuminating story about John Sloan, one of the leading American painters of the first half of the twentieth century. An important New York daily learned that he was employed by the PWAP and sent a reporter to get him to justify his need, presumably in the hope of exposing scandalous malfeasance.

Sloan invited the reporter into his studio, waved a hand toward racks of numerous canvases and said, "Here is virtually my entire life's work. I have *never* made a living from the sale of my creative art!" Newspaper illustration (before the days of high speed photography), poster design, and teaching had been his means of livelihood. "Give me an income of $50.00 a week, guaranteed for the rest of my life so I can paint, and you can have the lot of it!"

Despite herculean efforts to get federal programs for employment under way, mostly on large construction projects which required lengthy periods of negotiation and planning, the unemployment problem did not recede, and the New Deal administration decided that federal funds must be placed more quickly and more directly into the hands of the needy unemployed. The Works Progress Administration was set up to hire people certified locally as in need, on any project not provided in the regular budget of a tax-supported agency that would request, plan, and supervise it. The federal government undertook to meet the payroll, while the local community supplied the cost of materials.

By January 1935 the Artists' Union had begun agitating for a "Federal Art Bill" to set up a national department of fine arts. Artists' unions had begun to function in several large cities, notably Baltimore, Chicago, Cleveland, and St. Louis. As a consequence of such pressures, special provisions were made for the employment of artists, as well as actors, musicians, and writers, under the WPA program.

Thus the employment pattern was stabilized to a degree, but the quantity fluctuated on an annual, appropriation-to-appropriation basis. Project rolls quickly reached a national figure for the WPA/FAP in the neighborhood of 5,000, but they were reduced by annual cuts of sizable proportions. Under these conditions, the Artists' Union settled into a regular pattern as collective bargaining agent for Project employees. Regular meetings with the grievance committee of the union were held by Mrs. McMahon or members of her immediate executive staff, and occasionally with heads of various departments. Sufficiently important adjustments of policy might call for a picket line of several hours' duration, not to cut down operations but to publicize the issue.

The Artists' Union however, also stood ready to endorse and actively support other activities connected less immediately with the personal welfare of its members. For example, a campaign was undertaken to protest a jury's rejection of *all* the designs submitted for murals in the Department of Justice Building in a nationwide competition conducted by the Section. A Municipal Art Gallery to exhibit works by artists who had no representation with regular dealers, which had long been sought by artists' organizations, was opened by Mayor LaGuardia on January 6, 1936. The union raised several questions, and opposed the requirement that exhibitors be limited to citizens of the United States.

Organizational activity of various sorts engaged the union's attention. It consulted with organized workers on other WPA projects through the City Projects Council. Attempts were made to organize non-Project artists in a commercial artists' section, and to gain recognition from the labor movement. Applications for charters were made to the AFL in July 1935, and to the CIO in January 1937. A national conference of artists' unions, then numbering about twelve, was held in Baltimore, Maryland, on January 16, 1937. In December 1937 the Artists'

Union received a charter from the CIO as Local 60 of the United Office and Professional Workers of America and changed its name to United American Artists.

Standard trade union negotiations of individual grievances and general working conditions were supplemented in two areas. One was agitation to keep the job in existence. The other was promotion of a broadened response to art that would give the artist a deeper and more extensive relation to the life of the community. Holger Cahill, national director of the WPA/FAP, pointed out that American artists had suffered a "permanent depression" long before the unemployment emergency struck. He carefully documented this statement in the introduction to an exhibition of Project work throughout the nation after its first year of operation, held under the very apt title of "New Horizons in American Art" at New York's Museum of Modern Art in 1936. Beyond the purpose merely of creating work for artists in temporary financial need, he and many others saw in the Federal Art Project an opportunity to illuminate and promote the artist's role in the life of his time—a role his predecessors had in other ages. Since it could not be predicted whether this exciting prospect was to be achieved by means of a permanent government agency or simply through recognition by the artists and the community of their respective needs and interdependence, the Artists' Union worked toward both these ends.

The first of the two objectives necessitated extensive campaigns for renewal each year of the Congressional appropriation for the WPA and maintenance of the "quota" assigned to the arts. Emergence of "industrial unionism" about this time, with massive and often violent demonstrations, including use of the new "sit-down strike," inspired similar militancy in the ranks of the Artists' Union. Massive, raucous picket lines were routine, and a few sit-in demonstrations were staged at Project headquarters.

On one occasion Harold Stein, then New York representative of Federal Project No. 1, was held captive in his office overnight. Considerable violence by the police was reported in the arrest of 219 members of the Artists' Union who had invaded Mrs. McMahon's office on November 29, 1936 in protest against cuts that had been announced following reduction in the appropriation. On this occasion, Mayor LaGuardia went to Washington to appeal for restoration of the funds.

The union also applied considerable effort toward inspiring public recognition of more important roles artists might play in the life of the community. Support was given to legislative campaigns for establishing a federal department of fine arts with cabinet status. This centered mostly around a bill introduced in Congress by Senator Pepper and Congressman Coffee, which provided virtually for permanent continuance of the federal art program. The Public Use of Art Committee was formed to promote expanded use of art by other agencies. The

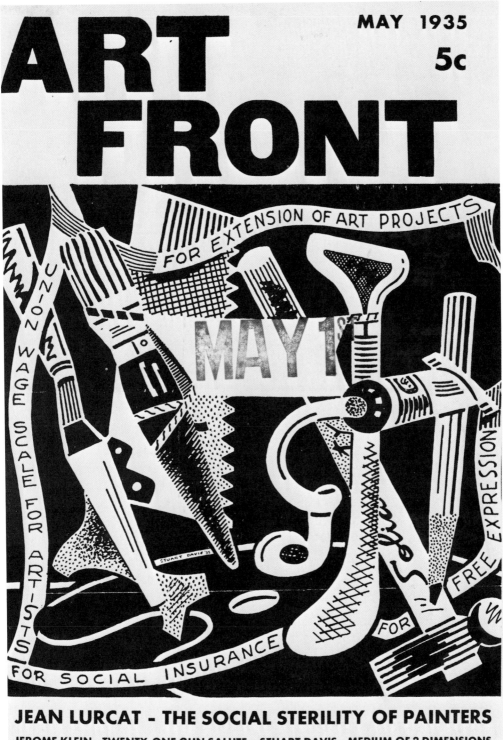

FIGURE 40.   Stuart Davis (1894–1964). Cover design for *Art Front*, May 1935. (Courtesy of Robert B. Hunter)

most spectacular proposal of this group, backed up by an active promotional campaign, was for thorough-going decoration of the New York City subways with murals and sculpture.

Perhaps the most interesting activity pursued by the Artists' Union to advance a new understanding of art as a vital medium for expression of the entire community, rather than simply its more privileged sections, was publication of the magazine *Art Front*. Appearing from November 1934 irregularly through December 1937, and edited first by Stuart Davis, followed by Joseph Solman in 1936 and Clarence Weinstock in 1937, it presented lively, penetrating, up-to-date analysis of developments in the world of art locally and internationally. Not all the articles were written specifically for *Art Front*, but they represented an awareness and breadth of interest on the part of the editors to a degree comparable with, if not overshadowing that of any other art publication appearing in the United States at that time.

Several figures of intellectual prominence in the art world were contributors. Meyer Schapiro, then starting his rise to eminence in the Department of Fine Arts at Columbia University, published articles on "Race, Nationality and Art" (March 1936) and "Public Use of Art" (November 1936). Harold Rosenberg, who later achieved prominence as an avant-garde critic, is represented by a lengthy review of a Van Gogh exhibition at the Museum of Modern Art (January 1936) and an essay on "The Wit of William Gropper" (March 1936). Jerome Klein, who had been assistant to Edward Alden Jewell, art critic of *The New York Times,* and was then writing art criticism for the recently regenerated *New York Post*, appeared frequently in brief reviews of books and exhibitions.

Some notable articles were "Scenery for Theatrical Dancing" by Lincoln Kirstein (January 1936), "The Artist and His Audience" (May 1936), a paper read by Max Weber at a meeting of the American Artists Congress, and "What Kind of World's Fair" (July-August 1936) written by Ralph Pearson as part of a general campaign by artists' organizations to expand the inadequate art exhibition planned for the New York World's Fair in 1939. Berenice Abbott wrote on "The Photographer as Artist" (September-October 1936) introducing the work of the noted French cameraman, Atget. Architect-decorator Frederick Kiesler wrote about the murals by Arshile Gorky at Newark airport under the title "Murals Without Walls" (December 1936).

One of the most vital and original exchanges in *Art Front* was with the noted and articulate regionalist painter Thomas Hart Benton, who was in his last term as a teacher at the Art Students League during the spring of 1935. Angered by an article by Stuart Davis (February 1935) and refusing to accept a challenge to public debate, he agreed to answer ten questions in writing. The complete dialogue was printed along with a rebuttal by Jacob Burck (April 1935) and prompted some lively letters to the editor (May 1935).

The pages of *Art Front* were also livened constantly by articles from foreign sources, several of which were written or translated by the then well-known author Samuel Putnam. Among these were his reports on "French Art and the Economic Struggle" (July-August 1936) and "French Art Today," a translation of some criticisms of European culture by Henri Barbusse (May 1936), and a paper by Fernand Léger on "The New Realism Goes On" (February 1937) delivered at the Maison de Culture in Paris. Another paper prepared for the same institution by Louis Aragon on "Painting and Reality" (January 1937) was reprinted from the avant-garde magazine *Transition*.

A discussion on "Surrealism and Reality" (March 1937) included an article called "I Defy Aragon" by Salvador Dali, "Marxism and Surrealism" by Samuel Putnam, and "The Man in the Balloon" by Clarence Weinstock.

A recurring editorial viewpoint is embodied in a review by Kenneth Rexroth of Herbert Read's well-known book *Art and Society* (June-July 1937). "For a supposedly Marxist book," he wrote, "*Art in Society* is remarkably barren of any discussion of the function of art and its emergence in the daily life of people as a whole." Despite the fact that considerable admiration was expended on some abstract artists in *Art Front*, and efforts were made to explain the reality of their art, Clarence Weinstock stated early on in "Contradictions in Abstraction" (April 1935) that "*No* meaning is the same as *any* meaning. Thus abstract painting is at the mercy of whatever physical associations the spectator has in mind...." The position—or double standard—seemed to be that at any other time art—even abstract art—could have a subtle or complex reference to reality; but in an America torn by economic and political conflict, anything but clear narrative exposition of social problems was either romanticism or escape.

The Union of Supervisors

In order to procure the technical and administrative skills necessary for WPA projects, regardless of whether people so qualified happened to appear on the relief rolls in any given area, a provision was included for employment of ten percent of the staff from other sources. This figure was considerably exceeded in the early days of the Art Project, but strict adherence was soon enforced. Some of the supervisory staff "rose from the ranks," and may have been members of the Artists' Union; but many came from academic and other backgrounds and were not ready to participate in the boisterous and, for them, excessively violent tactics of this organization. Some were drawn to the Project through personal contact with the director and other administrators, and had the usual feeling that they could negotiate better on a personal basis than in concert with others.

There were two additional reasons, however, for not recruiting supervisors into the Artists' Union or a separate section. One was the technical fact that supervisors were required to participate in or consult on the processes of hiring and firing, placing them on the side of management in the traditions of the labor movement. The other had reference to the pervasive aim of practically everyone on the Art Project of working toward some permanent government agency in the cultural area based on the on-going need for such services rather than as a measure of temporary economic relief.

Supervisors were not necessarily working on the Project because of their need for support, but because of the Project's need for their talents. Strictly speaking, they were *government employees!* Here, perhaps, was a "foot in the door." A supervisors' association was formed in the first year of the Project's operation. In July 1938, the association, swelled by supervisors from the other cultural projects, was granted a charter as Local 100 by the government employees' union known as the United Federal Workers of America, CIO.

Fringe benefits were negotiated for supervisors, comparable to those then in existence throughout government agencies, chiefly standard allowances for sick leave and vacations with pay, and the organization tried to do what it could in the campaigns for a permanent art project and the annual renewal of the appropriation. This was more apt to be done by letters and telegrams, and an occasional delegation to the offices of Congressmen and government agencies in Washington, than by mass demonstrations. The Association, before it became a CIO local, also published a little pamphlet called *Art as a Function of Government,* presenting research by several members on the extent to which bureaus of fine arts and other such activities were supported by foreign governments.

Eventually the organizations of the various other arts were separated and Local 100 contained only supervisors from the WPA/FAP. It achieved membership of 100 percent of those eligible, excluding "top administrative" personnel who were considered ineligible. This indicates the spirit of acceptance generally accorded any sort of organizational activity that grew up as a response to the complex needs of the situation, and to the further cultural ideals everyone on the Project was trying to promote.

Perhaps with a feeling that the program was based to a degree on the influence of organized artists during the early days of unemployment, Mrs. McMahon was quite responsive to group action and friendly with the leaders of the Artists' Union. On the occasion of the sit-in at her office she was "out of town," and it was rumored that this coincidence was due to a chivalrous tip in recognition of her cooperative spirit. Such was not always the case elsewhere, and two regional directors (in Philadelphia and Chicago) were removed as the result of protests against arbitrary, excessively personal patterns of command, in which violence was aroused by their opinionated intransigence.

The American Artists Congress

Many artists who were not directly involved in the federal relief projects were nevertheless interested in their progress and especially in using them as a springboard from which to develop permanent government support for the arts. Others were engaged in regular submission of sketches for the numerous competitions conducted by the Section, where no certification of need was required and many important artists participated. Revival of earlier concepts that an artist might become active in the affairs of the community, instead of continuing the romantic Bohemian role that had been gradually imposed on him during the Victorian era, aroused wide sympathy. In this connection, some felt forced by the shock of the Depression to seek social adjustments in order to avoid such drastic dislocations in the future, and sought means of joining with others to learn how to bring about what changes they could in their own areas, and to support broader developments for general improvement.

Feeling that the professional societies described above, and organizations limited to those actually employed by the government, were unable to lead the campaign for general cultural growth and failed to include all the artists willing to join in active support of the new objectives, a group of artists issued a call to others to meet for discussion and action upon problems facing the art world and possible means for their solution. Among over one hundred early signers were individuals of such prominence as Ben Shahn, Lewis Mumford, Raphael Soyer, Isamu Noguchi, David Smith, Margaret Bourke-White, and Yasuo Kuniyoshi. Almost four hundred signers were listed in the program of the open session. The name of Stuart Davis was given as secretary. The text was as follows:

CALL FOR AN AMERICAN ARTISTS' CONGRESS

This is a Call to all artists, of recognized standing in their profession, who are aware of the critical conditions existing in world culture in general, and in the field of the Arts in particular. This Call is to those artists, who, conscious of the need of action, realize the necessity of collective discussion and planning, with the objective of the preservation and development of our cultural heritage. It is for those artists who realize that the cultural crisis is but a reflection of a world economic crisis and not an isolated phenomenon.

The artists are among those most affected by the world economic crisis. Their income has dwindled dangerously close to zero.

Dealers, museums, and private patrons have long ceased to supply the meager support they once gave.

Government, State and Municipally sponsored Art Projects are giving only temporary employment to a small fraction of the artists.

The wage scale on these projects has been consistently below the standard set by the House Painters Union. Present Government policy on the Works Program will drive it below subsistence level.

All these attempts have failed conspicuously to provide that economic base on which creative work can be accomplished.

In addition to his economic plight, the artist must face a constant attack against his freedom of expression.

Rockefeller Center, the Museum of Modern Art, the Old Court House in St. Louis, the Coit Memorial Tower in San Francisco, the Abraham Lincoln High School, Rikers Island Penitentiary—in these and other important public and semi-public institutions, suppression, censorship, or actual destruction of art works has occurred.

Oaths of allegiance for teachers, investigations of colleges for radicalism, sedition bills aimed at the suppression of civil liberties, discrimination against the foreign-born, against Negroes, the reactionary Liberty League and similar organizations, Hearst journalism, etc., are daily reminders of fascist growth in the United States.

A picture of what fascism has done to living standards, to civil liberties, to workers' organizations, to science and art, the threat against the peace and security of the world, as shown in Italy and Germany, should arouse every sincere artist to action.

We artists must act. Individually we are powerless. Through collective action we can defend our interests. We must ally ourselves with all groups engaged in the common struggle against war and fascism.

There is need for an artists' organization on a nation-wide scale, which will deal with our cultural problems. The creation of such a permanent organization, which will be affiliated with kindred organizations throughout the world, is our task.

The Artists' Congress, to be held in New York City, February 15, 1936, will have as its objective the formation of such an organization. Discussion at the Congress will include the following:

'Fascism and War; Racial Discrimination; Preservation of Civil Liberties; Imprisonment of Revolutionary Artists and Writers; Federal, State and Municipal Art Projects; Municipal Art Gallery and Center; Federal Art Bill; Rental of Pictures; the Art Schools during the Crisis; Museum Policy in the Depression; Subject Matter in Art; Aesthetic Directions; Relations of Media and Material to Art Content; Art Criticism.'

We the undersigned artists, representing all sections of the United States, ask you to show your solidarity with us by signing this Call and by participating in the Congress.

The records of artists and others who signed the Call were checked to see if they qualified as "of recognized standing in their profession," and some were asked to serve on an executive committee that met approximately at weekly intervals to prepare for the organizational sessions. Topics were assigned for preparation by small groups or individuals. As the proposed "papers" took shape, they were read to the group for criticism and suggestions, each meeting generally being devoted to no more than one or two subjects.

About twenty or thirty members were generally present at these Thursday night gatherings, weekly when a public meeting drew close, less frequent at other times. Those on the executive committee were regularly notified by card and could vote, but any member was permitted to attend. The artist who had been selected to analyze a given problem would read what he had prepared, and the floor was thrown open for criticism, suggestion, or additional information. A

FIGURE 41. Peppino Mangravite (b. 1896). Caricature of the First American Artists' Congress. From left to right on stage: Heywood Broun, George Biddle, Stuart Davis, Julia Codesida of Peru, Lewis Mumford (Chairman), Margaret Bourke-White, Rockwell Kent, José Clemente Orozco of Mexico, Paul Manship, Peter Blume, and Aaron Douglas. In the background: Members of the presiding committee sing their praise of the Congress. In the foreground: The audience in different moods, mostly creative. (This caption quoted from Peppino Mangravite, "Aesthetic Freedom and the Artists Congress," *American Magazine of Art*, April 1936, pp. 234–237.)

decision was finally made as to whether the paper should be accepted or a revision presented for later approval. Thus each decision finally represented a consensus carefully arrived at, and more or less the official stand of the organization.

The open session of the first Congress was held at Town Hall on the evening of Friday, February 14, 1936, with the scale of prices for admission ranging from thirty-five cents to $1.65. Lewis Mumford, who had already achieved prominence as an art critic and author of *Technics and Civilization* (1934), was chairman. Stuart Davis, who had been the executive administrator of the activities to date, gave the keynote address, "Why an Artists' Congress?" Aaron Douglas spoke on "The Negro in American Culture," Joe Jones of St. Louis represented the nationwide outlook of the program in a speech on "Repression of Art in America," other professional spheres were reflected by Margaret Bourke-White and Heywood Broun, and the support of prominent artists was indicated by remarks from Rockwell Kent, Paul Manship, George Biddle, and Peter Blume.

Private sessions for members and their guests, to which no admission was charged, were held morning and afternoon, on Saturday and Sunday in the large auditorium of the New School for Social Research. The general topics of the four sessions were (1) The Artist in Society, (2) Professional and (3) Economic Problems of the American Artist, and (4) Delegates' Reports. Many artists of considerable prominence at the time spoke on various aspects of these matters, as they appeared in different mediums, different countries, and different parts of America, and organizational efforts that were being made to meet them. Ten delegates from three Latin American nations were present including the Mexican painters Orozco, Siqueiros, and Tamayo. Papers presented by Orozco and Siqueiros were printed in a small pamphlet which also contained the catalogue of an exhibition at the A.C.A. Gallery of work by thirteen Mexican painters, and drawings of Puerto Rican life by Bennett Buck. Forty of the papers delivered were published later in a 112-page booklet that sold for fifty cents (1936).

As a result of the interest in these meetings, it was decided to set up a permanent organization to seek the objectives discussed throughout the Congress, under the slogan, "For Peace, Democracy and Cultural Progress." Max Weber was named chairman; George Biddle, Rockwell Kent, Paul Manship, Arnold Blanch, and Joe Jones, vice chairmen; and Stuart Davis was continued as executive secretary.

With the dues of a rapidly growing membership augmented by proceeds from the sale of tickets to the open session, it was possible to open an office for headquarters at 66 Fifth Avenue, later moved to West 13th Street. The annual membership fee was one dollar, raised to two dollars following the second Congress, and by that time the number of members had risen almost to seven hundred.

Carnegie Hall was the site of the public session of the second general meeting of the American Artists Congress, held on Friday evening, December 17,

1937, after a long series of organizational meetings in which drafts of most of the papers were read as before the first Congress. A feature of the meeting was a message sent by the German writer, Thomas Mann, from his place of exile in Switzerland, which was read by his daughter, Erika Mann. He advocated the intellectual and cultural world face the importance of political issues, and commended the stand being taken by American artists "against those barbaric elements which today endanger all that we understand by civilization and culture and all that we love."

Arrangements had been made for Pablo Picasso, whose concern for the defense of the Spanish Republic—exemplified in his *Guernica*—had drawn him into public life, to address the open session by transatlantic telephone. Picasso was sick at the time.

Bill Mangold, head of a committee of information representing the Spanish Republic, kept assuring us that everything would be all right on the night of Picasso's phone call. I was put in charge of making the mechanical arrangements. The possibility of the artist's cutting a disk was raised—tapes were not yet known—if confined to a sickbed, and a turntable was set up backstage in readiness. The telephone company kept a transatlantic line open, but all to no avail. Jerome Klein had collected a few contributions to help defray the expense of hearing the great artist's voice across the ocean on which he had vowed never to travel, but they all had to be returned. Picasso's illness prevented what would have been a dramatic gesture, but a personal message was read instead.

Subjects featured in prepared papers were the federal art bill for a permanent government program in the arts, which was described by a representative of Congressman Coffee, opposition to discrimination against negro and oriental artists, criticism of the lukewarm attitude of American museums toward American art and alliance with the trade union movement.

The procedure that proved so successful in working up the papers for the first Congress broke down rather amusingly in connection with two of the "big guns" of the open meeting. George Biddle, a prominent mural painter credited with having helped to develop New Deal interest in the arts, was assigned the topic of Artists' Organizations. Reservations he expressed in his first draft about some of the tactics that had been used were interpreted as unfavorable to the Artists' Union, and he was asked to change them and report back. Not living in the city, Biddle was unable to get to many of the meetings, and turned up finally with a paper that had still not been approved. Trying to navigate between Scylla and Charybdis, he ad-libbed interpolations to tone down ideas that had aroused opposition. As he wandered equivocally in this way far beyond his time limit, Yasuo Kuniyoshi, who was chairing the meeting, twice called him to order. Then he went forward and genially pushed the speaker, a full head taller than himself, away from the rostrum, much to the amusement of the audience.

Bill Gropper, convivial cartoonist for *The New Masses* and other leftist publications, never bothered to write out his talk. When challenged he would say "Don't worry about me. I'll know what to say when I get up there." On the platform, however, before 2,000 people, he seemed completely at a loss and after fumbling for a minute or two sat down with a sheepish grin.

Closed sessions for members and invited guests were again held morning and afternoon of the two succeeding days at the New School for Social Research. Among the speakers at these meetings were Holger Cahill on "Cultural Aspects of Government Support of Art," Gwendolyn Bennett, delegate of the Harlem Artists' Guild on "The Negro Artist," Ralph Pearson on "The World's Fair," and Kuniyoshi on the subject of discrimination. Many other prominent speakers including Philip Evergood, president of the New York Artists' Union, Martha Graham, Rockwell Kent, George Biddle, and Stuart Davis covered a variety of subjects. Delegates reported on the activity of branches in St. Louis, Chicago, Washington, D.C., Cleveland, Philadelphia, and Baltimore. A national executive board was elected, consisting of forty-four members from the New York area and sixteen from other parts of the country.

As a promotional adjunct to the Congress, an exhibition of the work of two hundred members was held "In Defense of World Democracy—Dedicated to the Peoples of Spain and China." A section of work by Japanese artists condemning Japanese militarism and the invasion of China was featured. Parallel shows were arranged locally by branches in Cleveland, St. Louis, New Orleans, Los Angeles, Portland (Oregon), and Cedar Rapids.

Preparation of the general sessions, of course, was only an intermittent part of the organization's activity. Exhibitions were arranged so that members could reinforce the program of the organization using their professional mediums. Annual shows were arranged in which any member could enter his work on payment of a small fee. The first, held April 1937 in the International Building of Rockefeller Center, comprised almost three hundred items. The exhibition committee also arranged an opportunity for Congress members to exhibit at the Contemporary Arts Building of the World's Fair in New York. Interesting experimental devices were pioneered by a committee for the graphic arts, to promote the print media for reaching the widest possible public on a more intimate and economical basis than could be done by other art forms.

A novel venture of this group was the open exhibition called "America Today," for which one hundred prints were selected from a vast number of submissions by a jury of Congress artists. Each entrant agreed to submit an edition of thirty prints, if his work was selected, for simultaneous exhibition in as many centers throughout the country. Subsequently sets were sent to artists' associations for showing abroad, in London and Mexico City. The entire group was reproduced in book form for sale by the Equinox Press. Another was a "theme show" of prints and drawings on the subject of war and fascism. After showing in New York, this group was circulated throughout the country by the American Federation of Art, as part of its recently established program of traveling exhibitions that went mostly to small museums and colleges. One hundred of the items were reproduced in a 35 mm film strip which could be rented or purchased for a small fee. Smaller theme shows were arranged for various locations including art galleries in department stores, on the subjects of Sport Satires, America at Play, America at Work, and Artist's Holiday. A small group of prints was also assembled to be sent to the Far East with Jack Chen, a visiting Chinese artist, as a fraternal gesture.

Several symposia were arranged, including promotional events at the large membership exhibitions, on topics similar to those discussed at the general Congress. In March 1938, Lewis Mumford chaired a meeting at the New School to honor the visiting Spanish artist Luis Quintanilla. Picasso's painting of *Guernica*, exhibited in May 1939 at the Valentine Gallery under the auspices of the American Artists' Congress, was the focus of a discussion there by Leo Katz, Walter Pach, and Arshile Gorky.

Two meetings were held at the Museum of Modern Art in February 1940 in which the general subject "What is American Art?" was discussed by distinguished panels of artists and writers, before audiences averaging about 450, as an answer to current attacks by patriots of various sorts, both on types of subject matter they did not like, and on the growing trend toward abstraction, as un-American. The question, "Is American Art Menaced by Alien Trends?" was answered by Katherine Schmidt, Reginald Marsh, Stuart Davis, Yasuo Kuniyoshi, Philip Evergood, and a western artist, Frank Mechau. In the second of the series, "What is American Tradition?" was discussed by the well-known writer on American art, Elizabeth McCausland, as chairman, with Jerome Klein, another art critic; Gwendolyn Bennett, painter and supervisor for the WPA art teaching division in Harlem; and Lynd Ward, noted graphic artist.

In connection with the fourth membership exhibition held in April 1940, a symposium on "The Voice of the People" was held the first Sunday afternoon it was open, and a session of questions and answers in the manner of the then familiar radio program, "Information Please," was staged two weeks later.

Another type of activity was attempted with other artists' societies to hold an Artists' Conference of the Americas, in the fall of 1939, as a gesture for implementation of President Roosevelt's campaign to stimulate inter-American relations. Difficulties, mostly financial, in the way of bringing a sufficient number of artists here as delegates from the Latin American countries proved insuperable, and the effort had to be abandoned. A more successful organizational effort to gain the support of young artists, ineligible for membership in the congress as not yet outstanding in their profession, and to assist them in promoting their careers, was the formation of the Young American Artists Association.

Besides these activities, in which ideas of the organization were publicized and programs advanced for cultural growth, the national executive board frequently put the organized artist on record in relation to various current issues. Firm support was expressed to the American Society of Painters, Sculptors and Gravers in its effort to establish a boycott of all group exhibitions that refused to pay a modest rental fee to the artist for the use of his work, and members were urged to participate in this action. The Congress branch in Washington, D.C., sponsored a special showing of Peter Blume's anti-fascist painting, *The Eternal City*, now in New York's Museum of Modern Art, after it was rejected by the jury of the Corcoran Gallery for its 16th Biennial Exhibition. A protest against discontinuance as an economy measure of the art page in New York's daily newspaper *PM*, was registered with Robert Ingersoll, editor, and Marshall Field, publisher.

What was hoped might be a pilot attempt was made to broaden economic opportunity for the professional fine artist and to break down the sharp distinction between "fine and applied" art that had been generated in the 19th century by romantic, spiritual pretensions regarding the purpose of the arts. With the cooperation of a friendly manufacturer, a competition was held to obtain novel pictorial designs for gift-wrapping papers. The immediate results were far from impressive, but a series of similar competitions on a much grander scale were held by the Hallmark greeting card corporation in the forties, and other contacts between art and industry were developed.

Announcement of the gift to the nation of Andrew Mellon's great collection of old masters, with funds to build a large museum to house it under government auspices in Washington, D.C., brought forth criticism of the administrative arrangements because of failure to include representation for professional artists in its governing body, and lack of concern for American art and the living American artist in the program of the museum.

Opposition to emerging forces of totalitarian repression on the international front were expressed by sending a fraternal delegate to the Peoples' Congress of the American League Against War and Fascism held at Pittsburgh, Pennsylvania on November 26, 27, and 28, 1937, where an art exhibition was arranged in cooperation with the Artists' Union of New York. According to the *American Artist*, then the official news bulletin of the American Artists' Congress, its delegate "spoke briefly on the value of art exhibitions, low priced prints, and similar means of focusing attention on vital issues, and asked support of the League in various campaigns of protest against suppression and destruction of art by vigilantes, reactionary officials and others."

Members were urged to support the nation-wide boycott of Japanese goods, instituted following Japan's Manchurian invasion of China. Inclusion of German artists in a print show at the Chicago Art Institute was protested in view of Hitler's suppression of anti-Nazi artists, and rigid control of cultural activities by the Nazi government, especially in connection with work sent abroad. Opposition was also expressed to the McReynolds "Neutrality Bill" in view of the provision that the discretionary powers of the President to lift the embargo, which it provided on shipments to warring nations, was limited to exclude trade with either side in a civil war, thus precluding sale of arms and medical supplies to the Spanish Republic.

A severe blow to the power and prestige of the organization was suffered as the result of a position it was forced to take on the Russo-Finnish conflict, in which widespread sympathy was felt in America for the smaller nation. A request for funds and support of a promotional exhibition from a committee for Finnish War Relief, headed by ex-President Herbert Hoover, was turned down by the national executive board on the grounds that it was not a basically professional or cultural matter.

More extensive explanations, which the board was later required to make, attempted to identify the defeated Finnish regime as quasi-Fascist, citing military violence by its leader, Baron Mannerheim, against democratic political processes at the time of the emergence of the Soviet Union, and his cooperation with Kaiser Wilhelm II in helping the reactionary White Russian campaign. Questionable undemocratic actions in Herbert Hoover's career as relief administrator and also during his presidency were also mentioned.

The refusal to support Hoover's Finnish relief committee, stated as carefully as possible to avoid the appearance of political action where professional issues were not involved, was nevertheless interpreted as a partisan action by a number of individuals. A statement carrying seventeen names including those of such prominent figures as George Biddle, José de Creeft, Adolph Gottlieb, Lewis Mumford, and Meyer Schapiro, was mailed to the membership, stating that the executive board had been requested to set up a special meeting to discuss its position on war and fascism. It asked if it were true that "the Executive Board has adjusted the policy of the Congress to the line of the Communist Party without consulting the membership?" In answer, the board invited all members interested to attend its next regular meeting, April 4, 1940, for which a reconsideration of Finnish relief had already been scheduled.

Following a vote at this meeting of 125 to 12 in favor of the position of neutrality taken by the board, a wave of resignations took place that were extensively publicized in the press. Many withdrew simply to protect themselves from the sort of attack that would be leveled in some quarters on the basis of mere suspicion of radicalism. Stuart Davis resigned his leadership of the organization at this time without reference to the political issue, stating only that he felt the organization was "no longer in a position to carry out its original objectives."

What he meant may be indicated in a remark he made to the writer shortly before taking this step. After a late meeting in which some evidence of a fixed position by a few of those present was apparent even to my own inexperienced eye, I asked Davis for his estimate of Communist influence in the organization. After a brief reprimand for my naivete in asking a direct question on this sort of political affiliation, he added, "When I agreed to accept this job, I was assured there would be no fraction activity, and there hasn't been any—up to now."

Weakened in its previously prestigious position of spokesman for prominent progressive artists throughout the nation, and with its income cut drastically by the defection of a sizable portion of the membership, the Congress continued as best it could. Its swan song was a call issued jointly with the United American Artists to a "Congress of American Artists in Defense of Culture" to be held June 6, 7, and 8, 1941 at the Hotel Commodore. The open session was held at Manhattan Center, and its program listed the writers Edgar Snow, Richard Wright, and Dashiell Hammett, as well as Congressman Vito Marcantonio along with several noted artists.

Entry of the United States into the war following the Japanese attack on Pearl Harbor made it clear that new organizational patterns for artists would have to be developed. The Artists' Union ceased operation with the demise of the WPA/FAP. The resources of other groups diminished and their focus shifted as prosecution of the war effort intensified. The manpower that continued to be available under the circumstances, formed a joint body called the "Artists Council for Victory" following a crowded meeting called by a group of "Artists Societies for National Defense" at the Museum of Modern Art on December 17, 1941. An impressive list of organizations, including some highly conservative groups, was represented.

A conference on "Artists in the War" was held in June 1942 with Rockwell Kent as chairman of the public meeting and a list of speakers including the noted cartoonists and graphic artists, Art Young and William Gropper, with Yasuo Kuniyoshi, Fernand Léger, and the composer Marc Blitzstein. From this event emerged the Artists League of America which continued to function throughout the war.

Radical Participation

Failure to support the Hoover committee for Finnish relief was only the immediate reason that charges of conformity with the "Communist line" were raised

216

against the governing body of the American Artists' Congress. Throughout the Depression all organizations actively promoting hygienic social changes, the new movement for industrial unionism, the arts projects and the whole WPA, sometimes indeed the whole Democratic party and "that man in the White House," were all accused of being Communist puppets, fellow travelers, or dupes. Constant sniping and suspicion on this basis was directed against any active, assertive participant in attempts to alter the *status quo,* actually discouraging many of the fainthearted.

Accusations of "Communist domination" of the artists' organizations that were active during the Depression, the importance of leftist activity as an attempt to manipulate American society by a foreign power, cannot be disposed of satisfactorily by simple affirmation or denial. Any significant determination must take into account at least a *quantitative* factor: to what extent was any given organizational decision based on dictation of a group with ulterior motives; and to what extent was any given individual's vote based on adherence to dictates of a

FIGURE 42.   Artists picketing.

faction more intent on developing its own power and program than on the immediate social objectives of a particular action?

Participation of the Communist Party in artists' organizations of the Depression, sometimes even from their beginning, need not be denied. The nature and effect of such participation, however, should be given careful consideration to protect other participants from the easy condemnation of guilt by association. Begun by anti-New Deal forces in the Depression, this technique of unprincipled character assassination escalated in the McCarthy era to a point where it discredited itself. Untold irreparable personal damage resulted from whispering campaigns, and blacklists, as well as open accusations. Some aspects of the record still need clarification.

"Subversive activity" must be examined in terms both of tactical and ideological application. An important means of dominating a large corporate body, operating under democratic principles of rule by the majority, is the caucus, involving more or less formalized consolidation of sections of the membership behind decisions or candidates they favor. This might be a spontaneous decision of a group of neighbors to "stick together" on some local issue, or it might take the form of a carefully planned, permanent organization like the political machines that exercise such extensive control in the Democratic and Republican parties.

The Communist Party has made use of similar techniques in carefully organized "party fractions." This involves the simple practice of regular meetings by the Communist members of any given organization for the purpose of examining pending issues, formulating positions to be followed in discussing them, even deciding who will speak in the open meeting, and deciding on a stand to be taken in the final vote. All Party members are committed to these decisions, including those not present, and they may even be made for a numerous fraction in a large organization by a small executive group. One of the earliest and most revered agencies intended to combat social evils and work for progress in this manner, was the order of Freemasons, as described in Tolstoy's monumental novel of *War and Peace*. It is also used to less ideal purposes by college fraternities for wielding power in the management of campus activities.

In view of general recourse to such tactics of which many more instances might be cited, Communist use of the organized fraction cannot be condemned categorically, nor societies in which they operate categorized as "Communist dominated." A proportionately very small number of Party affiliates, for example, might be successful in gaining support for their policies by persuasion, where their influence could in no sense be considered "domination." Concerted action by a minority sufficiently large enough to influence the course of an organization consistently is subject to unfavorable criticism on two grounds. Many people object to the clandestine character of decisions taken prior to general discussion.

A kind of dishonesty or lack of candor is seen in the fact that someone votes on an issue or a candidate for office for reasons other than, or in addition to, those advanced on the floor of the meeting. A sense of unjust frustration may confront the others, since that invisible portion of the meeting presumably cannot be convinced.

A much more serious criticism of influence exercised by caucus techniques can be based on certain ideological aims for which they were sometimes used. Classical communism is based on the theory that radical social change can be accomplished only by violent seizure of power when a sufficiently large or crucial section of the populace becomes convinced of the fundamental evil or practical breakdown of the existing order. Therefore, revolution must be brought about, or may be accelerated, by convincing people of the unnecessary and unjust nature of privations of which they may even be unaware.

This theory may inspire actions that distort the program of the organization in which they are used, in order to reflect on the social structure as a whole. For they aim to expose evils *not* for the purpose of correcting them, but to condemn the current order for permitting them to exist. Thus, if a campaign, mounted presumably to correct an evil, should begin to show signs of success, Communists of this persuasion would try to advance the goal to impossible extremes, or would take steps to sabotage the effort in some other way. Likewise their support for the organization itself continues only so long as it remains a compliant instrument or mouthpiece for this type of agitation. An administration limiting itself strictly to accomplishment of tangible gains for its membership may be attacked, and if it cannot be dislodged, the entire organization may be wrecked or deserted.

A proper reconstruction of radical influence in artists' organizations of the 1930s must not ignore the fact that such unrest was not the primary objective of the Communist party at that time. Whether the tactic of disruption was rejected along with Trotskyite dedication to immediate world-wide revolution; whether a change in attitude made social reforms acceptable as steps toward socialism, rather than useless palliatives; or whether an attempt was being made to win friends with solid support for minor gains of their own choosing, instead of trying to foist on them dreams of broader ideological goals that had sufficed in European slums and ghettos, need not be decided here. However, a basic change resulting from the united front pattern proposed by the Bulgarian leader, Georgi Dimitrov, at an international Communist parley early in 1935, must be recognized.

The new policy of "building socialism in one state" altered the role of international Communism from advancing the classical Marxist and Trotskyite "world revolution" to the cultivation of friendship abroad for the Soviet Union and support of actions favorable to its survival. This involved explaining the principles and patterns on which it operated, and offering of local Party organizations to help people improve their lot. Working with and through popular groups (even in the political arena as in support of the "united front" government in France headed by the Socialist, Leon Blum), meant relaxation of social disruption and of the "rule or ruin" pattern. Missionary and educational functions were given priority over revolutionary political action, and candidates for public office in America were run largely to "expose the face of the party," publicize its analysis of current issues, and "give the people a voice" on progressive issues in the elections.

Even requirements for membership in the party were relaxed in a brief attempt to create a mass organization. No challenge was made to the all-out dedication of new applicants, and activism was placed largely on a voluntary basis, with little strict discipline imposed. (Probably there was an inner core or cadre of members based on the strict, earlier requirements, but in general this was obscured, in fact denied.) The underground character of operations was largely abandoned. Fraternal delegates were invited to regional conventions, and in some situations influential non-members were invited to "open fraction meetings" for development of policy respecting the activity in which they were involved.

Thus the accusation of Communist domination in the artists' organizations under discussion, must be discounted to the extent that policies and actions were pursued strictly in accordance with the interests and objectives of the entire membership. An American Group and the Painter-Gravers probably contained too few to accomplish anything else. The Artists' Union, however, and to a lesser extent the American Artists' Congress, at least in their respective governing bodies, contained sizable proportions of Communists, fellow travelers, sympathizers, or people who were simply unafraid to accept cooperation from any source toward what they considered important professional aims.

In the case of the Artists' Union, representing the rank and file of the Federal Art Project, organizational solidarity was too deeply based to be upset by political name-calling. Employment on WPA involved several onerous, unpleasant, and often obscure steps, first in qualifying for home relief, and then in getting transferred to the government payroll. Advice and encouragement from informed and sympathetic people were exceedingly helpful, and for some a virtual necessity. When given a meal ticket, and then a real job with a better income, a person is not inclined to criticize a friendly agent's political affiliations, or to dissociate himself if the label happened to be unfamiliar or a trifle bizarre.

Personal welfare was not equally at stake in the American Artists' Congress. For the artist who had to struggle for a living in good times or bad, however, even if as prominent a figure as John Sloan, such proposals as a permanent

Bureau of Fine Arts, development of new and wider audiences, liberalization of museum policy regarding exhibition and purchase of American art, and payment of rental for the use of artists' work to benefit audiences and institutions that rarely bought pictures, were powerfully attractive. Why question their source or other social ideas of those who advanced them? Such purely professional benefits were only incidentally or not at all political, and even a Communist artist might advance them more in terms of his personal interest than of any possible revolutionary eventuality.

Occasionally, excessively contentious or doctrinaire Communists over-stepped the line of demarcation between the precise objectives of a group and less germane political actions. But it was the Nazi regime in Germany and Italian Fascism in its wake that became intensely violent, and an increasing threat to popular influence on national governments elsewhere. Agitation on international political issues loomed to noticeable proportions in artists' professional organizations. At the outset, whatever influence the Communist Party may have exercised was channeled strictly toward furthering the personal welfare of the individual members, and the allegiance of the vast majority to the program of the group included no further commitment than what they could be shown was for their own immediate gain.

Revelations of Communist influence in artists' organizations need not be regarded as an argument against public support of welfare or cultural activities on the grounds they present an opportunity for revolutionary ferment. The lesson to be read from the experience of the Depression decade is rather that such needs engender militancy to the extent that they are ignored, and that radical influence was tolerated in the professional groups described, only within the limits of their expressed purposes.

ROSALIND BENGELSDORF BROWNE was born in 1916 in New York
City. She received her early education in the New York public schools and
at New York University. From 1930 to 1934 she studied at the Art Students
League where she was a pupil of Anne Goldthwaite, George Bridgman,
John Steuart Curry, and Raphael Soyer. From 1934 to 1935 she went to the
Annot Art School and studied with Hans Hofmann at his school from 1935
to 1936. She was emloyed on the WPA/FAP in New York from 1935 to 1939.
In 1936 she became a charter member of the American Abstract Artists and
has exhibited in many of that organization's annual and national exhibitions.
She was also a member of the American Artists' Congress and the Artists'
Union. In 1940 she married the painter Byron Browne. At present she
teaches courses at the New School for Social Research as well as private
studio classes, and writes monthly exhibition reviews in her capacity as editorial associate of *Art News*.

FIGURE 43. Joseph Solman. *Rosalind Bengelsdorf Browne.* 1958. Collection of
Chatham College, Pittsburg, Pennsylvania. (Photograph by Walter Rosenblum,
Courtesy of Joseph Solman)

The American Abstract Artists and the WPA Federal Art Project

ROSALIND BENGELSDORF BROWNE

As a founding member of the American Abstract Artists (AAA) in 1936 and an employee of the WPA Federal Art Project from 1935 to 1939, I shall attempt here to describe their contributions and to correct misconceptions which minimize their value.[1]

I shall focus on the activities of New York abstract artists of the 1930s, their working conditions and/or difficulties under government patronage and the prevailing prejudices of the time. In retrospect, our difficulties were rather easily surmounted, and, for most of us, working conditions on the WPA/FAP were excellent. I attribute much of the privilege and understanding we enjoyed to the liberal policy pursued by the Project. From my viewpoint, the most significant aftermath of the fertile environment for art supplied by the WPA/FAP has been the incredible transition and proliferation of abstract art in America and the powerful influence of American abstract art on international styles.

The fertile environment the government provided for the very few abstract artists working during the 1930s was "freedom from the pressure of cliques, the insistence of dealers, the noise of publicity."[2] It also prompted the Artists' Union, probably the largest artist's organization ever to be formed in this country. The Artists' Union had chapters in major U.S. cities and its membership included artists of every persuasion who had banded together to get Project jobs, to improve wages, hours and requirements, and to prevent dismissals.

This unity of purpose was paralleled by the latitude artists allowed each other in the Artists' Union. As a body, the union's purpose was to insure every member's economic *and* creative security. The majority of the membership, however, was engaged in illustrating social commentary about the American Depression scene—what they termed "art for the proletariat." They were really alien to an abstract art form that seemed remote from human problems. What helped was being thrown together. A continuous contact, born of joint economic need, overcame these differences, and made possible the reciprocal indulgence that induced this majority to listen receptively to a series of lectures on abstract art given by Balcomb Greene, myself,[3] and Arshile Gorky—in that chronological order.

The union evolved from a group called the Unemployed Artists' Association (UAA). It was formed in 1933 largely through the efforts of Bernarda Bryson (later Ben Shahn's second wife), Max Spivak, and Ibram Lassaw. Lassaw was treasurer for the group and remembers that the UAA picketed the Whitney Museum of American Art on 8th Street because its director, Juliana Force, was appointed regional director for the newly established Public Works of Art Project (PWAP).

From the outset the government art projects avoided official restrictions on the style of art submitted. Edward Bruce, director of the PWAP, succinctly outlined the Project's attitude in the catalogue of an exhibition of the work of PWAP artists held at the Corcoran Gallery of Art in the spring of 1934:

Artists were selected on the basis of their qualifications as artists and their need for employment. The subject matter assigned to them was the American scene in all its phases. Within this scope the artists were given the utmost freedom of expression.

The fact that this policy was not just talk but actually put into practice was confirmed by this exhibit's inclusion of an abstract painting by Paul Kelpe and semi-abstract pictures by A. S. Baylinson, Francis Criss, and Jan Matulka. Further confirmation is found in the PWAP final report[4] which lists the names of the following artists who were working more or less abstractly then:

Byron Browne	Werner Drewes	Pietro B. Lazzari
Martin Craig	Arshile Gorky	Louis Schanker
Stuart Davis	John D. Graham	Max Spivak
José Ruiz de Rivera	Harry Holtzman	
Burgoyne Diller	Ibram Lassaw	

Ilya Bolotowsky and Ralph Rosenborg told me they were employed by the PWAP before it ended but their names weren't in this report. True, the roster is small. But there weren't many more abstract artists around in New York in 1933–34.

The consensus among the above listed artists still living, is that work was rarely rejected by the PWAP or the WPA/FAP that followed because it was abstract. If such rejection occurred, it reflected the individual prejudice of an immediate supervisor or sponsor, not Project policy. Lassaw, who has done only non-representational sculpture since 1933, said all the PWAP demanded from artists were interim reports on the progress of work.

I say all this despite a letter Byron Browne wrote sometime before the fall of 1934. Apparently Byron had just been fired from the PWAP and he was mad. I quote his long hand-written complaint in full:[5]

Received your PWAP booklet and read with interest the items in it. My reason for writing is to offer a complaint. The PWAP like the NRA is not above criticism.

I offer myself as a case in point. The PWAP does not help the real creative artist. In the first place the subject matter is dictated to the artist. As my work contains little or no emphasis on subject matter I was ignored for a long time after the PWAP began to function and then cut off after a period of four weeks. This has also happened in many other cases. So here we have a great art movement in the country with the idea of aiding the artist. As far as I and many others are concerned we might be at the North Pole.

One case in particular I know of which I should like to bring to your attention. People receiving incomes from various sources are getting the government check regularly while the ones in need have barely a roof over their head. This is not laying it on too thick as I know from first hand information. Now about the case I spoke of. Here is an artist who receives a steady, reliable and comfortable income and is employed by the PWAP. This person's contribution consists of 2 small etchings done from photographs of historical buildings. This, you can readily see, does not come under the heading of creative art. The project, in inspecting the works on the fifteenth, finds this contribution to its liking.

I myself, upon entering the project, set to work to make a large 5-foot canvas of an imaginative nature, and not dealing with any subject matter upon the so-called American scene, which I believe has nothing at all to do with art. My idea must certainly have been disliked by the committee as I was cut off a whole week before the 15th. As to the quality of my work: I am the youngest man in America to win an award from the National Academy Exhibition. I had exhibited at the Corcoran Gallery in Washington, Pennsylvania Art Academy, Art Institute of Chicago, Buffalo Museum, and many other shows in different parts of the country. If I am qualified to exhibit my work in the best shows why does not this great art movement give me assistance. God knows I need it and would gladly take it at half the sum now being given out.

Sincerely,

[signed] George Byron Browne

Perhaps Byron's experience on the PWAP *was* the norm. Perhaps Lassaw and others I interviewed who had had some PWAP experience have undergone the mellowing of time. Perhaps the years softened or eliminated memories of their bad times. I met Byron in October of 1934. I didn't know him well enough at that time to have been his confidante, and I had never been on the PWAP myself. I do know Byron was very thin when I met him. I remember his telling me he lived on a quart of milk, a box of cornmeal, a head of lettuce, and some raisins a day. But the WPA/FAP started about that time and things looked up.

Certainly I'm on more secure ground relating WPA/FAP experiences because I shared them. I submit a positive evaluation of the PWAP on the premise that Byron and others who had similar experience were simply unlucky. Docu-

FIGURE 44. Byron Browne (1907–1961). *Rima Mosaic*. WPA/FAP, 1936.
U.S. Passport Office, Rockefeller Center, New York City. (Oliver Baker)

ments *do* record that some abstract work *was* accepted and exhibited by the PWAP and I am trying to relate a broad perspective that years and scope afford.

Abstract art on the WPA/FAP was practiced by a truly dedicated minority, determined to win acceptance and understanding. We organized the American Abstract Artists, we exhibited, and we proseltyzed via our most articulate spokesmen and skilled writers. We even had minor assistance from a few rich, influential members of our group like Albert Gallatin and George L. K. Morris, who gave us small sums for publicity and bought work from some members.

The WPA/FAP created our immediate and most valuable audience—an audience of our peers. It is entirely conceivable that figurative artists of the 1930s, who are internationally famous for an abstract idiom today, were stirred to experiment partly by our ardent efforts to spread abstract gospel then.

More important to our strength was the fact that we practiced democracy within our own ranks. Under the aegis of abstract art, the AAA harbored conflicting credos stemming from opposing sources—the Bauhaus, Kandinsky and Klee versus Cubism and Neo-Plasticism. There *was* occasional dissension about hairline boundaries dividing figurative from non-figurative art when we voted on the eligibilty of new members. But, by and large, we got along. And we had success. Our contribution to the popularity abstract art enjoys now has become part of history. Credit, however, should really go to one man who, almost single-handedly, achieved the first concrete public recognition and dissemination of abstract art in New York City—Burgoyne Diller, head of the WPA/FAP mural division from its inception until he left to join the Navy in the early forties.

All heads of divisions and supervisors of the WPA/FAP were artists—at least to the best of my knowledge. Artists usually have a basic empathy with artists, and, in those days, this empathy mitigated any ideological breaches. Diller had even more to go on. His interest in a group preoccupied with his own creative ideas was inevitable. He encouraged and expedited transfers of abstract artists to the mural division, gathering them, so to speak, "under his wing." He appointed Harry Holtzman as his special assistant to supervise abstract mural artists from 1936 to 1937. He enlisted the cooperation of modern architects such as William Lescaze (Williamsburg Housing Project) and Ian Woodner (Health Building, 1939 New York World's Fair), and persuaded the New York City Art Commission, WPA/FAP administrators, and many sponsors to accept abstract and semi-abstract murals for public buildings. I was told he even managed to get de Kooning (who had to leave the Project because he wasn't a U.S. citizen) an off-project commission to do a mural for the Fair's Hall of Pharmacy.

My own connection with Diller began at the Art Students League when I studied there from 1930–34. Diller entered the League in 1928 and left earlier than I—in 1933. His most influential teachers there were probably William von Schlegell, A. S. Baylinson, Jan Matulka, and Hans Hofmann. I clearly remember that he sold art materials at the League's supply shop, that he had longish, curly black hair, and wore knickers. Three of his bosom friends were Harry Holtzman, Albert Swinden, and a slight, Christ-like man called Albert S. Wilkinson. They exhibited their work at the League, which held its first show of abstract art about 1932. They awed me. To a youngster (I was about 16) they seemed aloof and way up on some transcendental plane. I also recall, less vividly, the first picture I saw of Diller's at a League exhibition. It was gray-green and citron—a cool, somewhat rigid synthetic cubist still-life (à la Braque) of a wine glass and lemons.

The next sharp image I retain of Diller places him with the small group of abstract artists who met at Ibram Lassaw's studio at 232 Wooster Street, New York, early in 1936. The gathering consisted roughly of Byron Browne, Gertrude and Balcomb Greene, Harry Holtzman, George McNeil, Albert Swinden, Lassaw, Diller, and myself. It was on this occasion that we decided to form a cooperative exhibition society. Therefore, this occasion became the first actual meeting of the American Abstract Artists, and we were, in fact, its founders.[6]

To obtain the minimum number of participants required for an exhibition of abstract art at the Municipal Art Galleries (see below) we immediately invited our colleagues and friends to join the enterprise. Toward fall, a large meeting was called where all those contacted came together. Many had been or still were Hofmann students. Vaclav Vytlacil, who had studied with Hofmann in Munich, brought Holty, Turnbull, and Morris among others. Holty had also studied with Hofmann in Munich. George L. K. Morris urged the group to invite Gallatin.

The charter members were:

R. D. Turnbull	Gertrude Peter Greene	Ilya Bolotowsky
George McNeil	Byron Browne	Giorgio Cavallon
Mercedes Jeanne Carles	Rosalind Bengelsdorf	Leo Lances
A. N. Christie	George L. K. Morris	Alice Mason
Carl R. Holty	Vaclav Vytlacil	Esphyr Slobodkina
Harry Holtzman	Paul Kelpe	Werner Drewes
Marie Kennedy	Balcomb Greene	Richard Taylor
Ray Kaiser	Frederick J. Whiteman	Josef Albers
W. N. Zogbaum	John Opper	
Ibram Lassaw	Albert Swinden	

The names are listed in the same order in which they were printed in our first publication, *Prospectus*, dated January 1937. It outlined the AAA's reason for being and its purpose.

Before we structured ourselves into an organization, elected officers or formed committees, there was some dissension about what the nature of the group should be. Our first large meeting was explosive. Harry Holtzman tried to convince those present to concentrate on a seminar workshop arrangement for the development and exchange of ideas instead of exhibitions. As I remember it, his presentation was unfortunate. His semantics were obscure and led to misunderstanding. Many of us surmised that *he* intended to teach *us*. Certainly Gorky did. He had come with de Kooning to see what the meeting was about. Greene recalls that Gorky vied with Holtzman for leadership. As though saying to Holtzman that if anyone was equipped to teach the group, he, Gorky, was. Greene recalls how Gorky "thought we should all limit ourselves to painting in red, white and black for a certain length of time."

In any case, Gorky walked out of that meeting in disgust. Before he left, Gorky said, "What do I need an exhibition group for? I can exhibit anywhere I want to." Greene believes that de Kooning didn't join because Gorky didn't. Gorky was Bill's idol (mine and Byron's too, for that matter) and he tended to follow Gorky's lead. I remember, however, that Bill usually met us after AAA meetings at a cafeteria on Fifth Avenue near 15th Street. He was always warm and friendly. He'd often complain to me about not being able to finish a picture. I had the distinct impression that he didn't feel ready to exhibit at that time. Perhaps that was really why he didn't join us.

Thus it all started—from associations in art classes, from common sources of inspiration. I first knew Holtzman, Diller, Swinden, even Gorky at the Art Students League. Gorky frequented the League, though he taught at the Grand Central School of Art. He introduced the Museum of Modern Art to me when it was still housed in the old building that stood on its present site. He was responsible for my first view of Picasso's *Green Still Life*. It puzzled me. Ashamed of my ignorance, I timidly admired a lush Renoir nude with flowing titian hair instead. But these experiences and these men aroused my curiosity and stimulated the development that led me to study with Hofmann. Byron Browne met me at the Artists' Union in 1934. We both attended Hofmann's art school on East 57th Street where we met Cavallon, McNeil, Opper, Carles, Zogbaum, and others who became part of the AAA. That was in 1935. Byron Browne, Ilya Bolotowsky, and Cavallon had studied previously at the National Academy of Design where Lee Krasner met them about 1929. Lassaw shared Holtzman's studio on Bedford Street during my League years, which is probably how I met Lassaw. The networks meshed and all roads led to the formation of the AAA and to Diller.

Our first exhibition as a group was held at the Squibb Galleries in April 1937. Jacob Kainen, the critic for *Art Front,* wrote the following about our show in the spring 1937 issue:[7]

For various reasons, abstract painters in this country have had to put up with a fierce cross-fire of general opposition. The insolence of office as well as the dictates of the market have conspired against them; the supineness of the critics, the howl of the yellow press, the philistinism of the museums and the host of pressures, great and small, which a predatory society can exert has been brought to bear against the relatively small number of native abstractionists. Under such circumstances it is natural that abstract artists should sooner or later get together on the basis of mutual defense and general popularization of their viewpoint. The recently formed American Abstract Artists has already swung into action with a membership showing at the Squibb Building in New York, where thirty-nine painters and sculptors exhibited more than one hundred pieces.

Most of the abstract work was "total," that is, completely non-representational. Not a glimmer of the external world intruded itself into the pieces of most exhibitors.

For the opening of this first AAA exhibit, the members prepared a loose leaf portfolio of thirty-nine original lithographs—one by each exhibitor. It is an interesting commentary on our market value at the time to note, from AAA minutes of a meeting on March 19, 1937, that we decided to set our own worth at fifty cents for each portfolio (not each print!) for sale at the exhibition.[8] We valued our ideas more, perhaps, and, on occasion, wrote letters to editors, like the one to *Art Front* which appeared in the October 1937 issue. It was written in response to certain rather narrow views of the purpose and implications of "non-objective" art stated by the Baroness Hilla Rebay on the occasion of the establishment of the Solomon R. Guggenheim Foundation. The Foundation's purpose was to provide for the "promotion and encouragement of art and education in art" with emphasis on abstract art. The Baroness was then curator of Mr. Guggenheim's collection—and, let it be said, probably of Mr. Guggenheim.

I remember my reaction to the Baroness Rebay very well. I didn't like her. I found her esthetic ideas unsound, her manner condescending, and the combination of both a threat to the democracy we abstract artists practiced among ourselves. After all, she had Guggenheim's money in back of her. My impression was formed at a cocktail party the AAA and Beverly Silverman arranged to welcome her to this country. The party was held in the duplex of Beverly's brother, Ian Woodner. In return she lectured to us—or rather it amounted to a lecture. She firmly stated that all young artists should support themselves at a full-time job and paint in their spare hours—say from 6 to 9 A.M. Evidently she changed her rules about a Spartan regime for young artists, or perhaps she wanted more control over American abstract art activities, because in the late 1930s she began to assist artists, Ralph Rosenborg and Jackson Pollock for example, by hiring them as guards for her Museum of Non-Objective Painting. Whatever, the last five paragraphs of our letter to *Art Front*[9] provide a good idea of how *we* were thinking about abstract art a few months after our first exhibition:

We wish it understood that with the works of the art themselves and with the artists who created the works in Mr. Guggenheim's collection, we will not disagree. But we cannot accept with approbation the opinions which Baroness Rebay seems to have that abstract art has "no meaning and represents nothing," that it is the "prophet of spiritual life," something "unearthly": that abstractions are "worlds of their own" achieved as their creators "turned away from contemplation of earth." The meaning implied in these phrases is that abstract artists preclude from their works, and lives too (for after all, an artist must live some super-worldly existence in order to create super-worldly works of art), worldly realities, and devote themselves to making spiritual squares, and "triangles, perhaps, less spiritual," which will exalt certain few souls who have managed, or can afford, to put aside "materialism."

We abstract artists are, of course, first to recognize that any good work of art has its own justification, that it has the effect of bringing joyful ecstasy to a sensitive spectator, that there is such a thing as an esthetic emotion, which is a particular emotion, caused by a particular created harmony of lines, colors and forms. But the forms may not be so ghostly-pure-spirit-suspended as Baroness Rebay would wish. Who knows whether the divorce of cosmic atmosphere and earthly air is so absolute? Who can tell us into what reaches the intuitive soul of an artist must extend? Perhaps there are some spectators who behold and enjoy a square, more or less, of fine color, and go away refreshed, but not frozen into the state of sublime non-intellectuality that Baroness Rebay described.

It is our very definite belief that abstract art forms are not separated from life, but on the contrary are great realities, manifestations of a search into the world about one's self, having basis in living actuality, made by artists who walk the earth, who see colors (which are realities), squares (which are realities, not some spiritual mystery), tactile surfaces, resistant materials, movement. The abstract work of an artist who is not conscious of or is contemptuous of the world about him is different from the abstract work of an artist who identifies himself with life and seeks generative force from its realities.

FIGURE 45. First exhibition of the American Abstract Artists, Squibb Building, New York City, 1937. From left to right: Mrs. Balcomb (Gertrude) Greene, a painting by Albert Swinden above her, unidentified works through arch, two paintings by Rosalind Bengelsdorf Browne. (Courtesy of Rosalind B. Browne)

Einstein is as "pure" a scientist as can be found. His work is applicable perhaps to no immediate practical end. He deals with cosmic space and ideas. In face, he is an "abstractionist." Yet his theories are realities, they are based upon certain life-forms, and they help us to understand the world we live in. They are themselves a new form, which we can enjoy, just as abstract art. His theories are not valuable to us as an aid in escaping into purity trances: they renew and extend our contact with life, just as the work of a realist-abstractionist, which is based upon manifestations of life and is itself a manifestation of life, can be seen, enjoyed and used by the greatest number of people.

Abstract art does not end in a private chapel. Its positive identification with life has brought a profound change in our environment and in our lives. The modern esthetic has accompanied modern science in a quest for knowledge and recognition of materials in a search for a logical combination of art and life. In no other age has art functioned so ubiquitously as in our own. One has only to observe the life about him to see that abstract art has been enormously fecund, and remains a vitally organic reality of this age.

Hananiah Harari	Leo Lances
Jan Matulka	Rosalind Bengelsdorf
Herzl Emanuel	George McNeil
Byron Browne	

In order to act on those views without the Guggenheim's bank account, we turned to the WPA/FAP. At least half of the AAA membership was employed by the Project—a very active half. It was impossible to separate their welfare on the Project from the welfare of the AAA. As I have stated, most of us landed on the mural division sooner or later. Though some started there as assistants, Diller eventually located sponsors for each of us to do our own abstract mural.

All murals had to pass the New York City Art Commission and gain the approval of the architect, if a new building was involved. No mural jobs were undertaken without the sponsorship of the institution to receive the mural. This consisted not only of a signed agreement but also of money contributed toward materials. The government paid for the artist's time but the sponsor's contribution was desirable to insure interest in the work done. The rejection of work or its eventual destruction usually took place after a change in personnel in the sponsoring organization. Gorky's ten-panel abstract mural for Newark airport, *Aviation: Evolution of Forms Under Aerodynamic Limitations*, was destroyed on the order of a commanding officer when the airport was taken over by the U.S. military during World War II.

Some abstract murals which are still in their original locations are those by Byron Browne, John von Wicht, and Louis Schanker at Station WNYC in the Municipal Building, Ilya Bolotowsky's fifty-foot mural in the Hospital for Chronic Diseases on Welfare Island and Browne's semi-abstract mosaic mural in the U.S. Passport Agency Office in Rockefeller Center.

Other notable abstract or semi-abstract murals done at the time were Stuart Davis' panel for WNYC (now in the Metropolitan Museum of Art), murals by

FIGURE 46. David Smith (1906–1965). Abstract scultpure. Medium, date and whereabouts unknown. WPA/FAP. (National Archives)

233

Bolotowsky, Browne, Greene, and Schanker for the Health Building at the 1939 World's Fair and James Brooks' 325-foot mural at LaGuardia field—not to mention my own mural executed for the Central Nurses Home on Welfare Island.

These last, and many other murals created in New York City on the WPA/FAP are possibly lost or destroyed. A major research effort is needed to determine exactly the present condition and location of all the murals painted on the New York Project—and across the country, for that matter.[10]

Considering how few were producing them, the number of accepted abstract murals in proportion to the total output of the mural division was phenomenal. Of course there were rejections, but from what I gathered, vetoes had little to do with whether the art was abstract or not. There were other reasons for rejections and often they were amusing.

Balcomb Greene was assigned to do a mural for the Jewish chapel in an enterprise that had sponsored the Project to decorate three chapels on Welfare Island. Greene met the rabbi, who told him he was delighted at the prospect of having abstract art in his chapel. As part of his design, Greene utilized a gammadion symbol—the Greek cross—which looks like a swastika. He says he had been thinking about the insignia of the Roman legions. When he submitted the color sketches of the mural for approval, Diller exploded. Though the quote is not verbatim, the effect was, "Why did you put in a swastika!!?" The sketches were not accepted.

Other anecdotes were tragi-comic. The doctors welcomed Bolotowsky's mural at the Hospital for Chronic Diseases, Welfare Island. It was installed in the male patients' lounge and replaced a photo-mural of girls in bathing suits. The confined men, aroused by the sight of scantily clad females had defaced the photo-mural with pornographic graffiti. Very pleased with Bolotowsky's non-figurative substitution that "kept the patients quiet," the Doctors' Committee offered him another mural in the hospital and approved his sketches for it. Just about that time, Baroness Rebay, Solomon Guggenheim, Rudolf Bauer, and a professor from Yale University visited the hospital to see the finished mural. The next day *The New York Times* carried a news item about this visit, and the article implied that the distinguished visitors had sponsored the mural. Diller's immediate superior, Audrey McMahon, was annoyed by the incident because the mural had been accomplished under her auspices and not the Baroness Rebay's. Bolotowsky feels that her pique at the Baroness for giving a false impression to the press caused her to halt the completion of his additional mural for the hospital, though Bolotowsky himself was not at all involved in the incident or in her anger.

Tales of Mrs. McMahon's temperament are legion. Louis Slobodkin, who was a supervisor of the sculpture division of the WPA/FAP from 1941–42 recalls that artists who rubbed her the wrong way—if she thought they acted like "prima donnas"—were blocked in their freedom of expression. While Slobodkin was supervisor, she rejected the sculpture of Nakian, Raoul Hague, Peter Grippe, Louise Nevelson, and Polygnotos Vagis, to name a few, and would only accept their figure drawings as Project submissions. But none of these artists (except Grippe, who was semi-abstract) were doing abstract work then. On the other hand, it appears that she got along splendidly with David Smith, José de Rivera, Martin Craig, Ibram Lassaw, and Herzl Emanuel if one should judge by the number of allocations, commissions, and exhibits these abstract sculptors were given. Lassaw, for instance, told me his work was never rejected and often allocated. Perhaps she was just being an honest and objective critic.

Of those I interviewed, only Peter Busa thought work was refused because it was non-representational. In the particular case he cited, he may have been right. He, Jean Xceron, and Gorky were assigned to decorate the Catholic chapel on Rikers Island. Busa and Xceron were to do murals and Gorky, a stained glass window. His color sketches were disapproved by the priest in charge. The priest demanded a religious theme and Busa would not put halos on the saints. It seems to me that—with or without halos—figures are figures, and the problem here did not concern abstraction. Xceron's mural, however, never got beyond the cartoon stage and, according to Busa and Cavallon (Gorky's assistant on the window), Gorky's project in stained glass was not installed. So Busa's reaction does seem valid here. In such instances, I would tend to blame the individual sponsor rather than imply that such reception of abstract art was typical as Busa did in an interview published by *Art International*.[11]

This interview with Peter Busa and Matta conducted by Sidney Simon in Minneapolis in December 1966, was titled "Concerning the Beginnings of The New York School: 1939–43." At one point Busa says:

I was practising an idiom that came directly out of Léger and Picasso, but it was also related to American Indian art in the sense of being flat. It was also close to Stuart Davis. In those days I knew the work of Tony Smith, Steve Wheeler and Robert Barrell. I felt close to the abstract artists on the Project. But you know we couldn't submit any of that work. It wouldn't have been acceptable. It would have been considered blotchy, or simply "paint on canvas." What we did on the Project was colored by our having to do commissioned work.

Yet Busa contradicts his own statement in the very next paragraph:

It's ironic, but some of the best things were the murals. Those by Davis and Byron Browne for Station WNYC; and those by Xceron, Gorky, Von Wicht, Bolotowsky, Brooks, and Guston on the Rikers Island project. The murals were certainly of a different caliber than the U.S. Treasury Department murals, which were really deadly.

I do not quite follow the logic of Busa's thinking here. The "commissioned" work of Davis, Browne, Gorky, Bolotowsky, and Von Wicht was certainly abstract. Most of their output for the Project was approved, completed and installed.

Perhaps Busa is thinking just of easel painting. Yet George McNeil and Ralph Rosenborg offer contradictions to his assumption that blotchy—or painterly—work was unacceptable to the Project. McNeil used thick pigment quite freely in a style that stood somewhere between Picasso and Hans Hofmann. His pictures were not neat. Yet while on the easel division from 1935–1936 under Lloyd Le Page Rollins, he was given no restrictions and had no work turned down. Ralph Rosenborg was employed first on the PWAP, then largely on the teaching and easel divisions of the WPA/FAP with a short span on the mural division assisting Gorky. His work was not only "blotchy," it was abstract-expressionist! It would seem quite legitimate to call him one of the first American abstract expressionists. His style, then, merged the whimsy of Klee with the kind of automatic calligraphy found in Kandinsky. All in all, he was doing what Busa described as least desirable to the Project. If this were true, why does Rosenborg recall his experience on the easel division with pleasure? He said Mrs. McMahon herself had him transferred from the teaching division to easel and proceeded to circulate all the work he submitted in Project exhibitions that traveled throughout the country.

As early members of the American Abstract Artists, Rosenborg and McNeil also represent major refutations of statements made by Sidney Geist in his article "Prelude: The 1930s." Geist says that abstract art in New York during the 1930s was generally an art abstracted from nature and lacked the non-representational character of present-day styles. He also states that the WPA/FAP in general did not give birth to either an important artist or an important body of work and that it was not able to generate a new manner.[12]

These seem irresponsible statements in view of present evidence and the documentation available of the past. At best they are thoughtless. In the first place, nature is a big word. In the final analysis *all* abstract art is derived from nature. Insofar as the past is concerned, a cursory examination of the reproductions in the 1938 brochure published by the American Abstract Artists is enough to establish that work by Lassaw, Gertrude and Balcomb Greene, Smith, Christie, Bolotowsky, Browne, Shaw, Vytlacil, Glarner, Albers, Gallatin, Slobodkina, Bowden, Drewes, McNeil, Mason, Turnbull, Holty, Swinden, and Zogbaum (listed, for the most part, in order of reproduction) was completely non-representational in character. Frankly, the majority of current styles amount to a repetition of what was done then—only now production is done on a larger, costlier scale. Does the following description of Lassaw's sculpture project an image that is different from those on the scene today?

The box is hollow and is made of wood and is 5 inches deep and a yard in width and length. The cover has biomorphic shapes cut out with a jig-saw. Inside the box is an electric light and colored wire forming designs.

This was taken from a notation on Lassaw's "box" in a brief review of "a large group of novelties at the AAA exhibit at the Fine Arts Building, 215 West 57th Street," printed in a WPA/FAP news release dated February 25, 1938. Almost everything done today, was done before, if not by us then by our predecessors abroad. The real difference is that we didn't become prosperous doing it.

In this area Mr. Geist's perception seems keener. In other sections of the same article he aptly sums up the attitude of the power structure in the 1930s. Talking about artists included in the Museum of Modern Art's exhibition, "New Horizons in American Art," in 1936, he writes:

It is an interesting comment on changing tastes that *not* reproduced in this catalogue were mural designs by James Brooks, Ilya Bolotowsky, Byron Browne, Stuart Davis, Balcomb Greene, Arshile Gorky, Willem de Kooning and George McNeil.[13]

Whether the Museum's amazingly responsive attitude to current fads today is the reverse side of the same coin, I leave to conjecture. Or perhaps the AAA put too much pressure on MOMA in their campaign to induce the Museum to exhibit, encourage, and purchase abstract American art instead of European. The fact remains, that in the 1930s the Museum catered to the most popular art of the time, American Regionalism.

By contrast, the WPA/FAP encouraged everybody. Its purpose was not to promote an art market, but to develop better artists and disperse better art. In principle—and usually in practice—it was devised to extend as much consideration to creative personalities and experimentation as possible. When art submissions met with disapproval, effort was made to handle such situations tactfully.

Paul Bodin related an episode affecting William Baziotes. Waiting on line for art materials at Project headquarters at 110 King Street, Bodin stood behind Baziotes. Baziotes carried a large package containing about twenty semi-abstract watercolors. He was taking them to the easel division so his supervisor could select one in exchange for another that the Project officer thought looked too much like Picasso. Baziotes opened the package and showed the group to Bodin. "Do you think any of these look like Picasso?" he asked Paul. Paul said they didn't. This system of exchange was customary and, apparently, not offensive to most.

Often factors that had nothing to do with disapproval interfered with the completion of art. Much was left undone when the WPA/FAP switched to the war effort during the terminal years of the Project. Lee Krasner, finally assigned to do her own mural for Radio Station WNYC after years as a mural assistant to Max

Spivak, Harry Bowden, and others, was prevented from completing it because of the war. Instead, she was put in charge of displays in department store windows publicizing the war services and war courses offered by various colleges and schools. Jackson Pollock, her future husband, and Jean Xceron were members of her crew.

Though she missed a mural commission of her own, Lee Krasner feels the Project was very important to her as an artist. She is particularly grateful to Diller, who allowed her to use the Hofmann Art School as a studio address between assignments, so she could study during the day instead of at night. Artists on the mural division had to be on a specified work location—their own studio, or that of the master artist—where time keepers paid them periodic (unannounced) visits. It also struck Lee, as she talked to me, that her interest in collage really began when she assisted Harry Bowden on a mosaic. He asked her to transpose his finished painting into a plan for a mosaic with collage. (Lee has an abstract mosaic panel done by Jackson Pollock which was "rejected" by the Project for undetermined reasons.)

Many abstract artists, including myself, started their WPA/FAP experience on the teaching division. Some of the PWAP artists, Lassaw, Bolotowsky, Rosenborg, spent an interval teaching before they were established on the creative divisions.

Nathaniel Dirk directed one of the major WPA/FAP art schools at the YMHA Contemporary Art Center on Lexington Avenue and 92nd Street where Lassaw conducted a sculpture class for a year before moving to the sculpture division of the Project. The Brooklyn Museum Art School got its start under WPA/FAP and Peter Busa, Ralph Rosenborg, and Werner Drewes were part of its original faculty under Director Augustus Peck. Art classes were set up in every feasible location—in settlement houses, Federal Art Galleries, public elementary and high schools (after regular school hours)—for both children and adults. Dispersed throughout these locations were teachers of abstract art. Balcomb Greene spent about two years teaching at various community centers such as The Gramercy Boys Club. I taught art to nurses in training at Beth Israel Hospital and to children at a community center in Washington Heights. Rosenborg also taught at Public Schools 9, 43, and 72.

Alex R. Stavenitz, director of the art teaching division in New York City, also managed his department without bias. His teachers operated without restriction regardless of their persuasions. Abstract teachers were publicized and respected, a condition exemplified by a news release in an art project bulletin dated October 11, 1937:

Frederick Whiteman, instructor of abstract art, will leave the Contemporary Art Center at 92nd Street and Lexington Ave., to become Director of the Greensboro, North Carolina Art Gallery and School. Both centers are units of the W.P.A. Federal Art Project.

It went on to outline Whiteman's biography and career, stating that he had studied with Jan Matulka, was a member of the American Abstract Artists, and had developed his own teaching method at the Whiteman School of Art in New York for eight years before he joined the Project.

Probably the most effective endeavor of the WPA/FAP to promote art appreciation and to build a wide art audience was the establishment of Federal Art Galleries, community art centers, art tours, and a program of traveling exhibitions. It was really the first major national showcase for abstract art. Here, Robert Ulrich Godsoe, head of the exhibition division of the Project, helped I'm sure. During the early 1930s he ran the Secession Gallery on West 12th Street. It was one of the very few galleries featuring a roster of young moderns like Byron Browne, Louis Schanker, and Pietro Lazzari. It was not surprising, therefore, that WPA/FAP art exhibitions in New York and throughout the country included the work of abstract artists. In fact, federally sponsored shows were usually advertised as "running the gamut from . . . to abstraction."

In at least one instance, the WPA/FAP sponsored a traveling exhibition that was totally abstract. The minutes of an American Abstract Artists meeting on November 30, 1940, read:

It was reported by Holtzman that the Federal Art Project, through Mildred Holzhauer, Assistant Administrator in Washington, D.C. has invited the group to send approximately 25 paintings 30″ × 40″ outside maximum measurement, for a travelling show to last about one year. It will be shown in various art centers throughout the country.

Apart from federally sponsored outlets, however, opportunities to exhibit abstract art were far more limited than they are now. One democratic showcase, the Municipal Art Galleries, was run by the Municipal Art Committee of the City of New York and partially funded by the WPA/FAP. I recall especially two of their exhibitions. The seventh, which took place from April 29 to May 17, 1936, included thirteen abstract artists, eleven of whom were charter members of the American Abstract Artists: Rosalind Bengelsdorf, Henry Bowden, George Byron Browne, Mercedes Jeanne Carles, Giorgio Cavallon, Ivan Donovetsky, Balcomb Greene, Ray Kaiser, Marie Kennedy, Leo Lances, George McNeil, Albert Swinden, Albert Wein. The thirty-seventh exhibition from October 26 to November 13, 1938 was devoted entirely to an exhibition of abstract art by thirty members of the AAA and two guests, John Graham and Martin Craig.

Fiorello LaGuardia, present at the opening of one exhibition at the Municipal Art Galleries, commented about a painting of Ilya Bolotowsky's titled *Engineer's Dream*. "That's not a dream," he said with a twinkle in his eye, "that's a nightmare." Bolotowsky was more amused than offended. He knew the Mayor was just trying to get laughs.

Not everyone, however, was joking. In the fall of 1939—when the New York WPA/FAP was in bad shape, having just been removed from the jurisdiction of Holger Cahill's national office in Washington and put back under the control of the local WPA administrator, Colonel Brehon Somervell (who ran the whole WPA operation in New York: ditch diggers, sewer maintenance, etc.)—the ever-hostile Hearst paper, the *New York Journal American*, published a harsh editorial attacking modern art in the United States. In response, the A.C.A. Gallery at 52 West 8th Street, which was the outgrowth of one of the predecessors of the Artists' Union, the Artists' Committee of Action, organized an exhibition from September 18 to 30 which included most of the abstract artists. In the preface to the catalogue, Herman Baron, director of the gallery announced:

We are glad to give this group of artists an opportunity to answer the attack made on their democratic right to self-expression. This assault on progressive art and artists evidently has spread to the New York WPA art project. The United American Artists are now appealing to the public to stay the wrecking tactics of Colonel Somervell. The A.C.A. Gallery cannot remain indifferent to this appeal and is bringing it to the attention of the gallery visitors.

In addition to such exhibition opportunities for abstract art in the 1930s and early 1940s, there were the galleries of a very few courageous dealers—The Artists Gallery, run by Hugh Stix, and Rose Fried's gallery, the Pinacotheca, where Byron and others of our number exhibited. There were the annual American Abstract Artists exhibitions which began, as discussed earlier, with our first at the Squibb Galleries in April 1937. Members also exhibited at Columbia University and the YMHA on Lexington Avenue and 92nd Street.

Actually we had things to be grateful for. On the credit side we had the WPA/FAP, the Artists' Union and the American Artists' Congress to make our existence, development, and struggle for recognition possible. We had a powerful and articulate fighter for government patronage of the arts on our side—Stuart Davis, national chairman of the American Artists' Congress. We were treated well by *Art Front*, the official organ of the Artists' Union. We were concerned, however, with gaining appreciation of our art and its validity. To do so we had to overcome "the supineness of the critics, the howl of the yellow press, and the philistinism of the museums" as Jacob Kainen expressed the problem before. We utilized every means at our disposal. We lectured, took part in panel discussions and wrote articles. In 1940, the AAA picketed the Museum of Modern Art to stir them into some action on behalf of American abstract art. On this occasion we distributed a pamphlet titled "The Art Critics!", subtitled, "How do they serve the public? What do they say? How much do they know? Let's look at the record!" The pamphlet quoted the art critics writing for major newspapers of the 1930s and pointed up their embarrassing errors in judgment of masters like

Cézanne, Picasso, and Matisse. I do, however, want to repeat its introduction because many of the issues raised still have bearing today and many similar problems involving the cleavage between the artist and the press remain unsolved:

There can be no question that the American Abstract Artists maintains itself as the most authoritative group of its kind in the United States. Since 1936, the members of this group have carried the heaviest part of the burden of education and promotion of the creative effort it represents in this country. We have seen, to our regret, not only the initiative of the Museum of Modern Art, the most influential institution of its kind, decay, but we have also witnessed political intrigue to prevent abstract artists from executing work in public buildings.

It has also been extremely obvious that a systematic campaign against the most advanced efforts in modern art, and against abstract art in particular, is being waged by the greater part of our press. It is indeed a mockery that these professional amateurs, the critics, should even write of Seurat, Cézanne, Van Gogh, Matisse, Picasso, Kandinsky, Mondrian. With little or no compunction and with the most blatant complacency, these gentlemen of the press have often confronted us with their piquant discussions concerning the sanity of the most significant artists of our time. With the utmost condescension, an already confused public is being treated to such barefaced and shameless effronteries as a so-called *"regional esthetic,"* among other things. Most encouraged of all recently is the barren negativism expressed by our professional primitives and provincialists. These typically flagrant expressions of a *total* lack of *any conception of the form problem* and the vital significance of its continued development, betray at the same time the failure of these self-appointed administrators of American art and traditions to accept their cultural responsibility. It is perfectly apparent that the task of objectively reporting creative accomplishment, effort and experiment has been *peremptorily obscured by endless and unsubstantiated personal opinions.* These facts are further proved by their *super-annuated platitudes concerning eclecticism.* It makes evident that their *inability to differentiate between one abstraction and another* is simply *an inability to experience form in terms of plastic, spatial unity.* Unless the forms are based upon the arbitrary shapes of heads, trees, turnips, et cetera, the experience seems not to exist at all for these gentlemen and they are left quite speechless so far as any constructive or analytical conceptions are concerned.

It should be clearly understood that we do not attempt to place the artist above criticism. The point is that *any* expression of mere personal opinion and prejudice, either *for* or against, *has no place* and right to existence on the pages of art criticism *unless substantiated by an authentic conception of form relationships.*

My italics pinpoint the barriers that I believe still exist between artist and critic—barriers that could possibly be lessened by a re-creation of an environment for action and reflection such as the wpa/fap afforded abstract artists.

In 1940, George Biddle stated in his article about art under federal patronage:

The wpa rarely censors its artists. It has fewer bureaucratic facilities than the Section of Fine Arts to do so. Occasionally, therefore, the Project gets very bad pictures—and occasionally the best an artist is capable of. But, for the first time in history, many thousands of artists are working for the government almost without censorship. I be-

FIGURE 47. Ilya Bolotowsky (b. 1907). Abstract mural in the Hall of Medicine at the New York World's Fair. WPA/FAP, 1939. (Courtesy of the artist)

242

lieve this is the most quickening impulse in America today. And I believe it will form a record of the deepest value to the psychologist or art critic of future generations.[14]

Biddle proved to be a perceptive prophet. "Future generations," caught in the frenzied art explosion today, are continuously involved in polemics about it and what led to it. Few historians would be likely to deny that this current phenomenon is the outgrowth of the unprecedented, unequaled product of the Depression, the WPA Federal Art Project. A huge organization that allowed artists to supervise artists was bound to bear rich fruit. And the group to benefit most from a condition wherein art was created for the government "almost without censorship," was the most unpopular *avant-garde* minority, the abstract artists. The reciprocal effect the Project and the abstract artists had upon each other and upon art and the public at large is incalculable. Certainly it was enormous.

1. I have incorporated in this memoir information obtained from the following colleagues who shared my experience on the American Abstract Artists and the WPA/FAP: Ilya Bolotowsky, Peter Busa, Giorgio Cavallon, Balcomb Greene, Lee Krasner Pollock, Ibram Lassaw, George McNeil, John Opper, Ralph Rosenborg, and Louis Slobodkin. I want to thank Miss Dorothy C. Miller for making available her files on the PWAP and the WPA/FAP at the Museum of Modern Art. For the purpose of this discussion, I am defining as *abstract* all works wherein any figurative source is impossible to detect except by conjecture or the professional eye of another abstract artist. By the same token, *semi-abstract* art retains recognizable, fragmented semblances of original subject matter. Thus Bolotowsky's murals for the Williamsburg housing project are *abstract* while James Brooks' mural for LaGuardia Field is *semi-abstract*.

2. Excerpt from a statement by Constance Rourke which is quoted in a news release issued by the Smolin Gallery, New York, for the exhibition "Art of the Thirties" held there from September 16 to October 7, 1961.

3. I delivered a slide lecture on Cubism titled "A Basic Approach to the New Realism in Art," to approximately 400 members of the Artists' Union on September 23, 1936.

4. PWAP Report of the Assistant Secretary of the Treasury to the Honorable Harry L. Hopkins, Federal Relief Administrator, dated 1934.

5. National Archives, Record Group 121, PWAP Files, Entry 108, Box 1.

6. Barbara Rose, in her *American Art Since 1900* (New York, 1967, p. 146) states, "By 1938–39 the group also included Josef Albers, Ilya Bolotowsky, Fritz Glarner, Burgoyne Diller, Alice Mason, Albert Swinden, I. Rice Pereira, Lee Krasner, Willem de Kooning and David Smith." De Kooning was *never* a member, not in the beginning years of the AAA when I was active (1936–40) and, according to long-standing members, not since. He *did* attend one of the first large meetings with Gorky, but neither of them joined the group. Swinden was one of the founding members and subsequent meetings were held in his studio loft (shared by Balcomb Greene) at 13 West 17th Street, for many months. It is true that Diller joined after the initial meeting, but not that much later. According to the minutes of AAA meetings, the members Miss Rose mentioned entered the group on the following dates: Josef Albers, January 29, 1937; Ilya Bolotowsky, a charter member, 1936; Burgoyne Diller, March 12, 1937; Fritz Glarner, December 21, 1937; Lee Krasner, 1940; Alice Mason, a charter member, 1936; David Smith, September 28, 1937. Miss Rose deprived all but Glarner and Smith of roughly a year's membership. A small point, but history is history. The minutes referred to are in the possession of Leo Rabkin, the AAA's current president. The year skipped over lightly was an important year, the year we jumped in growth, the year of our first big exhibition at the Squibb Galleries— 1937. Incredibly, Miss Rose does not discuss the American Abstract Artists in her recent *American Painting: The 20th Century*, Skira, 1970.

7. "American Abstract Artists," vol. 3, nos. 3–4, p. 25.

8. The only complete folio in existence that I know about is owned by Theo Hios. An incomplete copy is held by Leo Rabkin.

9. Vol. 3, no. 7 (October 1937), pp. 20–21.

10. Their existence and that of other work preserved in museums, private collections and storage areas, challenge Barbara Rose's flat statement on page 127 of *American Art Since 1900:* "Outside of a few murals known *only* through sketches and reconstructions such as Gorky's Newark Airport mural and de Kooning's sketch for the Williamsburg housing project, the WPA produced *almost no art of any consequence* that has *survived.*" The italics are mine. I leave to history to decide whether superb early examples of Stuart Davis, Ilya Bolotowsky, Byron Browne, Gertrude and Balcomb Greene, José de Rivera, Louis Schanker, and John von Wicht is art of "any consequence." In any case, this work survives. Housed in various collections I know about are Cavallons, Reinhardts, and the early figurative work of famous contemporary artists, such as Adolph Gottlieb, Jackson Pollock, Mark Rothko, Morris Graves, Loren MacIver.

11. Summer, 1967, p. 17.

12. *Arts* (September 1956), p. 52.

13. Ibid.

14. "Art Under Five Years of Federal Patronage," *The American Scholar* (Summer 1940), vol. 9, no. 3, p. 335.

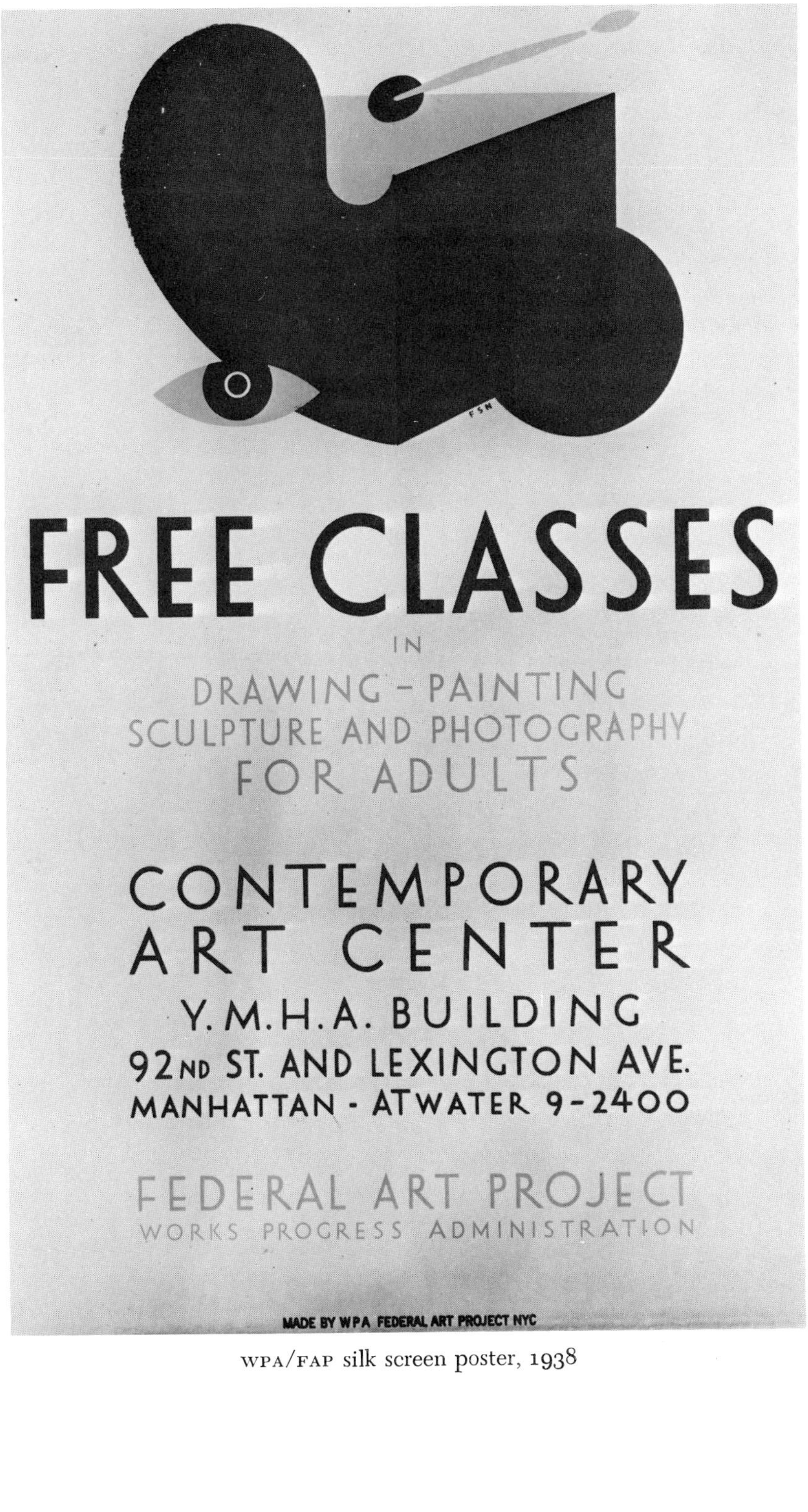

WPA/FAP silk screen poster, 1938

OLIVE LYFORD GAVERT has long been engaged in art activities. During the early 1930s she organized volunteer service in museums and art organizations for the Association of Junior Leagues of America. She was employed as a supervisor and assistant to the regional director on the New York WPA/FAP from 1935 to 1937. At the time of the 1939–1940 World's Fair in New York, she was in charge of art demonstrations and, during its second year, coordinated its art exhibitions. Later her interest in art led her to work for the Museum of Modern Art, New York, the Office of the Coordinator of Inter-American Affairs in Washington, and the American Red Cross. She is a former board member of the American Federation of Arts and is currently on the board of the Institute of Modern Art. As an artist, her work has appeared in a number of one-man and group shows in this country and Europe.

FIGURE 48. Olive Lyford posing in costume in the Victorian room of an Index of American Design exhibition at the WPA Federal Art Gallery, New York City, March 1939. (Archives of American Art)

The WPA Federal Art Project
and the New York World's Fair, 1939–1940

OLIVE LYFORD GAVERT

Twentieth-Century World's Fairs

The presentation of programs sponsored by the WPA/FAP at the New York World's Fair in 1939 and 1940 marked a milestone in the steadily widening interest in American art and artists which began in the early years of the 20th century.[1] The rapid changes in the social and economic scene were, of course, vividly reflected in the esthetic expressions of the 1930s. Earlier formality and neo-classicism had been superceded in 1939–40 by broadly based, democratically orientated manifestations in art. If one looks at two former world fairs one realizes how great the changes were in a relatively few years.

In 1915 the San Francisco "Panama-Pacific International Exposition" celebrated the opening of the Panama Canal. Interest was focused on the heroic and majestic, the noble and ideal. Language was couched in rather grandiose and sentimental terms and optimism reigned. Although World War I was in its second year, the United States was not yet involved.

The first paragraph of the introduction to the official catalogue reads: "This is but the counsel of a comrade anxious that you should realize the joy of just rambling 'round. . . . Catch the spirit of these 'sermons in stone' which preach our present-day gospel of 'Get There' none the less eloquently because they follow rather the simple phraseology of the Beatitudes than the labored language of finance."

The quotation is not to belittle the Exposition itself, which was a magnificent achievement of post-Victorian splendor. The Palace of Fine Arts was considered to be one of the wonders of the age. The acting chief for the abundance of heroic sculpture was A. Stirling Calder, who was aided by 160 men. The great colonnaded buildings, their curved facades decorated ornately with relief and

247

free-standing sculpture, the huge equestrian statues of Cortez, Pizarro, and others in armor, enormous fountain groups, far exceeded in size and elaborate detail any in later exposition sculpture. Those for the Fountain of Energy by Calder, a column designed like the Aurelian column in Rome entitled Column of Progress; vast allegorical murals, Labor Crowned, Achievement, Earth, Air, Fire, and Water by Frank Brangwyn of London, bespoke the firm faith of the day in the romantic and ideal. (A footnote to the exhibition of American Art was that women painters had a gallery to themselves. One wonders whether they thought this was desirable or whether it was forced upon them.)

Matthew Arnold's words inscribed on one of the reliefs was in keeping with the spirit of the times: "What good gifts have we but they come through strife and toil and loving sacrifice."

The title of the 1933 World's Fair in Chicago, "A Century of Progress," as far as art was concerned, referred principally to *progress in collecting* works of art during the preceding century. It was the proud position of the Chicago Art Institute that the works shown had been entirely assembled from American sources with one exception, Whistler's *Mother*. In 1833 very few works of importance were on this side of the Atlantic, but by 1933 "treasures of an amazing quality" had been transported to the United States for private and museum collections. At last artists and the public could see an extensive exhibition of great works without crossing the Atlantic, which had been impossible for all but the very few.

The emphasis on European art was still strong, however, and American art was not yet known as an entity important enough to stand on its own. It was combined mainly with that of Paris, still considered the capital of the art world. The titles of the three sections of paintings were: European Painting, 13th to 18th Centuries; Nineteenth Century Painting; and Twentieth Century Painting: National and International. The sculpture section was a combination of American and European works of the 19th and 20th centuries.

In the sculpture section twenty Americans were shown, all still living at that time. The eldest, Lorado Taft, was seventy-three, the majority were over forty, and the youngest was thirty-three. Among them were George Gray Barnard, Jo Davidson, Gertrude Whitney, Paul Manship, Jacob Epstein, Gaston Lachaise, and Mahonri Young; a notable group, but it would seem that on the whole the attitude that only successfully established and well-known artists were worthy of representing their country at a World's Fair was still the rule. The exception was a small exhibition of work by younger artists in the abstract artists section. There were only twenty-six American and European painters in the whole group, five being Americans. These were Peter Blume (27), Stefan Hirsch (26), Saul Schary (29), Albert Bloch, and Theodore Roszak. The abstract paintings were shown in a room entirely separated from the rest of the Exhibition. Perhaps this was to spare the feelings of World's Fair visitors to whom these manifestations would seem too alarming or ridiculous.

Between 1933 and 1939 the feeling was being dispelled that art was for museums and remote from daily living. The emphasis moved from the inspiring and instructional toward involvement in the everyday life in which the artists and citizens found themselves.

The plans for the two fairs of 1939 and 1940 in San Francisco and New York demonstrated a change in attitude toward art, which came more and more to be seen as an existing and necessary part of life.

The Golden Gate International Exposition, 1939–1940

In San Francisco at the Golden Gate International Exposition, there were three sections in the Contemporary Art Building: Art in Action, Art in Use, and California Art Today. These titles indicate the desire to draw the public into a closer contact with the art exhibits. According to the catalogues, the Art in Use section was to bring about a practical alliance between modern architecture, household furnishings, and abstract art. The California Art Today show included non-professional painters who produced "some of the strongest paintings." The demonstrations set up in Art in Action were made by painters, sculptors, print-makers, mosaic artists, ceramic craftsmen, and textile designers. The latter was under the direction of Anita Breuer and a group of WPA/FAP artists.

There was a complete mural workshop and a mosaic mural, 22 by 44 feet, was constructed during the summer at one end of the great hall. Diego Rivera and a group of WPA/FAP workers made a fresco of similar size at the other end. Rivera generously loaned his talents in the interests of good will, with the understanding that the mural would be permanently preserved.

There was a "Pageant of Photography" designed by Ansel Adams about which it was stated: "It is a pleasure to say that photography is here recognized for the first time in an exhibition of Fine Art at an Exposition."

The WPA/FAP's imposing art exhibit, "Frontiers of American Art" in the de Young Museum was selected by Herman More of the Whitney Museum and was "peculiarly American" although it ranged from literal realism to abstraction. Many of the exhibits were by artists on the New York Project. From the mural section were David Margolis, Eric Mose, Walter Quirt, Max Spivak, Lucienne Bloch, Francis Criss, and Paul Kelpe. From the easel section were paintings by Manuel Tolegian, Joseph de Martini, Don Forbes, Robert Archer, Louis Guglielmi, Perkins Harnly, Louis Ribak, Austin Mechlin, Elizabeth Terrel, and Julian Levi. Among the sculptors were Robert Cronbach, Hugo Robus, Robert Russin, Max Baum, and Eugenie Gershoy.

Herman More wrote in the catalogue that painting was losing its esoteric character. The same could be said of all other art media at the time as local committees became accustomed to accepting manifestations of art as a natural element in life. At this fair the public could see for the first time the work and art processes of the artists of their own country in buildings especially designed and equipped for the purpose. Visitors could watch artists at work, thus establishing a human dimension to their experience in art. New techniques and media were recognized as valid esthetically and were explained, as were the art exhibits, by guides and lecturers. Films were shown illustrating the fundamental principles on which an understanding and appreciation of art depend.

The most dramatic demonstration of this change in outlook toward art's role in the community, however, was to be found in the art activities at the New York World's Fair.

The New York World's Fair, 1939–1940

Consultations and planning for art activities at the New York World's Fair began as early as 1935 when Holger Cahill was asked by Grover Whalen, president of the Fair, to give his advice in regard to exhibitions and the role of the WPA/FAP.

Over a period of time Cahill met with members of its board of design, appointed in 1936. These were Stephen Voorhees (chairman), W. A. Delano (architect), Gilmore Clark (landscape-architect), Jay Towner (engineer), and Walter Dorwin Teague (industrial designer). Ernest Peixotto, painter member and secretary of the New York City Art Commission, became consultant to the subcommittee on murals, and Lee Lawrie consultant to the subcommittee on sculpture. The architects on the board of design had recommended to the Fair directors that in order to insure cooperation during the period of the creation of a finished design for the Fair, the directors also appoint a landscape architect and an engineer. A landscape architect was not to be called in merely to give an exterior setting to a structure previously designed or an engineer to provide merely a supporting skeleton for an architect's plan.

As an editorial in the *Art Digest* (May 15, 1939) expressed it: "Fairs are no longer haphazard displays of things amazing and spectacular but are a new 20th Century art form. The New York Fair is an entity in itself and an independent expression of a people."

From the start Cahill advocated a liberal attitude toward art and architecture, with a program demonstrating social betterment and recognition of industry as an aid to life. He also was in accord with the views of the majority of the board of design that community living should be stressed and that this could be accomplished by the construction of buildings for this purpose. For the program of art at the Fair he suggested that a complete picture of the rise and development of the arts in the United States be shown, and that it should not be local or international but solely national in character. The atmosphere should be that of a festival in keeping with the spirit of a world's fair.

From the very start, the planning on the part of the Fair administration made it evident that a new democratic spirit was in the air. It appeared first in a statement by the New York World's Fair Board of Design: "Let it be remembered that past World's Fairs in America have all been more or less mannered in style and steered in a certain direction in regard to their aesthetic expressions. Therefore it became consistent with the principles endorsed by the New York World's Fair that it should demonstrate a liberal reflection of the aesthetic forces at work among contemporary artists. And for this reason the Fair Designers have not been dictated to as to style." The only control exerted by the board was in relation to scale, color, and relationships between architecture, landscaping and placing of sculpture. Murals and sculpture were commissioned in relation to the three color sectors: white to bright gold, pale to Pompeian red, light to ultramarine blue. There were many protests, however, that the board exerted far too much control despite its official statements.

The board of design also stated later that artists who were chosen to embellish the buildings and grounds of the World's Fair included men and women of distinction, with well-known names, and also talented younger artists who heretofore had little chance to demonstrate their abilities to the public. This marked a departure from the attitude and policies of the controlling boards of former world's fairs, such as the quite recent 1933 Chicago Fair or the 1915 San Francisco Fair.

By 1937 specific recommendations were offered by the WPA Federal Project No. 1. In a letter addressed to Mrs. Ellen S. Woodward, (assistant federal administrator in charge of the womens and professional division, of which the art projects were a part at that time) Cahill states that several ideas had been brought forward and discussed between Audrey McMahon, Hallie Flanagan (national director of the WPA Federal Theater Project), Paul Edwards (administrative director of the WPA Federal Project No. 1 in New York, who was appointed as coordinator of all WPA arts activities at the World's Fair), Commander Flanigan (executive vice-president and chief administrator of the Fair), and himself.

Among the recommendations it was suggested that the WPA/FAP decorate the various State buildings at the Fair, making sure that "we would not be competing with private enterprise or taking jobs away from artists who should be paid commercially for doing this work"; that a plan be implemented for a community art center at the Fair in which all the Federal Art Projects would collaborate and carry on activities; and that a pageant be staged. The latter was vetoed because of trouble between the Theater Project and the government, while the first two recommendations were gradually adjusted to meet practical requirements.

Constant effort in subsequent conferences was to determine how the Project could best contribute to the Fair and the cause to which it was dedicated. Although recognizing the fact that the WPA/FAP was in constant danger of being curtailed, this group hopefully outlined further plans for art as basic to the community center idea, the general theme of the Fair.

Cahill, Thomas C. Parker (his assistant and later his deputy), and Audrey McMahon all felt strongly that the whole WPA national program should be dramatically presented to the public, and that the art program should be part of a whole concept of community life enriched by community activities in which all participate. The Project should present demonstrations of various art media in work shops where could be shown such activities as the design and execution of posters, mural processes, painting and printmaking, sculpture in wood and stone. In this way the lay public would become more interested, their appreciation broadened, and possibly their desire awakened to take part in creative activities—or to purchase art.

These plans for an ideal community center finally materialized in the program for the WPA Building. The WPA exhibit was to include Federal Art Project's exhibits and demonstrations. It was natural that the displays were made up of WPA activities that had already been functioning as part of the nation-wide WPA community center program. Represented were the divisions of recreation, education, libraries, music, theater, and, to some extent, art.

In December 1938, the organizational arrangements for the WPA Building were officially set forth as follows:

Appointed: *Executive Committee,* to define the manner in which participation by the WPA administration in the New York World's Fair would be conducted. They were the following:

Mrs. Ellen S. Woodward, Assistant Federal Administrator
  in charge of Womens and Professional Division
Mr. David K. Niles, ditto, in charge of Information Service
Col. F. C. Harrington, ditto, in charge of Engineering Division
Lt. Col. Brehon Somervell, WPA Administrator for New York City
Mr. Holger Cahill, Director, Federal Art Project
Mr. Allen H. Eaton

This committee was responsible to Mr. Harry Hopkins for the general conduct of the enterprise. It defined general policies, made all major decisions, and acted upon the recommendations submitted to it by the *Exhibition Committee.*

The *Exhibition Committee* consisted of the following:

Mr. Roscoe Wright, Director on Information, Chairman
Mr. Leonard C. Rennie, Chief of the Exhibits and Displays Section
Mr. John G. Curran, representing the N. Y. C. WPA
Capt. G. E. Textor, representing the Engineering Division

Mrs. Charley T. Cole, representing the Womens and Professional Division
Mr. Holger Cahill, Director of the Federal Art Project
Later: Thomas Parker, Deputy Director
     Burgoyne Diller, FAP Representative from December, 1938

The Exhibition Committee, subject to the approval of the Executive Committee, was responsible for the detailed planning of the exhibit and for the production of murals and other material and their delivery to New York City in time for installation in the building. The committee met on a weekly schedule.

One of the first ideas to be considered and launched was a very ambitious plan for a photo-mural "rising to the ceiling and extending the entire 520 square feet, over which will be applied statements in cutout letters . . . also colorful graphs as factual backing of the statements."

The work was well under way in November when at a meeting of the Exhibition Committee, Mr. Rennie, reported that the first draft was 40 percent complete. Several hundred photographs were then in his possession for use by the artist assigned to the project. The FAP, through Thomas Parker in Washington, would provide a mural expert to supervise the assembly and production of the photo mural. There were difficulties in finding a qualified expert and in assigning photographers to assist, although a report on December 3rd stated that the photo mural was "in work." By the end of the month, however, the Exhibition Committee finally rejected it and less ambitious plans were made. These finally culminated in a series of large but simple photo-murals not executed by the FAP. They were entitled: "Work Adds to the National Wealth," "Work Preserves Skills," "Work the Basis of Culture," "Work Enriches Daily Living," "Work Increases Knowledge," "Work Holds Homes Together."

At the November 18th Exhibition Committee meeting, Thomas Parker, acting for Cahill, accepted the responsibility for presenting details of how the WPA/FAP would handle all murals and sculptural decoration for the WPA Building, the tower, entrance foyer, and courtyard. On December 15th the final plan was submitted and accepted. Burgoyne Diller, supervisor of the Mural Division, was put in charge of securing working space and materials. The Fair administration offered all the necessary canvas, which was accepted, other supplies to be discussed later. (After December 1938 neither Cahill nor Parker attended the Exhibition Committee meetings, and Diller became the point of contact between the Fair and the New York WPA/FAP.)

Four interior and two exterior murals were decided upon, as well as a mural curtain for the auditorium. The artists chosen were Philip Guston, Eric Mose, Seymour Fogel, Anton Refregier, Ryah Ludins and Louis Ross, the curtain to be designed by Ruth Reeves. The artists were employed according to the usual WPA/FAP procedures. Sketches were submitted to Mrs. McMahon and Burgoyne

Diller, and were approved by Ernest Peixotto of the New York City Art Commission. For this work the artists' pay was raised from $23 a week to $35 a week, the assistant painters' salaries remaining at the former figure.

Trouble was encountered with the United Scenic Artists, which insisted that all artists at the Fair must be members of their union. (Mr. Whalen had agreed to this, a decision denounced by an editorial in the *Herald Tribune*.) Philip Guston recounted that one day as he was painting his exterior mural, unaware of this requirement, a limousine drove up and a man got out and demanded to see his union card. Not having any, he was obliged to stop painting until he obtained one. Fortunately the Project paid the fee, which would have been quite an embarrassment for him on $35 a week. One good thing about it, he said, was that a union membership made it possible for him to continue to work on the mural himself whereas many mural painters at the Fair had accepted the limitation of simply submitting their designs and then turning them over to be blown up by anonymities of the Mural Artists Guild, a branch of the United Scenic Artists. This union (AFL) had threatened to strike the Fair unless it was given jurisdiction over all murals, their design, execution, and placement. Emphatic statements against this requirement appeared in art magazine articles and editorials. The artists themselves differed as to the necessity of union membership or non-membership.

The theme of the Fair read: "To contribute A Happier Way of American Living by demonstrating how it can be achieved through the growing interdependence of men of every class and function, and by showing the things, ideas and forces at work in the world which are the tools of today and with which the better world of tomorrow is to be built." Forbes Watson, commenting in the May 1939 issue of the *Magazine of Art*, stated that "Mr. Whalen's philosophical waggeries about 'a world of tomorrow' and a 'happier way of American living' are tributes to academic advertising." There were many people who felt as Mr. Watson did, that since the Fair was a 150 million dollar commercial enterprise it should not endeavor to be too profound in its attitudes. The artists, however, were deeply involved in the serious aspects of life and wished to express their genuine feelings.

For the WPA Building the subjects of the murals related to the WPA program. Philip Guston's mural was over the main entrance of the WPA Building and was entitled *Maintaining America's Skills*, the inference being that this was one of the main purposes of WPA employment. There were four large, stylized figures: an engineer, a woman scientist, a surveyor, and a laborer. Besides the trouble previously mentioned, Guston had difficulty with his original color scheme. He found that at a distance the subtle colors he had at first planned did not carry the length of the ramp approaching the building, 200 or 300 feet. After two or three weeks' work he had to entirely reevaluate the colors to be used,

FIGURE 49.   Philip Guston (b. 1913). *Maintaining America's Skills*. Exterior mural for WPA Building at New York World's Fair. WPA/FAP, 1939. (National Archives)

and finally employed the primary ones; black, white, red, yellow, and blue. In the meantime the wpa kept urging him to speed up the completion of the mural as the budget for scaffolding was being exceeded. Another delay was caused by specks of silver leaf from the rca Building which were blown onto the wet paint of the mural, necessitating a crew to be rushed from the New York Project to aid in obliterating them. Forbes Watson, writing on an early visit to the Fair (*Magazine of Art*, May 1939, p. 318), said of the painting on the façade of the wpa Building, still behind scaffolding, that it "looked as though it might really come to something." That this was indeed true was brought out later when Guston was awarded a first prize for outdoor murals at the Fair. One other comment is worth recording, made a year later by Geoffrey Norman, assistant to the director of the fap in New York City, in a memorandum to the wpa administrator at the Fair, Colonel Somervell: "I am sure it will be of interest to you . . . to know that during a visit to the World's Fair grounds last week it was remarked that while most of the exterior mural decorations were badly faded in color, the outstanding exception was Philip Guston's fresco over the entrance of the wpa Building. This appeared as fresh and clean as the day it was painted and has not been affected in any way by an unusually severe winter. It is a fine example of good craftsmanship and a commentary on the excellence of the mural division of the n.y.c. Art Project."

For years the technical service department of the wpa in New York City, headed by Raphael Doktor, had experimented with pigments, adhesives, canvasses, and many other art materials. The effectiveness of these experiments was demonstrated by the quotation above.

Other murals were as follows: *The Relationship of the WPA to Rehabilitation,* by Seymour Fogel, an interior mural on the left side wall of the lobby, covering 748 square feet. It was described as "showing how people can be raised from starvation and hopelessness to self-support and self-reliance." The medium was oil on canvas.

Anton Refregier's interior mural (8 panels) was called *Cultural Activities of the WPA,* and portrayed the education, art, music and writer's projects. Refregier won a second prize for indoor murals at the Fair. He was also represented by a painting in the contemporary American art exhibition, *Accident in the Air,* and a mural in the main gallery of the American Art Today Building in 1940.

Building and Construction was the title of a mural by Eric Mose, portraying wpa activities and accomplishments in those fields, and Ryah Ludins, using "rubber paint" on wooden forms, combining low relief and painting created a mural described as "a gay and colorful picture of childrens' recreation under wpa supervision." Although another mural by Louis Ross is mentioned in the original plan no description of it could be found.

Not included in the list of mural painters in the WPA Building was the name of Ruth Reeves, well-known designer and one of the originators of the Index of American Design project. (Dorothy Liebes, textile designer of California, was one of the others.) She had designed a "traveling curtain" for the auditorium of the WPA Building. The curtain was described as a "mural curtain, in tones of brown and dull pink and was painted in casein on linen." Its subject was "community activities." It was 650 square feet.

Also on view were a series of Index of American Design plates, four pieces of sculpture, and three oil paintings, loaned by the WPA/FAP. The sculptures were: *Girl With Sheep*, by Concetta Scaravaglione, *Girl With Deer*, by Berta Margoulies, *Natural Resources*, by William Zorach, *Young Lincoln*, by James Hansen. It was requested by the administrator of the building that the paintings "bridge the gap between the ultra-conservative and the ultra-modern." Also on loan from the WPA/FAP were three demonstrators, a sculptor, a woodcarver, and a silk-screen printer.

Allen Eaton, author of an extensive report on the WPA professional and service projects at the Fair, (mainly in the WPA Building), wrote: "This division (FAP) is best represented in the mural paintings and decorations over the general entrance to the building, in the courtyard, in the large entrance hall, in the entrance to the theater, and by the theater curtain. I feel that the artists deserve a great deal of credit for what has been done in a very limited time and often under difficult circumstances."

The WPA/FAP also sponsored murals in the Fair's Medicine and Public Health Building. These were painted by Ilya Bolotowsky, Byron Browne, Balcomb Greene, Louis Schanker, A. Lishinsky, and Irving Block and included some interesting abstract designs.

Several mural painters and sculptors currently or formerly working for the WPA/FAP received commissions directly from the Fair or private exhibitors.

Eric Mose composed a mural, *Chemicals and Plastics*, in collaboration with José de Rivera, sculptor, using a plastic "now available which is crystal clear, in a variety of colors which the artist related to the spectrum." Also used were metals, strong lights, and aluminum tubes. This was for the Hall of Industrial Science.

Louis Ferstadt was commissioned to do a huge exterior mural on the walls of the Court of Communications Building. It was called: *Here You Are—The Greatest Show on Earth*. He is quoted as saying, "Man Alive is the subject of my mural, the understanding and use of the phenomenon of nature."

Arshile Gorky received a commission for the Aviation Building. Willem de Kooning together with Michael Loew and Stuyvesant Van Veen designed and executed a mural entitled *Production* for the Hall of Pharmacy Building.

William Zorach, whose sculpture *Benjamin Franklin* was shown in the Contemporary Art Building, also received a commission from the Fair. His monumental *Builders of the Future* was dedicated to manual labor which he felt was vital to the development of civilization and the family. He wrote: "It will be noticed that I have eliminated all scientific contraptions from the design and stripped my monument of everything except the essential details."

For the board of design, Waylande Gregory, formerly supervisor of the WPA/FAP sculpture division in New Jersey, created a fountain called *The Fountain of the Atom*. The general design was based on the octet theory of the atom, symbolized by eight figures representing electrons, boys and girls dancing a joyous, energetic dance around the nucleus. The fountain was at the foot of a ramp from a subway exit, and near the entrance of the Contemporary Art Building. Gregory also had two equestrian pieces in the United States Federal Building.

Chaim Gross, Louis Slobodkin, Concetta Scaravaglione, and Milton Hebald, all government sponsored sculptors, also received commissions from the Fair.

Louis Slobodkin's statue, variously called *Lincoln, the Rail Joiner,* or *Unity,* portrayed a young frontiersman joining two split rails (ploughshares?) symbolizing federal unity. There was a pleasing lack of pretense in this piece, but apparently it offended Edward J. Flynn, political boss of the Bronx, who had it "sledge-hammered into oblivion" by some accounts, others saying it "disappeared." Naturally there was a great outcry of anger against such an unwarranted and totally unforgivable and illegal act.

Another WPA sculptor by the name of Thomas G. Lo Medico won an $8,000 commission for a sculpture at the Metropolitan Life Building. It was a three-figure group symbolizing the average American family. Lo Medico had been on the Section and also the WPA/FAP, about which he wrote that he was indebted "for freedom from economic pressure which is necessary for an artist and encourages him to do his best work." An honorary mention for his art went to William Van Beek, a supervisor in the WPA/FAP sculpture division.

The Contemporary American Art Exhibition, 1939

An article in *Life* magazine (March 3, 1939), reported:

For a while it seemed as if statues and murals would constitute all the art at the Fair. No attempt was made to have a formal exhibition. But spurred by the San Francisco art coup, the Fair is hustling together a worthy collection of Old Masters, and will also have some modern American works.

This casual statement hardly describes the outcry on the part of artists and the public on learning that no art exhibitions as such had been planned for the Fair. The public furor brought about an intense revision in the thinking of Fair officials and resulted in the construction of two buildings known as the Master-pieces of Art and the Contemporary Art buildings.

For the "Masterpieces" exhibition, William R. Valentiner, director general of the exhibition, made a trip to Europe and in five months collected a group of celebrated paintings from museums and private collections. At the same time, he made arrangements with the officials of the Milan Exposition (May 9–September 30, 1939) to receive from their "Leonardo da Vinci Exhibition" a group of paintings by da Vinci's imitators, as well as two original da Vinci's from collections in the United States—an interesting development in relation to the 1933 Chicago Fair with its emphasis on the growth of collections of European masterpieces in the United States, mentioned earlier.

In the meantime, an elaborate plan for the exhibition of contemporary American art was inaugurated. Mr. Whalen, president of the Fair Corporation, placed the exhibition under the direction of a governing committee and an artists' committee. A. Conger Goodyear, president of the Museum of Modern Art, became chairman of the Governing Committee, the members of which were Juliana Force, director, Whitney Museum; Holger Cahill, national director, Federal Art Project; Lawrence P. Roberts, acting director, Brooklyn Museum; Herbert E. Winlock, director, Metropolitan Museum.

The Governing Committee named the nine members of the Artists' Committee, which established the procedures for the exhibitions and, after consultations with artists' organizations and museum directors, set up a system of Committees of Selection to handle work throughout the country. The Artists' Committee was composed of: Holger Cahill, chairman; Anne Goldthwaite, chairman, American Printmakers Association; John Taylor Arms, president, Society of American Etchers; Stuart Davis, national chairman, American Artists Congress; Hugo Gellert, chairman, Artists Coordination Committee; John Gregory, president, National Sculpture Society; Jonas Lie, president, National Academy of Design; Paul Manship, sculpture; Eugene Speicher, painter; William Zorach, sculptor.

It was the philosophy and experience of Holger Cahill which most strongly influenced the procedures determined by the Artists' Committee. He felt that contemporary art in the United States could not be adequately chosen by traditional methods, and was particularly interested in removing the power of selection from the élite few to a much larger, broadly based representation. This had become possible because of the growing decentralization of art, especially during the five years previous to the Fair, during which time the WPA/FAP had established art centers and projects across the country. Previous to this, it was said that 85 percent of the artists had congregated in nine metropolitan areas. Local art organizations had also begun to develop their own cultural resources and were given every encouragement by the WPA/FAP. As a result the public had become aware of the value and importance of the artist in their communities, finding him an interpreter of the life and design of everyday living. All of this was reflected in the final selection of paintings chosen for the contemporary American art exhibition.

In order to bring about a thoroughly democratic selection, the Artists' Committee, under Cahill's guidance, consulted with leading art organizations, artists and museum directors, in appointing the "Committees of Selection" to choose the work of artists from all parts of the country. This effort had never been attempted or thought desirable before. Each state within the seven regions had three committees of three each, for painting, sculpture, and graphic art. The three members in each category were to represent "American art in all its tendencies, conservative, middle-of-the-road, and modern." A number of consultants who had wide knowledge of art in their regions were appointed also, to aid the committees of selection. All committee members and consultants were persons professionally concerned with art: artists, museum directors and curators, or officials of art organizations. Finally, 25,000 works from thirty-six states were viewed by the regional committees (numbering approximately 500 persons), 1,200 chosen and sent to the central Artists' Committee in New York.

The fact that many of the artists whose work was accepted were currently or formerly on the payroll of the WPA/FAP gives proof again of the importance of the encouragement and support they had received from the government.

The building to house this exhibition was designed by Frederick L. Ackerman, Joshua V. Lowenfish, and John V. Van Pelt. Julian Garnsey was color consultant. It was built of California redwood and had a dignified, quiet façade composed of simple but interesting geometric forms. There were twenty-three galleries of various shapes and sizes from the great circular rotunda at the front entrance to smaller and more intimate rooms extending toward the rear. A more detailed description of the uses for the galleries and demonstrations of art processes will be given (p. 262) describing the building in 1940 under the jurisdiction of the New York Federal Art Project.[2]

The comments of A. Conger Goodyear and the members of the Artists' Committee, writing the prefaces for the three sections of the exhibition catalogue (*American Art Today*), reveal the important aspects of what was shown.

The policy of the board of design to include talented young artists who had not had the chance of coming before the public was carried out in the "American Art Today" exhibition. "Many new names will be found in this catalogue," reads the preface by Goodyear, "They are the names of those who in the best judgment of the most experienced artists [the jurors in the committees of selection] of the United States, show promise of carrying on the great tradition of American Art in the larger field that the life of tomorrow will offer."

The introduction to the painting section, written by Stuart Davis (modern), Jonas Lie (conservative), and Eugene Speicher (middle-of-the-road), states that "full representation of every aspect of contemporary American Art is to be found, . . . is a fact of such great importance that it cannot be stressed enough, . . . significant of a new point of view and the result of democratic principles . . . is the vitality and freshness of the painting section. New names appear, new sections of the country are given well-earned prominence with a force and power that in many examples indicates something ruggedly American in spirit and strikingly healthy in action."

John Gregory, Paul Manship, and William Zorach gave a constructive criticism in the catalogue's section on sculpture. They felt that contemporary sculpture was too localized in urban centers and that "all that has been done is a program that must be pushed much further to give us the base we need for the development of our national art. The show could stand more abstraction at one end and classic academic work at the other." (The "middle-of-the-road" sculpture was evidently considered too nondescript?) They spoke of the reaction of contemporary sculptors against the rococo and baroque and of how some had turned to early sculpture and the primitive for vitality and freshness. "To visitors from small communities will come a revelation of new materials and design."

John Taylor Arms, Hugo Gellert, and Anne Goldthwaite wrote the preface for the print section. "Lacking the sophistication of modern French and the uniformly high degree of technical excellence of the English, we yet are rapidly developing a school [of printmaking] which, in its spontaneous expression of national spirit, its directness and individuality of approach, its sensitivity to all the influences of our national life, and the complete honesty of its manifestations, is unsurpassed in any other country in the world."

Cahill strove toward a comprehensive grasp of total situations and conditions. This was evident not only by his attitude toward the selection of work for the art exhibition, but also in the relationship of the exhibition to the Fair as a whole. He wrote of this in his brilliant foreword in the *American Art Today* catalogue: "The New York World's Fair may be called an expression of the contemporary arts . . . the Fair as a whole is a vast mosaic of our present-day culture which everywhere shows the skill and talent of the artist . . . in this great cooperative demonstration of the creative and productive forces of modern civilization which the World's Fair is, its exhibition "American Art Today" is an integral part."

The artists of the exhibition were successful in revealing the needs, interests, ideas, and sentiments of the people as a whole rather than adhering to the former personalized expression by artists in relation to sophisticated coteries. Emily Genauer, art critic for the *New York Herald-Tribune*, expressed her reaction to what she found in the "American Art Today" exhibition: "It looks like America itself, its broad prairies, its teeming cities, its pleasant valleys, its dust bowls, its slums. And it is beautiful as life itself even in its grimmer aspects where 'beauty' lies in intense vitality. . . . The public will be astonished at the high level of competence."

The Fair administration planned to earmark 5 percent of the entrance fees for the purchase of works of art from the exhibition. The fees, however, did not realize the estimated amount and only $1,800 became available. From this sum four paintings, one sculpture, and ten or twelve prints were purchased by the Fair and donated to several museums.

The American Art Today Exhibition, 1940

Early in 1940, Mayor LaGuardia and the Fair administration agreed to contribute the use of the Contemporary Art Building to the New York City WPA. Holger Cahill would not directly supervise the project, but his authority would be the same as it was to any art project operated by a State administration. It was hoped that Clement Haupers, state supervisor of the Minnesota WPA/FAP, would be in charge of the building and program. It was found, however, that he could not be spared and Joseph Danysh, regional director for California, was appointed in his place.

The exhibition was the culmination of the nation-wide program begun in 1935 and was the largest display of the WPA/FAP art yet seen. About one-third of the exhibits were gathered from many parts of the country through the Washington office of the Project, and about two-thirds from New York City and State, for a total of about 800 items. It reflected the confidence and enthusiasm which the public had given the work of the WPA/FAP artists, which, in turn, made them realize that their work was appreciated and wanted. Their work showed a marked advance in power, decisiveness, and flexibility in interpreting the spirit and experience of the people of the country.

The murals and mural cartoons ranged from straight-forward realism to pure decoration, but all were keyed to an architectural whole. These were shown in the great rotunda of the WPA Building, placed high above the usual line for pictures. Smaller paintings and sculpture were shown below. The large murals came mainly from the New York City project because of the difficulty of transportation, but smaller sketches and cartoons gave a general survey of the work in this field from other sections of the country. The murals were allocated to such tax-supported institutions as schools and hospitals.

Except for the murals and large sculpture, the exhibits in the first eight galleries were changed periodically to give representation to the thousands of WPA/FAP art works in all media produced during the past five years. Partly because of the interest of the mayor in providing as broad an opportunity as possible to all New York City artists, the work of artists from collaborating organizations was shown on a three-week schedule in other galleries. The collaborating organizations were The Society of American Etchers, The National Society of

Mural Painters, An American Group, The National Association of Women Painters and Sculptors, The New York Society of Women Artists, The American Artists Congress, The National Academy of Design, United American Artists, Harlem Artists' Guild, Society of Modern Artists, National Sculpture Society, Sculptors' Guild, Allied Artists, New York Water Color Club, American Artists' Professional League, American Abstract Artists, and American Society of Miniature Painters.

Four galleries were devoted to rotating exhibitions, the first by the WPA/FAP followed by other groups. The Project exhibition was selected and arranged by the Museum of Modern Art in three groups of about twenty each and were given theme titles: "The Face of America," a group of landscapes from every section of the country; "Painters of Mystery and Sentiment," a selection of oils and watercolors; "Painters under 35," consisting of oils and watercolors. These three exhibitions were sent on a traveling circuit to the WPA community art centers. Other rotating exhibitions first shown in these galleries were "Graphic Art" arranged by the Society of American Etchers, an exhibition of fifty prints in all media from the Honolulu Print-Makers Club, and "100 Contemporary Mexican Prints." Practically every print process was represented in this collection, and some new techniques appeared, such as the carborundum and silk-screen prints, developed by the artists on the WPA/FAP. They gave a rich and vivid record of the contemporary scene which Cahill described as "fresh as today's newspaper, masterly in craftsmanship, and highly individual in style."

Eight galleries were reserved for demonstrations by WPA/FAP artists and the collaborating societies, with wall spaces for small associated exhibits. The demonstrations of the Project artists were conducted as their regular work assignments. The public had the opportunity of watching art in the making, the actual techniques employed for the making of a fresco, mosaic, prints, sculpture, posters, and Index of American Design drawings. The range of demonstrations was the same as that of the total exhibition.

The official opening ceremony of the WPA/FAP's "American Art Today" exhibition took place on May 21, 1940, at which time the speakers were Mayor La-Guardia, Commander Flanigan representing the Fair, Colonel Somervell for the City WPA, Mrs. Audrey McMahon, director of the city WPA/FAP, and Joseph Danysh, director of the World's Fair art project, who read a message from Holger Cahill. Another speaker was Ernest Peixotto, member of the City Art Commission and the mayor's representative on city-sponsored art projects.

The mayor spoke vehemently in favor of the WPA and launched a rhetorical war against detractors of its program. He inveighed against "cruel and unjust" statements being made in Congress against the WPA. "A great many jokes have been coined about the WPA," he said, "but I just can't laugh if anyone is so low as to joke about one who through no fault of his own is in distress." He said that all over New York City existed living proof that the WPA had paid for itself (referring to municipal pools, playgrounds, etc.) and now it could be seen by this exhibition that the WPA had proved itself again by the fine display of the artists' work. He especially liked the Index of American Design drawings but found the "modern" paintings hard to understand.

Before leaving, the mayor ran off the first impression of a souvenir print bearing the seal of the city, using a silk-screen process perfected by WPA artists.

The American Art Today Building, administered entirely by WPA/FAP personnel, was host to many other special events and demonstrations during succeeding weeks. Most of these were offered by the sixteen non-WPA art organizations which had been invited to put on rotating exhibitions at three-week intervals, each to have an "Opening Day" program. Two of the most interesting were presented by the Society of American Etchers and the Sculptors' Guild.

John Taylor Arms, president of the Society of American Etchers, and 38 members gave a demonstration of printmaking by three processes, lithography, etching, and wood-engraving. The presses and equipment necessary for the demonstration filled the large front gallery and transformed it into an immense print workshop. More than three thousand watched with fascination the various stages of printmaking. Mr. Arms himself etched and printed a plate all in the space of two hours while explaining each step without pausing.

Many aspects of sculpture-making were shown by members of the Sculptors' Guild: Chaim Gross, carving in wood; Saul Baizerman, hammering on copper; Louis Slobodkin, modeling in clay; Frank Epping, a portrait in clay; José de Creeft, carving in marble; John Hovannes, plaster casting; Dorothea Greenbaum, composition. Outdoor talks were also given by sculptors at the location of their own work: William Zorach, Louise Cross, Jean de Marco, Chaim Gross, Robert Laurent, Oronzio Maldarelli, Berta Margoulies, Charles Rudy, Concetta Scaravaglione, Louis Slobodkin, Marion Walton, Nat Werner, Paul Manship.

There was a special "WPA Art Project Day" when the art chairmen of the New York Board of Education were invited to come to the American Art Today Building to select prints from the FAP print exhibition. The prints were presented to the schools by Mayor LaGuardia. Mrs. Roosevelt had accepted an invitation to be present but was unable to do so.

Another event was called "American Designers Day" and was sponsored by the Fair's Fashion Committee and the administration of the American Art Today Building. The intention was to show how the extensive material of the Index of American Design—a cross-section of which was on exhibition—could be used as inspiration for modern designers of textiles, jewelry, household utensils, etc., and

FIGURE 50. Demonstration of painting by artists of "An American Group" in the main gallery of the American Art Today Building at the New York World's Fair, 1940. Artists are, left to right: Anton Refregier (whose mural can be seen on wall), George Picken, and Philip Evergood. (Courtesy of Mrs. Olive Lyford Gavert)

adapted for modern times. Ruth Reeves (textiles), John Vassos (industry and theater), Gilbert Rohde (industry), and Shepard Vogelgesang, were among those who gave talks and demonstrations. For example, Anne Frank chose a motif from an 18th-century wrought iron kettle tilter and arranged it in a rhythmic repeated pattern for a textile design, and a 19th-century pancake turner became a motif for a necklace of small metal pieces designed by Marguerita Mergentime.

Groups of New York students from the Art Students League, the Music and Art High School, the Washington Irving High School, and many others had special events arranged for them at the American Art Today Building.

Having been present at many of the demonstrations and special events in the American Art Today Building the writer is in a position to comment on the response of the public to them. As visitors watched the artists at work their keen interest was evident by their absorbed expressions and by the questions with which they plied the artists. To be allowed to touch the clay or stone, to discuss the tools or other equipment, to ask what inspired the work, to see a form emerging from wood or metal or paint, and more than any of these, to see and talk with "real, live artists" seemed to be an exciting experience. Sometimes they watched for a long time, sometimes the attention span was short, which was natural and depended on the type of visitor and on the ability of the artists to dramatize what they were doing to some extent.

The artists' response to an audience varied according to the temperament of each. A stone-cutter kept chiseling away all summer, not paying any attention to what was going on around him, others showed a real interest in wanting to explain what they were doing and with what tools and materials; Chaim Gross was one of these. Others were inclined to put on a real show, perhaps more histrionic than esthetic. Some came as members of a dedicated group like the Society of American Etchers and made a prodigious effort to communicate with their audience both by words and concentrated craftsmanship. Some came perhaps as a diversion and just enjoyed mingling with people.

On the whole, the mingling of artists and the public appeared to be quite exhilerating to both, and to some, an unforgettable experience.

This account has been an attempt to show the interaction of the WPA Federal Art Project with other activities at the New York World's Fair during the seasons of 1939–40. Allusions have been made not only to work by artists currently or formerly employed on the Project but also to a few connected with the Section.

In general it has shown that the WPA/FAP at the Fair illustrated in capsule form the great changes which had occurred since the turn of the century in social and esthetic attitudes and consequently in the visual expressions of the feelings and thoughts of the artists.

Cahill wrote in the foreword of the catalogue: "American Art Today shows that everywhere in the country there are artists who have the technique, the discipline and the will to maintain American art at the level of its best traditions, and that they are finding publics which are equal to the event." Visitors to the World's Fair did indeed seem to be "equal to the event" as they thronged to see what the artists had to say. The attendance of over a million visitors to the American Art Today exhibition during each of the two seasons of the Fair gave proof of Cahill's faith in the public's interest in contemporary American art.

1. In doing the research for this memoir, I have drawn on the files of the WPA Federal Art Project on file in Record Group 69 at the National Archives in Washington, D.C. and on official World's Fair documents and catalogs in the collection of the New York Public Library. I have also consulted articles published in *Parnassus, Design, Art News, The Art Digest,* and the *Magazine of Art.*

2. *Staff of Exhibition 1939:* Holger Cahill, director; Donald J. Bear, assistant director, specializing in the representation of outlying regions, loaned by the Denver Art Museum of which he was the director; Elizabeth Litchfield, assistant director; Olive Lyford, in charge of art demonstrations. *Catalog Committee:* Mildred Constantine, Edward T. Buxton, Charles E. Dancey, Frederick T. Fisher, Bernard Myers.

MARCHAL EMILE LANDGREN was born in Connecticut in 1907. As a youth he studied painting. As associate director and a member of the Board of Contemporary Arts, New York, 1931–32, Mr. Landgren set up a program offering artists their first one-man shows in New York City. During 1932–33 he directed exhibitions at the New School for Social Research. In 1935 he was appointed director of art activities for New York's Municipal Art Committee and until 1939 directed the Municipal Art Galleries, sponsored by the committee. He also directed three annual National Exhibitions of American Art, 1936–38, as part of New York's summer festival. He also arranged exhibitions for the Whitney Museum of American Art, the Museum of the City of New York, the Virginia Museum of Fine Arts in Richmond, and many New York galleries. After service in World War II, he joined the art division of the Washington, D.C., Public Library, and after retirement in 1967, he served as consultant to the art library at the University of Maryland. He also initiated and conducted graduate seminars in the historiography of art for its art department. At present he is director of the University's art gallery. Over his long career, he has contributed to many art periodicals, and has been a reviewer of art books for the *Library Journal*. In 1940 he published *Years of Art: The Story of the Art Students League of New York*. He is currently working on a cumulative exhibition record of the Municipal Art Galleries.

FIGURE 51. Charles Logasa (1883–1936). *Marchal E. Landgren.* 1931 Collection of Marchal E. Landgren.

A Memoir of the New York City
Municipal Art Galleries, 1936–1939

MARCHAL E. LANDGREN

New York's Municipal Art Committee

Fiorello LaGuardia was ushered into his first term as mayor of the City of New York by two significant and related art events. On January 29, 1934, the "First Municipal Art Exhibition" was announced. It opened in February in the RCA Building, Rockefeller Center, with the official recognition and support of the mayor. The exhibition, under the sponsorship of the leading art museums of the city, was to be a large and comprehensive showing of artists identified with New York. "In contrast to the recently initiated Federal program which aims to help artists through Federal and civic support, this exhibition is intended to stimulate private buying of the works of leading American artists."[1]

At midnight on February 9, shortly after the announcement of the exhibition, the fresco by Diego Rivera, *Man at the Crossroads of Life,* in the lobby of the same RCA Building, was destroyed by the Rockefeller interests that had commissioned it. It had contained a portrait of Lenin.

Eleven artists "indignant over the cultural vandalism of the Rockefeller Center Authorities," publicly announced that they would withdraw their work from the municipal exhibition "if it is held at Rockefeller Center," and they petitioned the mayor to find another location for it. They called on their fellow artists to join them in their protest, and a number did.[2]

The municipal exhibition, however, opened on February 28 as scheduled. It filled thirty-three galleries and a sculpture court. About one thousand works were included in the exhibition, and all the paintings were hung on a single line. It was dubbed "the mile of art," and the mayor officiated at the opening.

The protesting artists at first planned to set up a counter-exhibition, but decided instead to demand that the city establish a municipal art gallery and art center for its artists. They organized the Artists' Committee of Action and sent their proposal to the mayor on March 20. And on May 9, about 300-strong, they and their sympathizers marched on City Hall to demonstrate their demands. According to *The New York Times* (May 10, 1934), they "found a good friend in Alderman President Bernard S. Deutsch, who offered his aid in getting a vacant city building where they could exhibit their work."[3]

Sometime before their march, the mayor, interested especially in music, had called in Mrs. Henry Breckinridge to discuss what organized effort on the part of the city could do to better the welfare of the New York artist and musician, and to promote New York as a great art center. Mrs. Breckinridge was a public-spirited woman with known abilities as an organizer and publicist. By June 20, she had assembled an executive committee for a municipal art committee to be appointed by the mayor.[4]

The artists again pressed their demands for a municipal art center on the mayor when, on October 27, the Artists' Union and the Artists' Committee of Action, this time one thousand-strong and without a police permit, again marched on City Hall. They asked for jobs and for a center and gallery.

The mayor announced the formation of a Municipal Art Committee on January 7, 1935. The committee was a formidable one, with 118 members, drawn from a cross-section of the cultural life of the city. Mrs. Breckinridge was announced as its chairman.

In his letter of invitation to the members of this committee the Mayor said:

We are assembling a Municipal Art Committee of One Hundred to advise and cooperate with the city government in stimulating the artistic life and expression of the city.

Within the broad field of the committee special subcommittees will be concerned with art, drama, and music.

Outstanding experts and patrons in the different fields of art are being invited to membership in the Committee of One Hundred. You are cordially invited to accept membership on this committee. The executive detail administration of the committee functions will be in the hands of a professional staff. It is not such detail work that I am asking you to do, but I do need and invite the great benefit that will come from your advice, broad knowledge and well-known interest in the subject.[5]

The first meeting of the Committee of One Hundred was held at City Hall on January 15 in the Board of Estimate chamber. At that meeting the mayor outlined an eight-point program for the committee:

(1) the working out of a program of music for the people at popular prices; (2) a study of music in the parks and a music program for the parks; (3) a study of the community, art, and drama needs of the city and the development of a program; (4) establishment of a music and art high school; (5) development of an educational and cultural art program in cooperation with the municipal radio station; (6) cooperation with the department of public works in the gradual transfer of works division, music,

art, and drama educational and recreational projects of proved value and demand, to a permanent municipal program of selfsustaining and city-supported activities; (7) cooperation with the state and federal employment service in finding ways to meet the many community demands for music and art which the music department city-wide survey has disclosed; and (8) the creation and operation of a municipal art center where adequate provisions will be made for concerts, opera, drama, arts and crafts, in the endeavor, as we have said, "to increase the grace, happiness, and beauty of our municipal life."[6]

Although the mayor's Committee of One Hundred did include practicing artists in all fields, with members of the Artists' Union and the Artists' Committee of Action among them, the artists continued to protest.

And while the Municipal Art Center was being made the excuse for all this genteel back-scratching by the Mayor and his hand-picked committee of "New York's most splendid citizens"—yes, at that very hour on Tuesday, January 15th, representatives of the artists themselves clamored vainly to be heard. They represented hundreds of painters, sculptors, actors, writers, architects, musicians and dancers, professions whose very existence depends for the immediate future on action from the administration. They felt they had a right to a voice in the deliberations of the Mayor's committee. But the Mayor and his committee felt otherwise.[7]

The group excluded from the first meeting of the committee represented the inter-cultural organization. "Its members intended to demand that the municipal art centre be administered by working artists instead of the Mayor's committee and that a building at 62 West Fifty-third Street be turned over immediately as a temporary centre."[8]

The Municipal Art Committee eventually grew to include 147 members. Herbert E. Winlock, director of the Metropolitan Museum of Art, was the first chairman of the subcommittee on art, and when he retired from public life, Hardinge Scholle, director of the Museum of the City of New York, took his place. Artists on the same subcommittee included Herbert Adams, Wood Gaylor, Alexandrina R. Harris, Leonebel Jacobs, Leon Kroll, Jonas Lie, Michael Loew, Louis Lozowick, Wallace Morgan, Attilio Piccirilli, Abram Poole, Vernon C. Porter, John Sloan, and F. Ballard Williams.[9]

As a cross-section, [the committee] included the widest variety of working artists and art devotees—painters, actors and concert musicians, internationally known; directors of art schools and art institutions; heads of local work relief units for artists, and wealthy private patrons. Furthermore, every person who received an invitation to the meetings attended. Certainly this was no perfunctory response. Probably to a greater degree than the committee members themselves realized, it was a manifestation of the concern felt by responsible Americans in the adjustment of cultural life to changed economic conditions.[10]

271

FIGURE 52. Ben Shahn (1898–1969). *The Committee of 100 count 'em.*
Illustration for *Art Front*, February 1935.

The MacDowell Plan of Exhibitions

On April 8, 1935, a subcommittee of the Committee on Art Plans and Exhibits
met to work out a plan under which the Municipal Art Committee could exhibit
and offer for sale the works of the resident artists of New York. Leon Kroll was
the chairman of that subcommittee, and serving with him were four other artists,
Louis Lozowick, Vernon Porter, John Sloan, and F. Ballard Williams. Mr. Kroll's
report of the meeting read as follows:

The committee worked on the assumption that it is the desire and intention of the city
to give all of its artists an opportunity to exhibit when a permanent Municipal Art
Center, with an adequate number of galleries, is provided by the city.

For this permanent center, the plan of selection of works by the committee, is the
one which worked so well at the MacDowell Club exhibitions. In this plan, the details
of which can be worked out at future meetings, a group of ten, fifteen or twenty artists,
who respect each others work and wish to exhibit together, may self-organize a group
to exhibit for a period of three weeks.

If there are twenty artists in each group, and twelve large galleries, about 2000
artists could exhibit during the season of eight months. The exhibitions could be so
arranged on a stagger plan, that there be at least one new exhibition each week.

A permanent paid secretary be engaged to make arrangements and allot dates. The
secretary be under the supervision of a special committee representing all phases of art,
whose duty it will be, to see that no injustice is permitted.

A plan for a method of selection for neighborhood and community exhibitions: The
same plan used for the larger exhibitions, may also be used for regional shows, with

proviso that no work outside of the region or neighborhood, be invited, until all artists of the region have been taken care of.

While these two plans were considered by the committee, no plan need be absolutely fixed. Other plans may be tried if these are not found to be workable. Your committee thinks they are, and that they should be tried first.[11]

Robert Henri was probably the originator of the MacDowell Club exhibitions; he was, at least, their chief protagonist. It was, of course, Henri who led The Eight, that famous self-organized group of artists, which included, in addition to Henri, John Sloan, William Glackens, George Luks, Everett Shinn, Ernest Lawson, Maurice Prendergast, and Arthur B. Davies. The Eight, protesting the rejection of some of its members from the Academy exhibition of 1907, exhibited together at the Macbeth Galleries, New York, in 1908. It may have been in the memory of that experience that the MacDowell plan evolved.

The first of the MacDowell Club exhibitions was held at the club, then located at 108 West 55th Street, in November 1911. It was Henri's group, and it included nine exhibitors, who showed forty-two paintings. In addition to Henri, the group included George Bellows, Ben Ali Haggin, Paul Daugherty, John C. Johansen, and Jonas Lie.

John Sloan and Leon Kroll, who served on the subcommittee that recommended the MacDowell plan to the Municipal Art Committee, both participated in many of the MacDowell Club exhibitions.

The MacDowell plan was certainly one of the most democratic plans ever put to work to bring the artist before the public. As practiced at the MacDowell Club, any self-organized group of from eight to twelve members could show their work without approval by a jury. At the heart of the plan was the belief that any such group of artists, willing to exhibit together, had the right to be heard.

Throughout the history of American art, the question of the rights of the artist in a democratic society has been raised intermittently. At times, it has been answered that the artist should serve the people by creating an art for the people, a popular art; at other times, that the people should be educated to an understanding of art. Both answers, insofar as the living artist is concerned, call for a screen of patronage between the artist and the public: Someone must gauge the standards of popularity, at the one extreme, and, at the other, the standards of education.

The remarkable present-day growth of the public museum in America is based on the premise of educating the people to an understanding of art. Around it has grown a great network, in the universities and colleges of the country, of training specialists to serve the museums. It is now these specialists who form the screen of patronage between the living artist and his public.

There was a time in America, however, when the artist himself judged his peers, through his own professional associations. Today, however, the museum has usurped that privilege. It is a rare event today to find an artist serving on a jury of admission to an exhibition, and it is rarer still to find an artist serving in any capacity in the administration of a museum. The public interest in art is no longer focused on the professional associations of artists, although some still exist, but on the museum.

"Almost nowhere in the United States today," wrote Robert Goldwater in 1951, "do groups of artists initiate and control their own exhibitions. And the fact of the matter is that the artist today is not master of his own exhibition fate. Almost without exception he must now show through the intervention, if not by the grace, of a gallery or museum."[12]

Historical Implications of the MacDowell Plan

In 1826, when the National Academy of Design was founded in New York City under the leadership of Samuel F. B. Morse, it set out to be a democratic organization. The meaning of democracy in relation to art and the artist in this case was that the artists themselves should set the standards of their profession. The Academy and its school were planned to be governed by the artists themselves, independent of outside patronage. The Academy prospered, and it did become the center on which the standards of the profession were balanced, both in the training of the artist and in the recognition of his accomplishment.

In 1863, in order to raise money for a new building, needed "to raise American art to the highest excellence," the Academy amended its constitution to admit lay members to its body.[13] It succeeded in raising $100,000 to build its Venetian Gothic palace on West 23rd Street. And although the privileges of the 800 or more lay members it admitted were strictly limited, the prestige of the Academy soon became associated with its patrons, rather than with its professional membership.

In a decade, the repute of its school had so declined that a new, democratic school, the Art Students League of New York, managed by the students for the students, was founded in 1875 by dissidents from the Academy. Two years later, the Society of American Artists was organized by another group of dissidents, who felt that the academicians, by jealously protecting their own interests, were discriminating against them. In fact, the situation was such that Clarence Cook could write in the *New York Tribune* (June 5, 1877) that the Academy "is come to be an establishment for the sale of pictures, and the competition is no longer between artists as to who shall paint the best pictures, but between merchants as to who shall get the best stall in the market." The Academy has never regained its earlier prestige.

The Art Students League continued to prosper, and whatever distinction the Academy could give to the artists it exhibited, it had to share with the Society of American Artists.

In 1906, the Academy and the Society resolved their differences, and the Society merged back into the Academy. It was the Academy exhibition of the next year, 1907, that gave birth to The Eight. The exhibition of The Eight was originally planned as a much more inclusive affair; Robert Henri felt the need of a *salon des refusés*, a need that was not filled.

A year before the MacDowell Club exhibitions were launched, Robert Henri, John Sloan, and other artists imbued with the democratic spirit, supported the 1910 Independent Artists Exhibition, held in a building on West Thirty-fifth Street. "The total number of entries was 260 paintings, 219 drawings, and 20 pieces of sculpture. A hundred and three artists exhibited, many of whom were Henri's pupils."[14] And the Society of Independent Artists, which held its first no-jury, no-prizes exhibition in 1917, and which continued to hold such exhibitions annually for twenty-eight years, until 1944, was founded by the same men.

The 1910 Independent Artists Exhibition, in its turn, led to the great armory show of 1913, staged by the Association of American Painters and Sculptors.

These experiences of the American artist vis-à-vis his public are, of course, paralleled throughout the Western World. Ever since the Paris Salon of 1737, which established the public exhibition on a regular basis, the development of modern art has been inextricably tied to the artist presenting himself to the public.

275

It was the agitation of the artists themselves that brought about the *Salon des Refusés* of 1863; it was the artists themselves who formed the *Société Anonyme* that presented the Impressionists in their eight group exhibitions between 1874 and 1886; and it was the artists themselves who formed the *Société des Artistes Indépendants* in 1884 and the *Salon d'Automne* in 1903. In Germany, it was the artists themselves who banded together in 1903 as *Die Brücke* and in 1911 as *Der Blaue Reiter*. And, of course, there were *Les Vingt* in Brussels, the *Dadaistes* in Zurich, the Futurists in Milan, the Constructivists in Moscow, *De Stijl* in Amsterdam, and the Surrealists in Paris. It is impossible to review the history of modern art without finding that it was the artist himself, in association with his peers, who presented his work to the public.

When Leon Kroll and the other artist-members of the subcommittee of the Committee on Art Plans and Exhibits recommended the MacDowell plan to the Municipal Art Committee, it did so in full awareness of the rights of the artist in a democratic society. "I believe wholeheartedly," wrote Leon Kroll in 1936, "that the result of the municipal government's creation of a liaison between living artist and the public will be a greater understanding and appreciation of art, and a greater wealth and higher standards of creative expression."[15]

The plan eliminated any screen of patronage between the artist and his public. It allowed the resident artist of New York, regardless of pursuasion, to exhibit his work if a limited number of his peers were willing to exhibit with him.

The Temporary Galleries of the Municipal Art Committee

The Municipal Art Committee approved the MacDowell plan, and it was put into effect in January of 1936.

Early in 1935 the Municipal Art Committee was given the use of an old brownstone residence at 62 West 53rd Street. The building had been taken over by the New York City Board of Transportation and was scheduled for demolition during the construction of the Independent subway system.

The building was completely remodeled to the committee's specifications for use as the Temporary Galleries of the Municipal Art Committee. Interior walls were removed; remaining walls were replastered; new floors were laid; layers and layers of paint were removed from the original black walnut woodwork; steel beams were added to reinforce the structure; the entrance to the building was changed from the first floor to the ground floor basement; and the entire front of the building was refaced. All this was accomplished, at great cost, probably as much as $40,000, by WPA funds and labor.

The remodeling of the building took about a year. But when it was finished, the committee had four floors of galleries, well lighted by both trough lights and ceiling fixtures. The fifth floor was set aside for offices, and the cellar became a storage and work room.

The first three floors were opened into one room each for the exhibition of paintings and sculpture, and the fourth floor was divided into two rooms for the exhibition of graphics and watercolors. The window walls of each of the gallery floors, to the north and south of the building, were screened by false interior walls to provide maximum exhibition space. All walls were painted a light sand color.

The only furniture in the four floors of galleries, except for a reception desk on the main floor, were benches made of the black walnut, rubbed to a piano finish, salvaged from the many surplus doors. A dado of black walnut paneling ran along the stairway; there was no elevator in the building. The dado was rubbed down to the natural wood and waxed. A short time after the opening of the galleries, several artist-members of the staff designed an overall pattern based on the seal of the city of New York and, on their own time, stenciled the design on the walls of the stairwell. It was their contribution to their colleagues.

In December 1935, the committee was ready to accept applications from New York artists to exhibit in the galleries. The MacDowell plan was adapted to the space provided by the four floors of galleries. Four groups were to be shown at one time, each being allotted one floor; and the groups were to be made up of "not less than 10 and not more than 15 artists working in the same field or medium." The committee announced that:

Applications from existing groups and from groups of individual artists formed for the purpose of exhibiting in these Galleries, will be received and exhibition space will be allotted to not less than 10 and not more than 15 artists working in the same field or medium, who shall apply in a body and qualify for exhibition space. As nearly as possible, the members of each group will be allotted the space of one gallery, so that they may exhibit as a body. Each group will select a representative to work with the staff of the Municipal Art Committee on details of the exhibition. Exhibitions will run for a period of two weeks.

An artist who has been a resident of the state of New York for one year and of Greater New York City for six months is eligible to exhibit in the Temporary Galleries.

An edition of mimeographed check lists will be supplied each group. Printed catalogs may be furnished by the exhibiting group for free distribution.

All works exhibited shall be the property of the exhibitor.[16]

The committee charged no exhibition fees or commissions on sales. It did not, however, insure the works exhibited. A certain amount of wall space was allotted to each artist, so that the number of works he could show was determined by the sizes of his works.

The requirement that works in any one group would be in the "same field or medium" was made to give consistency to each exhibition. It was to the advantage of the artist that he be well presented. The mixing of prints, drawings, oils, watercolors, and works in other mediums, in any one group would not make for a successful presentation.

The first applications for exhibition space that went out to the artists in December contained a citizenship clause. Not only legal residence in New York City—one year in the state and six months in the city—but American citizenship was required of all exhibitors. The clause was inserted by the executive secretary of the committee and was a clear case of misguided patriotism. It was questioned internally, before publication, by some members of the executive staff, but it passed unnoticed by the subcommittee that had recommended the MacDowell plan.

The citizenship clause brought a great wave of protest from the artists themselves, who were quick to note that it excluded from the galleries all Japanese artists living in New York, including Yasuo Kuniyoshi, a highly respected member of the New York art community, who had lived in the city for twenty-nine years.

A meeting of artist-members of the committee was held early in January. Those present were George Pearse Ennis, Wood Gaylor, Mrs. Alexandrina R. Harris, Leon Kroll, Jonas Lie, Michael Loew, and Vernon Porter. The following motion was carried unanimously: "An artist who has been a resident of the State of New York for one year and of Greater New York City for six months is eligible to exhibit in the Temporary Galleries."[17]

The motion was released to the press, and in the same release Mrs. Breckinridge stated:

The purpose of this Gallery and the great desire of the Mayor is to give the resident artist[s] of this City of Greater New York a gallery that they may use to show their work. The Gallery is the first of its kind in any municipality, is temporary and experimental and upon the success of this experiment depends the continuance of the plan in the Municipal Art Center which I hope later may include invitations to other states and foreign countries to exhibit.

A "hospitality clause" was also included in the original application for exhibition space in the galleries, asking the artists not to abuse the hospitality of the city.[18] The clause was nonsensical, but in the view of the destruction of the Rivera mural in Rockefeller Center it took on a meaning far beyond its intent, which was to eliminate "any artist who seeks unwarranted publicity."[19] It was rescinded, and in no instance in the history of the galleries did any artist seek unwarranted publicity.

The first exhibition opened on January 7 and continued through January 18. One group exhibited sculpture; two groups showed oil paintings, and the fourth group showed watercolors and gouaches.

The sculptors were Jacob Paul Daniel, Irving Diener, Maurice Glickman, Ernest Guteman, Alonzo Hauser, Nathaniel Kaz, Helene Straube, and Louis

Wilks. Their works in marble, stone, granite, bronze, and plaster were installed on the ground floor, "a single commodious gallery, its gray walls serving as a background for sculpture."[20]

The second-floor gallery was taken over by a group of painters, all of whom, except the two women-artists, were national academicians. The members of the group were Roy Brown, George Elmer Browne, H. E. Ogden Campbell, Charles C. Curran, Edward Dufner, Frank Vincent DuMond, Eugene Higgins, H. L. Hildebrandt, Paul King, Ernest Lawson, F. Luis Mora, Chauncey F. Ryder, Marion Gray Traver, and Harry W. Watrous. Mr. Watrous was a former president of the Academy.

The group of painters on the third floor called itself The Ten. Its members had organized as an exhibiting group just before the Temporary Galleries opened and had shown together at the Montross Galleries, as Joseph Solman relates above.

The fourth group, showing watercolors and gouaches on the fourth floor, was a miscellaneous group, most of whose members had some association with the Art Students League of New York. It included Genevieve H. Augustin, Nathaniel C. Burwash, Hubert Davis, Gilberta D. Goodwin, Charles Trumbo Henry, Bernard Klonis, Stewart Klonis, Charles Lofgren, Lisbeth Lofgren, Bruce Mitchell, James Penney, and Harwood Steiger. Stewart Klonis was then president of the Art Students League; Charles Trumbo Henry and Nathaniel Burwash were artist-members of the staff of the Temporary Galleries.

At the preview of the exhibition on January 6, Mayor LaGuardia "expressed hearty approval of the undertaking, although his attitude was somewhat lukewarm toward a few of the modern paintings included in the first show. Even these, however, he found useful in proving that artists of all persuasions were permitted to exhibit in this municipal gallery without prejudice or favor."[21]

Mayor LaGuardia said at the opening of the galleries:

It may be just a boon-doggling exhibit, but here it is. You don't have to know anybody to have your pictures in it and we hope to make this exhibit something permanent where all the artists of the City of New York may have a place to show their work.[22]

The second exhibition opened on January 21. It was the only exhibit in the galleries to include five groups. Again, there was a sculpture group on the second floor. Its members were Paul Black, Martin Craig, Herbert Ferber, Eugenie Gershoy, Aaron Goodelman, Jacques Horwitz, Paul Hyun, Simon Kennedy, Golda Lewis, Sahny Olenikov, Simon Slifkin, William Van Boeck, and Edmund Weil.

The oil paintings on the second floor were by Maurice Becker, Ben Benn, Oscar Bluemner, Paul Burlin, Arnold Friedman, Lee Gatch, Leon Hartl, Yasuo Kuniyoshi, and Joseph Stella. George Grosz had applied to exhibit with this group, but he sent in a watercolor instead of an oil. He did not replace it at the gallery's suggestion, so he was not shown. His was the only rejection in the history of the gallery.

The third floor was taken over by a group of conservative painters: Johann Berthelson, Daniel R. Daly, Julius Delbos, Frederick K. Detwiller, Paul Fuerstenberg, Gordon Grant, Charles P. Gruppe, Kenneth How, J. Redding Kelly, Orlando Rouland, Howard R. Spencer, and Gustave Wiegand. Five of the twelve members of this group were later to become associates of the National Academy or academicians.

One group on the fourth floor exhibited drawings and prints. Its members were Isabel Bate, William Baziotes, Nathalie Beach, Harold Black, Srug Hovsep Chapian, Betty Eberle, Gretl Glogan Gold, Carl Jacoby, Sigmund Kozlow, Azio Martinelli, Charles Seide, Ann Hunt Spencer, William N. Thompson, Abraham Tobias, and Jane White.

Printmakers constituted the fifth group. They were Virginia Bill, E. N. Fairchild, Ray Goldsmith, Hedwig Haust, Carrie L. Housenfluck, Josephine K. van Ingen, T. Komara, Alexis Maltz, R. Gray Neff, Ada Raab, and Clara Thorward.

In their first two exhibitions, the New York artists set the pattern for all ensuing exhibitions. When the Temporary Galleries opened in January 1936, about one month after it had announced it would receive applications for exhibition space, more than seven hundred artists had already applied, and never in the history of the galleries was there a moment when exhibitions could not be scheduled well in advance, despite the ruling that artists could exhibit only once a year.

It was the expressed desire of the mayor and of his Municipal Art Committee that all resident artists of the city make use of the galleries. There was, of course, some criticism of this at the start. It was felt in some quarters that the galleries should not be open to established artists, who had other outlets, through their dealers or through their professional associations, such as the National Academy's annual exhibits. But, in truth, the New York artist, no matter how great his reputation, had few outlets for his work. And, if the galleries were to be open only to unknown or little-known artists, all who exhibited there would have been stigmatized at the start.

The democratic way was to accept all artists on an equal footing. The Temporary Galleries was a function of the municipal government; it was the city's way of recognizing the creative expression of its residents, not a private, charitable organization. The criticism died as soon as it was born.

The first two exhibitions set the pattern of not only including works in many mediums—carved and modeled sculpture, oils, temperas, watercolors, gouaches, drawings, and various forms of printmaking—they also included work by known and unknown artists of many persuasions. There were both academicians and academics. There were artists, such as Yasuo Kuniyoshi and Joseph Stella, who were leading figures in contemporary American art; there were artists, such as Mark Rothko and Adolph Gottlieb, who were to become outstanding contributors to American art; and, of course, there were those artists whose contributions were more modest, but who were, or were to become, an essential part of the art life of the country. There were also those time has forgotten.

The first two exhibitions were held for two-week periods, and the galleries were open to the public five days a week, Tuesday through Saturday, from ten o'clock in the morning to six in the evening. Ten days was found too short a period to do justice to the exhibitors. During the third exhibition (February 4 through 23, 1936), the exhibiting period was changed to three weeks, with the galleries open every day, except Monday, from noon to six o'clock. The change was recommended by the same subcommittee that had recommended the Mac-Dowell plan, and it was observed throughout the life of the galleries.[23]

The seventeenth exhibition in the Temporary Galleries (December 23, 1936, through January 10, 1937) completed their first year. Mrs. Breckinridge noted that 750 artists had exhibited in sixty-eight groups during the year.[24]

More than this [she added] these artists have succeeded in interesting tens of thousands of visitors [20,518 by actual count] to the galleries and have had their work brought to the attention of a buying public that has spent nearly one hundred dollars a week on them. They have also interested the dealers and several of the latter using the Municipal Galleries as a clearing house and a testing ground, have taken on the work of several of these artists.

"There is perhaps no way of counting the actual number of practicing artists living in New York City," Mrs. Breckinridge wrote, "all of whom are, because of their residence, eligible to exhibit in the Municipal Galleries." She concluded:

It would seem that the seven hundred and fifty who exhibited during 1936 would more or less complete the list of those who find it possible to organize in groups and present exhibitions, but such is not the case, for nearly one thousand, who have not yet shown have filed applications for exhibition space in 1937 before the new year has arrived. It is a credit to the artists of New York that they have been able to support municipally operated galleries in a way that has been profitable to both them and the public. The exhibitions have given the general public the opportunity to fully see and understand the creative expression that exists in their time.[25]

To review the year, the galleries staged a retrospective exhibition in which artists from each group that had shown during the first year were invited by the group itself to represent it. The exhibition, held from January 13 through 31, 1937, included 124 works by as many artists.

Among the artists chosen by their colleagues were Ilya Bolotowsky, George Elmer Browne, Maurice Glickman, Adolph Gottlieb, Abraham Tobias, Sacha Moldovan, Warren Wheelock, Philip Evergood, Helen Farr, Victor Perard, Louis Ribak, Will Barnet, Ary Stillman, Werner Drewes, Albert Groll, Zoltan Hecht, Sol Aronson, Saul Baizerman, Irving Marantz, Vincent D'Agostino, Milton Avery, Fred Nagler, Isaac Soyer, and Arline Wingate.

Only five subsequent exhibitions were held at the Temporary Galleries. The building, so suitable to its purpose, had to be demolished in the wake of the new subway construction. The twenty-second exhibition, April 28 through May 16, 1937, was the last of the series held there in which "nearly 900 artists showed their work and approximately 30,000 visitors saw the exhibitions."[26]

In February 1936 the Municipal Art Committee announced plans "to publish a catalogue for each exhibition":

It is the plan of the Committee to have this catalogue in the form of a magazine, each issue carrying a feature article closely related to the exhibition and the artists exhibiting. Whenever possible, the artists themselves will be the contributors to the catalogue. Mrs. Henry Breckinridge, Chairman of the Municipal Art Committee, will edit the catalogue which will be sold at the Galleries for a small fee. It is her belief that it will be of great value to all people interested in Art and a valuable medium for the artists of the City. Plans for the publication of this catalogue are now under way.

The problem, of course, was to find a way to finance such a publication. The committee felt that it should pay its own way through sales and advertising. A freelance agent was eventually found who would solicit advertisers and thus carry the main financial burden. The magazine was called *Exhibition*. The first issue appeared with the thirteenth exhibition (September 30–October 18, 1936). Only seven issues of *Exhibition* were published; it did not pay for itself and had to be discontinued.

It did not meet its potential except to provide a satisfactory and rather handsome catalogue of the exhibitions. The committee returned to the mimeographed checklists it had previously supplied for each exhibition, but added to them the publication of the short biographies it had launched in *Exhibition*.

The Municipal Art Galleries

The search for new galleries ended when the former private galleries of Thomas Fortune Ryan were offered to the Municipal Art Committee. The galleries, at 3 East 67th Street, were a separate building, connected by a passageway to the Ryan residence on 5th Avenue.

Designed by Carrere and Hastings, who were also responsible for the New York Public Library, the Frick Collection, and the Metropolitan Museum of Art, the galleries were built in 1913.

The entrance to the galleries at street level was through glass doors mounted with a grill of wrought iron. The facade of the ground floor was constructed of alternate wide and narrow stone courses, pierced by two small windows, one at each side of the wide entranceway. In the design of the building, the ground-floor façade served merely as the pedestal of the grand *piano nobile,* which was reminiscent of the upper story of the central portico of Alessandro Galilei's St. John Lateran in Rome. Between double pilasters with Corinthian capitals, was a loggia framed by a balustrade and an arch supported by Tuscan columns and pilasters. The abutments of the arch were decorated in high relief by Stirling Calder, with a male figure on one side, a female on the other. The walls of the loggia were decorated with grotesques in *graffito* on terra-cotta. An elegant lantern hung on a long chain from the center of its high ceiling.

At the back of the ground floor, opening on a garden, was a room, paneled in the style of Louis xvi, with a mantel of red marble, over which was a mirror. The approach to this room was by a hallway, paved in marble, to the right of the main entrance. And from this room, a marble stairway led to the gallery above, which was entered from the west, at one side of the north wall, through studded leather doors. A pair of large, marble, Ionic columns and pilasters, a few feet from the north wall, made a sort of vestibule between the columns and the wall, which was pierced by glass doors and windows, framed in walnut and arched in the Palladian style. The doors led to a balcony, with stairs to the garden.

In the review of one of the exhibitions held there, one critic noted that the pictures "are an interesting and lively lot." "They'd have to be," she quickly added, "to overcome the competition offered by the magnificent Ryan gardens which the galleries overlook and the singing of what sounds like a hundred birds outside in the trees."[27]

The gallery was a large room with a very high ceiling. Its walls were covered in a rose silk damask above a dado of walnut paneling, which was carved in fine detail, with moldings of an egg-and-dart motif and with dentils. A great mantelpiece of Renaissance style was on the east wall. The south wall, behind the loggia of the façade, was also paneled in walnut and had a musician's gallery. There were murals on the ceiling. The walls, designed for the display of paintings, were lighted by a series of troughs, cast in bronze of an open Lombardic design and lined with rose-colored silk. The floor was of walnut parquetry.

Louis xvi paneled walls and rose silk damask were hardly the backgrounds for the work of the contemporary New York artist. The problem that faced the staff of the galleries was to convert the space to modern use without damaging any of the existing decorations. It was solved by stretching monk's cloth over light wooden frames and securing the frames against the walls. This was done in both rooms. When the panels of monk's cloth were in place, a narrow upholsterer's gimp was used to finish their edges. Both the paneling in the Louis XVI room and the silk damask of the main gallery were thus covered. The silk in the trough lights in the main gallery was replaced with white rice paper. And with the advice of a lighting engineer, the Louis XVI room was lighted indirectly by two powerful bronze torchiers. Some of the black walnut benches from the Temporary Galleries were used in the new galleries.

Two tubs, painted with sand to simulate stone, were planted with greenery by the parks department and placed on the sidewalk, one at each side of the entrance door. And the flag of the city of New York was hung over the entrance from a pole attached to the balustrade of the loggia. A small display case, in a stainless steel frame, was attached to the stone to the left of the entrance.

The name of the galleries was changed from Temporary Galleries of the Municipal Art Committee to the Municipal Art Galleries, not because the galleries were considered more permanent, but because the name Municipal Art Galleries had become the popular name for the Temporary Galleries.

The galleries were opened on December 15, 1937, with the twenty-third exhibition. Although there were only two galleries in the new location, four groups of artists, as in the Temporary Galleries, were included in each of the exhibitions held there. The twenty-third exhibition included a group of sculptors—Nathaniel Kaz, Robert Cronbach, Milton Hebald, and Herbert Ferber were among them—who were shown in the ground floor gallery. "Indirect lighting," reported *The New York Times* on December 15, "makes the room . . . an excellent place to show sculpture." Three groups of painters occupied the main gallery. Altogether there were twenty-one pieces of sculpture and seventy paintings in the exhibition.

On June 1, 1938, following the thirtieth exhibition, a second retrospective exhibition was held at the galleries to review their second year of operation. From the thirteen exhibitions of fifty-two groups, whose members totaled 562 artists, held from February 4, 1937, through May 29, 1938, forty-seven artists were selected for this exhibition by the groups with which they exhibited. Among them were Eugene Bischoff, George Constant, Edward Dufner, Nan Greacen, Zoltan Hecht, Irving Lehman, Beatrice Levy, and Gertrude Nason. In addition, there were selections from each of the groups, voted for inclusion in the exhibition by the visitors to the gallery. Among the artists in this group were A. S. Baylinson, George Beline, Roy Brown, Herbert Ferber, Ben Galos, Lena Gurr, Riva Helfond, Harold Lehman, Moissaye Marans, Arnold Roston, Manuel Tolegian, W. Campbell Walsh, and Albert Wein. The artists' choices were hung together on the ground floor; those of the visitors were in the main gallery.

In pursuance of the policy established in the first year, no favor has been shown to either modernist or academician. Oils, watercolors, sculpture and prints have all had their day. So this resume of the year's activities is well diversified in type, subject-matter and media. It is perhaps not going too far to say that this is the best exhibition the Municipal Galleries have thus far put on.[28]

In its first two years, the galleries had shown the work of 1,225 artists, in 121 self-organized groups, in thirty exhibitions, which were attended by some 35,000 visitors.

Eighteen more exhibitions were held at the Municipal Art Galleries, the thirty-first through the forty-eighth, from June 22, 1938 through July 23, 1939. The galleries were closed at the end of the forty-eighth exhibition, and the Municipal Art Committee was dissolved.

During the three years of its activities, the galleries exhibited the work of 2,067 artists in 193 self-organized groups.

The pattern established by the artists in their first two exhibitions, which included artists, known and unknown, of all persuasions, from the most conservative to the experimental, was evident in all the exhibitions they held in the galleries.

Between the forty-seventh and the forty-eighth exhibitions, a third retrospective was held (July 14 through July 2, 1939), which was selected from the fifteen groups that exhibited from June 22, 1938, through April 30, 1939. Again, as in the second retrospective, the works were selected both by vote of the visitors and by the groups themselves.

Included among the visitors' choices were works by Walton Blodgett, Nick Buongiorno, Ann Coles, Charles C. Curran, Werner Drewes, May Fairchild, Fritz Glarner, Fay Gould, Hy Hintermeister, Albert Sumter Kelley, Paul Kelpe, and Pauline Law.

Among the artists' choices were works by Albert M. Canter, Beatrice Cuming, Antonio DeFelippo, Carolyn Keskulla, Albert P. Lucas, Sacha Moldovan, David Morrison, William Panchak, Chris Ritter, Ernest D. Roth, Mary Tyson, and Vaclav Vytlacil.

As Howard Devree pointed out in *The New York Times* (June 14, 1939), "Oils, water-colors, prints, and sculptures are included, the work ranging from the 'pretty picture' academism of the right to abstractions and brash paintings of the extreme left."

Effort was made in the hanging of each exhibition to assure both an equitable presentation of the work of each artist and a generally effective presentation to the public. Moreover, the galleries were well maintained. "The shoddiness which so often characterizes both the locale and the personnel of a city or state project is cheerfully absent. . . ."[29]

The Physiognomy of the Exhibiting Groups

The reviewer who reported on the first exhibitions at the MacDowell Club for *The New York Times* (Sunday, November 12, 1911), noted that it had "its own physiognomy.... The pictures," he wrote, "resemble each other as a family might whose features differed with each person."

Family resemblance is inherent in the MacDowell plan, which requires the artist to group together with his peers in order to exhibit his work, and it was recognizable in different degrees in the exhibitions held at the Municipal Art Galleries.

The student-master relationship was probably the first in which family resemblance was most easily seen, and many of the exhibiting groups in the Municipal Galleries were based on that relationship. The fourteenth exhibition (October 21 through November 8, 1936) included a group of watercolorists who had studied under George Pearse Ennis. In the sixteenth exhibition (December 2 through 20, 1936) the group of sculptors was made up of students of Alexander Archipenko. A popular studio during the 1930s was that run by Mme. Annot and Rudolph Jacoby; artists associated with that studio exhibited in the twenty-fifth exhibition (January 26 through February 13, 1938). They presented "decorative landscapes, still-lifes and portraits—a number of the pictures reminiscent of the Annot manner."[30] And a group that had worked with Robert Brackman was included in the seventeenth exhibition (December 23, 1936, through January 10, 1937).

An interesting group based on the same syndrome was shown in the eighteenth exhibition (February 3 through 21, 1937). Both Jackson Pollock and Philip Guston (then called Philip Goldstein) exhibited with it, and with them were George R. Cox, Millicent Cox, Bertram Goodman, Harold Lehman, Guy Maccoy, Sande McCoy (Pollock's brother), Genoi Grace Pettit, Bernard Schardt, J. B. Steffen, Manuel J. Tolegian, and Reginald Wilson. Many members of the group had studied under either Thomas Hart Benton or David Siqueiros, or under both. Several of its members had come to New York from Kansas, Wyoming, Missouri, Wisconsin, and California.

There was a resemblance, too, among the members of groups that had ties with various professional organizations. Some groups originated from the National Academy of Design. Members of the conservative Salmagundi Club exhibited as a group in the fourteenth exhibition (October 21 through November 8, 1936). And thirteen members of the New York Society of Women Artists showed watercolors in the twenty-eighth exhibition (March 30 through April 17, 1938); among them were Theresa Bernstein, Dorothy Lubell Feigin, and Beulah Stevenson.

In similar fashion, many groups originated in the Artists' Union. The thirty-eighth exhibition (November 16 through December 4, 1938) included three such groups shown together in the main gallery. *The New York Times* (November 20, 1938) clearly indicated the different kinships of the three groups by labeling them as "pseudo-primitives," "little 'expressionists,'" and "propagandists." And in the thirty-ninth exhibition (December 7 to 24, 1938) there was a group from the Modelers and Sculptors Union.

Regional groups, too, tended to show common characteristics. This was true of the two groups of Staten Island artists, one showing oil paintings in the fifth exhibition (March 18 through April 5, 1936), the other showing watercolors in the thirtieth exhibition (May 11 through 29, 1938). It was also true of the members of the Brooklyn Society of Modern Artists, who showed in the seventh exhibition (April 29 through May 17, 1936), and of the members of the Bronx Artists Guild in the thirty-second exhibition (July 13 through 31, 1938).

In the seventh exhibition (April 29 through May 17, 1936) the following group of abstractionists exhibited together: Rosalind Bengelsdorf, Harry Bowden, George Byron Browne, Mercedes Jeanne Carles, Giorgio Cavallon, Ivan Donovetsky, Balcomb Greene, Ray Kaiser, Marie Kennedy, Leo Lances, George McNeil, Albert Swinden, and Albert Wein. In November of the same year, eleven of the thirteen members of this group became charter members of the American Abstract Artists, whose contributions to American art are well known today, and in the thirty-seventh exhibition (October 26 through November 13, 1938) four groups, all members of the American Abstract Artists, made up the entire exhibition. Sculpture was included in their show, with works by Martin Craig, Ibram Lassaw, David Smith, and Warren Wheelock. Ilya Bolotowsky, Werner Drewes, Fritz Glarner, George L. K. Morris, Louis Schanker, and Vaclav Vytlacil, were among the painters in the group, who did not show with them in the earlier exhibition.

"Surrealism," reported the *New York Herald-Tribune* (August 7, 1938), "overruns the print group in the thirty-third exhibition of resident New York artists which opened last week at the Municipal Art Galleries. . . . The influence of George Grosz is also visible. Between the two influences the prints take on a nightmarish quality. Three prints especially, Claire Mahl's 'Juggernaut,' Ida Abelman's 'Homage to the Screw,' and Fred Becker's 'Death of John Henry' appear to be the expression of a series of traumas done in little pictures arranged around a central theme."

Some of the groups were bonded by the genre, rather than the style of their work. In the sixteenth exhibition (December 2 through 20, 1936), one group showed work in the decorative arts, which included overdoor panels, designs for painted furniture, decorative murals, and screens. Contributors to the *New Masses* formed a substantial part of the group exhibiting lithographs in the twenty-fourth exhibition (January 5 through 23, 1938), which included works by Ruth Gikow, John Groth, Helen Ludwig, Irving Marantz, Winifred Milius, and Eugene Morley. The forty-sixth exhibition (May 3 through 21, 1939) included sixty-seven works by fourteen miniaturists, among them Clara Louise Bell, Alexandrina R. Harris, Elsie Dodge Pattee, and William J. Whittemore.

A group of illustrators, organized by Alice Vetter, exhibited in the thirty-eighth exhibition (November 16 through December 4, 1938). Boris Aronson led a group, including David Burliuk, Eugene Dunkel, Josef Foshko, Serge Soudeikine, Nicholas Vasilieff, and C. Westchiloff, in the forty-seventh exhibition (May 24 through June 11, 1939), several of whose members were noted, like Aronson, for their work in the field of theatrical art as well as for easel painting.

Japanese-American artists living in New York came together in the thirty-first exhibition (June 22 through July 10, 1938). The group included work by Eitaro Ishigaki, Roy Kadowaki, Yasuo Kuniyoshi, Chuzo Tamotzu, Sakari Suzuki, Kaname Miyamoto, Thomas Nagai, Fuji Nakamizo, Takeo Watari, and Chikamichi Yamasaki. "Some of the Japanese artists," reported the *New York Times* on June 26, "apparently sympathize with China rather than Japan, or perhaps rather are distinctly anti-militaristic in their point of view." Originally, two groups of Japanese-American artists had applied to exhibit together—they did so in 1937 before the Japanese invasion of the northern provinces of China—but when the dates of their exhibition were set, several refused to send their works because of the insecurity of their position in this country during the Sino-Japanese conflict.

The association of Philip Evergood and William Gropper, also in the thirty-first exhibition, was perhaps understandable in that they both practiced an anecdotal art, although their means were quite different. Showing with them were Louis Ribak, John Lonergan, George Picken, Francis Criss, Moses Oley, Emptage, and H. Glitenkamp.

The make-up of some of the groups was somewhat puzzling. Milton Avery and Raphael Soyer exhibited together in the fourteenth exhibition (October 21 through November 8, 1936), with a group that also included Vincent D'Agostino, Rifka Angel, Milton Douthat, Charles B. Goodstein, Arthur Gunn, Bertram Hartman, Manfred Schwartz, and Jacques Zucker. The members were, however, more or less of the same age group, and their work comprised landscape and figure painting, based on the observation of their immediate surroundings.

No groups of photographers, architects, or industrial designers ever took advantage of the Municipal Galleries, although under the MacDowell plan they were privileged to do so.

If, as the above samplings would indicate, each group had a certain physiognomy or family resemblance, due to the democratic system of checks and balances of the MacDowell plan, no family of artists ever dominated the galleries. The sole arbiters of their exhibitions were the exhibiting artists themselves. The family resemblances of the members of each group were the same sort of resemblances that have prompted artists to associate from the time of the first public exhibitions. They were the resemblances that grouped the *Poussinistes* against the *Rubenistes* in the early days of the French Academy, the followers of Ingres against the followers of Delacroix in the first half of the nineteenth century, that brought the Impressionists together in the *Société Anonyme,* and that prompted the association of *Die Brücke, Der Blaue Reiter,* and The Eight in the twentieth century. The difference was that all families had their day. And the visitor, who came to see the exhibitions was in the same position as the artist; he could choose his friends.

A Profile of the Public

Thirty years ago, art exhibitions did not draw the large attendance they do to-day. And they were not staged with the showmanship that today so often makes events of them. The most popular exhibitions in New York during the thirties were those at the Museum of Modern Art. It was rare for the catalogues of those exhibitions to be published in editions of more than one or two thousand copies. Today, as an indication of the growth of the art public, they are published in tens of thousands.

The Municipal Art Galleries followed "one show with another with clocklike regularity."[31] With the aim of equity for all the artists who showed there, the exhibitions were called the first, the second, the third, and so on to the forty-eighth exhibition. The galleries gave no other labels to the exhibiting groups and did not in any other way evaluate the work of the artists it showed. As a result, if the visitor to the galleries were not merely curious, or a friend of the artist, he had to have some interest in what the artists of the community were doing. The galleries could not possibly draw the same public interest and attendance as a Picasso retrospective, for example, or a survey of Dada and Surrealism. Yet, during the seventeen days that each of its exhibitions was open to the public, well over a thousand visitors attended it.[32]

During its second year, when the galleries asked the visitors to vote on one work from each of the exhibiting groups for inclusion in its second retrospective exhibition, along with the artists' choices from the same groups, it was inevitable, that the difference between the visitors' and the artists' selections would be discussed. The discussion brought with it some speculation on the type of visitor that attended the exhibitions. The judgment of the visitors was generally respected.

"The contrast," said the *New York Sun* (June 4, 1938), "is somewhat marked, with the advantage it would seem, not by any means invariably in favor of the artists' choices. The visitors' preferences may incline a trifle more to the conservative but for all that they seem to have kept painter-like qualities and sound craftsmanship in mind."

"On the whole," wrote the *New York Evening Post* on the same day, "the public has made the more interesting selections."

It was Emily Genauer of the *World-Telegram* (June 4, 1938), who brought up the question of the visitors to the Municipal Art Galleries.

This doubting-Thomas-of-a-critic, still hesitates to fling roses at Demos for his fine taste. Because, after all, does Demos get to the Municipal Art Gallery or are its audiences composed of serious art lovers?

Will the public flock in as great numbers as do attend the Municipal Art Gallery shows to events that are not publicized with any great fanfare, that are not musts on the programs of the smart New Yorker who gets around, that are not part of chic dinner table conversation? One would like to think so, but hesitates.

So, perhaps, it is more reasonable to assume that people who visit the Municipal Gallery at least are more or less interested in art, and consequently have a more keenly developed appreciation than the public at large. No tyro in art would, it is safe to assume, have voted for Viola Anderson's delicate, finely brushed, sensitive but unpretentious little canvas called "Bootblacks," for example, or Lucy Thayer's near abstraction "Cemetery," with its subtle nuances of tone laid on in arbitrary planes, or A. S. Baylinson's "An Oriental" depicting a seated semi-nude woman as solidly modeled as a piece of sculpture and set against a background of intricately patterned, sketchily drawn and opulently colored Oriental fabrics. . . .

An editorial "Public Taste in Art," based on the popular selections in the retrospective exhibition, appeared in the Dayton, Ohio, *Herald* (June 18, 1938). It closed with the following paragraph:

A general belief has come into existence that the public taste, given time, will sort out the geniuses of the world and hand their work down to posterity. Now it would seem that the public taste is able to discriminate in its immediate decisions, or, at least, the New York Retrospective would so indicate.

A third retrospective exhibition, based on the works shown during the 1938–39 season, was also made up of selections by both the visitors and the artists. Held from June 14 through July 2, 1939, it did not receive as much attention in the press as the second retrospective, due no doubt to the amount of space given over to the art exhibits at the New York World's Fair. But Emily Genauer again commented on the quality of the visitors' choices.

The conclusion is obvious. The shows at the Municipal Art Gallery are achieving a purpose that to many will seem even more important than the opportunity they have to date given to 2034 artists to show their work without expense and without jury. They are developing constantly improving standards of taste for the general public.[33]

The MacDowell plan, a democratic plan for the artist, could not have been effective without its corollary, a belief in the judgment of the public. The second and third retrospective exhibitions, in which the public participated, gave some substance to that belief.

Benefits to the Artist

The material benefits to the artists who exhibited in the Municipal Art Galleries were small by today's standards. The years of the Depression were not, even with federal patronage, the best years for the artists of the country.

There is no full record of the sales or other benefits to the artists resulting from their exhibitions, but some are a matter of public record. The Metropolitan Museum of Art bought "Abandoned," a painting by George Elmer Browne, from the first exhibition. And Mrs. Breckinridge reported at the time of the seventeenth exhibition that, during the first year of the galleries, the "buying public [had] spent nearly one hundred dollars a week" on the work of the exhibitors.[34]

An examination of the Municipal Art Committee's books for the year 1937 showed sales of only $27.50 for that year.[35] It is possible, however, that other payments for sales were made directly to the artists and did not appear in the committee's books; and, of course, the galleries were closed from May 17 to December 15 of that year.

A review, in *The New York Times* (December 7, 1938) of the thirty-ninth exhibition, noted the "gratifying appearance of red stars indicative of sales."

There were financial benefits to the artists other than direct sales. A representative of *Scribners Magazine* visited the galleries during the eleventh exhibition. He commissioned Victor Candell, who was exhibiting drawings, to illustrate an article for *Scribners*. It was the first such commission for the artist. And during the fourth exhibition, in which Ramon Rebajes was exhibiting his work, surrealist in concept and constructed of unusual materials, including tacks and egg-crates, a tack manufacturer happened to stop in the galleries. He "was simply fascinated to see the new use to which his product had been put . . . and another misunderstood artist [had] found his patron."[36]

J. Warren Brady, whose pastel, "Joe, Bellboy," was included in the first retrospective exhibition, was given his first one-man show by a New York dealer as the result of exhibiting in the galleries.[37] There is no way of knowing today how many artists were similarly recognized.

Perhaps the greatest rewards to the artists were the intangible ones. Artists with little exhibition experience certainly gained much from seeing their works well presented in the company of their colleagues. In an interview on the Municipal Art Galleries, F. Newlin Price, then president of the Ferargil Galleries, New York, put it this way, "the best instruction to the student is the rude impact of a new eye on strange art."[38] Many of the artists who showed at the galleries, if not students, were at the start of their careers: Adolph Gottlieb, Philip Guston, Jackson Pollock, and Mark Rothko among them. The simple fact of having their work accepted by a group of their peers was undoubtedly a sustaining factor in the development of their careers.

The National Exhibitions of American Art

Three large annual national exhibitions of American art were put on by the Municipal Art Committee during the summers of 1936, 1937, and 1938.

The national exhibitions comprised state exhibits of paintings and sculpture by the resident artists of the then forty-eight states, the District of Columbia, and the territories and possessions of the United States. They were selected by the states that sent them to the exhibitions. The number of works each state could send was proportional to its population.

The first of the national exhibitions was held on the mezzanine floor of the International Building, Rockefeller Center. It opened on May 18, 1936, and continued through most of the summer. Forty-six of the forty-eight states—all but Louisiana and New Hampshire—were represented, and there were exhibits from

FIGURE 53. View of the First National Exhibition of the Municipal Art Committee at Rockefeller Center, New York, 1936.

Hawaii, Puerto Rico, the Panama Canal Zone, the Virgin Islands, and the District of Columbia. It was made up of over 700 works by almost as many artists.

The second and third of the national exhibitions were held in the somewhat smaller American Fine Arts Society Galleries at 215 West 57th Street. Both Louisiana and New Hampshire participated in the second exhibition; Maryland was the only state not represented. The third exhibition included all but Arkansas, Connecticut, Missouri, Ohio, and Tennessee. American Samoa entered the second exhibition, and Alaska, the third. There were 526 works in the second exhibition; 417 in the third.

The exhibitions were hung by regions: the New England states, the Plateau states, the Pacific states, and so on. As a result, regional differences, both creative and critical, were made apparent. Carlyle Burroughs, writing in the *New York Herald Tribune* (June 19, 1938) on the third exhibition, noted "the variety of regional subject matter depicted, especially the concentration of Negro themes in the South, the weakness of the showing made by the Plateau states and the Pacific Coast, the conservatism of New England, and the fact that in the territories and possessions, while there is little evidence of a well formed group activity, a definite art consciousness is perceptible."

The selection of works for the three national exhibitions created an almost simultaneous art activity throughout the country. Artists in many of the states were requested simply to submit works to a jury of selection appointed by the governor, and in some states the selection was by invitation. In many cases, the works so selected were put on exhibition, usually in the capitol, before being sent to the national exhibition. But in many states, such as Mississippi, Tennessee, Florida, and Wyoming, state-wide exhibitions were held, from which the works to be sent to New York were selected. In others, such as New Jersey, two or more regional exhibitions were held. Works selected from these made up another final exhibition from which the works to represent the state were chosen.

Because of the limited space allotted to each state, some method of selection had to be set up by each state. It was impossible to adapt the democratic Mac-Dowell plan to a single, large, national exhibition. The national exhibitions were nevertheless democratic in their organization. Selected by committees appointed by the governors of the states, official state exhibits were subject to the same checks and balances of a democratic society that apply to any of its official acts.

There were at least two instances when those checks and balances were used. A group of modern artists in New Jersey, dissatisfied with the selection that represented their state in the first national exhibition, marched on the state legislature, canvases under their arms, to demand that they be given a voice in the selection of works for future national exhibitions. They won their case.

In Wisconsin, an artist living in Milwaukee, protested that the state's committee of selection for the second national exhibition acted in an "arbitrary, capricious, whimsical, and self-serving" way, and that their selections in no way represented the work of "reputable or representative Wisconsin artists." He took his case to the courts and obtained a temporary order restraining the governor's committee from certifying their selections to the governor and the "artists from sending their paintings or sculptures to the national exhibition." He lost his case. But both the jury appointed by the governor and the artists they had chosen to represent the state were summoned before the public courts to show cause why the order of restraint should not be made permanent.[39]

The national exhibitions were unlike most of the large exhibitions of American art of the thirties, or of those of today. They did not, as other exhibitions did, reflect the screening of a single, small jury of experts, or the judgment of a museum's staff. Nor were they the free-for-all of the Independents. Every region of the country screened the work of its own artists. They presented the contemporary art of the country as it was known and respected throughout the country. Not only was the local art of various regions placed in open competition, so was local judgment of its art. As Howard Devree noted in *The New York Times* (June 19, 1938):

Such an exhibition is a point of departure for so many speculations that extend far beyond the burdened walls of the galleries—questions of art and democracy, of leveling up and leveling down, of whether American taste is being standardized by art as by radio, of whether any fundamental sectional differences exist or could be brought out in such a display. Questions that cannot be answered here or at this time . . . and if a visit raises questions such as those suggested above, the exhibition is surely far from being given in vain.

Federal Support of the Committee

The administrative staff of the Municipal Art Committee, as it was organized in January 1935, consisted of the chairman, an executive secretary, and the three heads of its three divisions: art, dance and drama, and music. The chairman contributed her services; the executive secretary and the three division heads were originally employed by the Temporary Emergency Relief Administration and assigned to the committee. On August 1, 1935, they were transferred to the WPA/FAP. On October 29, 1937, they resigned from the WPA and were thereafter paid from private donations to the committee. The sources of those donations were never revealed, but it was generally understood that they came from foundations. The executive secretary and the heads of the dance and drama, and the music divisions remained with the committee until it dissolved. I resigned on February 1, 1939, and was not replaced.

The art division had the largest staff of the three divisions. To operate the Temporary Galleries required a receptionist; five or six artists, who served as registrars and docents; two stenographers; two messengers; a porter; and two or three night watchmen. With the move to 3 East 67th Street, a smaller staff was required: four "registrars," two stenographers, and a messenger. The same staff that operated the Municipal Galleries also handled the national exhibitions.

All the gallery staff, excepting the division head, were on the WPA payrolls until July 1, 1938, at which time they were transferred to Federal Project No. 1. They were dropped from the latter, due to "reduction in quota," on January 16, 1939. Some of the staff of the galleries were kept on after that date, but whether the mayor, the city, or the chairman of the committee found the means of paying them is not known.

Salaries were paid from federal funds, as well as the costs of stationery, supplies, and the utilities at the Temporary Galleries.

The building occupied by the Temporary Galleries was owned by the city, but was, as noted above, remodeled at great expense by the WPA. The building at 3 East 67th Street was made available to the committee by the trustees of the Ryan estate at the nominal rental of $166.66 a month.

In December 1937, when the Municipal Art Galleries opened at 3 East 67th Street, membership in the galleries was opened to the public at five dollars a year. Income from membership fees was small, but it defrayed some of the expenses of maintaining the galleries.

The offices of the committee at 30 Rockefeller Plaza were donated by Rockefeller Center.

The city contributed very little to the support of the committee's activities. It did pay for the 1937 Summer Festival booklet. But in the same year, the mayor's office contributed only $644.28. The total income for that year was $62,981.89, and the disbursements, $62,628.20. The WPA contribution for the year was $28,631.63; and private donations were $8,000.[40]

At the time that federal support was withdrawn from the committee, Federal Project No. 1 was contributing about $14,000 in salaries for the staff, about half of which went to the staff of the galleries. Federal support of the arts was being greatly curtailed. Nevertheless, in retrospect, it seems unreasonable to have withdrawn support from an organization that was helping the artist to help himself on a permanent basis, in order to give temporary relief to others.

There are, in fact, some curious papers in the National Archives related to the withdrawal of support from the committee. One memorandum points to the fact that the twelve workers assigned to the Municipal Art Committee were taken over by Federal Project No. 1 in the hope that Mrs. Breckinridge's committee would be sufficiently interested in the Art Program to cooperate with it in various ways.

Mrs. Breckinridge, however [the report continues], although wishing to use WPA workers, does not, according to Mr. [Paul] Edwards [administrative officer, Federal Project No. 1] like to make public confession of alliance with the WPA. In fact, she informed Mr. Edwards that she could not hold her Committee together if she laid any stress on WPA. A request, for example, for the use of artists on the Project of the Municipal Art Committee's gallery to hang their own work, for sale, was at first refused, and finally granted for August 1939.[41]

The Municipal Art Committee was not a WPA project, any more than was the Metropolitan Museum of Art, or the New York Public Library, or the Museum of the City of New York, although all of them received considerable help in carrying out their programs from the WPA. The Municipal Art Galleries, however, continually exhibited and offered for sale works by artists who were on the WPA/FAP.

The committee was not set up to support the WPA, or to become one of its projects: It was searching for permanent means to help the artist help himself, serving as a liaison between him and the public. The mayor's plea for the retention of the twelve members of the staff was that their dismissal would probably destroy the work of the committee.

For reasons too complicated to be covered by telegram the future of the committee faces a present emergency which I hope means will be found to meet. I have the honor to ask you temporarily to rescind the dismissal of these employees so that the work can go on while measures may be attempted to save the committee which is working for the fulfillment of permanent projects which will furnish employment and be a credit to you and the WPA.[42]

Mrs. Breckinridge merely asked for time to raise a budget to keep the staff together, as she had previously done for the administrative staff. But federal support was withdrawn, and, as the mayor prophesied, that withdrawal probably destroyed the work of the committee.

There is no record of the collapse of the Municipal Art Committee, and no public announcement was made of it. Mayor LaGuardia's papers, however, indicate that at the time that federal support was withdrawn, the Mayor was working on the reorganization of the committee to keep it alive.[43] It would appear that Mrs. Breckinridge had, in a way, challenged the mayor to do so. She had given five full years of her time to the organization of the committee and to the development of the mayor's program for it. During all that time she received almost no financial assistance from the city.

In carrying out the mayor's program, the committee had steered the establishment of the Music and Art High School under the New York Board of Education; it had sponsored many programs of plays, symphony concerts, ballets, and other programs, at popular prices in the high-school auditoriums of the five boroughs; it had given wide promotion to the cultural events in the city during the summer months through the annual Summer Festivals; and it had established and operated the Municipal Art Galleries.

The greatest charge to the committee by the mayor was to establish a municipal art center, the plans for which were well under way. Briefly, the plans included new homes for the New York Philharmonic Symphony, the Metropolitan Opera, and the Municipal Art Galleries. A site for the center had been selected and about twenty million dollars raised to build it.

The center was to be located in the West Fifties. Rockefeller Plaza was to have been extended north to West 53rd Street—the Museum of Modern Art at the head of the Plaza on 53rd Street would have formed the cul-de-sac—and the center was to be located west and south of the museum, from Rockefeller Plaza extended to the Avenue of the Americas. In addition to the building housing the Opera, the Philharmonic, and the galleries, a number of other institutions were interested in building in the center.

The Opera and the Philharmonic now have their new homes in Lincoln Center, and the annual Summer Festivals have been revived. There was, however, a great difference between the plans for the Municipal Art Committee's center and the present-day Lincoln Center. Not only were the visual arts to be included with the performing arts, the Opera, the Philharmonic, and the galleries, but like the Metropolitan Museum and the New York Public Library, they were to be city-maintained. This sort of subsidy would undoubtedly have kept admission fees at reasonable levels.

The withdrawal of federal support from the Municipal Art Committee came at just the wrong time. It frayed tempers. Plans for the fourth annual national exhibition were cancelled; the Municipal Art Galleries closed at the end of their forty-eighth exhibition, and the committee collapsed.

The Need for Municipal Art Galleries Today

Today the public interest in art is much greater than in the thirties. Exhibitions of contemporary art enjoy large attendances, and the buying public has grown proportionately. Opportunities for artists to exhibit their works have, of course, also grown in proportion to the public interest.

The artist today, however, has almost no control over his exhibition fate. The artists who do come to public attention are brought there "through the intervention, if not by the grace, of gallery or museum."[44]

Because of the popularity of art today, many artists, especially those whose careers began during the thirties, are able to support themselves by their work, even when they are not favored by showings in the museums and galleries. Their work, however, is rarely brought to public attention.

Younger artists, on the other hand, are given little opportunity, except by favor or exploitation. Yet there are more art students, and hence more young artists, than at any other time in the history of the country.

These considerations of the situation of the artist today are generalities, known to almost all long-term observers of the art scene. They are difficult to document, for there are no surveys of sufficient merit and scope to support them.

Grace Glueck recently noted in *The New York Times* that "Manhattan's 40 or 50 leading dealers can only mount one-man shows each season for about 500 of the estimated 12,000 to 15,000 artists working in New York." She continued:

Most of the top dealers have waiting lists, and many are so solidly booked they refuse to consider new work. And of the 350 lesser galleries that also provide wall space, most leave something to be desired in the way of professional expertise (some even charge rental fees).

So, in the last few years, more and more downtown artists have been putting on their own shows, selling work directly from their lofts. . . . For some, it has proved a satisfactory way of doing business. . . .[45]

A recent survey of Washington artists pointed out, that after expressing that they "were not happy about their inability to support themselves from art alone," the "second, third and fourth on the list of professional problems mentioned by these artists was the absence of places to exhibit their works, the lack of critical acceptance, and the lack of public acceptance . . ."[46] The MacDowell plan, which can be adapted to almost any available space for community exhibitions, and to the needs of the artists of almost any community, has proven its popularity among artists over a period of eleven years in New York; eight years at the MacDowell Club and three at the Municipal Art Gallery.

Offering a direct liaison between the artist and the public, the plan could today go a long way to meet the needs of artists. It eliminates any screen of patronage between the artist and the public, and it gives the public a true opportunity to see the creative expression of their communities.

The present-day popularity of art would undoubtedly bring much greater benefits to the artists who would exhibit under the MacDowell plan than was brought to them during the years of the Depression.

If a way could be found for federal support, matched by local contributions, of galleries in metropolitan areas, and even of regional areas where there is any concentration of artists, to operate under the MacDowell plan, a great service would be rendered to both the people and the artists of those areas. Such support would constitute a renewal of the creative life of the country. It would bring to the surface the work of artists who rarely, if ever, come to public attention.

A society, such as ours today, which spends millions of dollars annually on works of art by deceased artists for its museums—in one recent case over five millions for a single work—should be able to spend something less in support of municipal or regional galleries as showcases for its living artists.

Every effort to locate the papers, press-book, and other records of the Municipal Art Committee of the City of New York, in the preparation of this memoir of its activities, has failed. It is quite probable that they were destroyed when the committee collapsed in 1939. Much, therefore, is based on my personal files and memory.

I am most grateful for the cooperation of the Municipal Archives, New York, which houses the papers of Mayor LaGuardia, and the National Archives, Washington, D.C., which houses the papers of Holger Cahill, a member of the Municipal Art Committee, as they relate to his work with the WPA Federal Art Project. I am also indebted to the New York Public Library, the Frick Art Reference Library, New York, and the Library of the National Collection of Fine Arts and National Portrait Gallery, Washington, D.C., which have preserved various reports of the committee and catalogues of the exhibitions it sponsored. I am especially indebted to Dr. Francis V. O'Connor who not only made this memoir possible, but gave me access to the many documents he has assembled in his studies of federal support of the fine arts during the 1930s.

1. *The New York Times,* January 29, 1934.
2. *Ibid.,* February 14 and 15, 1934.
3. The artists' proposals were contained in a pamphlet issued by the Artists' Committee of Action. Their proposals were:

1. A MUNICIPAL ART CENTER, with galleries for exhibitions, for the use of all artists throughout the year.
2. A fraternal meeting place for the artists enabling them to come in contact with their contemporaries.
3. A live forum for the discussion and exchange of ideas in art.
4. A center for traveling exhibitions from which art works would be sent to all sections of the country; also, where art from other parts of the United States could be studied.
5. A department for the popularization of art and art appreciation.
6. Studios and laboratories where advanced experiments will be conducted in all mediums.
7. A circulating library of art works to be rented and loaned to private individuals and public places.
8. An art committee to establish friendly relationships with art centers throughout the world.
9. The MUNICIPAL ART GALLERY AND CENTER shall be administered by and for the artists, by means of duly elected committees.
10. Any artist may join this institution who agrees to further its aims and purposes.
11. There shall be no discrimination whatsoever against any school of esthetic belief, no political discrimination, nor shall race, creed or color constitute a barrier to membership.
12. Regular meetings shall be arranged as agreed to by the membership.
13. A charter shall be drawn up by the artists covering the details of administration.
14. Members of the administration elected to serve shall be responsible for their assigned duties and subject to recall by the membership.
15. THE MUNICIPAL ART CENTER shall be a non-profit making project.
16. A comprehensive plan will be devised by capable advisors, subject to the approval of the membership, for the sale promotion of works of art and immediate payments to the artists.
17. Methods and means shall be planned for the economic benefit of all artists. A percentage of all sales and the income from other activities will be established in a common fund to be utilized for the benefit of the members.
18. There shall be no jury system. Exhibitions sufficient in number and of adequate character to satisfy the requirements of the entire membership shall be arranged throughout the year.

19. Artists members having common purposes or character of work may hold exhibitions subject only to the time and space limitations of the galleries in the MUNICIPAL ART CENTER. Exhibitions of special nature shall be scheduled, to which members will be asked to submit works.

20. The principle which will govern all activities shall be on a democratic basis, administered by and for the artists.

4. Letter from Mrs. Breckinridge to Mayor LaGuardia, June 20, 1934. (Municipal Archives, New York City).

5. *The New York Times,* January 7, 1935.

6. City of New York, Municipal Art Committee, *First Annual Report,* 1935 (New York, 1936), p. 14.

7. Alfred Sinks, "Potted Palms and Public Art," *Art Front,* I (February 1935), p. 4.

8. *The New York Times,* January 16, 1935.

9. The complete membership of the Art Division Committee was as follows: Herbert Adams, Mrs. Rogers Bacon, Alfred H. Barr, Jr., Alon Bement, George Blumenthal, James C. Boudreau, Holger Cahill, Mrs. Telesforo Casanova, Joseph H. Freedlander, Wood Gaylor, Forest Grant, Mrs. J. B. Handley-Greaves, Mrs. Harry F. Guggenheim, Mrs. Alexandrina R. Harris, Mrs. Ripley Hitchcock, Mrs. Leonebel Jacobs, Albert J. Kennedy, Leon Kroll, Florence N. Levy, Jonas Lie, Michael Loew, Louis Lozowick, Anne Morgan, Wallace Morgan, Mrs. Audrey McMahon, Mrs. Robert Patchin, Attilio Piccirilli, Abram Poole, Vernon C. Porter, Austin Purves, Jr., Ellen Ravenscroft, Mrs. Elihu Root, Jr., Dr. Joseph M. Sheehan, Mrs. John S. Sheppard, John Sloan, Mrs. William K. Vanderbilt, Sr., Dr. Ira Wile, F. Ballard Williams, Herbert E. Winlock and Philip N. Youtz.

10. Grace Overmeyer, *Government and the Arts* (New York, 1939), p. 177–8.

11. City of New York, Municipal Art Committee, *First Annual Report, 1935* (New York, 1936), pp. 19, 20.

12. "The Lost Independents," *Magazine of Art,* XLIV (December 1951), p. 302.

13. Thomas S. Cummings, *Historic Annals of the National Academy of Design* (Philadelphia, G. W. Childs, 1865).

14. Bruce St. John, editor, *John Sloan's New York Scene* (New York: Harper & Row, 1965), p. 406.

15. "Municipal Government and the Artist," *Exhibition,* I (September 30–October 18, 1936), p. 10.

16. City of New York, Municipal Art Committee, Application for Exhibition Space in the Temporary Galleries (mimeographed).

17. City of New York, Municipal Art Committee, Press Release, n.d.

18. *Art Front,* II (February, 1936), p. 4, 5.

19. Letter to Holger Cahill from Mrs. Breckinridge, January 7, 1935 (National Archives, Record Group 69, series 607.315).

20. *New York Times,* January 7, 1936.

21. *Ibid.*

22. *Art Digest,* X (January 1936), p. 6.

23. City of New York, Municipal Art Committee, *For Release Saturday and Sunday, February 15 and 16, 1936.*

24. The actual count was 663 artists in 69 groups. The groups sometimes fell short of the number of artists included in their original applications.

25. *Exhibition,* I (December 23, 1936–January 10, 1937).

26. *Art Digest,* XII (December 15, 1937), p. 11.

27. Emily Genauer in the *New York World-Telegram,* July 16, 1938.

28. Howard Devree, *The New York Times,* June 5, 1938.

29. Bertha A. Houck, "The Painter Sees America," *The Spur,* LXI (June 1938), p. 54.

30. *The New York Times,* January 30, 1938.

31. *New York Herald Tribune,* September 18, 1939.

32. This figure is based on various reports of the Municipal Art Committee and newspaper accounts of the galleries.

33. *New York World-Telegram,* June 17, 1939.

34. *Exhibition,* I (December 23, 1936–January 10, 1937), p. 5.

35. City of New York, Department of Investigation, *Report to Mayor LaGuardia Concerning Municipal Art Committee,* March 4, 1938 (in Municipal Archives, New York).

36. *New York Sun,* January 16, 1937.

37. *Ibid.*

38. "New York's New Municipal Gallery Knows How to Forfend Trouble," *Art Digest,* X (January 1936), p. 6.

39. *Milwaukee Journal,* May 22 and 23, 1937; *Milwaukee Sentinel,* May 22 and 23, 1937.

40. City of New York, Department of Investigation, *Report* (see footnote 35).

41. Memorandum to Mrs. Florence Kerr from Lawrence Morris, executive assistant, WPA, dated January 16, 1939. (National Archives, Record Group 69, series 651.315, Box 2109, January 1939)

42. Radiogram to Colonel Francis C. Harrington, January 16, 1939. (National Archives, Record Group 69, series 651.315, Box 2109, January 1939)

43. In Municipal Archives, New York.

44. Robert Goldwater, *loc. cit.* (see footnote 12).

45. "Artists Arrange Multi-Loft Show," *New York Times,* April 19, 1968.

46. Cornelia Noland, "A Documented Portrait of the Washington Artist," *Washingtonian,* III (March, 1968), p. 48.

PART 4

A DIALOGUE

FVO'C

Photograph by Thomas Beck

OLG

JK

AM

MEL

A Dialogue

Participants: AUDREY McMAHON
OLIVE LYFORD GAVERT
MARCHAL E. LANDGREN
JACOB KAINEN
FRANCIS V. O'CONNOR

FVO'C Let us explore first the cultural situation in America before and during the New Deal period. What was American art like? What access did the people have to it prior to 1930? What did the government projects do to increase and broaden access later on? Perhaps we can begin by directing these questions to Mrs. McMahon since she worked in the early 1930s surveying the American art scene for the College Art Association.

AM I would say that in the early days of the CAA knowledge of art and the understanding and enjoyment of it was strictly an eastern seaboard matter. Art had not got beyond the Alleghenies. There were all sorts of misconceptions, if there was any thinking at all. It was these misconceptions that led the CAA to hire me to try to do something to popularize, broaden, and bring art to other places, especially where there would be students. The teaching of art in the Middle and Far West was largely in the hands of maiden ladies who knew little about art, had not seen any original or important works, had often not been to Europe and had, to say the least, very narrow esthetic views. So the artist hadn't very much of a chance for any real self-expression.

FVO'C Can you describe what a mid-western art museum was like at that time?

AM Yes, I remember vividly a day something like today in temperature in Sacramento, California. There was a beautiful, beautiful mansion filled with paintings and they were largely *Mona Lisa* by Miss Jones, *Mona Lisa* by Miss Smith, *Mona Lisa* by Miss Raymond, and there would be manifold other paintings of similar nature. There was not one original painting in that whole museum. Then there was the de Young Museum in San Francisco, which is, after all, a very respectable museum today. It was empty. It was ready for exhibitions, it was hopeful of them, but was empty. There were no accessions. Then in the South there were accessions that were gilded baby shoes! They had been worn by the founder of the museum!

305

MEL   Well, think of what the Walker Art Center in Minneapolis was then, and now it is one of the leading museums in the country.

AM   Yes, how right you are. And in the southwest they had things like antimacassars and embroidery with here and there some old Americana that, probably accidently, might be excellent. I doubt that they knew very much what they had. There was some building, there was some teaching, but the quality of accessions and exhibitions was really appalling.

MEL   The Art Institute of Chicago was a little bit different.

AM   Yes, as was the Detroit Institute of Art because William R. Valentiner was there and doing a good job. He had good Dutch paintings there and many other fine things.

JK   Every museum, including Chicago and the Metropolitan, had large rooms devoted to plaster casts. You could see the seams. It took me a long time to realize they were not originals. It was a great letdown to look at famous works like the *Discus Thrower* or *Dying Gaul* which seemed so wrong—so flimsy.

MEL   I think it is of special interest that on the eastern seaboard, even where money was available, very little was being spent for American art, except in a few places.

AM   You're right.

MEL   The Metropolitan, for instance, had the Hearn fund for contemporary American art which it had for years and which was growing and growing and growing. They refused to spend it because they didn't know what to do with contemporary American art. When they did buy, they bought some of the most ridiculous things I have ever seen. They acquired a painting from the first exhibition in the Municipal Art Gallery at what was then a very good price, $2,500. It was called *Abandoned*. It was the biggest thing in the show and pretty awful. After it was delivered, I called Harry Wehle then curator of painting and said, "You've made a very nice gesture to the city but now why don't you buy something worthwhile?" (Laughter)

AM   Well I discussed this at length many times with Wehle and I think he quite honestly had no idea what was good American art. There were guidelines for Renaissance, for European art, and so on. There were no guidelines for American art—and a primitive painting was something of which curators had no conception. It wasn't until the Museum of Modern Art, and Alfred Barr and Holger Cahill came onto the horizon that this became accepted at all. Newark had some good primitive art and this was because of Cahill and Beatrice Winser, who understood and valued it.

FVO'C Mrs. Gavert, you traveled a great deal for the Association of Junior Leagues during the very early 1930s. What did you find?

OLG   Yes. I went all over the country. My job was to find whatever cultural institutions existed in various cities and to persuade their directors to use volunteers. I remember very well some of the places I went where culture was supposed to flourish. In West Virginia—I've forgotten which city it was—I remember being so depressed by the very poor things they had to show. What art there was was all mixed up with stuffed birds and things like that. In Nashville, Tennessee, the museum was an exact replica of the Parthenon. That, for them, was the last word in contemporary culture. Then in Oklahoma City we found a lot of Indian material but mainly photographs of the early legislators in Oklahoma—who were Indians—all got up in their white collars and big cravats. This was all very interesting but a little difficult to tie in with volunteers working for cultural organizations.

FVO'C Did the institutions that displayed this type of material—photographs, gilded booties, stuffed birds—did they claim to be art museums?

OLG Well I think the one in West Virginia certainly did.

AM By and large the ones I visited claimed to be museums. They had been erected as museums and the reason we of the CAA were so welcome was because we were going to send something that would hang on those empty walls.

JK This was a time when American art was really at about its lowest ebb. At the end of the 1920s and the beginning of the 1930s there were few commercial galleries. The art museums were dominated by people with 19th-century notions of what a museum's functions were. The American artists of the 1920s who were influenced by Cubism and foreign art saw that there was a chance to break our insular tradition. But these artists were so neglected, so spurned by the museums and the critics, that several, such as Alfred Maurer, committed suicide. Many went to Paris and others left their radical styles and went back to more acceptable work. So those who were interested in doing something fresh had no place to show. The New Deal projects actually stimulated the development of new galleries.

MEL Very much.

JK There was that irrepressible Irishman, Pat Codyre, who used to work for the Newhouse Galleries and the Museum of Modern Art when it first opened. He went on to the Contemporary Arts Gallery in the early 1930s. You, Marchal, and Pat helped the young expressionists who suddenly began to emerge at that time. Remember The Ten—Adolph Gottlieb, Mark Rothko, Ben-Zion, Joseph Solman, Ilya Bolotowsky . . . ?

AM Of course. And don't forget J. B. Neumann's gallery, The New Art Circle.

JK For the first time we could see Max Beckmann . . . and Neumann selected some good Americans.

AM And Curt Valentin's Gallery of Modern Art. . . .

JK Well, he came in a little later, in 1937.

MEL Also, you can't forget a man like Charles Daniel, who was very important, or Dorothy Paris. They both ran important galleries in the early 1930s.

AM   Yes, there were a few dealers among the people who really did recognize the artist. They knew and they dared. They were risking their own money whereas the museum curators were risking their donors' money and they didn't dare. They had absolutely no confidence. With the exception of the Whitney you couldn't get a living artist into a permanent collection. Even an up-and-coming museum person like Francis Henry Taylor who was director of the Worcester Museum never bought for his collection. He wrote about American art. We published articles in *Parnassus* in which he wrote good criticism and encouraging things. But so far as I know, he never bought anything of the contemporary artists.

MEL   He was a great idol for the American artist at the time.

AM   Yes, he was a great idol because he did understand it, but he didn't risk money on it.

MEL   The dealers were coming up. People like Valentine Dudensing. I hate to praise him too much; I didn't like him.

AM   I couldn't stand him either, but he did a good job. First he had the Valentine Gallery and later it was called the Dudensing.

MEL   I knew Milton Avery from around 1930. He was not selling, of course, at all. But it was Dudensing who came in one day to see his work and he bought up a great quantity of it and gave him a flat rate. It was very little, but to Avery, who had just had a daughter born to him, this was a tremendous thing. It got him started, really got him started.

AM   The commercial galleries by and large were more advanced and more daring than the museums.

MEL   But we should also recall that the Museum of Modern Art, which opened in 1929, held several shows of American art in its first years. Its second show was "19 Living Americans" and later it showed Max Weber, Burchfield, Homer, Ryder, and Eakins. I think it is also very interesting that the first exhibition of Paul Klee's work in America was at MOMA. It was one of the very early shows in 1930. The catalogue was the first publication on Klee in English. It was published in an edition of 1,000 copies.

JK   At the same time abstract art was at such a low ebb that the artists had to band together—like the American Abstract Artists.

MEL   In the seventh exhibition of the Municipal Art Gallery—that was 1936—thirteen abstractionists got together and put on a show. In November of that year eleven of them became charter members of the American Abstract Artists. The next year they had their show in the Squibb Building, the following year they had another show in the Municipal Art Gallery. Léger came to speak at the opening. But the American Abstract Artists were nothing to the critics. There were nasty little cracks about echoes of the School of Paris. Of course, this was a time when people looked down on the School of Paris in a funny way.

AM   Yes.

308

MEL   When I was at the Contemporary Arts Gallery helping Miss Emily Frances and Pat Codyre put on first one-man shows for young unknown artists—we gave Mark Tobey and John Kane their first one-man shows—I had the opportunity to observe many artists just starting their careers. They came from all parts of the country. I remember one evening sitting with a group of them and they started to ask me questions about modern art. In the course of that evening I learned that this particular group had learned about modern art from the John Quinn catalogue. They had never seen an original painting by Picasso or Matisse, but they had seen the 1926 catalogue of the sale of the famous John Quinn collection and their whole knowledge of modern art came from it. Milton Avery told me that the greatest influence on his life was the Quinn sale where he first saw Maurice Prendergast. There was something else in the 1930s that I think was very interesting and I have never seen it brought up critically. The artists, the young artists, were looking for roots in America and they turned to Albert Pinkham Ryder. Ryder had a certain abstract quality that appealed to them. He was a tremendous influence on many of the young painters—like Jackson Pollock.

AM   That's right.

MEL   Also, I think something should be said here about Mrs. Katherine Dreier. She was a very strange, though, certainly, very well-meaning, woman. In 1920 she organized the *Société Anonyme,* which was an international association to promote the study of modern art in America. Kandinsky was its vice president and Marcel Duchamp its secretary. It sponsored a so-called Museum of Modern Art and brought some marvelous exhibitions to New York.

AM   Katherine Dreier did something remarkable for the CAA. She gave us those exhibitions when she was finished with them and we circulated them. This was one of the great aims of the CAA. But the sad fact is that those exhibitions, as well as others we organized ourselves were not accepted very well outside New York, Chicago, and San Francisco.

MEL   Exactly. I tried in 1940, I think it was, to circulate a small inexpensive show of watercolors, temperas, gouaches by the members of the American Abstract Artists—at their request. I was able to get three bookings in the country; the fee was $25.

AM   Yes, I know. Those fees were nominal. Yale refused one show after another including one of Maurer's. Couldn't possibly have that. Much too distorted, you know. And so on. There was just no acceptance. Compared to the museums, the colleges were a hundred times more reactionary. It was almost impossible to get them to accept anything abstract; even School of Paris was too much for them.

MEL   That's right.

FVO'C   Aside from commercial galleries, where could an artist exhibit his work during the 1930s? What were the most prestigous shows?

MEL   The Corcoran Biennial and the Carnegie International were the two most desirable places for an artist in America to show.

AM   Not only desirable, there wasn't anything else! They were the only big shows and then you were all hemmed in by regulations: one oil, two watercolors, etc.

MEL   The Whitney was another when it started its Biennials. I made every effort to get the artists that I was working with represented in three places: the Corcoran, the Carnegie, and the Whitney. And I would go on my hands and knees and beg! I remember the first Whitney Biennial of Contemporary American Painting in 1932. I wanted Charles Logasa in it. The Whitney policy was to look at an artist's work and invite him, permitting him to select whichever picture he wanted to be seen in the show. Well, they finally decided to take Logasa in but they insisted on picking the picture. They wouldn't trust him. But I did manage. I got him into the Carnegie and the first Whitney.

AM   It was an enormous event in the life of an artist to get his work seen. Enormous! This is one reason the CAA had such phenomenal success. I think we were the first or the only people who really circulated living art to small galleries and libraries and halls and colleges at that time. But our policy of trying to get one painting bought per show failed dismally. Practically no one bought anything.

FVO'C What was the price-scale of those paintings?

AM   They started at $10 and went to about $150; $250 was high.

MEL   The painters who got a good price in those days were people like Eugene Speicher and Leon Kroll.

JK   But John Sloan couldn't sell. I remember when he offered his whole set of New York etchings—*Turning out the light* and all those—for about $2 each.

MEL   Yes, I remember that.

AM   Isn't that awful.

FVO'C This suggests a question. Was the state of the artist in 1928 before the Depression any better than in 1932? Did the crash have any effect at all on the ability of the young artist to make a living from his art?

AM   To make a living *from his art?*

FVO'C Yes.

AM   So far as I recall he never made his living from his art at any time! But he made a living. He moonlighted. He did all sorts of allied things. He taught, he did commercial art, he lettered. There were a lot of letterers. The Depression wiped out the secondary employment that kept him alive. But, to my knowledge, he was never able to make a living through his art in those days.

MEL   Well, there were a few. Milton Avery was one of the few artists I knew who could exist. He never did anything but paint. He was supported by his wife who was a commercial artist and had faith—actually great devotion—in him. She kept him going. There were artists who didn't even have homes—who had to live with friends. Some were pretty tragic.

AM   Yes, but you see, this is exactly my point. The artist was not living on producing art as art in those years. He was making a living elsewhere or his wife or parents were supporting him. And the means of support failed.

MEL   That's true.

AM   Therefore he became, to some degree, a derelict person, who had no means of support.

OLG   Surely, Francis, the answers to the questionnaires* you sent out to former New Deal artists show that even today some artists can barely live without outside support.

FVO'C Definitely yes. Only 7 percent of the artists who responded make their entire living from the sale of their work and only about 30 percent make over half their income from that source; 75 percent teach to make ends meet. The median yearly income of all the artists responding was around $8,000—which is a scandal.

AM   It is really only a few that are eminently successful.

MEL   Always in the history of art there are those few.

AM   Yes, except that in the history of American art it is only since the end of the Second World War that there are even those few.

MEL   Well I don't know. Eugene Speicher used to get about $8,000 per canvas.

AM   Yes, but he was a rare exception. I would say we are having today the only boom in American art in my lifetime. The only time that even a small number of people can live the way people in other professions live from the product of their work. I got into a taxicab recently and the driver said to me, "You're Audrey Mc-Mahon, aren't you?" He was a former WPA/FAP artist who had never made it. He still paints—and drives that cab for a livelihood. It's sad, but we still cannot provide a market for the people we educate.

FVO'C Let us turn now to the early Depression years, to the years between 1929 and 1933 when the government first tried to help the artist. This period is almost entirely undocumented.

AM   Are you speaking of the Emergency Relief Administration days?

FVO'C Yes, and also before that, during the last years of the Hoover administration.

AM   The CAA was in touch with artists primarily because we did exhibitions. Frances Pollak was very social minded. She and I went to see the mayor and he agreed to support a small group of artists. His budget was so limited—I think it was about $15 a week was all he could offer. Then Albany agreed to give a part of its relief funds from the state. We got that through Fred Daniels who was a social worker and knew Harry Hopkins. This was when Roosevelt was governor of New York. Hopkins was chairman of the state's Temporary Emergency Relief Administration and I know he

---

* These questionnaires are part of the files of "Federal Support for the Visual Arts: The New Deal and Now," which are deposited in the Library of the National Collection of Fine Arts, Smithsonian Institution in Washington, D.C.

311

knew about our project because he referred to it in conversation when we were setting up the WPA/FAP years later.

MEL   I remember Harry Hopkins came to one of my exhibitions at Contemporary Arts. I told the poor man—even then—that if he took the burden of his office as seriously as he was doing, he wasn't going to live very long. That man had the utmost sympathy for everyone.

AM   The small program the directors of the CAA allowed us was very hit-or-miss. It was a very minor, very small, very unsatisfying program. All the artists came to us strictly from the relief rolls. As the needs grew, it became less effective. But of course, as the needs grew, then other measures came into effect—such as the PWAP. But later, in 1935, we became the natural model for the WPA/FAP. Since I was the director of the CAA project I think that is how I became the natural director of the WPA project in New York. I really don't know the thinking of the people involved, but it would seem to me now that that is what must have happened.

FVO'C But that was a very long five years for the artists.

AM   A very long five years and a dreadful, dreadful five years! All we did really was dole out this tiny little pittance and hope some good would come of it. Then we would try to explain why there was not more and try to get wealthy people to help out the weeks we couldn't and so on and on. It was a starvation thing. Out of my window I could see people who were working for us sleeping on park benches. That was just how stark things were.

FVO'C Jacob, you were an artist then. What was it like?

JK   I graduated from Pratt Institute in 1930. I did manage to get a job in a place called the Intaglio Gravure Co. I drew greeting cards in pen and ink. The drawings were reproduced by photogravure. It was fascinating. But, of course, the job lasted about six months and they went out of business. Then I was absolutely indigent. I lived on relief in a condemned house and paid $10 a month rent. I had an extension cord so I could get electricity through the transom.

AM   You were not unique in that!

JK   I know I wasn't—I got the idea from the painter Max Schnitzler. (Laughter) I had a heater and I lived on beans. I saw the beginning of cafeteria modern. Now Roy Lichtenstein is using the "moderne." But the cafeterias were just beginning to adopt this style. That's how I lived—in style! It was fortunate we were young—we could exist that way.

MEL   Remember that wonderful place on University Place where we could get hot pastrami sandwiches for 10¢—or was it a nickel?

JK   That's how we lived. Then there was home relief—and later the art project. And we *lived* on relief. It was positively Lucullan! The food we could get from the relief money! We could even buy books on 4th Avenue with all that extra money. The surrealist painter Walter Quirt lived down 14th Street. We would work, then walk along 2nd Avenue. It was great to be young, but we had absolutely nothing. No one dreamed of selling a painting.

AM Of course. The public had no purchasing power—especially when it came to art—or novels—or buying a theater or concert ticket. You ought to know that even people like myself, who had a job that paid—though not always—and a husband with a Harvard PhD were in trouble. The first year my husband Philip McMahon taught he earned $360 as a lecturer at the Metropolitan. He gave up a job working with some advertising firm because he was unhappy. So he went into teaching and made $360 the first year. I well remember this. But despite it all we were financial aristocrats in those years because between us we might have an income of say $3,500 or $4,000. We were doing very well—but we didn't have money to go to the theater. We were supporting relatives, and parents, and friends who needed a meal. Who could buy theater tickets?

JK There was a real Bohemia in those days. The artists, writers, musicians all lived in the same section of town and were all in the same boat. The Bohemia of the Village was genuine and it lasted until the end of the Project in the early 1940s. Then of course it became popular. The lawyers came down to get culture. But the artists lived on the fringes of society and the Bohemian sections were our Hoovervilles. All that is gone though. Everyone is so successful these days that no one can be radical anymore.

FVO'C Young people fleeing affluence make up the radical Bohemia we have today.

JK But that's incredible!

FVO'C When did the artists begin to organize in their own interests? I am thinking about the Artists' Committee for Action and the Artists' Union.

MEL There was the John Reed Club. I was never a member but I know it was certainly an organizing point before the Artists' Union.

JK Would I be compromising myself if I say that I was a member?

MEL No, I don't think so at all. I think it is quite to your credit.

JK I remember when Diego Rivera came down and spoke. He was attacked from the floor and accused of betraying the revolution. The meeting was disrupted. Many members threatened to quit the John Reed Club.

MEL The only thing I can say about my radical days was that I absolutely loved Mother Bloor.

JK She was a wonderful, warm-hearted woman.

MEL Nothing excited me more than sitting down and having a scotch and soda with Mother Bloor. She was a great radical and had been jailed over and over. I remember going to an enormous birthday party for her one year. I never saw so much schmaltz—but it was fun.

AM But the artists were not really organized that early. They came in to us en masse and presented their many grievances which often were justified. But they didn't know how to present them and we didn't know how to receive them. It took a period of months or even years for *us* to learn to organize, and that was well after the WPA/FAP got started.

FVO'C In the early 1930s the CAA was the only organization dispensing some sort of relief to unemployed artists. Late in 1933—December 6 to be precise—the PWAP was set up. In New York it was operated through the Whitney Museum under its director, Juliana Force, and Lloyd Goodrich. Thus there were two agencies working for the benefit of the artist through June 1934. Can we discuss the PWAP dispensing largess through the medium of Mrs. Force?

AM Well, as far as the CAA was concerned, our artists all wanted to be on the PWAP for any number of reasons: recognition was better, salary was better, work was regular. We were night to its day. We were merely a little organization trying to do a stop-gap job. Here was a real program. All the artists tried to get on it.

MEL Before Mrs. Force began to operate the PWAP, Mrs. Gertrude Vanderbilt Whitney, the founder of the Whitney Museum, had a private relief project. There were quite a few artists in New York who received $50 a month by check. This was private and was all very secret. No one ever said much about it.

AM We had some people working on the CAA who received the $50 a month. But this was kept very undercover.

JK What did the Baroness Rebay do? Didn't she sponsor some people?

MEL She was mainly interested in musicians. She gave grand pianos to young musicians.

FVO'C What was the relationship between the CAA project and Mrs. Force and the PWAP? Was there any coordination?

MEL No one ever coordinated anything with Juliana Force.

AM We had an armed truce. We agreed to co-exist. And that is about what we did. She had the upper hand, usually; we had the upper hand, occasionally—as when we would have something very distinguished happen by pure chance and get some public acclaim. But it was co-existence, not coordination.

FVO'C The PWAP's policies were rather strict. They demanded the American scene as apt subject matter. There was endless dunning of artists to produce on schedule. There is a letter from Edward Laning in which he has to explain in infinite detail what he is doing so Mrs. Force will continue sending the checks. The PWAP in New York seemed an autocratic system for the artists and I know many were dismissed because of Mrs. Force.

AM And then others left on their own.

FVO'C Yes. Now in June of 1934 the PWAP ceased to function though the CAA continued. What was the situation then? The Federal Emergency Relief Administration was functioning nationally. In New York the Emergency Relief Bureau was set up.

Between June 1934 and that winter there was a statue cleaning project going. Many artists who had been on the PWAP were continued under the federal emergency program. This meant that they were back on the old CAA project which was now funded by the government.

AM   That's right. That was when Mrs. Pollak shifted her responsibility to me because she wanted to take on a teaching and service project which was her major interest. I switched over exclusively to the creative artists. That was when the PWAP artists applied for employment with us. Of course we could only help them if they were on home relief. There was no non-relief quota until the WPA/FAP.

FVO'C Mrs. McMahon, could you tell us in greater detail how you got involved with the WPA/FAP during the summer and fall of 1935?

AM   So far as I know the initiative was from Washington. Harry Hopkins then director of the FERA got in touch with the CAA. He asked us if we could make any personnel recommendations. After a great deal of consideration, we recommended that Francis Henry Taylor, then director of the Worcester Museum, become national director of the WPA/FAP. We asked Taylor, since Hopkins thought well of this, but he didn't want the job. Then there was a conference with a number of people. Taylor was there, Mildred Holzhauer (later Mrs. Jacob Baker) and many others. Holger Cahill was suggested. He was then at the Newark Museum and was someone who specialized in American art. He was asked and he said he would be delighted. Then the CAA was asked whether I could be lent, on a temporary basis, to advise. I went to Washington quite early in the situation and met with Harry Hopkins, his deputy Jacob Baker, and Cahill. We talked. Then I went back to my CAA job. A little later I was informed that Cahill had been formally appointed national director and that I would be a regional director. That, as far as I know, was the beginning.

FVO'C Can you tell us something of the early planning? Was the new project seen solely as a relief operation or as a creative enterprise that would take advantage of the relief set-up for broader cultural goals?

AM   Hopkins saw it as a relief set-up; Cahill as a cultural opportunity. In the beginning there was great stress on the 25 percent non-relief quota. I remember we sent Cahill a list of our artists divided as relief and non-relief and he said "Thank God for that 25 percent." The relief aspect was stressed by the local WPA administration rather than by the national office. In later years, of course, even the national office was forced to emphasize the relief aspect and that 25 percent went down to 10 percent and eventually to 5 percent, but in the beginning the WPA/FAP was conceived and presented to us at the CAA as a chance for American art and artists.

FVO'C Yes. That leads us very nicely to the art and artists who were involved in the WPA/FAP. We have been all looking through the Museum of Modern Art's 1936 catalogue of the Project's first big exhibition, "New Horizons in American Art." Perhaps we could talk about the art in that show.

JK   You know, it was a very odd selection.

AM   Well when you say that, Jacob, you have to remember it was really the beginning. It was awfully early for them to do that—especially in the light of what came after. So much better work came late in 1936—when that show appeared—and in '37 and '38. Those were the peak years. In 1935–36 it had hardly started.

JK   It is true that the artists really began developing after a year or two. They were new to their media, rather timid, and they inherited certain traditions. I know when I went to the printer, George C. Miller, before the project to work on a stone, Miller handed me a group of lithographic crayons in holders beginning with No. 5, which is the hardest. You were supposed to take the point and carefully build up tones. Well that is a lot of work to begin with—to get a nice dark, like Goya. The artists who had come on the wpa/fap's graphic division had to break reflexes if they had had training under a conservative printer. It took some time to get acquainted with the stone.

FVO'C Going through the New Horizons catalogue it seems that most of the art is orientated toward the social scene or regionalism.

AM   It is interesting to me, Francis, that you asked in your questionnaire if artists were required, or requested, to depict the social scene—and they all say no. They all say they could do what they pleased except on pwap. Yet, as I look over the lithographs I still have and the many I see around, that is exactly what they depicted and little else. By and large it is a record of the social scene. Yet there really was no emphasis on the social scene from on high—though I do not know if that is true for projects outside New York. But nothing was ever rejected in New York because it was too close to the truth, shall we say. That is certain.

OLG   Wasn't this just about the time when America discovered regional art? I mean Thomas Hart Benton and Grant Wood became great heroes because they had discovered something in America to paint.

MEL   Well the painters of the American scene came up in the early 1930s and many people who are abstractionists today were painters of the American scene then.

JK   But American scene was still progressive in its way. The established academies and art organizations turned out confections. Impressionism was domesticated and sweetened. You could practically eat up the pictures including frame, glass and all. Absolutely no feeling, no observation. It was something that looked pretty. Regionalism at least was an attempt to see life as it was. It was naive artistically but at that time artists were cautious of following advanced European trends and winding up with a disaster. They steered away from European influences. As a matter of fact, some of the regional artists who had been influenced by Benton and others renounced European modernism completely. They didn't want anything to do with the sort of thing that had destroyed their fathers.

AM   How remarkable it is, if you think about it, that a few short years afterward, just because it was recognized and underwritten by Washington, we had art where the social scene was depicted truthfully. The complaints from my superiors in the

WPA/FAP at that time were "Does it all have to be so grim? Does it all have to be so drab?" But this was the reality of the moment. Isn't it extraordinary that we went from the plaster casts and total artificiality almost in one leap right down to the bones. And there were hundreds of people ready to put down on canvas and paper what was true.

JK   Was anything rejected because it was too true, or too wild esthetically? Was the artist allowed to fail?

AM   I don't recall any rejections for that. A work could perhaps not be allocated to a public building, you know. That's of course certainly true. Also, I recall there was some sort of myth that if your work wasn't allocable you couldn't be a creative artist. That was never true.

MEL   I was never on the WPA/FAP, but my memory is that the artists did pretty much what they wanted to do.

AM   They say so, by and large. I've spent the day reading Dr. O'Connor's questionnaires at random, not picking people I knew but going through alphabetically, and I found some extraordinary things. The consensus was that if a person could not do creative work he didn't do creative work, but if he could then he did creative work along his own preferences.

JK   But it was a very unsophisticated period in American art.

MEL   Yes, it was. Yet the social scene in that day was a very vital scene. You had the activities of the Communists, you had the American League Against War and Fascism. Social concern was very strongly in the air. Artists in the great metropolitan areas were very alive to social events. The artists in more rural areas were, of course, painting the American scene in a different context entirely; they were more sentimental than radical. In the national exhibitions which I helped to organize for the Municipal Art Committee, walking through the galleries was like taking a tour of the country. You could walk from one region to another. And it was perfectly natural for the artists from the urban centers to paint the social scene. That was what was in the air—and in the streets. The very fact that the urban artists were able to organize some 2,000 strong into a union at that point shows a kind of social awareness you wouldn't expect to find in rural communities. So there was plenty of local color and private commentary.

JK   There were distinct groups among the socially concerned artists, especially among the graphic artists. Some were artistically naive, sentimental, illustrative, who rendered things without any conception of form. Then there were others who knew Rouault or Orozco and who were more expressionist in treatment. They were the better artists because they were more aware of artistic traditions. This expressionist development actually led to later developments after the 1930s. But at the time it was eclipsed by social pot-boilers. The same was true of painting to an extent. But it was on the graphic division—aside, of course from the mural division—that valuable things

317

happened. There were a number of artists who became bolder in their handling and outlook and nothing like that had happened before in American art.

MEL   Well, of course, there you had practically a whole graphic workshop opened up to artists for the first time.

JK   Oh, it was certainly the first time.

AM   That's just why I feel to have had an exhibition at the end of that first year can not indicate to us today anything of the stature that this program was to attain.

JK   Sure, I see now why I was disappointed in this New Horizons catalogue.

AM   It's bound to be disappointing because it illustrates all too well a great period of trial and error. If you look through the wpa/fap records of the artists, you will find a great many awfully well-known artists today who had not yet found themselves— even to the extent of knowing what medium they were going to work in definitely. They were given the opportunity to experiment. Many were young in years and art. So the New Horizons show, important as it was, seems not too fortunate now for posterity to look at or judge by.

FVO'C The documentation concerning the organization of the New Horizon show indicates Cahill thought of it as a means of publicizing the Project. It was conceived almost as soon as the wpa/fap was under way—along with the illustrated report which was to become *Art for the Millions*—as a means of publicizing and justifying itself. This is certainly understandable, considering the pressures from Congress for results; but it does raise a question about the whole attitude the Project had towards its own product and the obsession with publicity that seems to have set in after a while. The reports to Washington even include the number of inches of copy about the Project in the newspapers every week.

AM   There was a tremendous need to show that the tax-payers' money was not being wasted and that the criticism leveled at the wpa program in general, if merited, was certainly not applicable to its Federal Art Project. This was important to Cahill; it was important to the artists; it was important to us. And the only way you could do that was to give some kind of graphic demonstration. The theater project had been able to show its works to the public, the music project had concerts, everybody else could do it. We allocated our works, but one man would know it, or maybe ten. There was no real way to go before the public except on a big exhibition basis.

FVO'C But let us turn to something more pertinent. We were talking about the artist and his subject matter. What is the basic influence behind social realism as opposed to the American scene? Is it simply something that spontaneously develops out of the realities of the Depression, or is it influenced by others doing similar things in Europe or the Soviet Union?

OLG   There was a great influence from Mexican art about this time.

AM   I was amazed to read in the questionnaires that many artists were enormously influenced by the Mexicans. They felt that art in Mexico had made so much progress that art in America should do likewise. They speak of the Mexicans as "giants" and feel themselves "pygmies" in comparison. All this comes through as rather naive. Yet it is true that all the major Mexicans—Orozco, Rivera, Siqueiros—painted murals here during the early 1930s.

MEL   There is a great deal more to it than that. Consider the social realities themselves. I can't emphasize this enough. Anyone who can remember a May Day parade in New York would know what I'm talking about.

AM   Yes.

MEL   . . . and the turnout of hundreds of thousands of people. And then the poverty. Washington Square was one big bed at night—not a blade of grass uncovered. Hoovervilles in the drained reservoir in Central Park, on the banks of the Hudson, on the lower East Side.

JK   There was a "Resurrection City" like the one over on the Mall now° on the outskirts of almost every city in the nation. Shanties made of cardboard and tin. People couldn't pay rent anywhere.

MEL   Mrs. John D. Rockefeller's Christmas card one year was a lithograph of a bread line.

AM   So the artists weren't expressing anything but day-to-day reality. If it now seems they were expressing a political or sociological point of view, this is merely because it was the only attitude anyone could have of anything in the midst of such a situation.

OLG   I think it is very interesting that this question of the mix of influences should come up. As we talk about it, it seems so natural that the wpa/fap artists would be affected by the social condition. They depicted workers, people in the fields, city children in a most down-to-earth way, without any effort at elegance or scenery or sunsets. Just what was there.

MEL   Do not forget, it was the Mexican government that supported the Mexican artist.

AM   And don't forget that in those Mexican paintings there is very little evidence of oppression or want or any real depth of trauma or overt deprivation.

OLG   But the great weights the people carry. . . .

AM   That's right; the burden of labor and a great deal that is factual that we would, perhaps, not think happy. But there was not anything similar to that which our artists had to mirror if they were going to mirror the truth.

MEL   Yes, yes.

JK   Another thing. We had no real painting tradition in this country such as France or Italy. Good painting in itself would have seemed so frivolous. "What! Just

° Southern Christian Leadership Conference's campsite in Washington, D.C., July 1968.

good color?" It would mean nothing. As a result color was one of the weakest aspects of the art of the 1930s. What could have been further from the general public's mind—or for that matter the art world's—than a Matisse outlook? Hedonistic—the pleasures of life. It would have been wrong. It would not have reflected the mood of the country. It would have been an importation.

AM I know we do say, don't we, that the Project didn't influence the artist. But we did influence the artists in their subject matter to this degree: that we said "Paint what you see—paint what you feel—paint what you know." In other words, copying the modern masters was discouraged by the supervisors, who were themselves artists. Suppose we had had all art critics or art teachers, or ladies who collect art, as supervisors. The subject matter would have been quite different.

MEL Now you are making one of the strongest points you could make!

FVO'C Many of the artists who were on the WPA/FAP say it was the only college the 1930s offered them. We ought to explore this. What did the young artist learn on the Project about art?

JK Artists came to the Project with different backgrounds. Some had taken classes at the Art Students League. Others, like myself, had longer training. Still others had very little training. But they could draw and paint, they were technically competent. They had no notion, however, of what went into a work of art. Some of the older artists knew about Cubism—and Surrealism which was beginning to influence a very small number. But everybody's heros were Eugene Speicher, Henry McFee, Leon Kroll—artists of that sort. The Project was a great purgative. Artists entered it from all levels and they began to see the limitations of the acclaimed American contemporaries. The reason for this is in the fact that working on the Project they were under no real pressures. They could experiment. A lot of what they did was bad but the freedom to be bad acted as a sort of purgative. Finally, gropingly, they found roots by pulling together certain aspects of Expressionism, Surrealism, abstraction—but always in American terms, in terms of their own experience. It was very tentative but out of it I think American art suddenly came of age because it had this big experience. Right after the Project American art developed enormously. It couldn't possibly have done it without the WPA/FAP. The artists still would have been uncertain, still would have had all the provincialisms.

AM Yes. It is very interesting when you read the questionnaires to find some saying in answer to one question that they never had anything rejected for allocation, while others say they did indeed have works rejected and—extraordinary for artists and extraordinary to me, they say . . . .

JK They say the rejection was justified . . . .

AM Yes!! They say it was right. They say they came to see that the work in question wasn't any good! This I didn't remember. I was amazed to read it. One artist says "I took it back and gave my supervisor something else and he accepted it as my assignment for the month." Well, this is extraordinary. On the other hand, we are walking a tightrope here because, in theory at least, and I think in practice, the artist was supposed to be a professional or he couldn't be a creative artist on the Project. He could be a mural assistant or a poster-maker or something of that sort, but to be a creative artist he had to have demonstrable art training or have had a one-man show or the equivalent. He had to have been in the Carnegie, or the Philadelphia Watercolor show, or something. By and large I find that this is substantiated by fact. So, therefore, we were naive as well—we the public, we the art viewer. We shared the artists' naiveté.

JK   Most of the artists knew nothing of composition. I went through three years at Pratt Institute, six hours a day. I had, of course, been to the Art Students League before, and the Educational Alliance Art School when I was sixteen. I had all sorts of courses. I learned to draw, I learned anatomy. That didn't do me any harm. But when I came out I knew nothing about composition—about what made a picture.

AM   I'm not saying you were educated; I said you'd had education. (Laughter)

JK   But this applied to a lot of people on the Project. I remember when I began to see Arshile Gorky and John Graham. They could take a painting by Titian or Poussin and explain its structure; how something began as a circle on a car and that circular movement was carried through. It was incredible to me that there was this kind of organization.

MEL   You studied under the wrong teachers. (Laughter) Certainly Tom Benton was teaching composition, and Reginald Marsh.

JK   All Reggie Marsh did was take a group of bums and arrange them in a triangle. (Peals of laughter) We didn't know what to do with areas. We didn't know. This is the whole thing. Only a handful of artists knew. It was only when we began to see Max Beckmann and the work of Milton Avery and Stuart Davis.

AM   Yes. And we had some artists who had this instinctively. People like Loren McIver, who from the very first would produce a sophisticated and intelligent piece of work.

OLG   How much influence did the wpa/fap supervisors have?

AM   Their role was to help the artist secure what was needed and give him comfort and support and then present his work properly to the allocation committee. Supervisors were chosen for their ability to lead people and to guide and help. They were chosen to relate rather than to teach. The only instruction per se was that which a supervising muralist would give his assistants. But an easel painter or a printmaker was on his own.

OLG   I didn't mean actual instruction but how the supervisor helped, how he related. Did the supervisor visit studios?

321

AM   Oh yes. Burgoyne Diller visited muralists' studios. But not easel or graphic. Their work was brought in when finished. I would say that the artists had more of an influence on one another than any supervisor ever had on them. Now Diller and the mural supervisors had an influence on the artists in their groups. They got to know them very well. They were very much involved in long-term projects. But this was a by-product. In looking back, that may have been one of the flaws.

JK   Perhaps another flaw is that the supervisors didn't let the artists know that they could really cut loose if they wanted to.

AM   They didn't? Yet they all say there were no restrictions.

JK   There were no restrictions; but artists knew, or felt, that the work had to be allocated and that the supervisor would look at it.

AM   That didn't hold them down, surely.

JK   That didn't hold them down; but it was expecting a great deal for the artist, who was a relief recipient . . . .

AM   Yes, to break loose.

FVO'C Just as in any bureaucracy there are unspoken policies, expectations . . . .

AM   Yes, of course. And there were other flaws, since we are mentioning flaws. The artists in the easel division—and some in graphics—all say that they never knew where their work went when it was allocated. "I was never told." There must have been some order, but I recall no order to that effect. I could never have invented a thing like that. There was no earthly reason for it. It was a lack of communication.

FVO'C On just this point. A few months after the first allocations to Washington were made from the New York Project, some of the artists apparently petitioned you to find out what happened to the work. I think they wanted it back for a show, or something. Cahill's deputy, Thomas Parker, wrote back to say that no one knew where the work was. It was in a traveling show and just not available. I think this was something everyone knew: once allocated, goodbye. But today there is a great deal of resentment that the art has disappeared. Many of the artists writing to me are trying to find their paintings, their plates or copies of their prints, and they are coming up against a blank wall.

AM   It was very shortsighted of us and of those behind us not to know that this would happen. But we were confronted with this overwhelming, horrible need. Apparently our policies were very shortsighted. If we had any faith in these artists we would have had to believe that they would go on, that a certain percentage would develop and become known. But we didn't think beyond the moment. That's the worst flaw.

MEL   Probably just the effort of getting things allocated was so great that it never occurred to you . . . .

AM   No, the demand was enormous. It was not a great effort to get things allocated. It was certainly always a great effort to get certain artist's work allocated. This is why I am so vehement when anyone says that an artist was not kept on if his work wasn't allocated. That was never true. There were all kinds of artists whose work was never allocated. If they were extreme in their depiction of the social scene some public officials just wouldn't put it into public buildings. But this did not influence us in employing them.

FVO'C   Was really good art produced on the Project? Does the WPA/FAP deserve the disparagement one finds so frequently?

AM   Why of course good art was produced—wonderful art. I didn't know that the disparagement was so general. It seems to me that the disparagement was greater at the time when the work was produced.

FVO'C   Well, in the standard textbooks on American art, the projects are hardly mentioned and, of course, little attempt is made to distinguish between them. The tenor of judgment is that there is some sociological interest but that they were esthetically pointless and valueless.

MEL   I think it is the 1930s as a whole that are frowned on. Do any of these authors know anything about the art of the 1930s?

FVO'C   This is the general attitude toward the projects.

AM   But that's an outrageous thing to say. An uninformed thing to say. It is certainly true that the sociological need preoccupied everybody and so perhaps that comes out more strongly afterwards as well. But good art was surely produced.

MEL   No one knows the work. Most of the history books point out the 1930s as the period of Thomas Hart Benton, Grant Wood, and John Steuart Curry. Well these three artists were detested, absolutely detested, by most of the artists.

AM   I want to know how you think we would have felt about the art of the 1950s and 1960s if we hadn't had the art of the 1930s? I would like to know that?

JK   Rothko, Gottlieb, Gorky, Graham, Joseph Solman, Louis Schanker . . . .

AM   Gottlieb was better then than he ever has been since.

MEL   Gottlieb was excellent then. And I think he is today. It's what happened in between that I don't care too much about. I think what he's doing now is superb painting. Back in the 1930s he did those beautiful big nudes.

AM   Yes, beautiful . . . .

JK   And Louis Schanker was doing superb color woodcuts. They were his best work.

AM   They're the most beautiful color woodcuts I've ever seen.

OLG Speaking of prints, we should not forget the experiments being done with the silk-screen process in those days.

AM The Project got it started as a medium of creative expression.

JK That was Anthony Velonis and Guy Maccoy. They developed what was essentially a commercial process. A small group gathered with Velonis. Harry Gottlieb, Elizabeth Olds, Hyman Warsager, Leonard Pytlak. They got started about 1938–1939. Then in 1939 or 1940 a group of artists outside the Project formed the National Serigraph Society together with the Project artists to promote the new medium.

FVO'C One of the more overwhelming boxes at the National Archives is stuffed solid with requests coming into the Washington office for copies of Velonis' two little books on the techniques of silk-screen printing. Letters from all over the country asking for copies. It was a very popular medium. Also, for the record, perhaps it should be mentioned that the New York Project produced a whole series of technical manuals. There is one on how to paint a fresco—as well as a movie on the same subject.

AM Then there was Raphael Doktor, with his technical laboratory and his new adhesives. He made all the paint used on the Project, and Grumbacher didn't mind.

JK I would like to bring up one more point as far as American art in the 1930s is concerned. It is that critics, especially recent critics, have tended to underrate, or to minimize art that has any socially disturbing quality in it. Look how long it took for the German Expressionists to get any real recognition. The French are preferred. In this country there is a reaction against expressionism of any kind. We are intolerant or blind to the kind of art that is socially disturbing. I know people who wouldn't want a Beckmann or a George Grosz or an Otto Dix. Going back to the 1930s—people don't want to look at it. Their idea of art is something that looks handsome in a luxurious home.

AM It's more the decorator's art today, really.

FVO'C In view of the wpa/fap as essentially a relief organization, what steps were taken to make it permanent?

AM Well, Cahill and all of us were perfectly aware that the very premise of the Project was its impermanency. This was pointed up later by the Congress' attitude. We were totally governed by the yearly appropriation. We were strictly a relief project. The qualitative aspect, the art, was actually a by-product. The main goal was to keep these people alive, housed, and eating. What they did was to be an expression of their training and competence, rather than make-work. That's the distinction, in my book, between what we did and what many of the other big wpa projects did. This wasn't make-work; it was the preservation of the artists' skills.

FVO'C Why didn't you all resign in the fall of 1939 when Congress cut the appropriation drastically and put you back under local control? Wouldn't that have been better than to have had to drag on through to 1943, losing your creative motivation and in the end becoming just another war-services project?

324

AM   Better from what point of view? There was still a great deal of very creditable work going on, even though under enormous handicaps. Our mandate, really, was to employ people who needed employment as long as possible within their skills. It really was our job—at least I saw it as my job—to stay until the last artist was no longer employed. Then, of course, no one in 1939 foresaw the war. Had we known the war was coming, we might have taken a different view. But this is hindsight. To give up then just because we were being cut by 600 people—which was dreadful—would have been fallacious. We always believed that maybe we could get an appropriation and get those 600 back. No one ever accepted these cuts. This really must be remembered. We had to cut. We had to endure Somervell all over again after 1939. This was certainly horrible. Looking back, maybe it would have been better to have quit. But it certainly didn't seem better then. Besides, it surely would not have been tolerated by the artists themselves or by the Artists' Union or any of the art organizations—nor by me, for that matter.

JK   What would the artists have done without any means of livelihood?

OLG   What did they do in 1943—go in the army?

AM   Not many, as far as I know, but there was ever so much more general employment as the years—and the war—went on. There could have been no validity in continuing the Project once there was a war and an absorption of manpower. There is no question about that. It was a hard time for the artists—almost impossible, I would say.

FVO'C   We are getting near the end of the tape. I would like to ask a more general question that takes in more than the Projects but which concerns something that fascinates me as an art historian. During the 1930s art and artists seem focused on the environment—on what's going on. However personal the individual reaction, the artist is reacting to very palpable social pressures. Then, after the war, you have the development of Abstract Expressionism which, as Jacob has already mentioned, brought American art to the attention of the rest of the world. But Abstract Expressionism seems the other side of the coin. It is almost solipsistic in its introversion. Surrealism, of course, had a lot to do with its early stages, with the engendering and exploiting of unconscious imagery. Later, many of the artists who started out on the WPA/FAP find what I like to call their "signature styles." I am thinking of Pollock, de Kooning, Rothko, Gottlieb, James Brooks. This starts about 1950. Art is focused on the self. It is seen as a process of becoming for the personality. Then, from the late 1950s through the decade of the 1960s you get first the pseudo-sociology of Pop Art with its satire and camp and then what is dominant today: an optical or coloristic pattern-making where method, materials, the intricacies of form become art's content. How do you account for these radical changes in artistic style and esthetic mentality over four decades?

MEL   I have many ideas on this. Number one is the artist no longer has a voice in his own affairs. Everything is directed, everything is done for the artist through intervention. It is done through scholars, critics, museum directors, or galleries. Perhaps this is why contemporary art is repeating everything that happened from 1907 on. You get surrealist emphasis at one moment, you get the so-called search for the real. You get these peculiar changes of emphasis all the time, not on the part of the artist necessarily,

325

but on the part of people who intervene and present the artist to the public. I am wondering if there hasn't been too much art education. When you talk of artists moving from this on to that I am not sure it is the artist who is moving; it's the people who are presenting the artist who have moved.

AM   The times have moved too. The scene the artist is portraying has moved—and he is still a person who portrays. The demand on him is shifting and he is responding. Hasn't he always done that? Hasn't the artist always responded rather directly to the demand on him through the ages? When the Church made a demand, he made a response; when the State demanded, he made a response.

FVO'C Yet you find few artists of the past who go through these radical stylistic changes.

AM   Because society didn't. We are responsible for the change in the artist; it's what we ask of him that he gives us. So does the playwright. The artist isn't making any greater change than the playwright is making. Same with the musician. They are responding to change and isn't it natural that they should?

OLG   But the change has come so rapidly . . . .

MEL   Are these truly responses to changes in society? I don't believe it for a minute.

AM   I believe so. Everything is kaleidoscopic. Space has vanished and time is vanishing. Everything is much faster, everything is much closer, everything much more one-upon-the-other. There's much less interval for consideration, for thought—and for repentance, if you will.

JK   It's a patron's society. It expects certain things of the artist. But to go to your basic question of the change beginning with Abstract Expressionism, I think there are other reasons. The Abstract Expressionists came out of the 1930s and the war into the period when the witch hunts began. Suddenly anyone who had any feeling for social betterment in the 1930s was considered an enemy of society in the late 1940s and 1950s. The artist, or anyone, who had signed a petition for Spain is suddenly hunted down and exposed on the front pages of the newspapers. Certain artists I know didn't even want to show in New York because they would be fingered in Washington by the various committees. Russia was the hope of the world at one time, the hope of Utopia. After all, most artists are idealists. They have a great feeling for justice and social order. And then everything is turned upside down. Anyone who was an idealist in his youth is now not only an enemy of society but the worst kind: a traitor. So that when he started working again there was a kind of anguished generality in it, a savagery. He had no image. This is the art of Abstract Expressionism.

AM   But you're not accounting for the outlook of the man who was born between then and now. Your explanation is all right but it doesn't take into account the ideology of the younger man, who comes along now and thinks that today is the answer.

MEL   Well, I've heard informed persons say that this art of Abstract Expressionism was definitely Cold War art, anti-Communist art. And in a sense they are saying exactly the same thing you are saying.

AM   Yes, well, its a refuge action . . . .

JK   Yet what can they do? Artists have to have some values to express. And everything is shattered. They're being pursued as the dangerous element in society.

AM   They're being pursued for being what they are.

MEL   I think that the tragedy in the art world today is that the artist no longer has any control of his exhibition fate. I think this is the greatest tragedy.

AM   Well, that is another thing.

MEL   I think this is the greatest tragedy. I don't think we see what art is today. We only see what people want us to see.

AM   Are you talking of the country or of New York?

MEL   I think it is true of New York.

AM   Yes. It's true of New York. I am not sure it's true of the country.

JK   I am talking for the world! What Abstract Expressionism did was to make art really respectable. The point is it is obvious that these artists had great integrity. Kline, David Smith. They see the sublime, the reaching-out quality that is in it. Then suddenly so many of them became nouveaux-riche. Suddenly they are famous. And they become really horrified.

MEL   This is very cruel, I know, but I really quite mean it. I can see no difference between the success of Pollock and the success of Bouguereau in the 19th century. I see absolutely no difference. They are both tastes. Their works both appealed to a bourgeois taste at one moment and took the whole Western world by storm. I see no difference between the two.

FVO'C I object! (General laughter)

MEL   I see a different social setting, but I see the same result.

JK   Oh, there is more to it than that! Abstract Expressionism opened the way. Then when critics like Clement Greenberg, who is basically a Marxist, starts to think in terms of historical change, we must have the exact opposite of Abstract Expressionism—the post-painterly.

AM   I know.

JK   So you soak it into the canvas—and no paint standing out.

FVO'C This is the antithesis.

JK   The antithesis—no emotion.

AM   It is only the momentary response, I feel, to a momentary demand. Such terrific flux in all kinds of progress, in evaluations of time and space. Such enormous flux is bound to be reflected in the arts. What else is the artist except another person who lives in a dumb society?

327

MEL   The artist has always been something more than another person who lives in society. The great artist has been the man who prophesied the currents of society.

AM   More than the writer?

MEL   Much more than the writer, much more than the musician, and well in advance of it. Always.

FVO'C   Pray, what is Bouguereau's prophecy? (Laughter)

MEL   The same as Jackson Pollock's.

FVO'C   Bouguereau was a pornographer. Pollock was not.

MEL   Bouguereau was not a pornographer. He was the product of a bourgeois society—the worst bourgeois society known in the 19th century—that of Napoleon III.

AM   But how can you divorce the artist from the society in which he lives? I am not saying that he is the meanest person in the society, or that he is the most advanced. In this society and in a technological age, I don't know where he is, but I do know that he's a part of his society. If he isn't, who is he?

MEL   Well, I am saying that the artists whom we see today are not necessarily the real artists of today.

JK   We don't even know who the artists are today.

AM   Well, I would agree with that.

JK   What the artist does is sense the vitality of his period, the meaning of it.

AM   That's right.

JK   The artist will use the most modern materials because he's a reflection of his times. But that reflects a superficial quality of a society. Take Ryder. He came in just about the time industrialization was taking over. You would think he would reflect such a society. On the contrary, he began to think in terms of the most basic qualities of modern life. He wanted to get at real truths. He found the sea . . . . I think he somehow felt this. He recoiled from his society.

AM   That is one reaction. I don't say that the reaction has to be favorable always—but there has to be a reaction.

JK   Absolutely, I agree. But I think that's what the reaction of the first generation Abstract Expressionists was—the real ones. Not the second generation who began just empty slashing. It became then just a technique. Society ladies were doing it. It was taught in colleges. That's what ruined it.

MEL   At the time of Bouguereau you had some wonderful people who could not show publicly. So they organized together and showed themselves. They were the Impressionists, under the Société Anonyme. The whole history of modern art is the history of artists organizing and showing themselves.

AM   It's a history of revolution.

MEL   There is a smattering in this country today. Artists are beginning to have loft shows in New York. The establishment won't take them. There's no room for them and they're beginning to organize their own shows. What I am saying—and I repeat—is that the voice of the artist has been absolutely lost, and all we get is the voice of the person who acts between the artist and the public.

AM   I do not think that is the real reason. I think it is so much deeper than that. I think we have a basic change now.

FVO'C Yes . . . .

AM   A basic change in what we're looking for and living for and living by—and how the artist could not reflect that I cannot imagine.

FVO'C Yes, but we are running out of tape and I must answer this Bouguereau business. (Laughter)

AM   Oh, all right.

FVO'C I think it is essentially invalid to make comparisons between 19th-century situations and 20th-century situations. The psychology, the point of view, the whole process of evolution has advanced radically in the last hundred years.

MEL   No, I disagree!

FVO'C I know you do, Marchal, because you're a 19th-century man.

MEL   No, I'm not! (Laughter)

AM   No . . . but I object to only one word in what you said, Francis, and that is *advanced*. It has *changed* so radically . . . .

FVO'C I think the change *is* an advance.

SELECTED BIBLIOGRAPHY

American Art Annual, vols. 32 to 36, 1935 to 1945. Contain valuable articles on the history and activities of the various projects, including, in volume 35, a complete listing of Section murals through 1941 and WPA Community Art Centers.

American Heritage, October 1970. "Memoirs of a WPA Painter," by Edward Laning and "A Sampler of New Deal Murals," selected by Francis V. O'Connor, pp. 38–57. Illustrated.

Art as a Function of Government. New York: Supervisors Association of Federal Art Projects, 1937.

Bruce, Edward, and Forbes Watson. *Art in Federal Buildings: An Illustrated Record of the Treasury Department's New Program in Painting and Sculpture*. Washington, D.C.: Art in Federal Buildings, Inc., 1936.

Cahill, Holger. *New Horizons in American Art*. New York: Museum of Modern Art, 1936. Illustrated.

Carr, Eleanor. "The New Deal and the Sculptor: A Study of Federal Relief to the Sculptor on the New York City Federal Art Project of the Works Progress Administration, 1935 to 1943." Unpublished PhD Dissertation, Institute of Fine Arts, New York University, 1969.

Collier's Yearbook: 1935 to 1943. Contains yearly articles on the New Deal art projects by Dorothy C. Miller. Cf. "The U.S. Government Art Projects: A Brief Summary" based on these articles and published in mimeo by the Department of Circulating Exhibitions, Museum of Modern Art, New York.

Contreras, Belisario R. "Treasury Art Programs: The New Deal and the American Artist, 1933 to 1943." Unpublished PhD dissertation, American University, 1967.

McDonald, William F. *Federal Relief Administration and the Arts: The Origins and Administrative History of the Arts Projects of the Works Progress Administration*. Columbus: Ohio State University Press, 1969.

330

McKinzie, Richard D. "The New Deal for Artists: Federal Subsidies, 1933 to 1943." Unpublished PhD dissertation, Indiana University, Bloomington, 1968.

Marling, Karal Ann. "Federal Patronage and the Woodstock Colony." Unpublished PhD dissertation, Bryn Mawr College, 1971.

Monroe, Gerald M. "The Artists Union of New York." Unpublished EdD dissertation, New York University, 1971.

O'Connor, Francis V. *Federal Art Patronage: 1933 to 1943.* College Park: University of Maryland Art Gallery, 1966. Illustrated.

——————. *Jackson Pollock.* New York: Museum of Modern Art, 1967. See especially pp. 20–27. Illustrated.

——————. "New Deal Murals in New York," *Artforum,* November 1968, pp. 41–49. Illustrated.

——————. "The New Deal Art Projects in New York," *American Art Journal,* Fall 1969, pp. 58–79.

——————. *Federal Support for the Visual Arts: The New Deal and Now.* Greenwich, Connecticut: New York Graphic Society, 1969. Contains comprehensive bibliography and a guide to New Deal art project documentation.

Overmeyer, Grace. *Government and the Arts.* New York: W. W. Norton, 1939.

Purcell, Ralph. *Government and Art.* Washington, D.C.: Public Affairs Press, 1956.

Rubenstein, Erica Beckh. "Tax Payers' Murals." Unpublished PhD dissertation, Harvard University, 1944.

——————. "Government Art in the Roosevelt Era," *Art Journal,* Fall, 1960, pp. 2–8. Illustrated.

INDEX OF NAMES

Note: Figure numbers in parentheses following page references indicate person is depicted in illustration; page references in italics indicate works of art.